Shojo Beat

Vol. **2**

Story & Art by
Chica Umino

honey and clover

Volume 2
CONTENTS

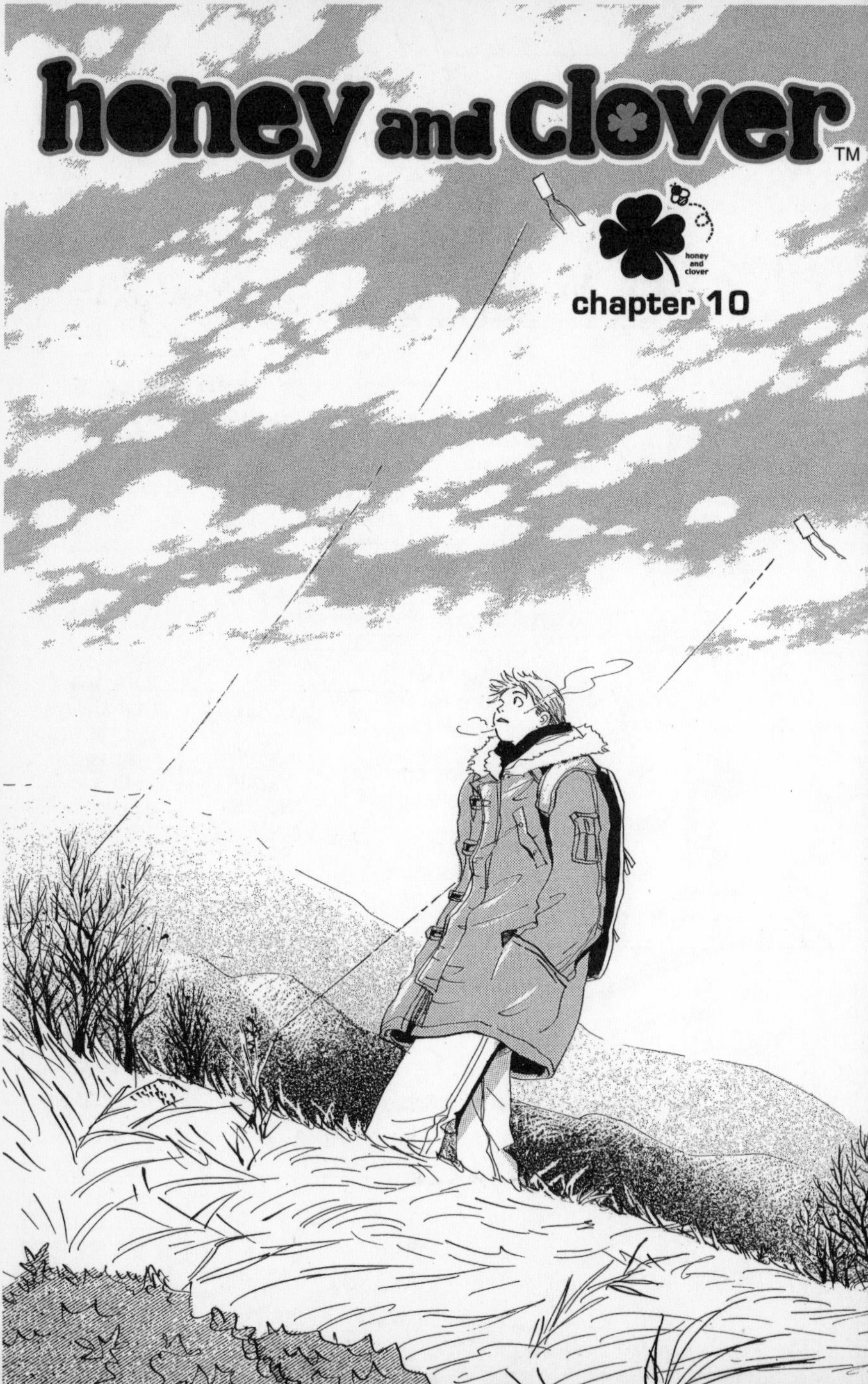
honey and clover™
honey and clover
chapter 10

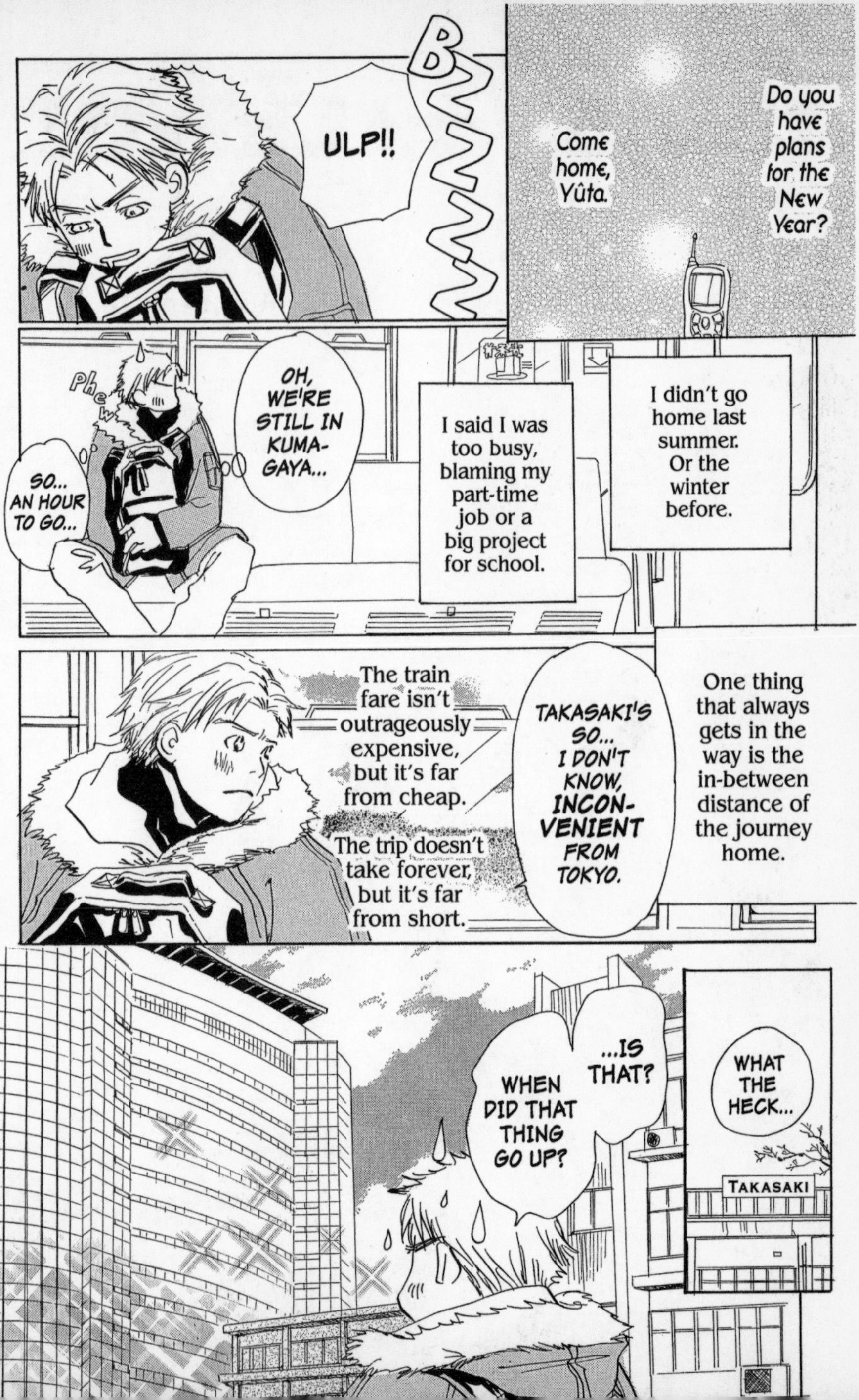
Do you have plans for the New Year?
Come home, Yûta.
BZZZ
ULP!!
I didn't go home last summer. Or the winter before.
I said I was too busy, blaming my part-time job or a big project for school.
OH, WE'RE STILL IN KUMAGAYA...
Phew
SO... AN HOUR TO GO...
One thing that always gets in the way is the in-between distance of the journey home.
TAKASAKI'S SO... I DON'T KNOW, INCONVENIENT FROM TOKYO.
The train fare isn't outrageously expensive, but it's far from cheap.
The trip doesn't take forever, but it's far from short.
WHAT THE HECK...
TAKASAKI
...IS THAT?
WHEN DID THAT THING GO UP?

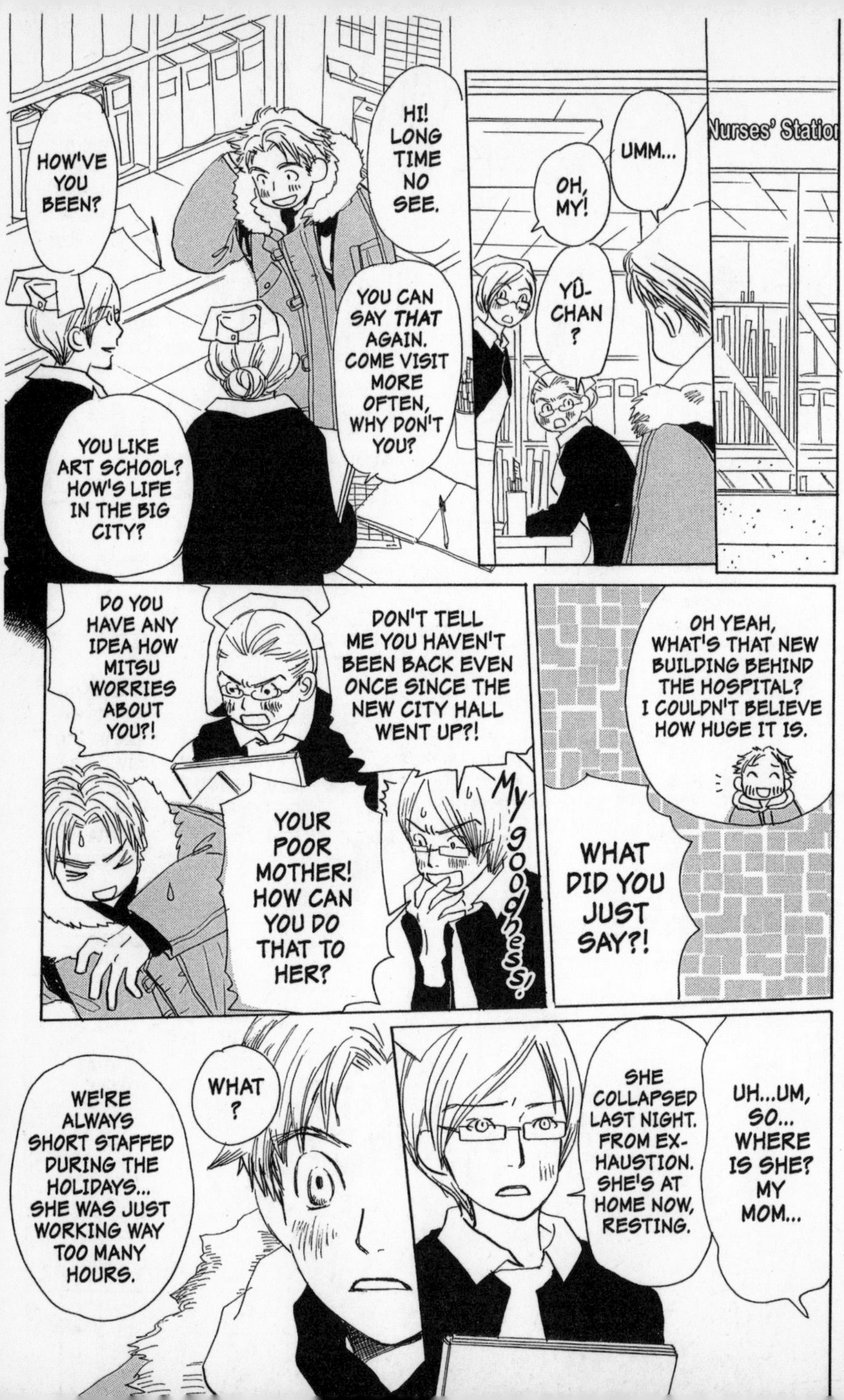
Nurses' Station
UMM...
OH, MY!
YÛ-CHAN?
HI! LONG TIME NO SEE.
HOW'VE YOU BEEN?
YOU CAN SAY THAT AGAIN. COME VISIT MORE OFTEN, WHY DON'T YOU?
YOU LIKE ART SCHOOL? HOW'S LIFE IN THE BIG CITY?
OH YEAH, WHAT'S THAT NEW BUILDING BEHIND THE HOSPITAL? I COULDN'T BELIEVE HOW HUGE IT IS.
WHAT DID YOU JUST SAY?!
DON'T TELL ME YOU HAVEN'T BEEN BACK EVEN ONCE SINCE THE NEW CITY HALL WENT UP?!
DO YOU HAVE ANY IDEA HOW MITSU WORRIES ABOUT YOU?!
My goodness!
YOUR POOR MOTHER! HOW CAN YOU DO THAT TO HER?
UH...UM, SO... WHERE IS SHE? MY MOM...
SHE COLLAPSED LAST NIGHT. FROM EX-HAUSTION. SHE'S AT HOME NOW, RESTING.
WHAT?
WE'RE ALWAYS SHORT STAFFED DURING THE HOLIDAYS... SHE WAS JUST WORKING WAY TOO MANY HOURS.

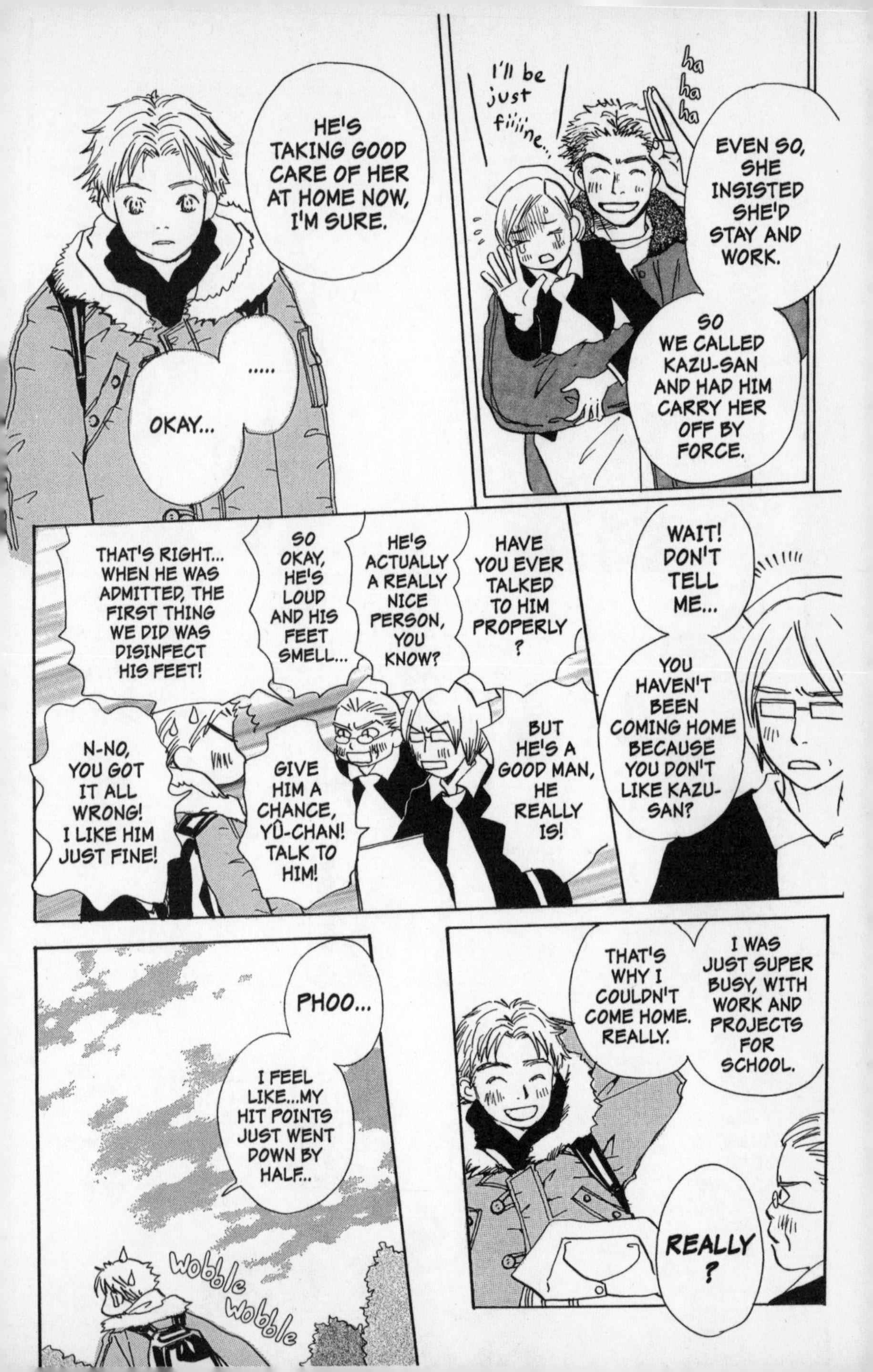
ha ha ha
EVEN SO, SHE INSISTED SHE'D STAY AND WORK.
I'll be just fiiine...
SO WE CALLED KAZU-SAN AND HAD HIM CARRY HER OFF BY FORCE.
HE'S TAKING GOOD CARE OF HER AT HOME NOW, I'M SURE.
.....
OKAY...
WAIT! DON'T TELL ME...
YOU HAVEN'T BEEN COMING HOME BECAUSE YOU DON'T LIKE KAZU-SAN?
HAVE YOU EVER TALKED TO HIM PROPERLY?
HE'S ACTUALLY A REALLY NICE PERSON, YOU KNOW?
SO OKAY, HE'S LOUD AND HIS FEET SMELL...
THAT'S RIGHT... WHEN HE WAS ADMITTED, THE FIRST THING WE DID WAS DISINFECT HIS FEET!
BUT HE'S A GOOD MAN, HE REALLY IS!
GIVE HIM A CHANCE, YÛ-CHAN! TALK TO HIM!
N-NO, YOU GOT IT ALL WRONG! I LIKE HIM JUST FINE!
I WAS JUST SUPER BUSY, WITH WORK AND PROJECTS FOR SCHOOL.
THAT'S WHY I COULDN'T COME HOME. REALLY.
REALLY?
PHOO...
I FEEL LIKE...MY HIT POINTS JUST WENT DOWN BY HALF...
wobble wobble

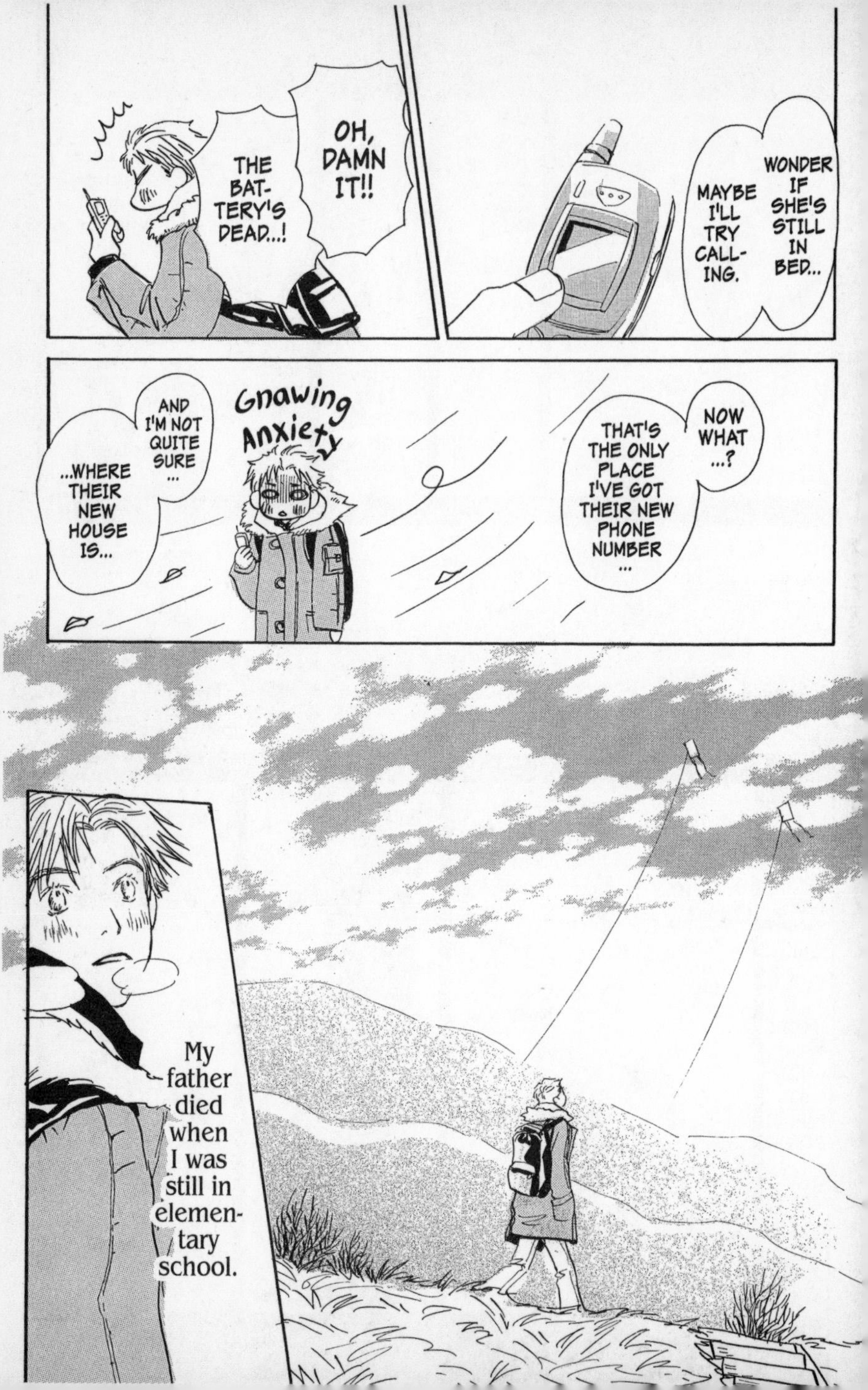
WONDER IF SHE'S STILL IN BED...
MAYBE I'LL TRY CALL-ING.
OH, DAMN IT!!
THE BAT-TERY'S DEAD...!
NOW WHAT ...?
THAT'S THE ONLY PLACE I'VE GOT THEIR NEW PHONE NUMBER ...
Gnawing Anxiety
AND I'M NOT QUITE SURE ...
...WHERE THEIR NEW HOUSE IS...
My father died when I was still in elemen-tary school.

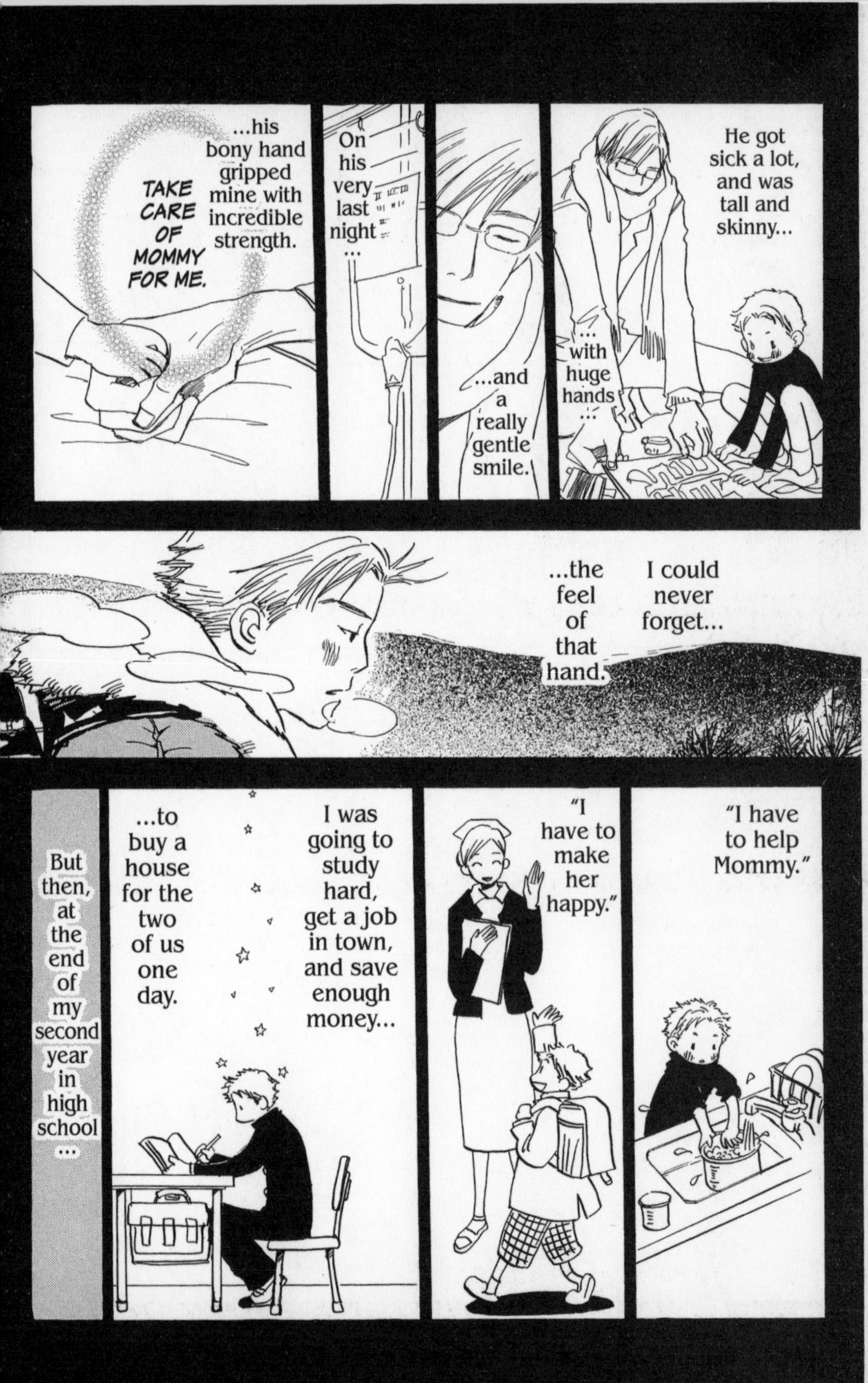
He got sick a lot, and was tall and skinny...
...with huge hands...
...and a really gentle smile.
On his very last night...
...his bony hand gripped mine with incredible strength.
TAKE CARE OF MOMMY FOR ME.
I could never forget...
...the feel of that hand.
"I have to help Mommy."
"I have to make her happy."
I was going to study hard, get a job in town, and save enough money...
...to buy a house for the two of us one day.
But then, at the end of my second year in high school...

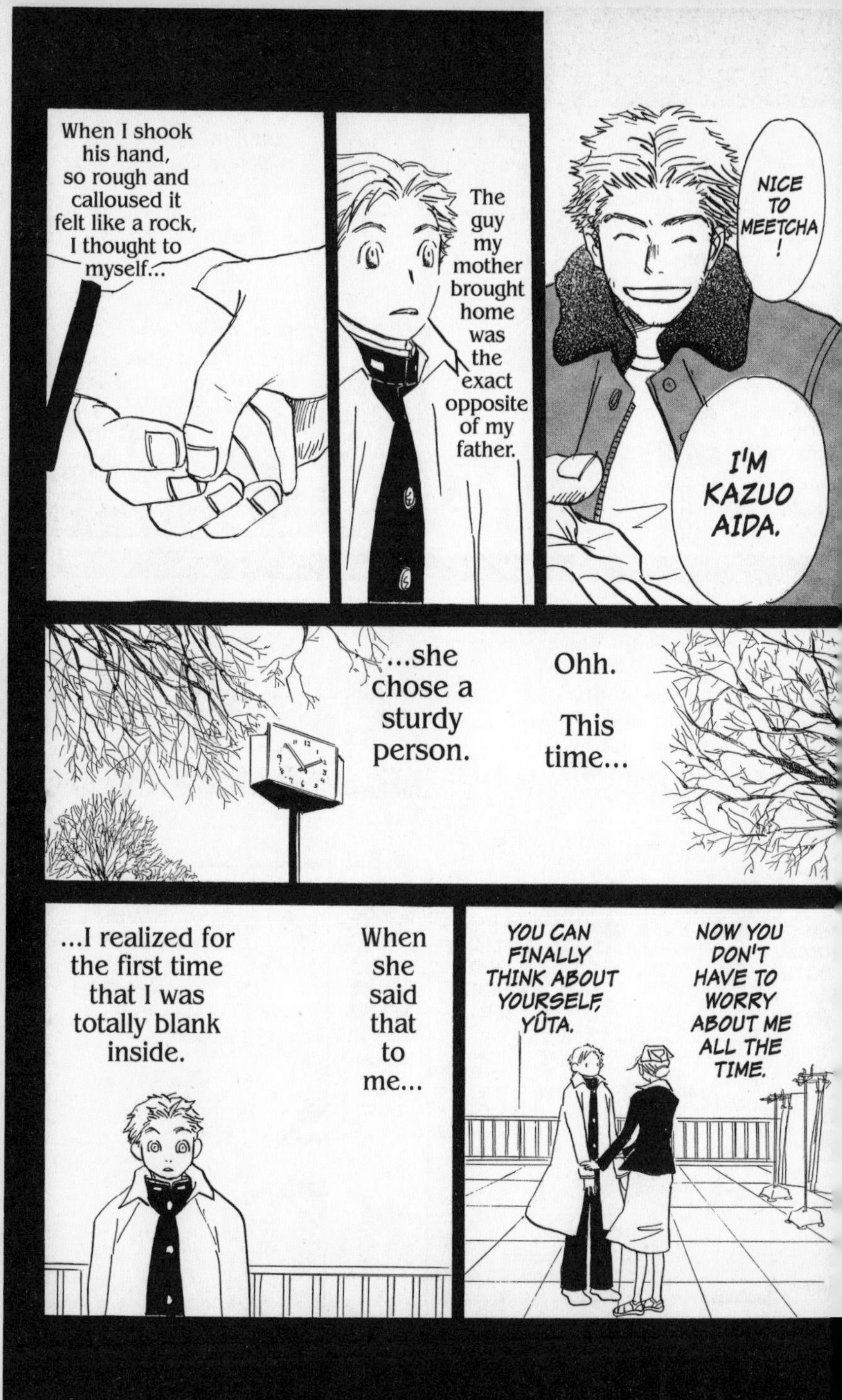
NICE TO MEETCHA!
I'M KAZUO AIDA.
The guy my mother brought home was the exact opposite of my father.
When I shook his hand, so rough and calloused it felt like a rock, I thought to myself...
Ohh.
This time...
...she chose a sturdy person.
NOW YOU DON'T HAVE TO WORRY ABOUT ME ALL THE TIME.
YOU CAN FINALLY THINK ABOUT YOURSELF, YÛTA.
When she said that to me...
...I realized for the first time that I was totally blank inside.

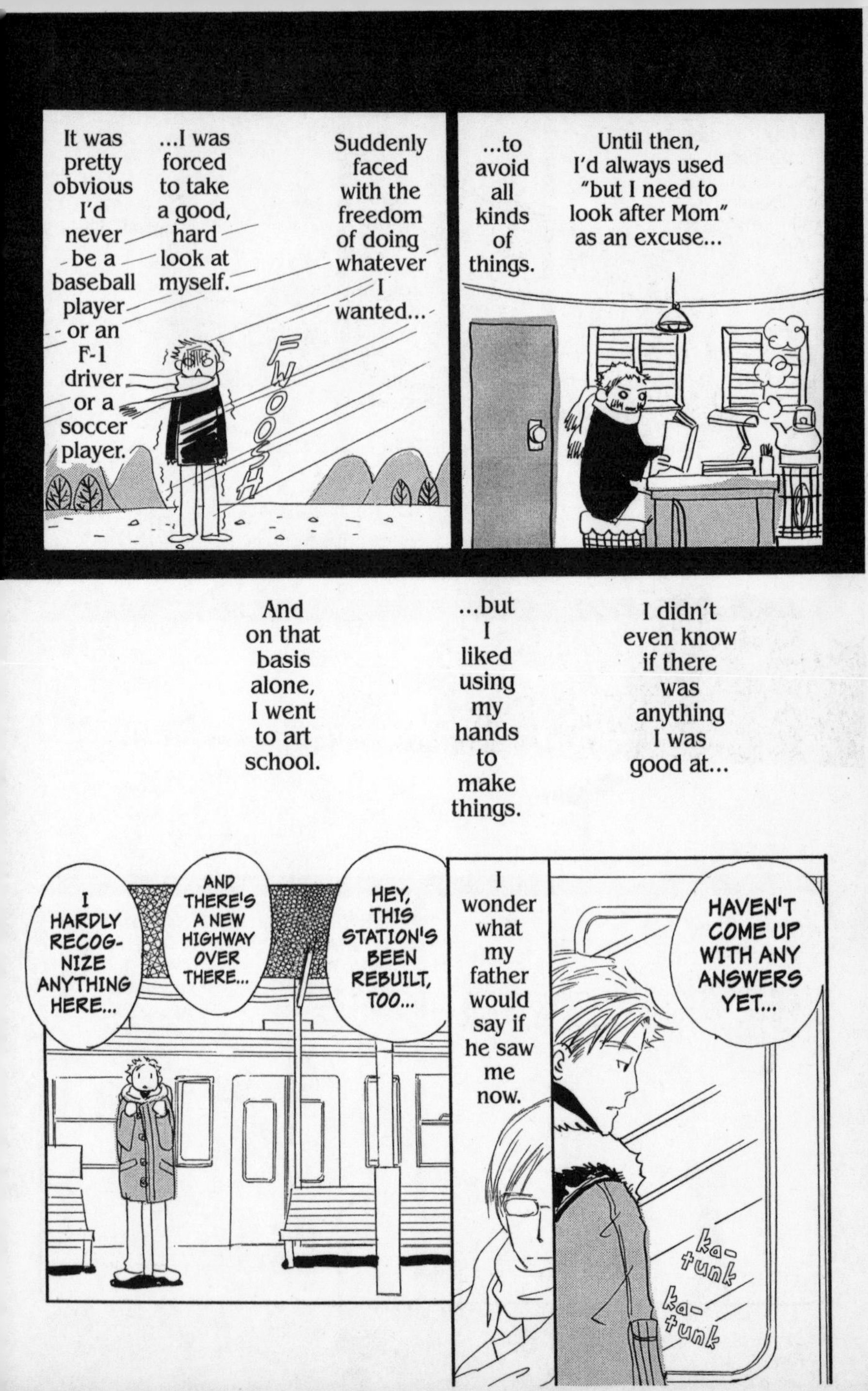
Until then, I'd always used "but I need to look after Mom" as an excuse...
...to avoid all kinds of things.
Suddenly faced with the freedom of doing whatever I wanted...
...I was forced to take a good, hard look at myself.
It was pretty obvious I'd never be a baseball player or an F-1 driver or a soccer player.
FWOOSH
I didn't even know if there was anything I was good at...
...but I liked using my hands to make things.
And on that basis alone, I went to art school.
HAVEN'T COME UP WITH ANY ANSWERS YET...
I wonder what my father would say if he saw me now.
ka-tunk
ka-tunk
HEY, THIS STATION'S BEEN REBUILT, TOO...
AND THERE'S A NEW HIGHWAY OVER THERE...
I HARDLY RECOG-NIZE ANYTHING HERE...

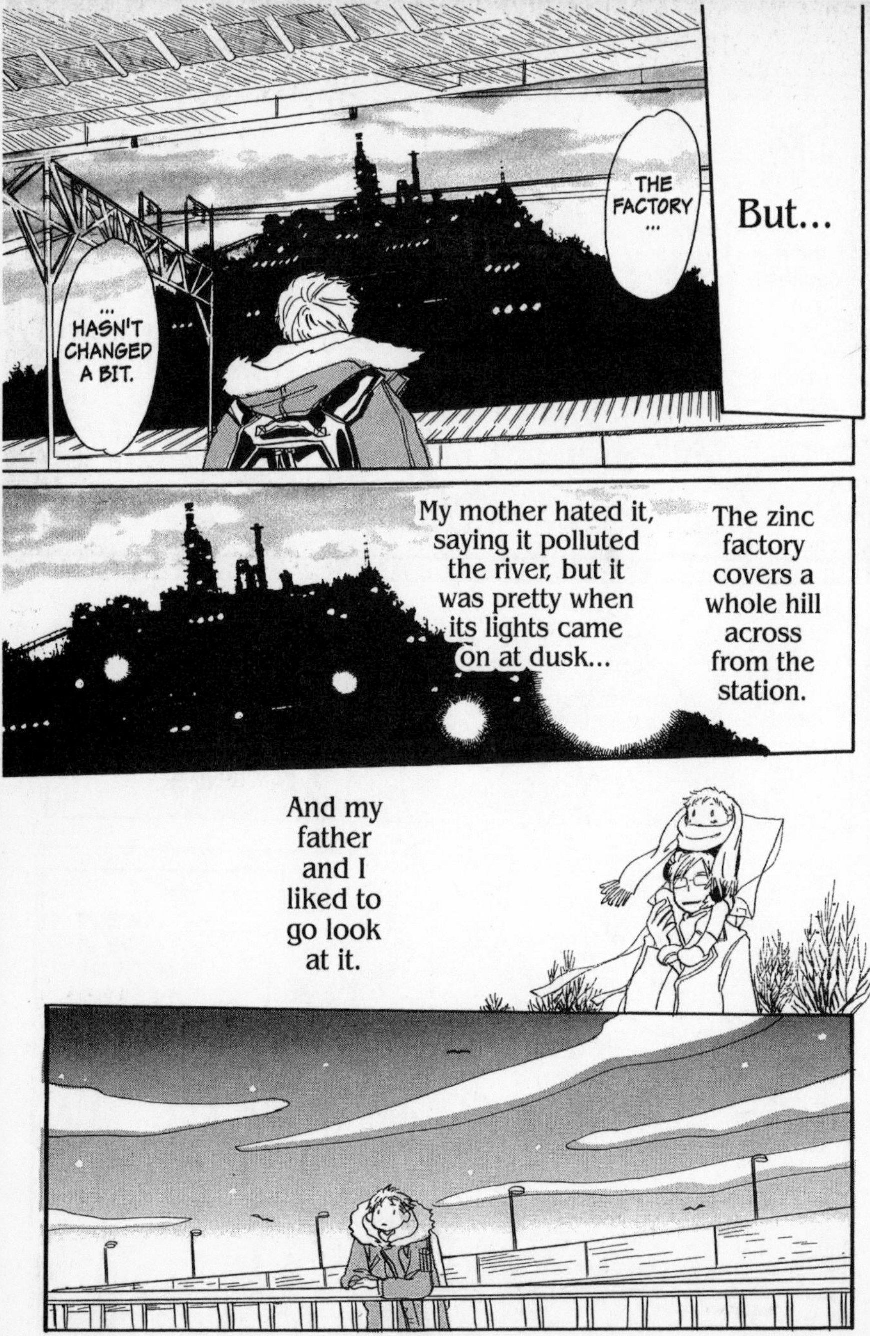
But...
THE FACTORY ...
... HASN'T CHANGED A BIT.
The zinc factory covers a whole hill across from the station.
My mother hated it, saying it polluted the river, but it was pretty when its lights came on at dusk...
And my father and I liked to go look at it.

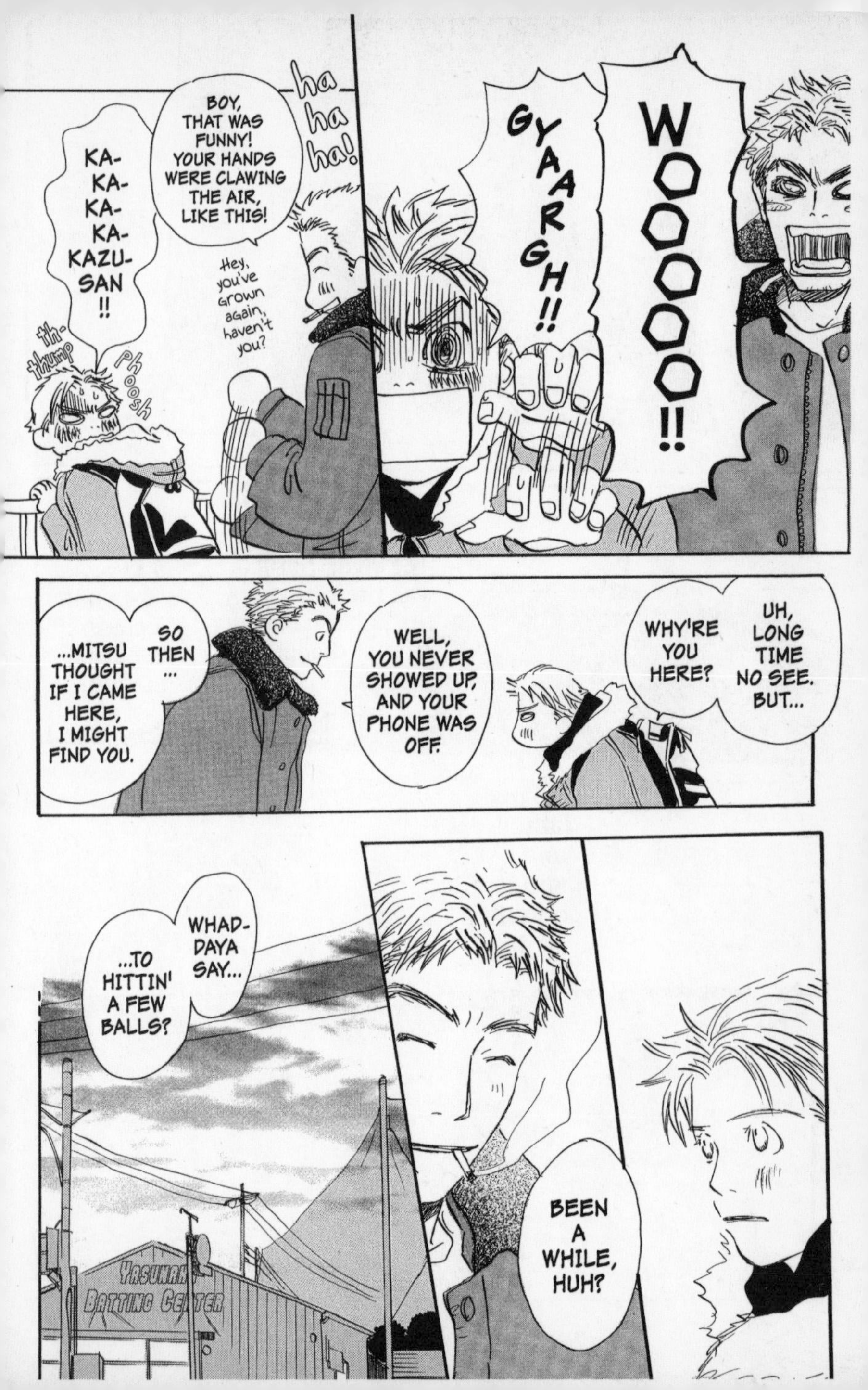
WOOOOOO!!
GYAARGH!!
ha ha ha!
BOY, THAT WAS FUNNY! YOUR HANDS WERE CLAWING THE AIR, LIKE THIS!
Hey, you've grown again, haven't you?
KA-KA-KA-KA-KAZU-SAN!!
th-thump
Phoosh
UH, LONG TIME NO SEE. BUT...
WHY'RE YOU HERE?
WELL, YOU NEVER SHOWED UP, AND YOUR PHONE WAS OFF.
SO THEN...
...MITSU THOUGHT IF I CAME HERE, I MIGHT FIND YOU.
BEEN A WHILE, HUH?
WHAD-DAYA SAY...
...TO HITTIN' A FEW BALLS?
BATTING CENTER

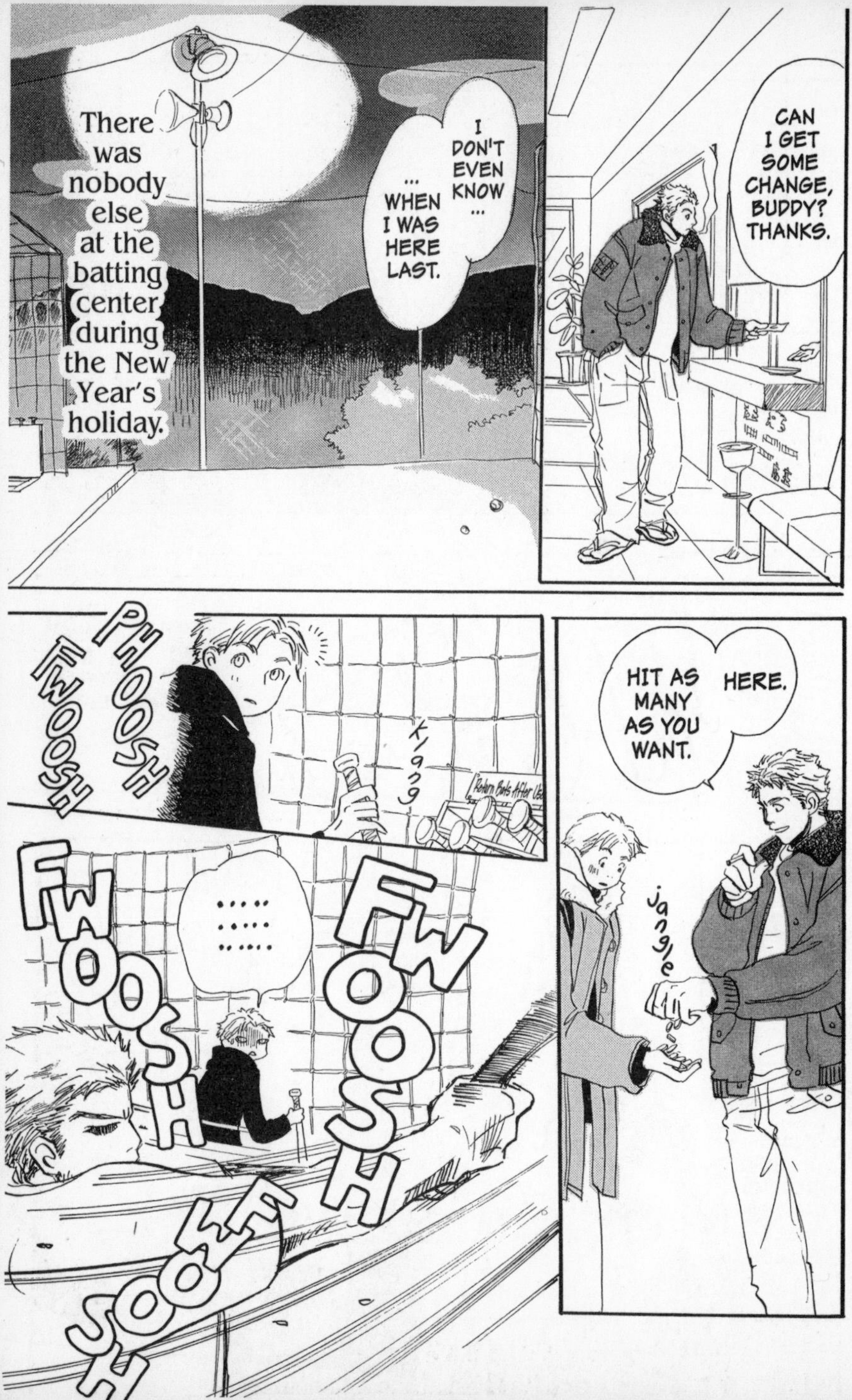
CAN I GET SOME CHANGE, BUDDY? THANKS.
There was nobody else at the batting center during the New Year's holiday.
I DON'T EVEN KNOW ...
... WHEN I WAS HERE LAST.
HERE.
HIT AS MANY AS YOU WANT.
jangle
PHOOSH
FWOOSH
klang
FWOOSH
FWOOSH
......
FWOOSH

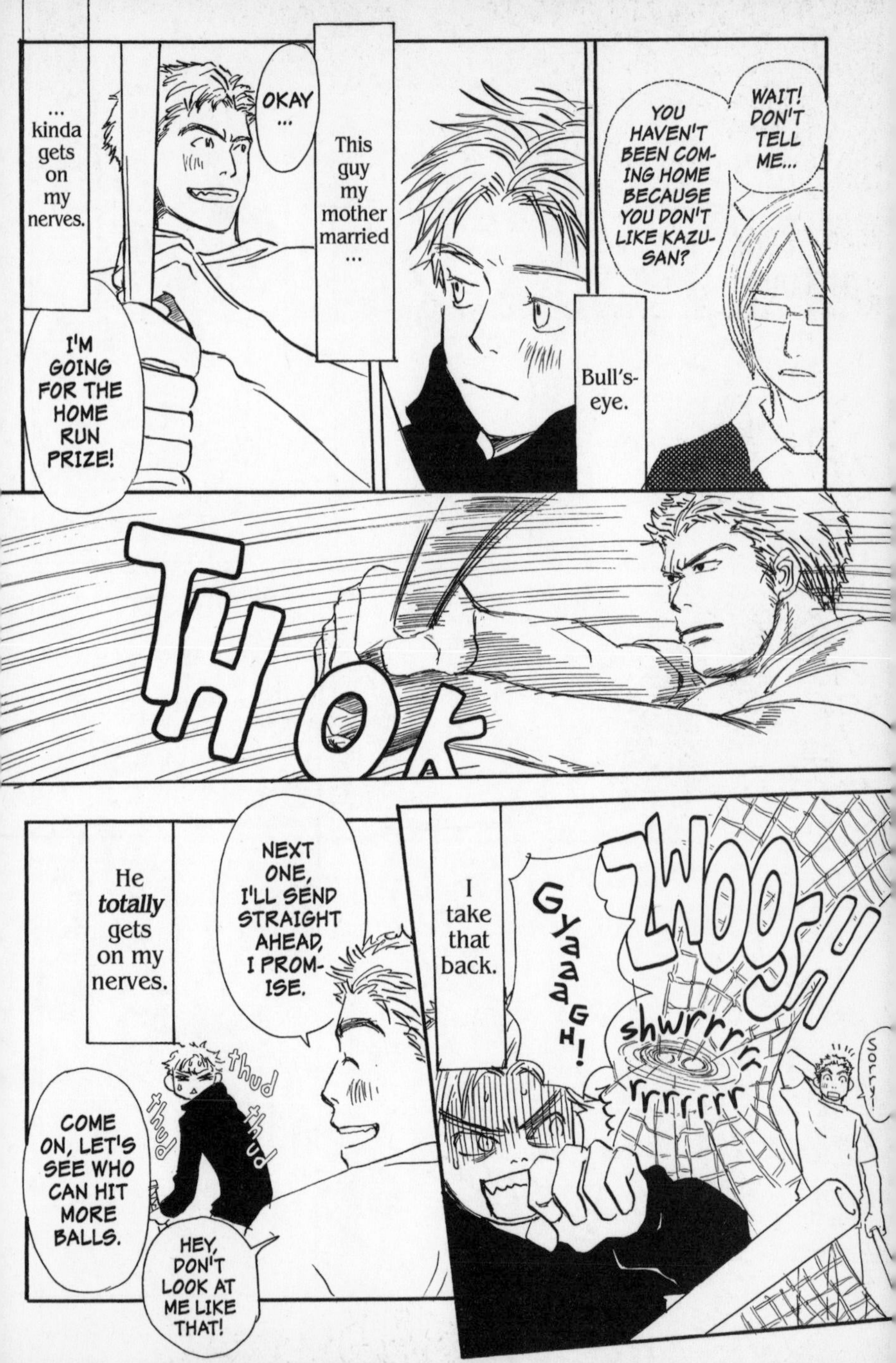
WAIT! DON'T TELL ME...
YOU HAVEN'T BEEN COMING HOME BECAUSE YOU DON'T LIKE KAZU-SAN?
Bull's-eye.
OKAY ...
This guy my mother married ...
... kinda gets on my nerves.
I'M GOING FOR THE HOME RUN PRIZE!
THOK
I take that back.
ZWOOSH
GYAAAAGH!
shwrrrrrr rrrrrrr
Sorry!
He *totally* gets on my nerves.
NEXT ONE, I'LL SEND STRAIGHT AHEAD, I PROMISE.
thud thud
COME ON, LET'S SEE WHO CAN HIT MORE BALLS.
HEY, DON'T LOOK AT ME LIKE THAT!

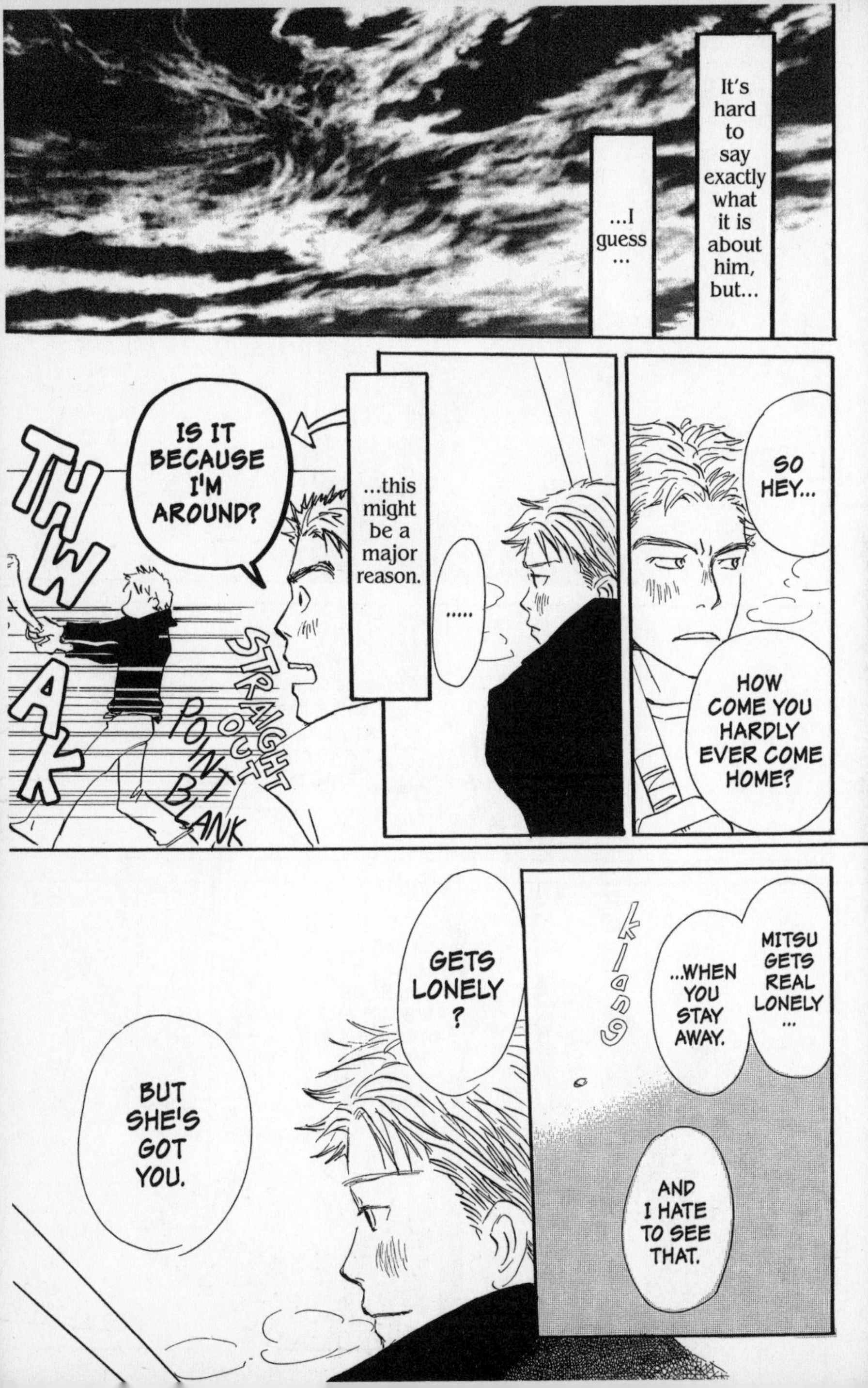
It's hard to say exactly what it is about him, but...
...I guess...
SO HEY...
HOW COME YOU HARDLY EVER COME HOME?
.....
...this might be a major reason.
IS IT BECAUSE I'M AROUND?
STRAIGHT OUT
POINT BLANK
THWAK
MITSU GETS REAL LONELY...
...WHEN YOU STAY AWAY.
klang
AND I HATE TO SEE THAT.
GETS LONELY?
BUT SHE'S GOT YOU.

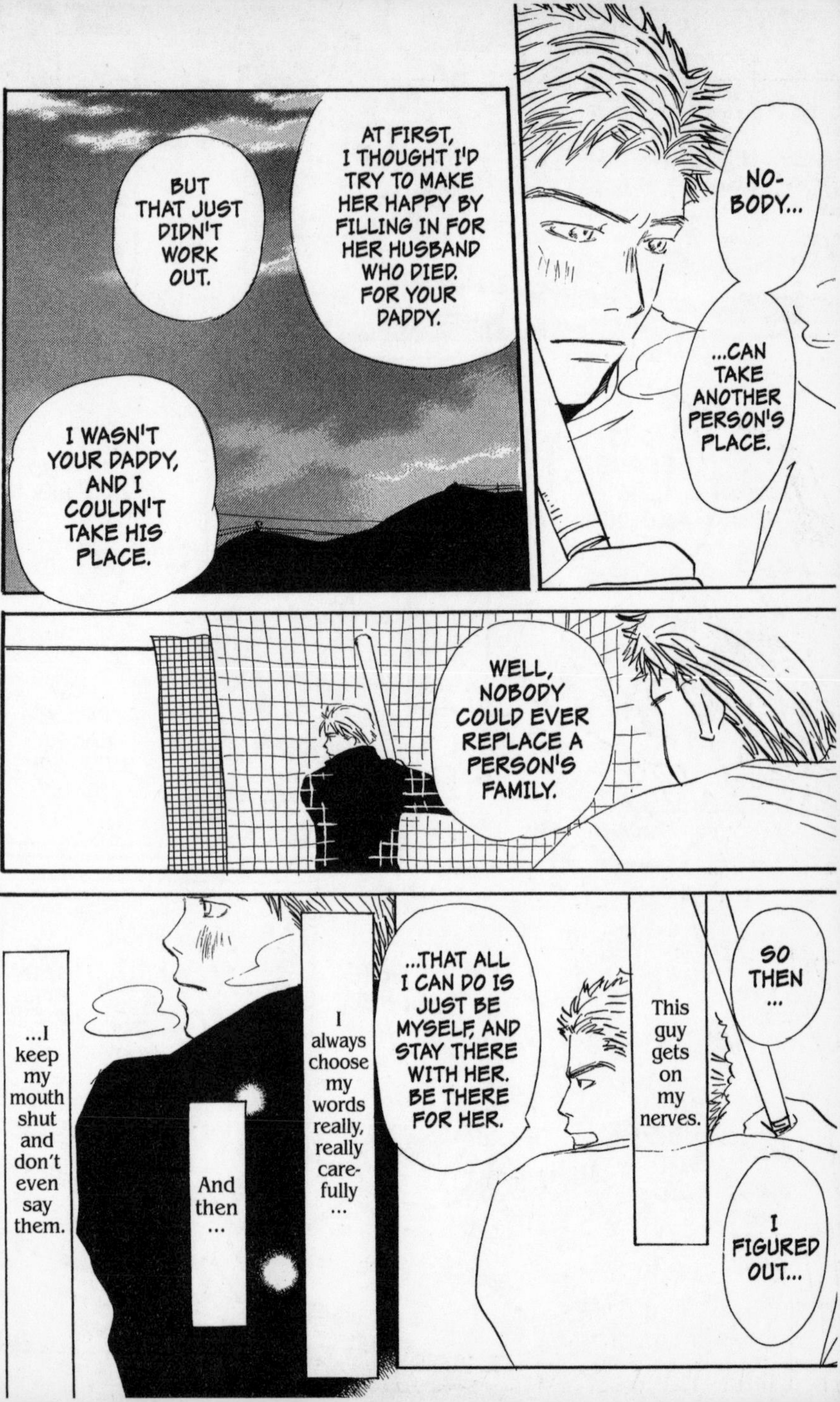
NO-BODY...
...CAN TAKE ANOTHER PERSON'S PLACE.
AT FIRST, I THOUGHT I'D TRY TO MAKE HER HAPPY BY FILLING IN FOR HER HUSBAND WHO DIED. FOR YOUR DADDY.
BUT THAT JUST DIDN'T WORK OUT.
I WASN'T YOUR DADDY, AND I COULDN'T TAKE HIS PLACE.
WELL, NOBODY COULD EVER REPLACE A PERSON'S FAMILY.
SO THEN ...
This guy gets on my nerves.
I FIGURED OUT...
...THAT ALL I CAN DO IS JUST BE MYSELF, AND STAY THERE WITH HER. BE THERE FOR HER.
I always choose my words really, really care-fully ...
And then ...
...I keep my mouth shut and don't even say them.

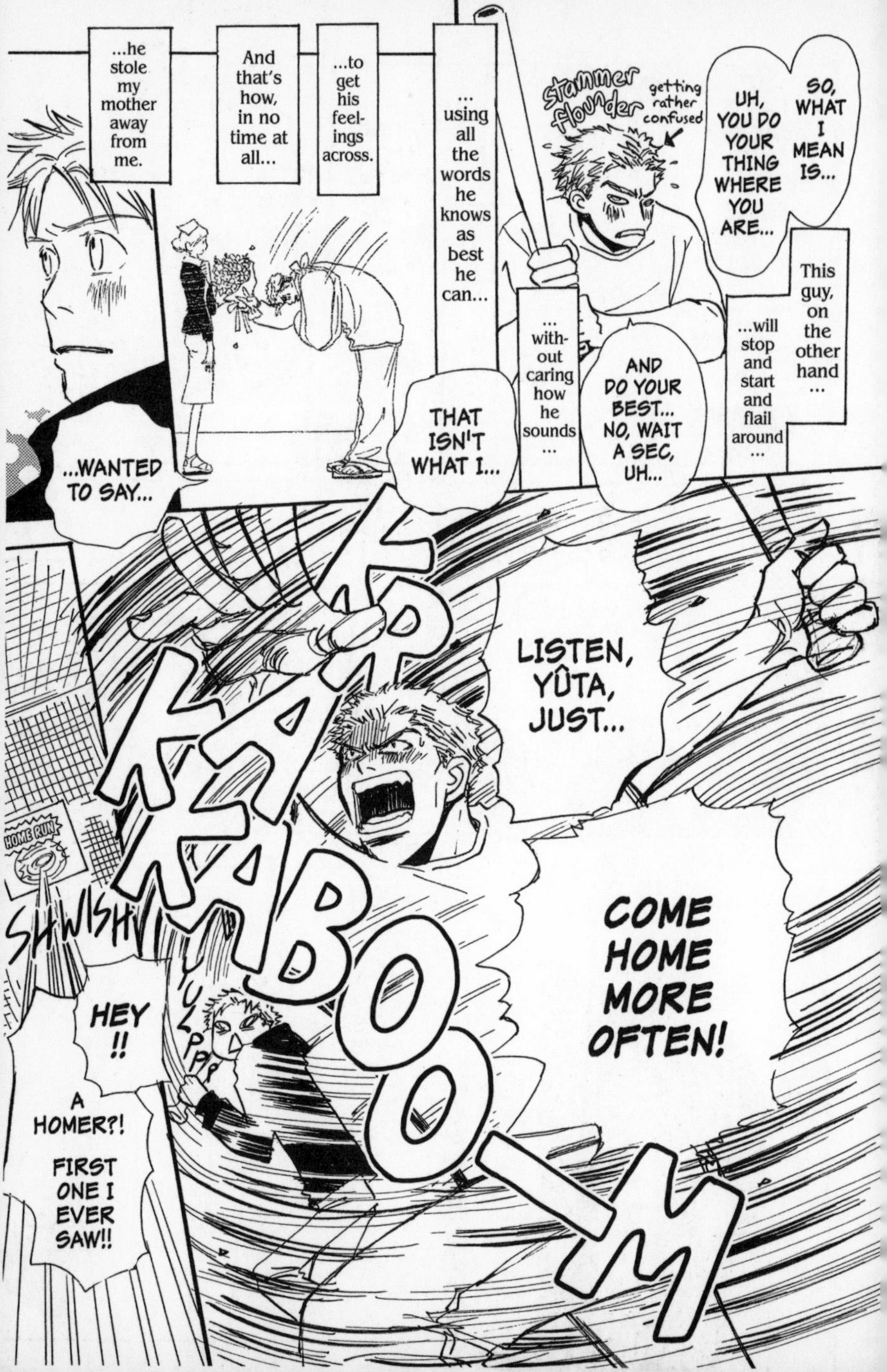
SO, WHAT I MEAN IS...
UH, YOU DO YOUR THING WHERE YOU ARE...
stammer flounder
getting rather confused
This guy, on the other hand...
...will stop and start and flail around...
AND DO YOUR BEST... NO, WAIT A SEC, UH...
...without caring how he sounds...
THAT ISN'T WHAT I...
...using all the words he knows as best he can...
...to get his feelings across.
And that's how, in no time at all...
...he stole my mother away from me.
...WANTED TO SAY...
LISTEN, YÛTA, JUST...
COME HOME MORE OFTEN!
KABOO-M
HOME RUN
SHWISH
HEY!!
A HOMER?!
FIRST ONE I EVER SAW!!

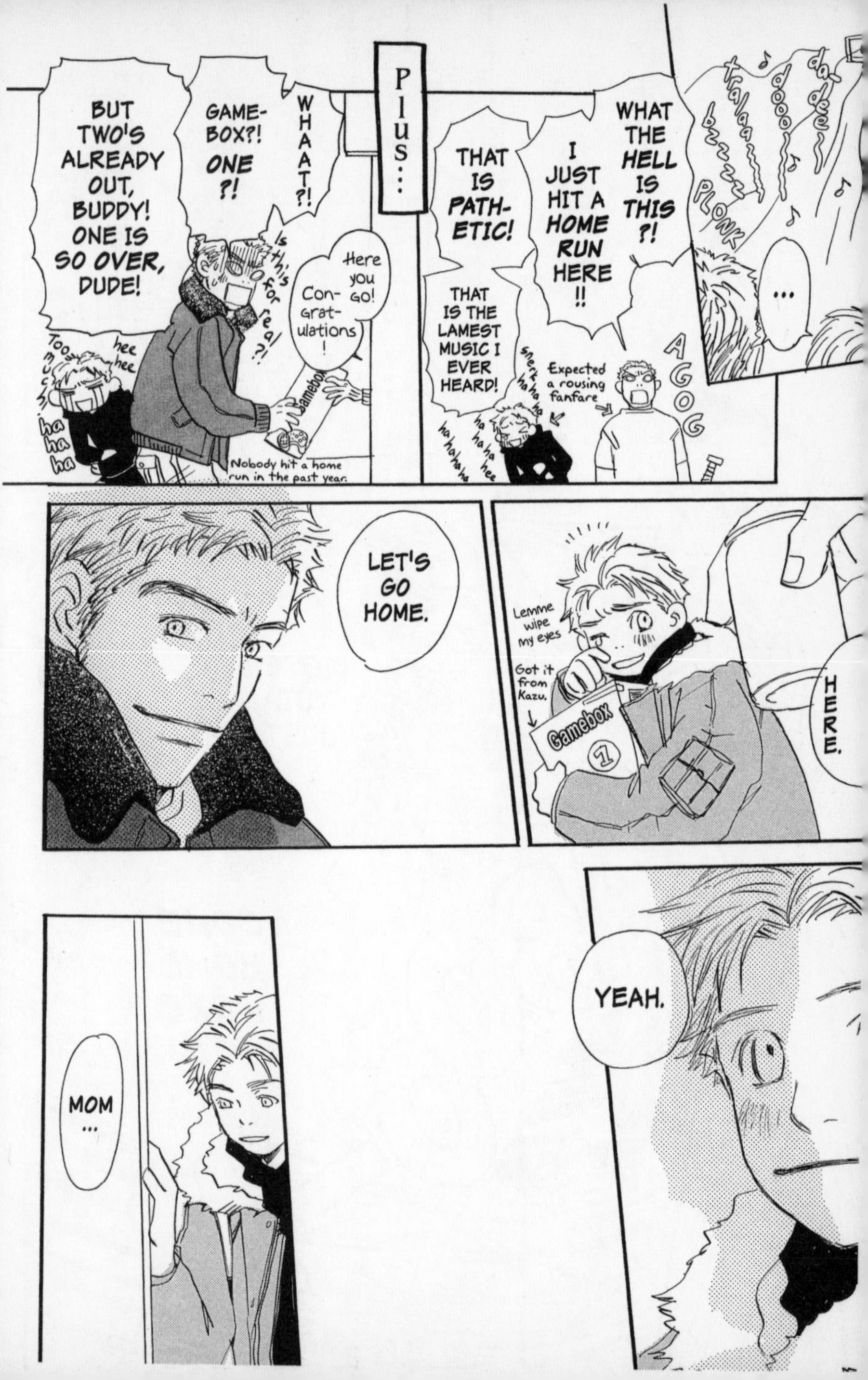
da-dee~
doooo~
tralaa~
bzzzz
PLONK
...
WHAT THE HELL IS THIS?!
I JUST HIT A HOME RUN HERE!!
THAT IS PATHETIC!
THAT IS THE LAMEST MUSIC I EVER HEARD!
snert ha ha ha
ha ha ha hee
ha ha ha ha
Expected a rousing fanfare
AGOG
Plus…
Here you go!
Con-grat-ulations!
Gamebox
Nobody hit a home run in the past year.
WHAAT?!
GAME-BOX?! ONE?!
Is this for real?!
BUT TWO'S ALREADY OUT, BUDDY! ONE IS SO OVER, DUDE!
hee hee
Too much!
ha ha ha
HERE.
Lemme wipe my eyes
Got it from Kazu.
Gamebox 1
LET'S GO HOME.
YEAH.
MOM
...

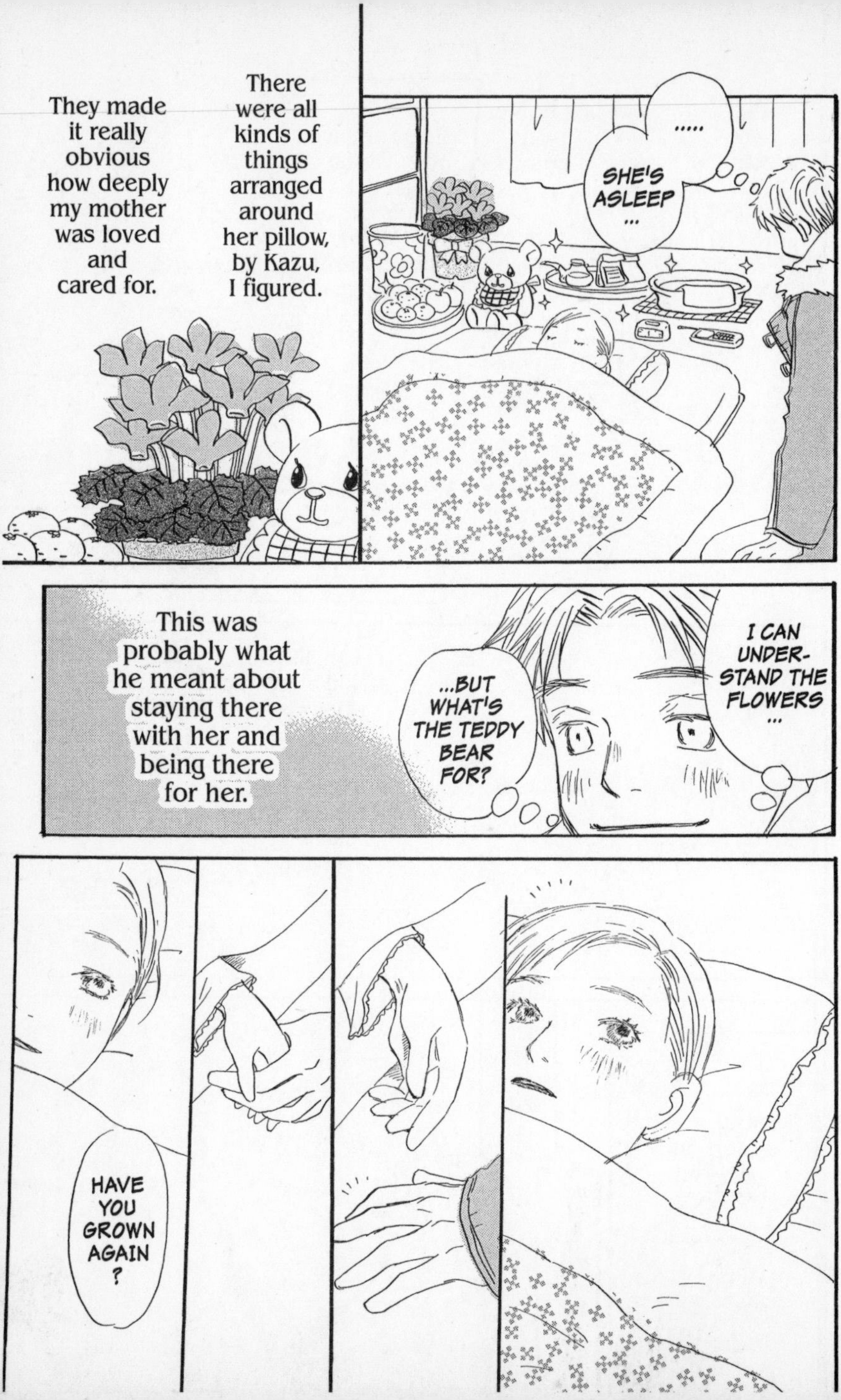
.....
SHE'S ASLEEP ...
There were all kinds of things arranged around her pillow, by Kazu, I figured.
They made it really obvious how deeply my mother was loved and cared for.
I CAN UNDER-STAND THE FLOWERS ...
...BUT WHAT'S THE TEDDY BEAR FOR?
This was probably what he meant about staying there with her and being there for her.
HAVE YOU GROWN AGAIN ?

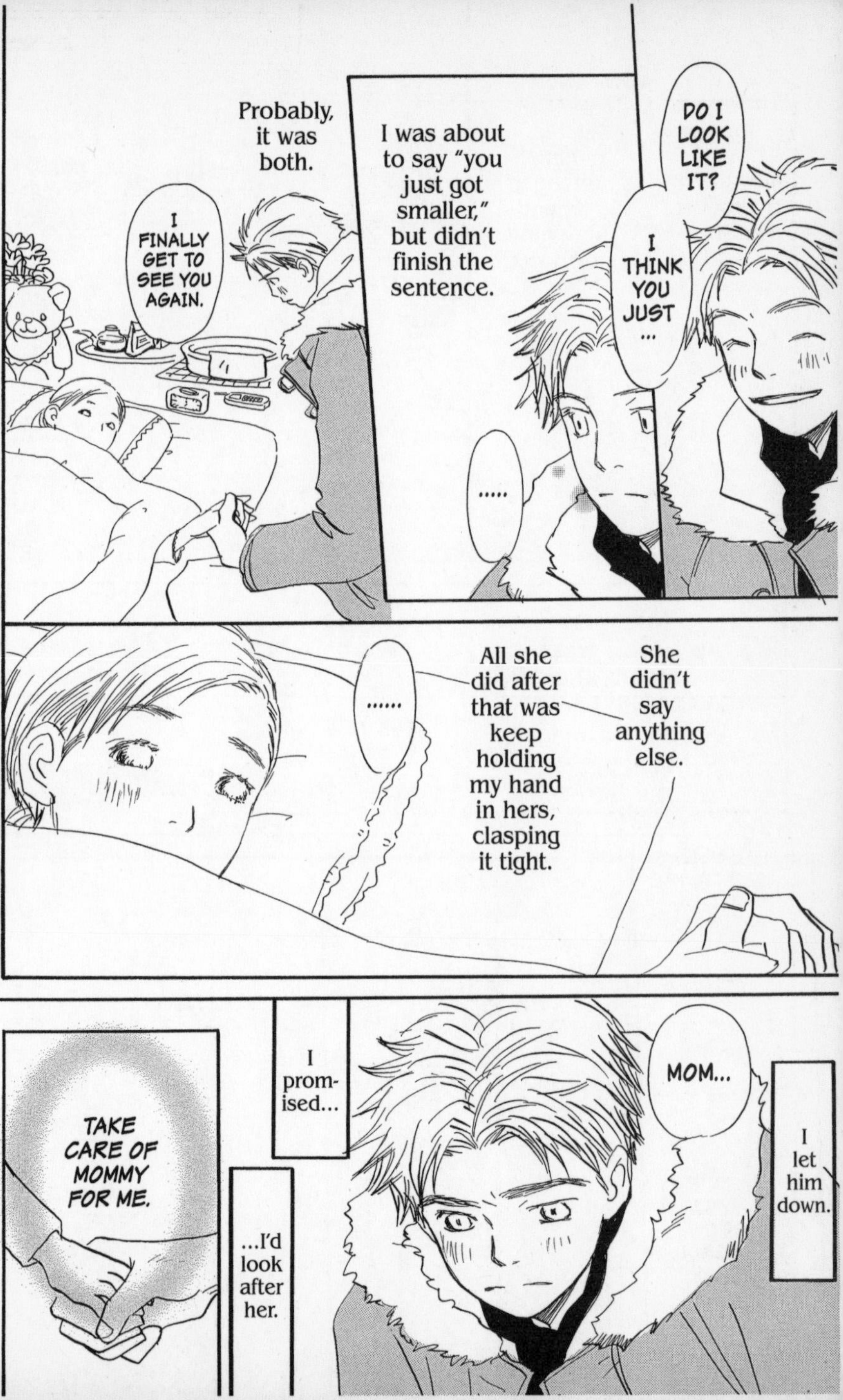
DO I LOOK LIKE IT?
I THINK YOU JUST ...
I was about to say "you just got smaller," but didn't finish the sentence.
.....
Probably, it was both.
I FINALLY GET TO SEE YOU AGAIN.
She didn't say anything else.
All she did after that was keep holding my hand in hers, clasping it tight.
......
MOM...
I let him down.
I prom-ised...
...I'd look after her.
TAKE CARE OF MOMMY FOR ME.

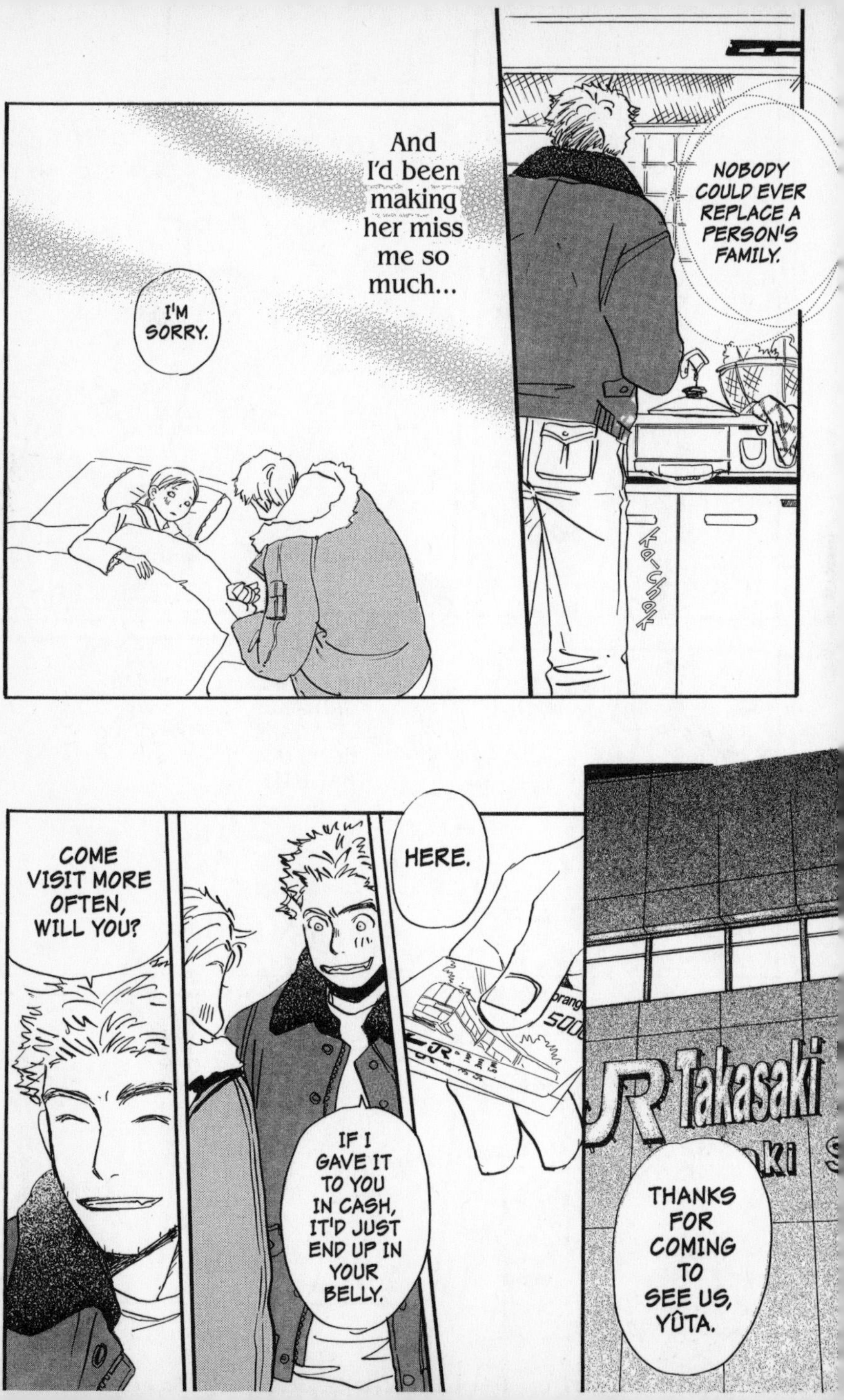
NOBODY COULD EVER REPLACE A PERSON'S FAMILY.
ka-chak
And I'd been making her miss me so much...
I'M SORRY.
JR Takasaki
THANKS FOR COMING TO SEE US, YÛTA.
HERE.
IF I GAVE IT TO YOU IN CASH, IT'D JUST END UP IN YOUR BELLY.
COME VISIT MORE OFTEN, WILL YOU?

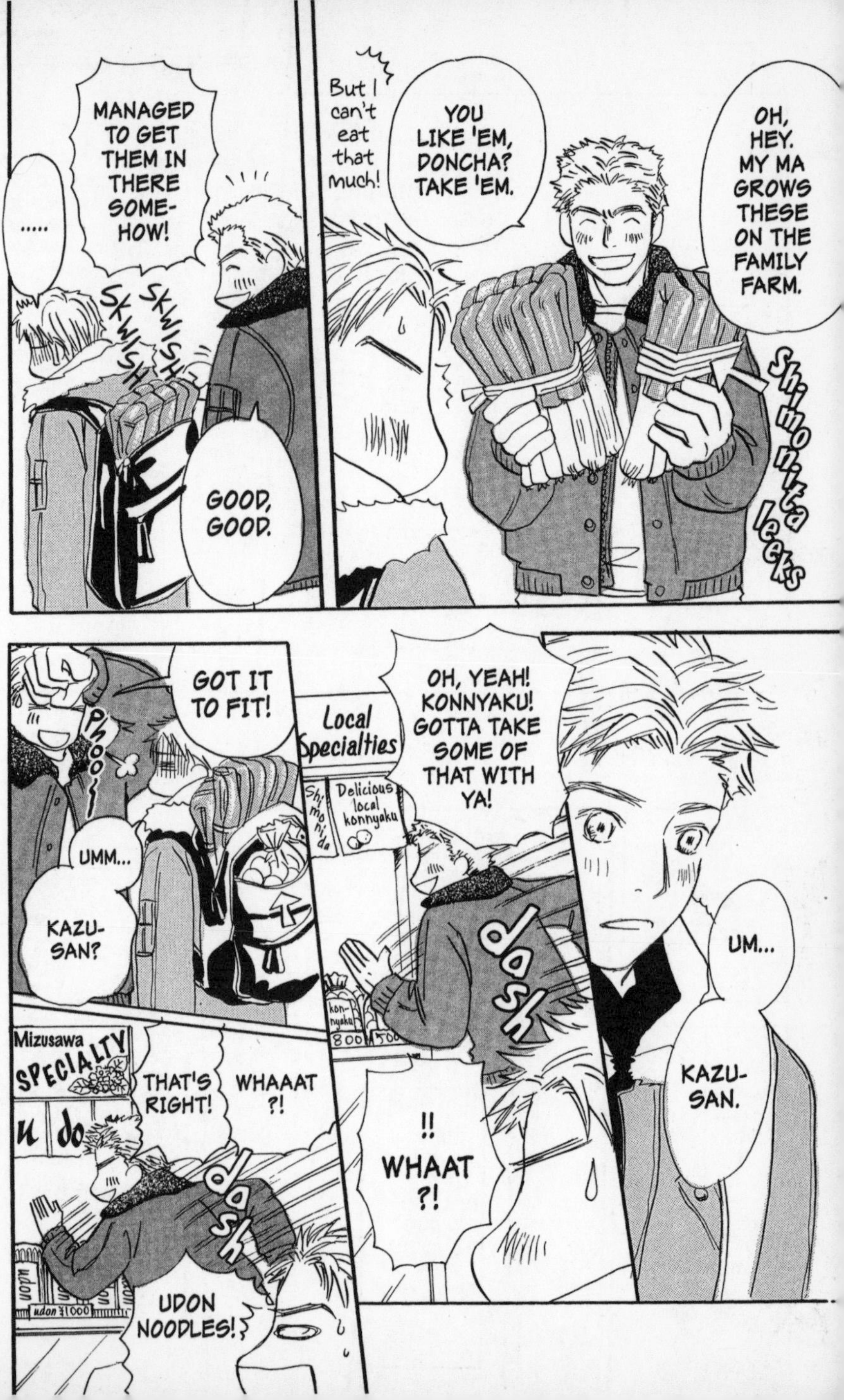
OH, HEY. MY MA GROWS THESE ON THE FAMILY FARM.
YOU LIKE 'EM, DONCHA? TAKE 'EM.
But I can't eat that much!
Shimonitta leeks
MANAGED TO GET THEM IN THERE SOME-HOW!
.....
SKWISH SKWISH
GOOD, GOOD.
OH, YEAH! KONNYAKU! GOTTA TAKE SOME OF THAT WITH YA!
Local Specialties
Shimonida
Delicious local konnyaku
konnyaku
800 500
dash
GOT IT TO FIT!
Phoooi
UMM...
KAZU-SAN?
UM...
KAZU-SAN.
!! WHAAT ?!
Mizusawa SPECIALTY
udo
THAT'S RIGHT!
WHAAAT ?!
dash
udon
udon ¥1000
UDON NOODLES!

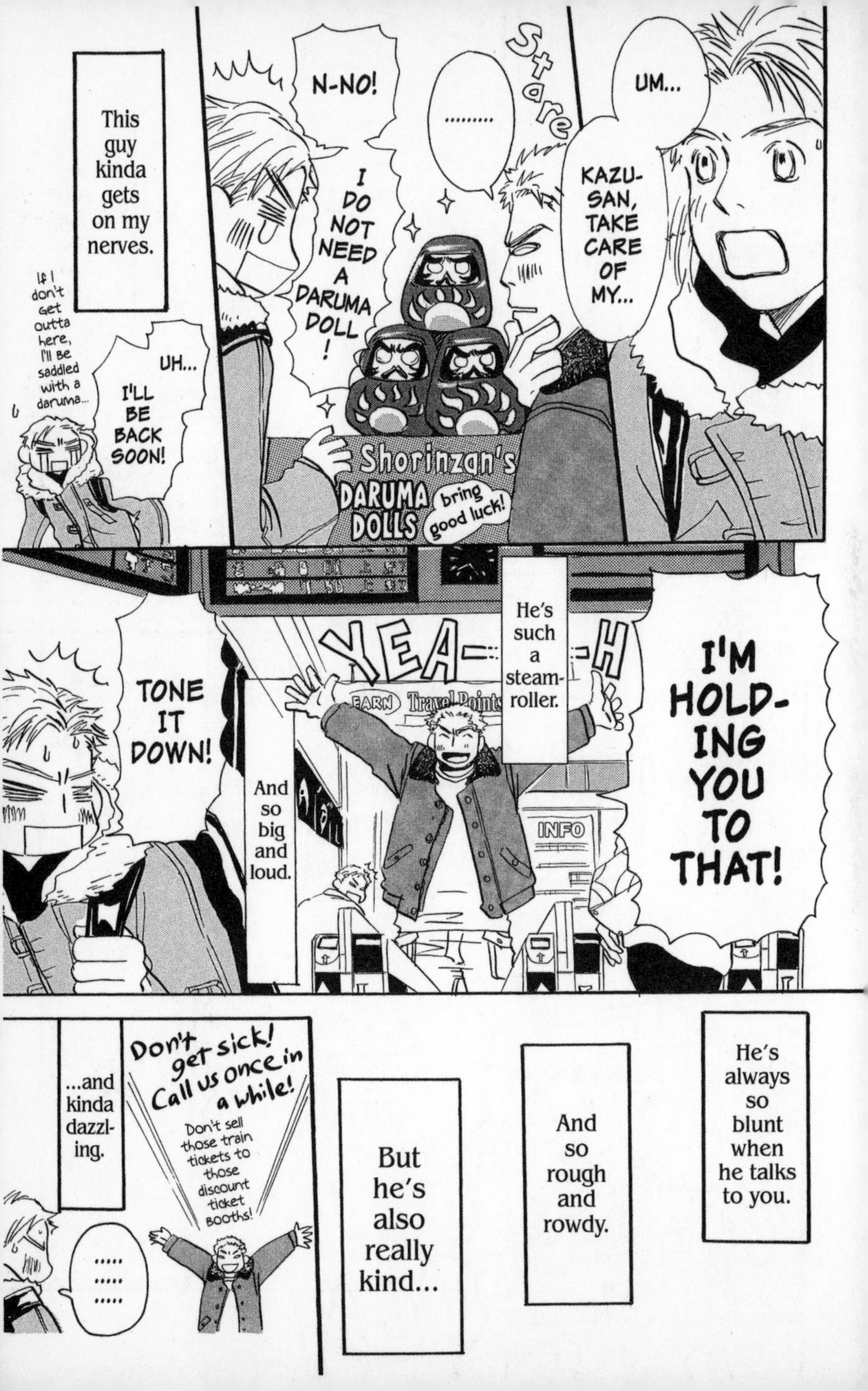
UM...
KAZU-SAN, TAKE CARE OF MY...
Stare
....
N-NO!
I DO NOT NEED A DARUMA DOLL!
Shorinzan's DARUMA DOLLS bring good luck!
This guy kinda gets on my nerves.
UH... I'LL BE BACK SOON!
If I don't get outta here, I'll be saddled with a daruma...
I'M HOLDING YOU TO THAT!
He's such a steamroller.
YEA---H
EARN Travel Points
INFO
And so big and loud.
TONE IT DOWN!
He's always so blunt when he talks to you.
And so rough and rowdy.
But he's also really kind...
Don't get sick! Call us once in a while!
Don't sell those train tickets to those discount ticket booths!
...and kinda dazzling.
....

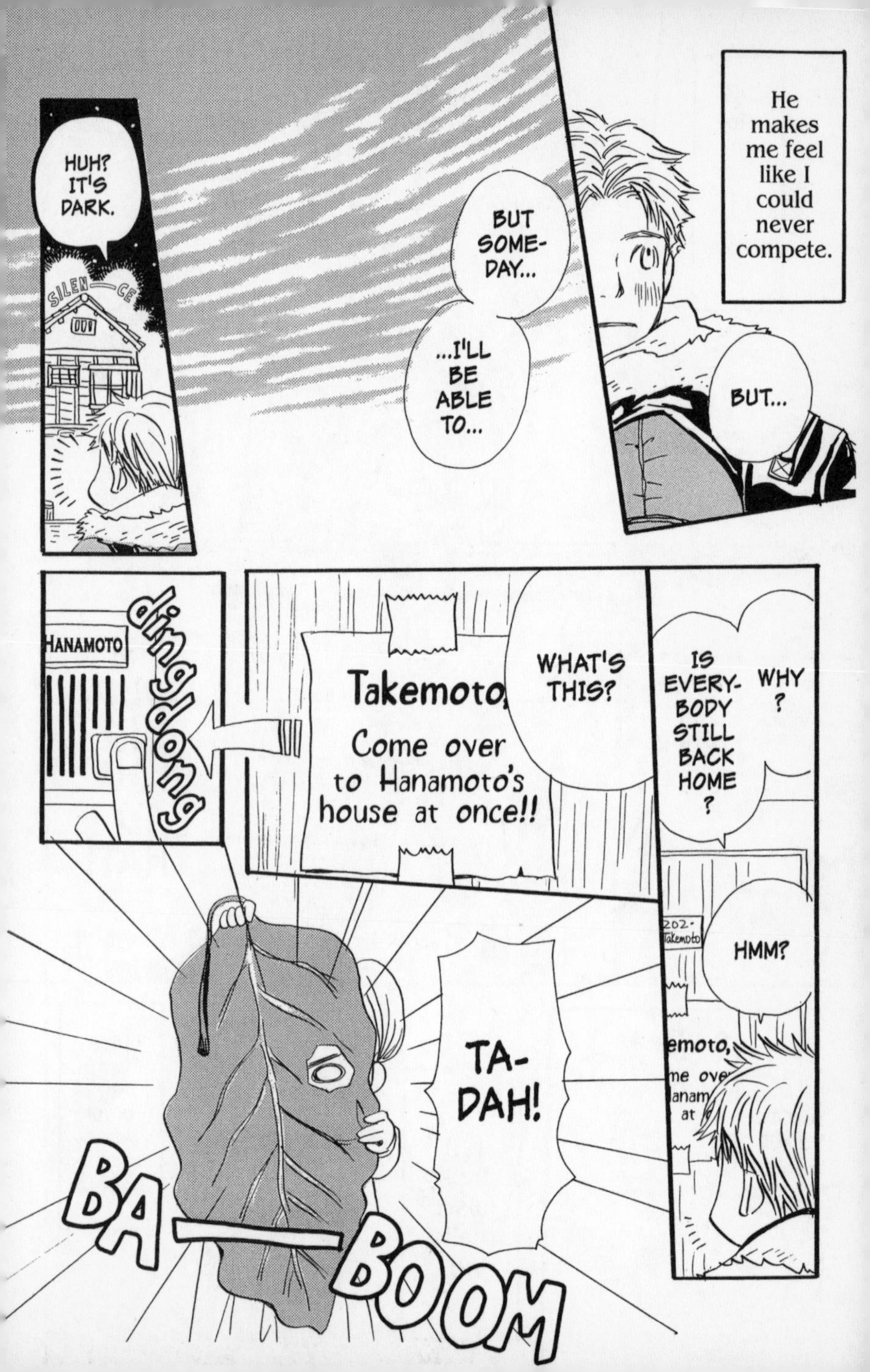
He makes me feel like I could never compete.
BUT...
BUT SOME-DAY...
...I'LL BE ABLE TO...
HUH? IT'S DARK.
SILEN—CE
WHY?
IS EVERY-BODY STILL BACK HOME?
WHAT'S THIS?
Takemoto,
Come over to Hanamoto's house at once!!
HANAMOTO
dingdong
202-
Takemoto
HMM?
TA-DAH!
BA—BOOM

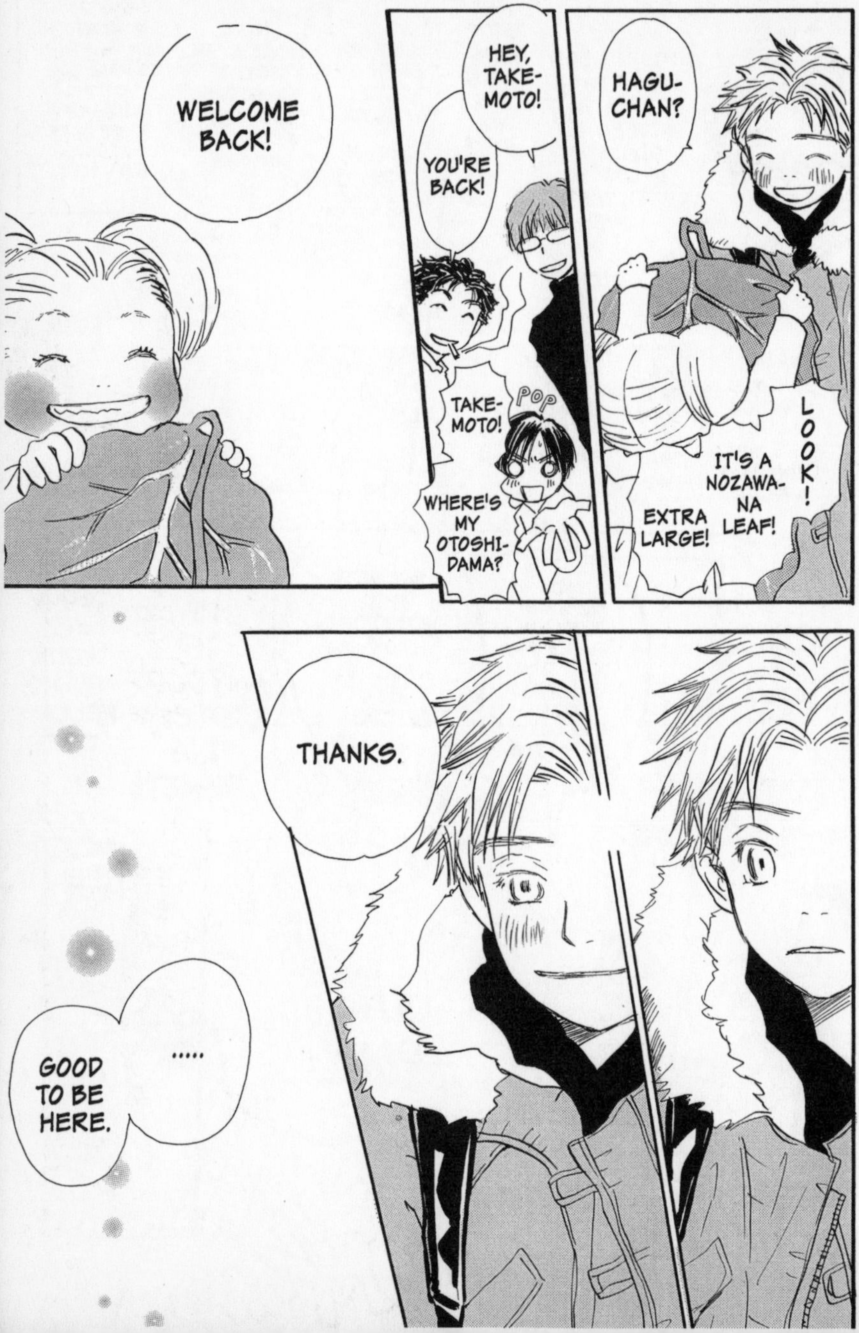
HAGU-CHAN?
LOOK!
IT'S A NOZAWA-NA LEAF!
EXTRA LARGE!
HEY, TAKE-MOTO!
YOU'RE BACK!
POP
TAKE-MOTO!
WHERE'S MY OTOSHI-DAMA?
WELCOME BACK!
THANKS.
.....
GOOD TO BE HERE.

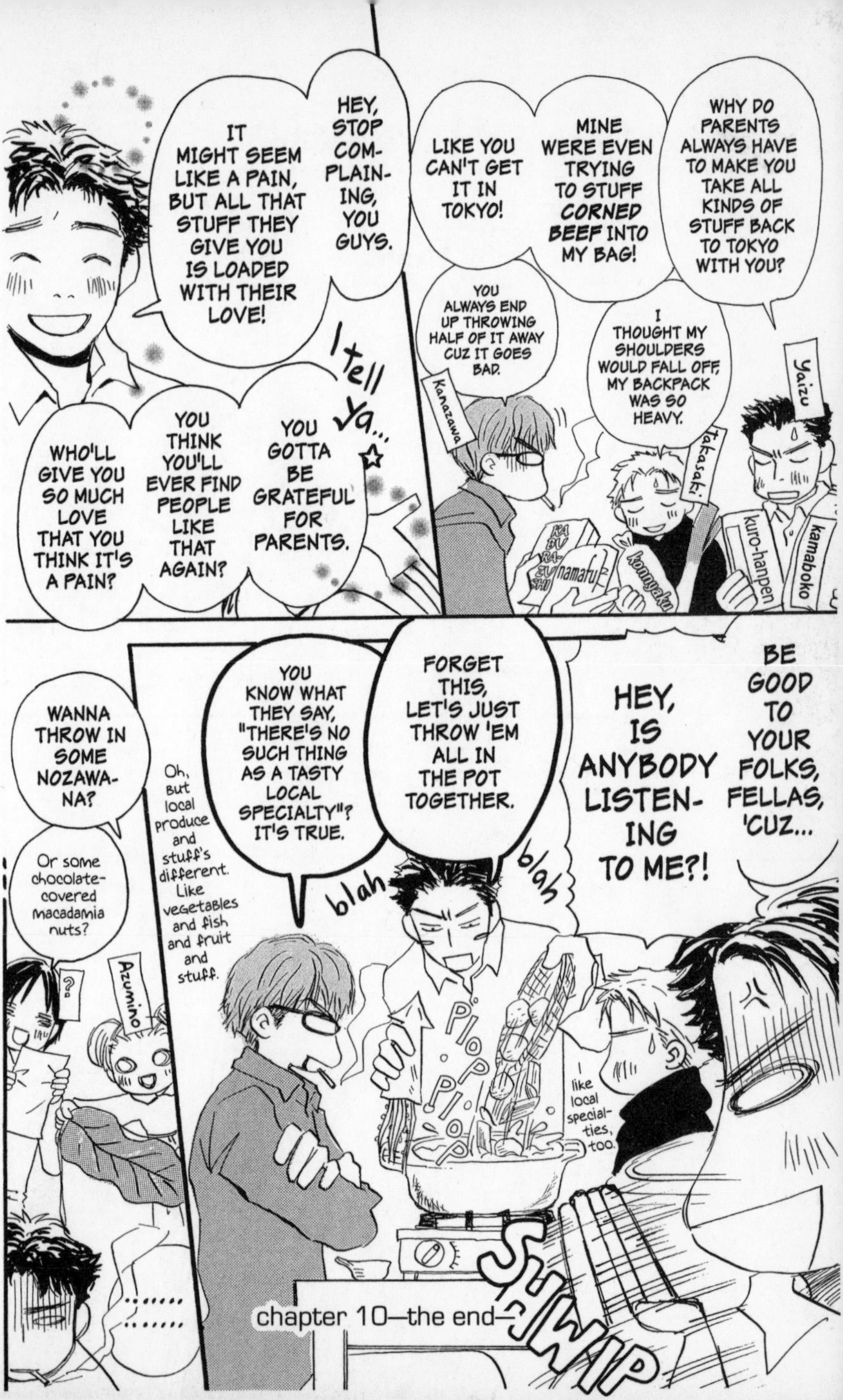
WHY DO PARENTS ALWAYS HAVE TO MAKE YOU TAKE ALL KINDS OF STUFF BACK TO TOKYO WITH YOU?
MINE WERE EVEN TRYING TO STUFF CORNED BEEF INTO MY BAG!
LIKE YOU CAN'T GET IT IN TOKYO!
I THOUGHT MY SHOULDERS WOULD FALL OFF, MY BACKPACK WAS SO HEAVY.
YOU ALWAYS END UP THROWING HALF OF IT AWAY CUZ IT GOES BAD.
Yaizu
Takasaki
Kanazawa
kamaboko
kuro-hanpen
konnyaku
namafu
KABURAZUSHI
HEY, STOP COMPLAINING, YOU GUYS.
IT MIGHT SEEM LIKE A PAIN, BUT ALL THAT STUFF THEY GIVE YOU IS LOADED WITH THEIR LOVE!
I tell ya...
YOU GOTTA BE GRATEFUL FOR PARENTS.
YOU THINK YOU'LL EVER FIND PEOPLE LIKE THAT AGAIN?
WHO'LL GIVE YOU SO MUCH LOVE THAT YOU THINK IT'S A PAIN?
BE GOOD TO YOUR FOLKS, FELLAS, 'CUZ...
HEY, IS ANYBODY LISTENING TO ME?!
FORGET THIS, LET'S JUST THROW 'EM ALL IN THE POT TOGETHER.
blah
blah
YOU KNOW WHAT THEY SAY, "THERE'S NO SUCH THING AS A TASTY LOCAL SPECIALTY"? IT'S TRUE.
Oh, but local produce and stuff's different. Like vegetables and fish and fruit and stuff.
WANNA THROW IN SOME NOZAWANA?
Or some chocolate-covered macadamia nuts?
Azumino
??
PLOP PLOP PLOP
I like local specialties, too.
SHWIP
......
......
chapter 10—the end—

honey and clover™

chapter 11

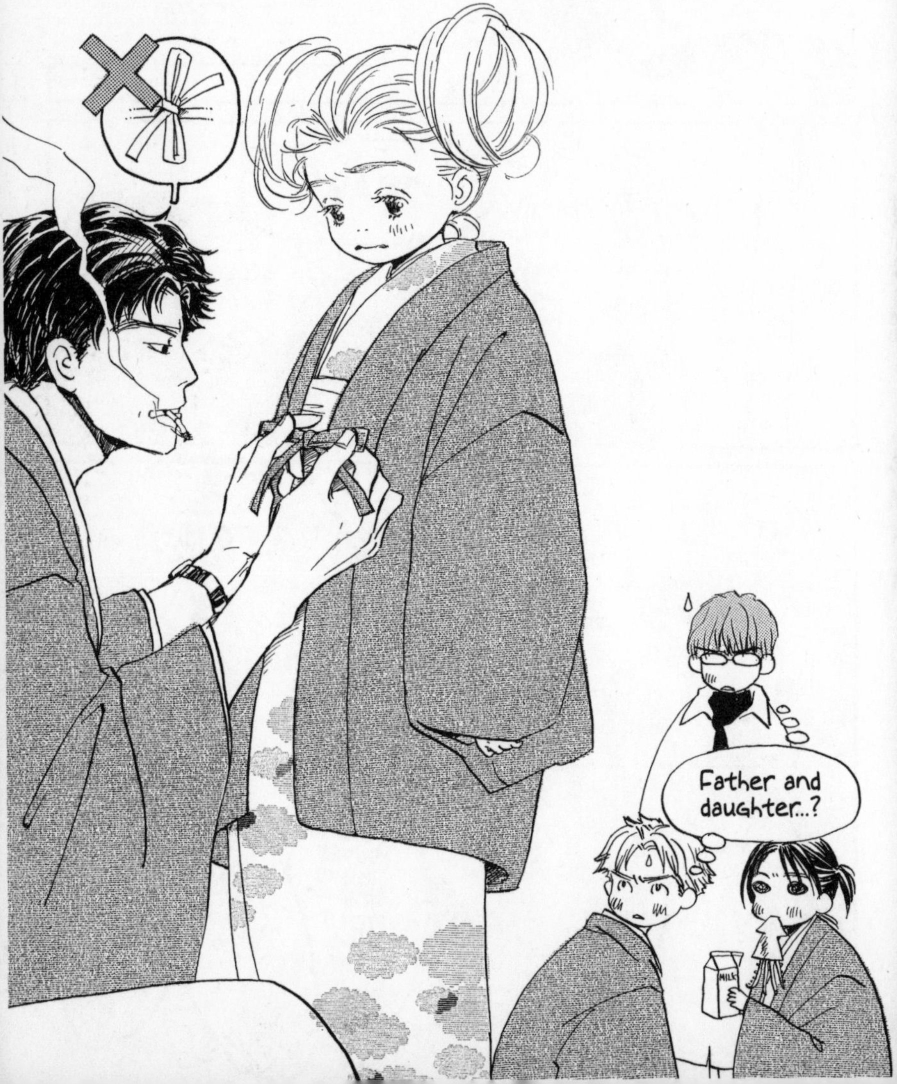
Father and daughter...?
MILK

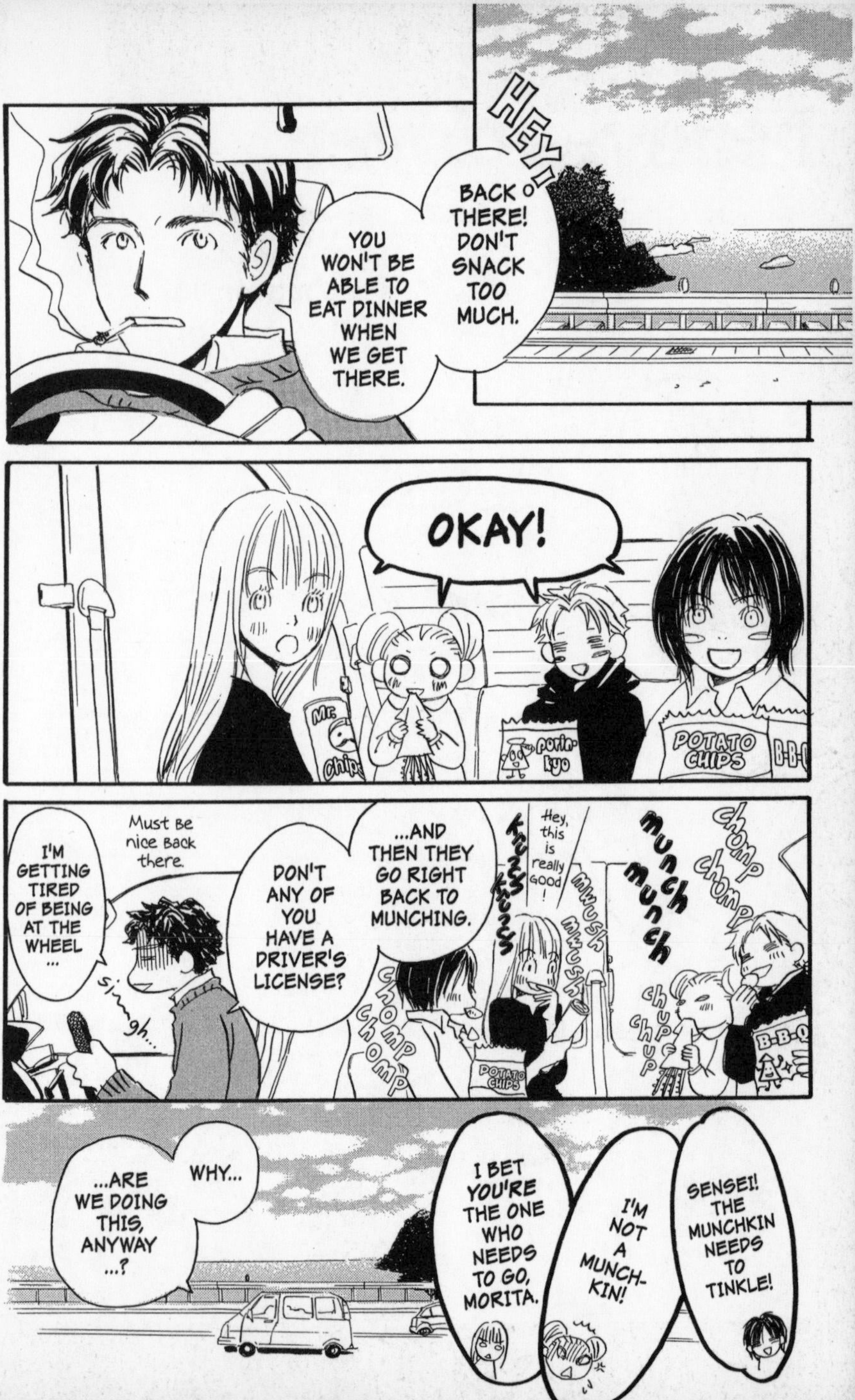

HEY!!
BACK THERE! DON'T SNACK TOO MUCH.
YOU WON'T BE ABLE TO EAT DINNER WHEN WE GET THERE.
OKAY!
Mr. Chips
porin-kyo
POTATO CHIPS
B-B-Q
chomp chomp
munch munch
mwush mwush
Hey, this is really good!
krunch krunch
...AND THEN THEY GO RIGHT BACK TO MUNCHING.
DON'T ANY OF YOU HAVE A DRIVER'S LICENSE?
Must be nice back there.
I'M GETTING TIRED OF BEING AT THE WHEEL...
chup chup
B-B-Q
POTATO CHIPS
chomp chomp
SENSEI! THE MUNCHKIN NEEDS TO TINKLE!
I'M NOT A MUNCHKIN!
I BET YOU'RE THE ONE WHO NEEDS TO GO, MORITA.
WHY...
...ARE WE DOING THIS, ANYWAY...?

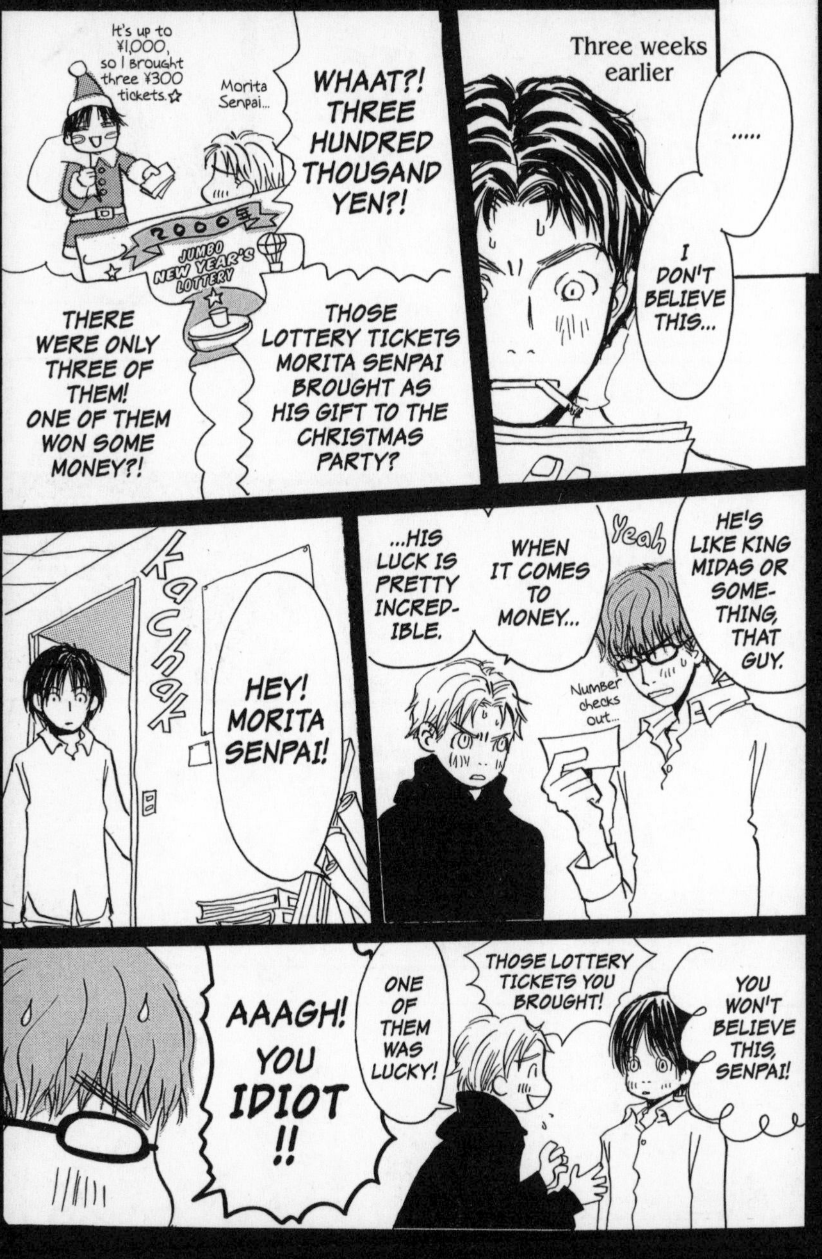
Three weeks earlier
.....
I DON'T BELIEVE THIS...
WHAAT?! THREE HUNDRED THOUSAND YEN?!
Morita Senpai...
It's up to ¥1,000, so I brought three ¥300 tickets.☆
2000年
JUMBO NEW YEAR'S LOTTERY
THOSE LOTTERY TICKETS MORITA SENPAI BROUGHT AS HIS GIFT TO THE CHRISTMAS PARTY?
THERE WERE ONLY THREE OF THEM! ONE OF THEM WON SOME MONEY?!
HE'S LIKE KING MIDAS OR SOME-THING, THAT GUY.
Yeah
WHEN IT COMES TO MONEY...
...HIS LUCK IS PRETTY INCRED-IBLE.
Number checks out...
Kachak
HEY! MORITA SENPAI!
YOU WON'T BELIEVE THIS, SENPAI!
THOSE LOTTERY TICKETS YOU BROUGHT!
ONE OF THEM WAS LUCKY!
AAAGH! YOU IDIOT!!

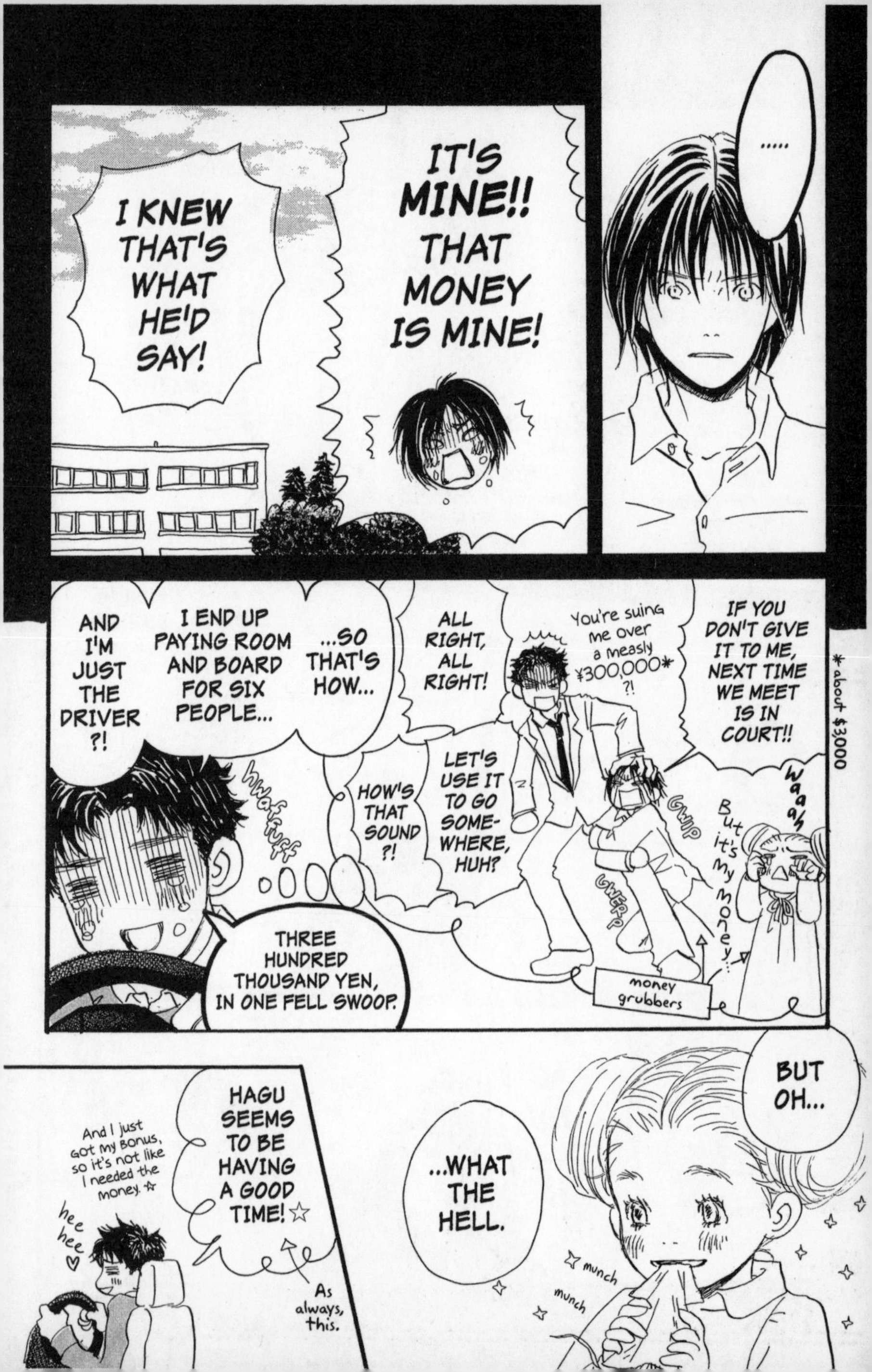

.....
IT'S MINE!! THAT MONEY IS MINE!
I KNEW THAT'S WHAT HE'D SAY!
IF YOU DON'T GIVE IT TO ME, NEXT TIME WE MEET IS IN COURT!!
* about $3000
You're suing me over a measly ¥300,000* ?!
ALL RIGHT, ALL RIGHT!
...SO THAT'S HOW...
I END UP PAYING ROOM AND BOARD FOR SIX PEOPLE...
AND I'M JUST THE DRIVER ?!
Waaah
But it's my money...
GWIP
GWEPP
money grubbers
LET'S USE IT TO GO SOME-WHERE, HUH?
HOW'S THAT SOUND ?!
hwafuff
THREE HUNDRED THOUSAND YEN, IN ONE FELL SWOOP.
BUT OH...
...WHAT THE HELL.
munch
munch
HAGU SEEMS TO BE HAVING A GOOD TIME! ☆
As always, this.
And I just got my bonus, so it's not like I needed the money. ☆
hee hee ♡

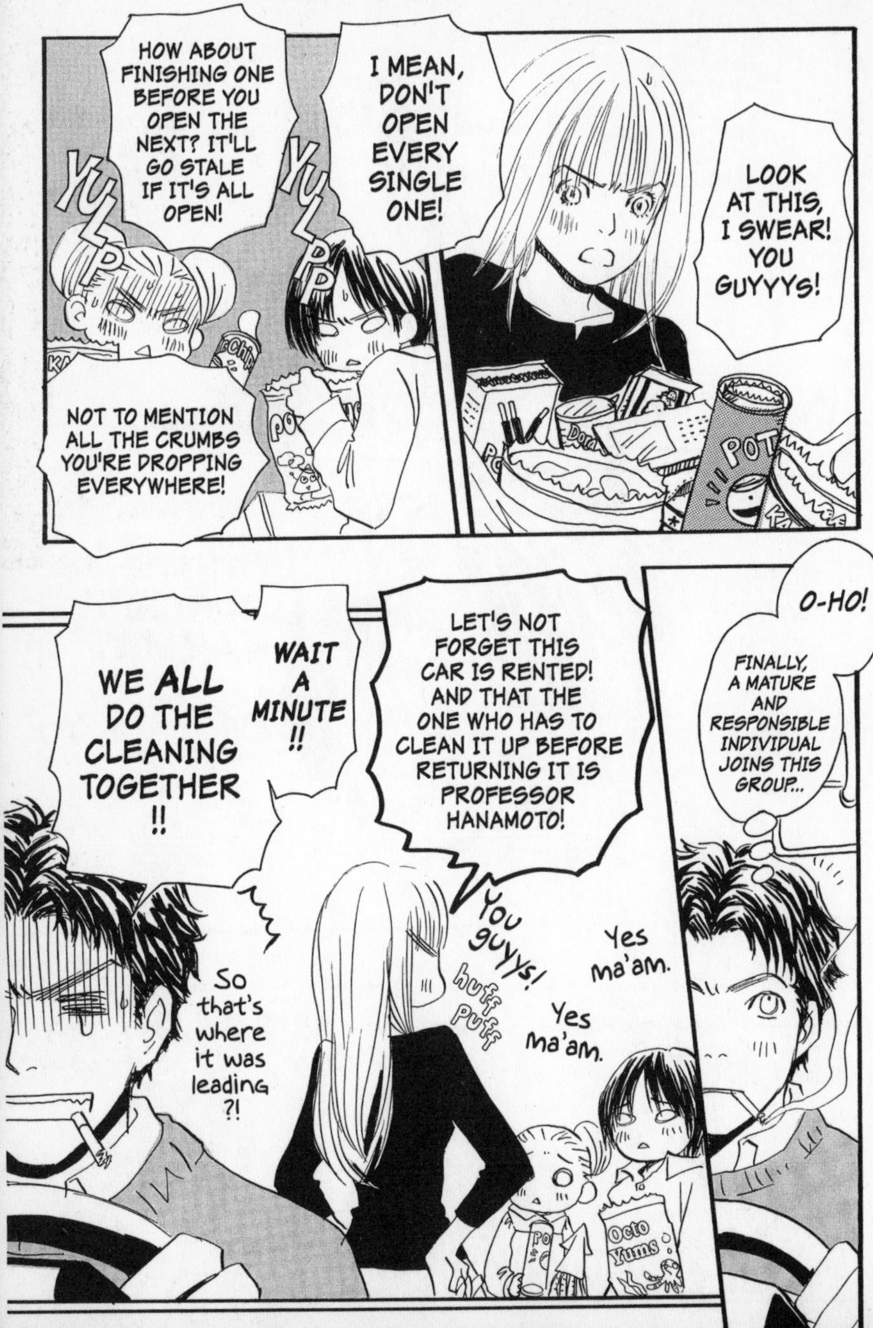
LOOK AT THIS, I SWEAR! YOU GUYYYS!
I MEAN, DON'T OPEN EVERY SINGLE ONE!
YULP
HOW ABOUT FINISHING ONE BEFORE YOU OPEN THE NEXT? IT'LL GO STALE IF IT'S ALL OPEN!
YULP
NOT TO MENTION ALL THE CRUMBS YOU'RE DROPPING EVERYWHERE!
POT
O-HO!
FINALLY, A MATURE AND RESPONSIBLE INDIVIDUAL JOINS THIS GROUP...
LET'S NOT FORGET THIS CAR IS RENTED! AND THAT THE ONE WHO HAS TO CLEAN IT UP BEFORE RETURNING IT IS PROFESSOR HANAMOTO!
WAIT A MINUTE !!
WE ALL DO THE CLEANING TOGETHER !!
You guyyys!
huff puff
Yes ma'am.
Yes ma'am.
So that's where it was leading ?!
Octo Yums

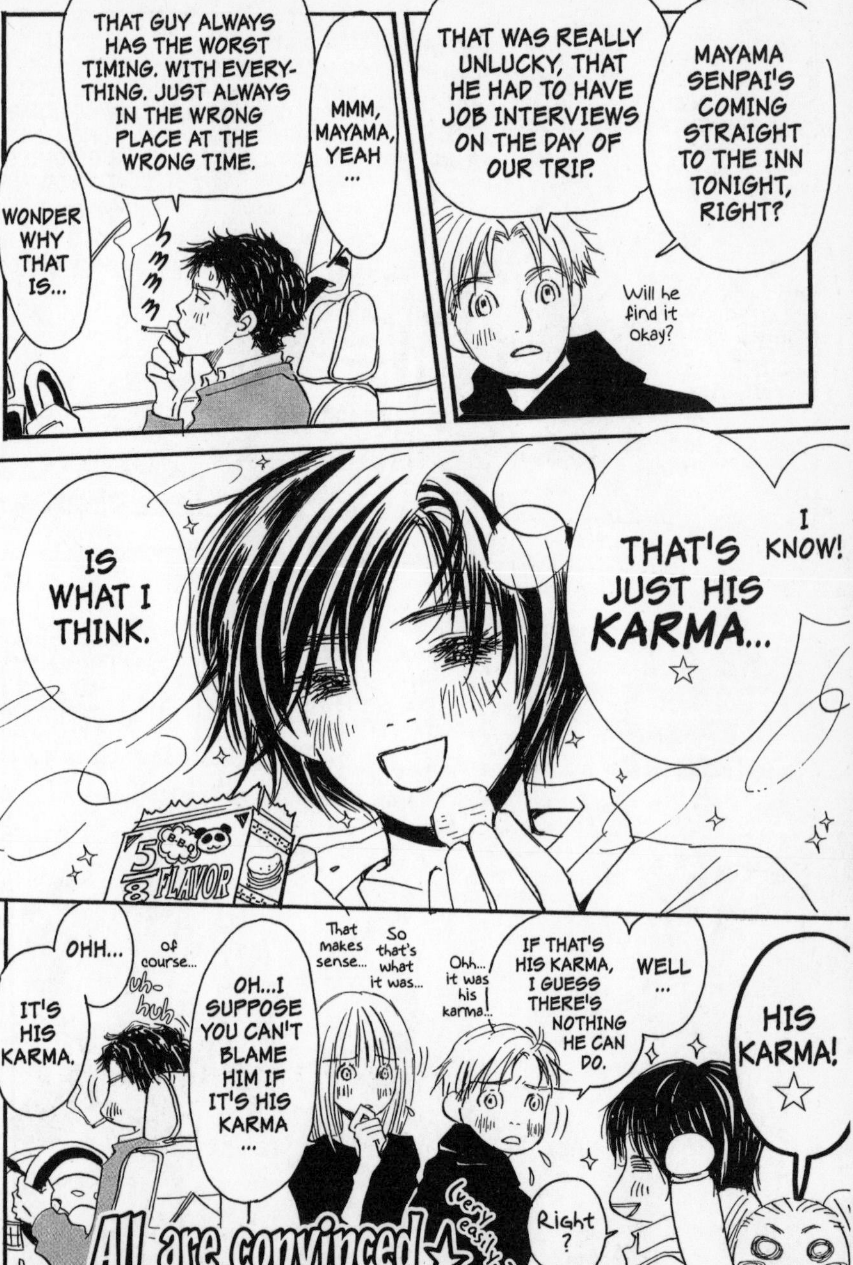
MAYAMA SENPAI'S COMING STRAIGHT TO THE INN TONIGHT, RIGHT?
THAT WAS REALLY UNLUCKY, THAT HE HAD TO HAVE JOB INTERVIEWS ON THE DAY OF OUR TRIP.
Will he find it okay?
MMM, MAYAMA, YEAH ...
mmmm
THAT GUY ALWAYS HAS THE WORST TIMING. WITH EVERY-THING. JUST ALWAYS IN THE WRONG PLACE AT THE WRONG TIME.
WONDER WHY THAT IS...
I KNOW!
THAT'S JUST HIS KARMA... ☆
IS WHAT I THINK.
B.B.Q
5/8 FLAVOR
HIS KARMA! ☆
Right?
WELL ...
IF THAT'S HIS KARMA, I GUESS THERE'S NOTHING HE CAN DO.
Ohh... it was his karma...
So that's what it was...
That makes sense...
(very easily...)
OH...I SUPPOSE YOU CAN'T BLAME HIM IF IT'S HIS KARMA ...
of course...
uh-huh
OHH...
IT'S HIS KARMA.
All are convinced ☆

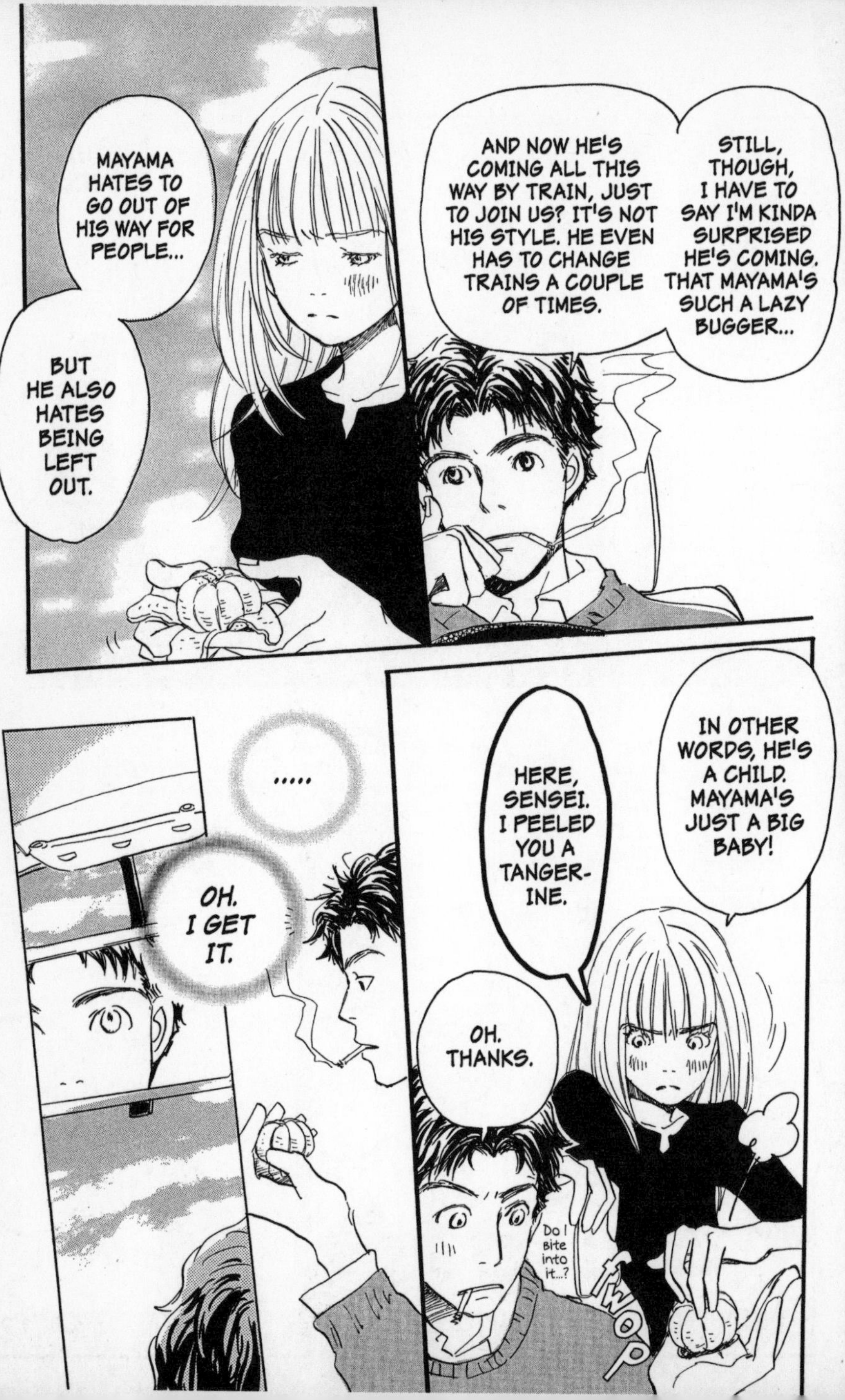
STILL, THOUGH, I HAVE TO SAY I'M KINDA SURPRISED HE'S COMING. THAT MAYAMA'S SUCH A LAZY BUGGER...
AND NOW HE'S COMING ALL THIS WAY BY TRAIN, JUST TO JOIN US? IT'S NOT HIS STYLE. HE EVEN HAS TO CHANGE TRAINS A COUPLE OF TIMES.
MAYAMA HATES TO GO OUT OF HIS WAY FOR PEOPLE...
BUT HE ALSO HATES BEING LEFT OUT.
IN OTHER WORDS, HE'S A CHILD. MAYAMA'S JUST A BIG BABY!
HERE, SENSEI. I PEELED YOU A TANGER-INE.
OH. THANKS.
Do I bite into it...?
TWOP
.....
OH. I GET IT.

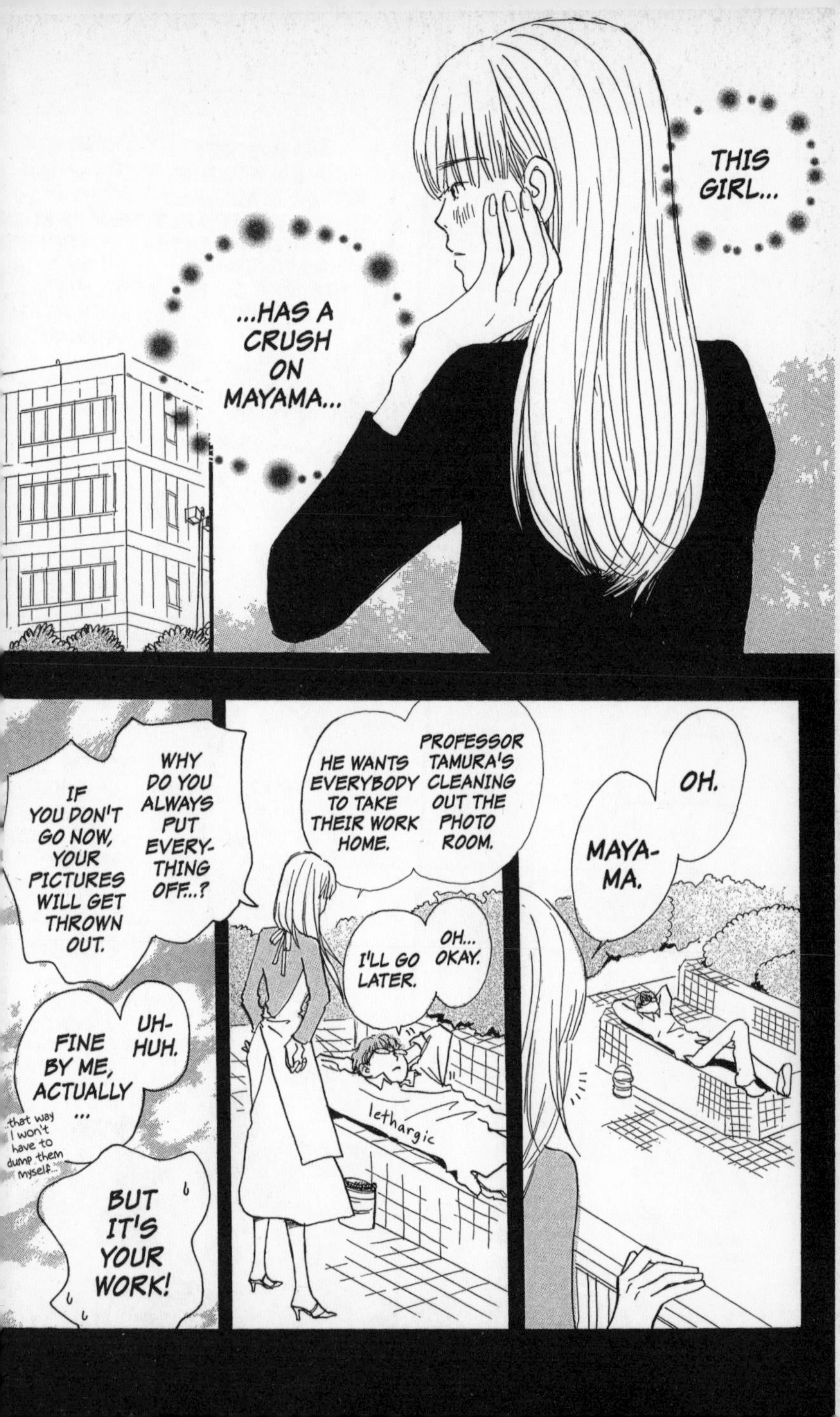
THIS GIRL...
...HAS A CRUSH ON MAYAMA...
OH.
MAYA-MA.
PROFESSOR TAMURA'S CLEANING OUT THE PHOTO ROOM.
HE WANTS EVERYBODY TO TAKE THEIR WORK HOME.
OH... OKAY.
I'LL GO LATER.
lethargic
WHY DO YOU ALWAYS PUT EVERY-THING OFF...?
IF YOU DON'T GO NOW, YOUR PICTURES WILL GET THROWN OUT.
UH-HUH.
FINE BY ME, ACTUALLY...
...that way I won't have to dump them myself...
BUT IT'S YOUR WORK!

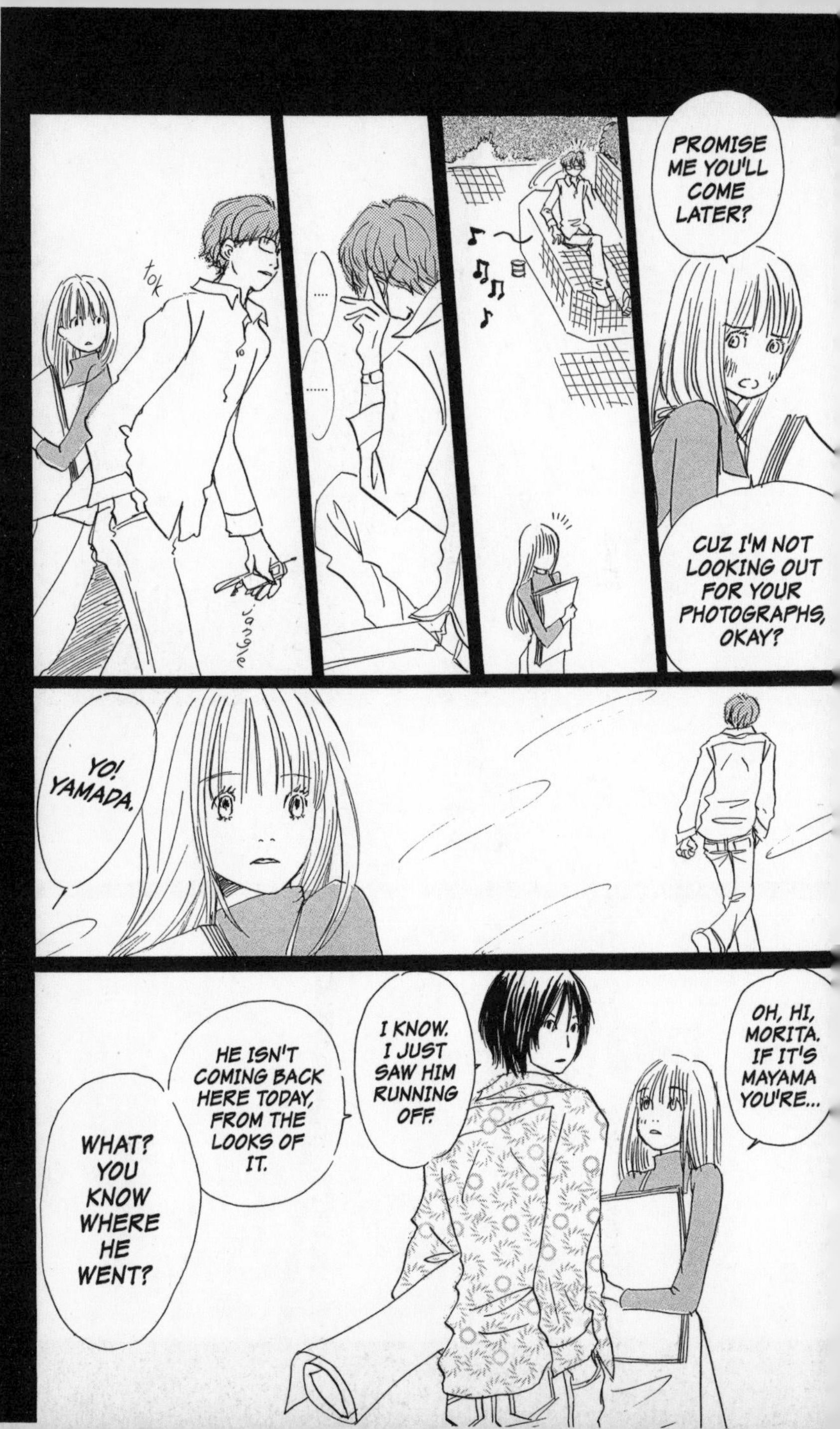
PROMISE ME YOU'LL COME LATER?
CUZ I'M NOT LOOKING OUT FOR YOUR PHOTOGRAPHS, OKAY?
.....
.....
tok
jangle
YO! YAMADA.
OH, HI, MORITA. IF IT'S MAYAMA YOU'RE...
I KNOW. I JUST SAW HIM RUNNING OFF.
HE ISN'T COMING BACK HERE TODAY, FROM THE LOOKS OF IT.
WHAT? YOU KNOW WHERE HE WENT?

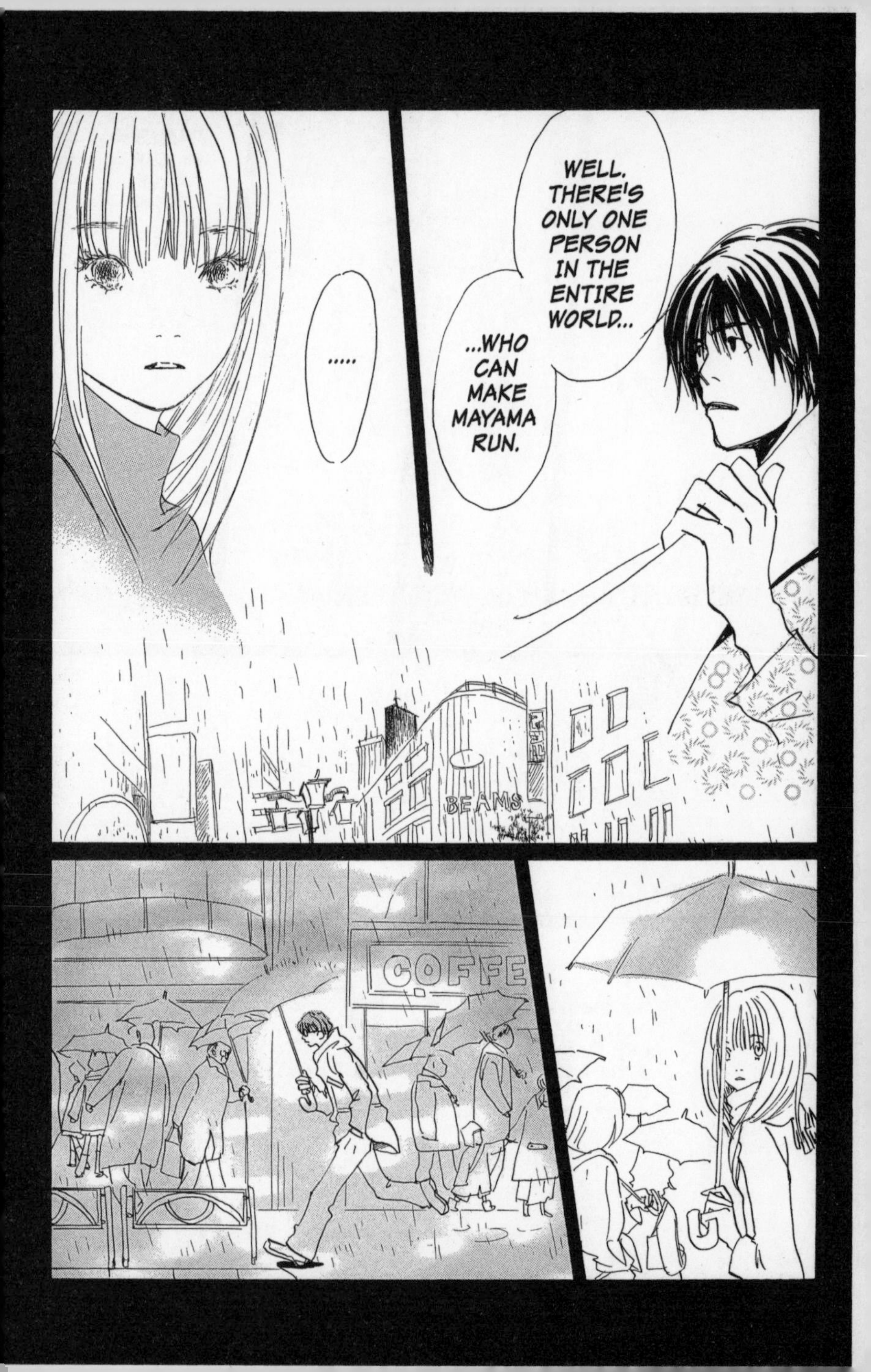
WELL. THERE'S ONLY ONE PERSON IN THE ENTIRE WORLD...
...WHO CAN MAKE MAYAMA RUN.
BEAMS
.....
COFFE

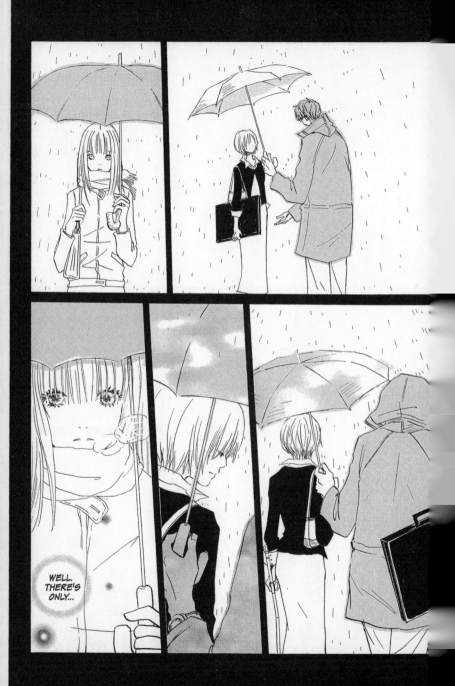

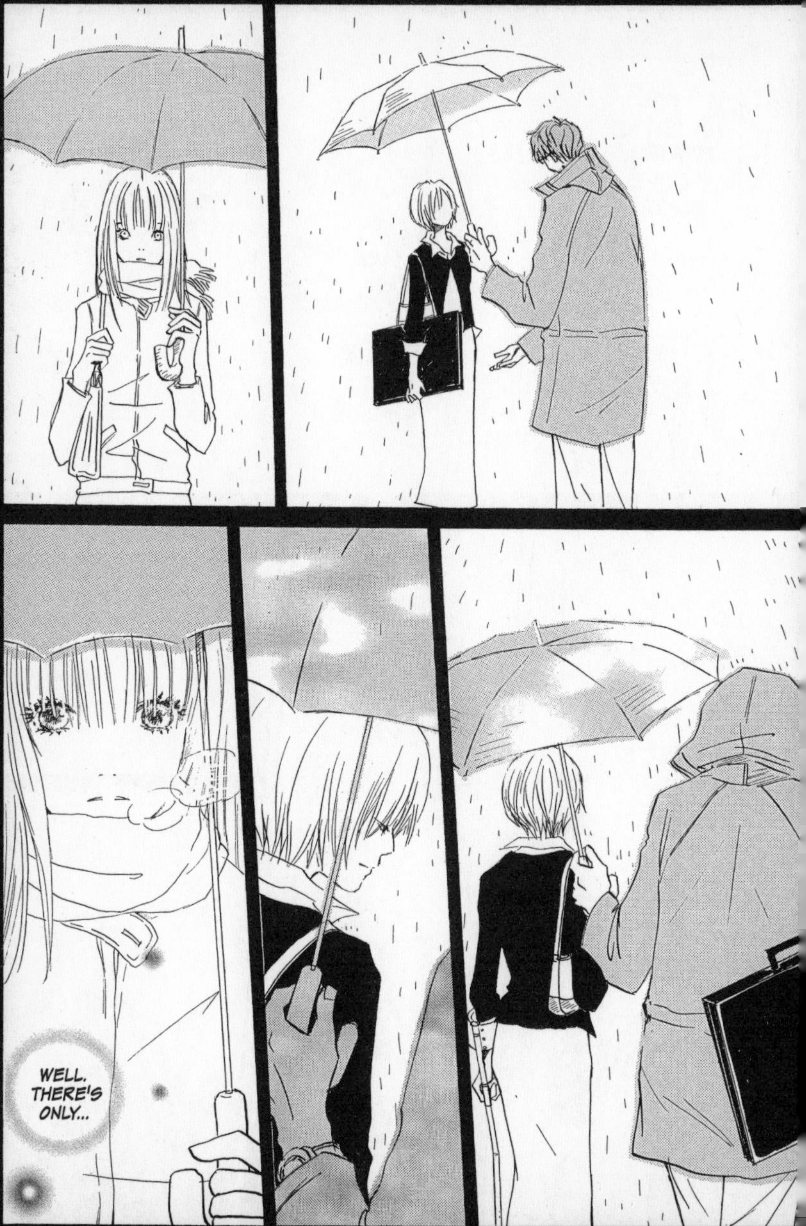
WELL. THERE'S ONLY...

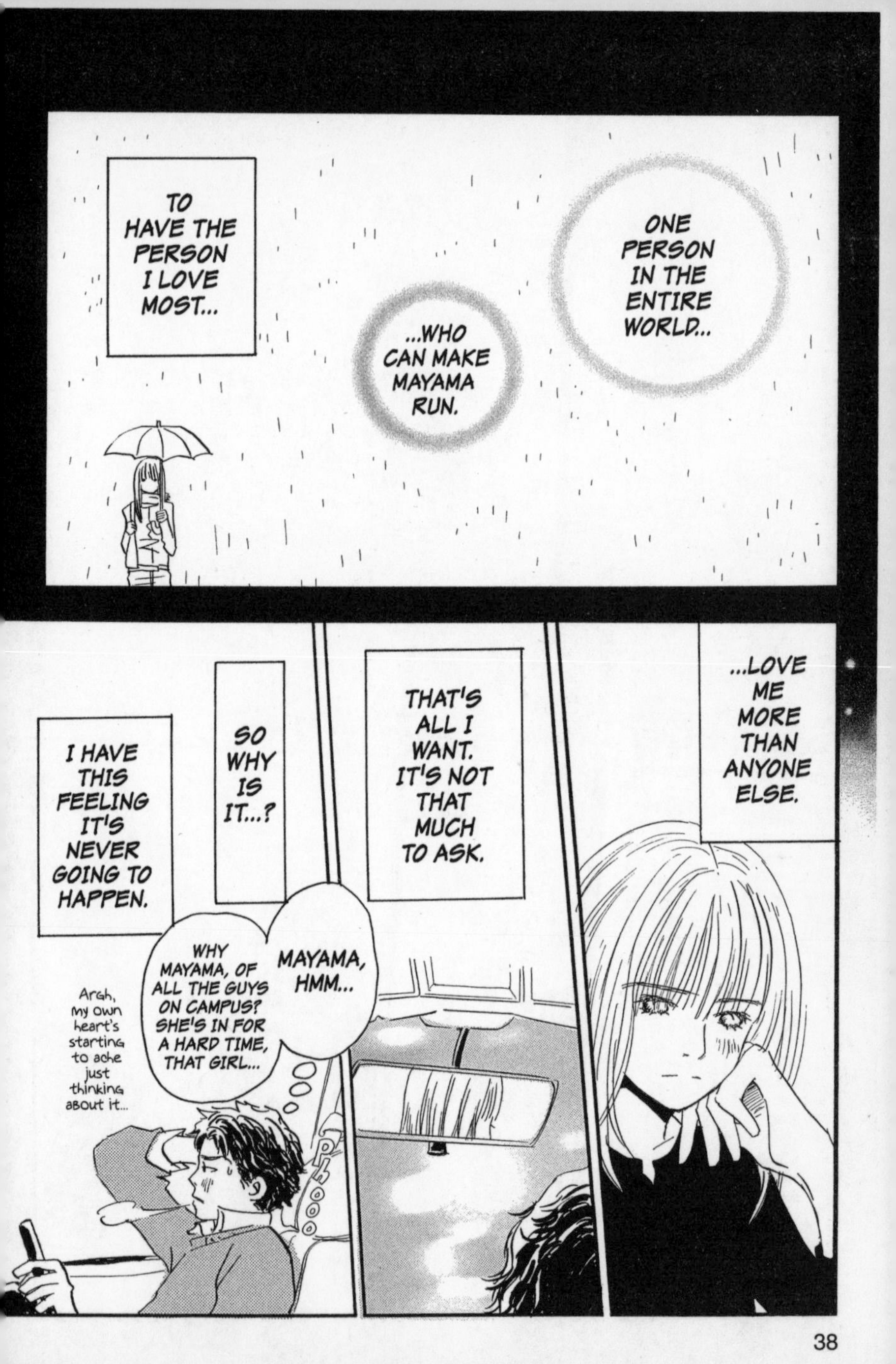
ONE PERSON IN THE ENTIRE WORLD...
...WHO CAN MAKE MAYAMA RUN.
TO HAVE THE PERSON I LOVE MOST...
...LOVE ME MORE THAN ANYONE ELSE.
THAT'S ALL I WANT. IT'S NOT THAT MUCH TO ASK.
SO WHY IS IT...?
I HAVE THIS FEELING IT'S NEVER GOING TO HAPPEN.
MAYAMA, HMM...
WHY MAYAMA, OF ALL THE GUYS ON CAMPUS? SHE'S IN FOR A HARD TIME, THAT GIRL...
Argh, my own heart's starting to ache just thinking about it...

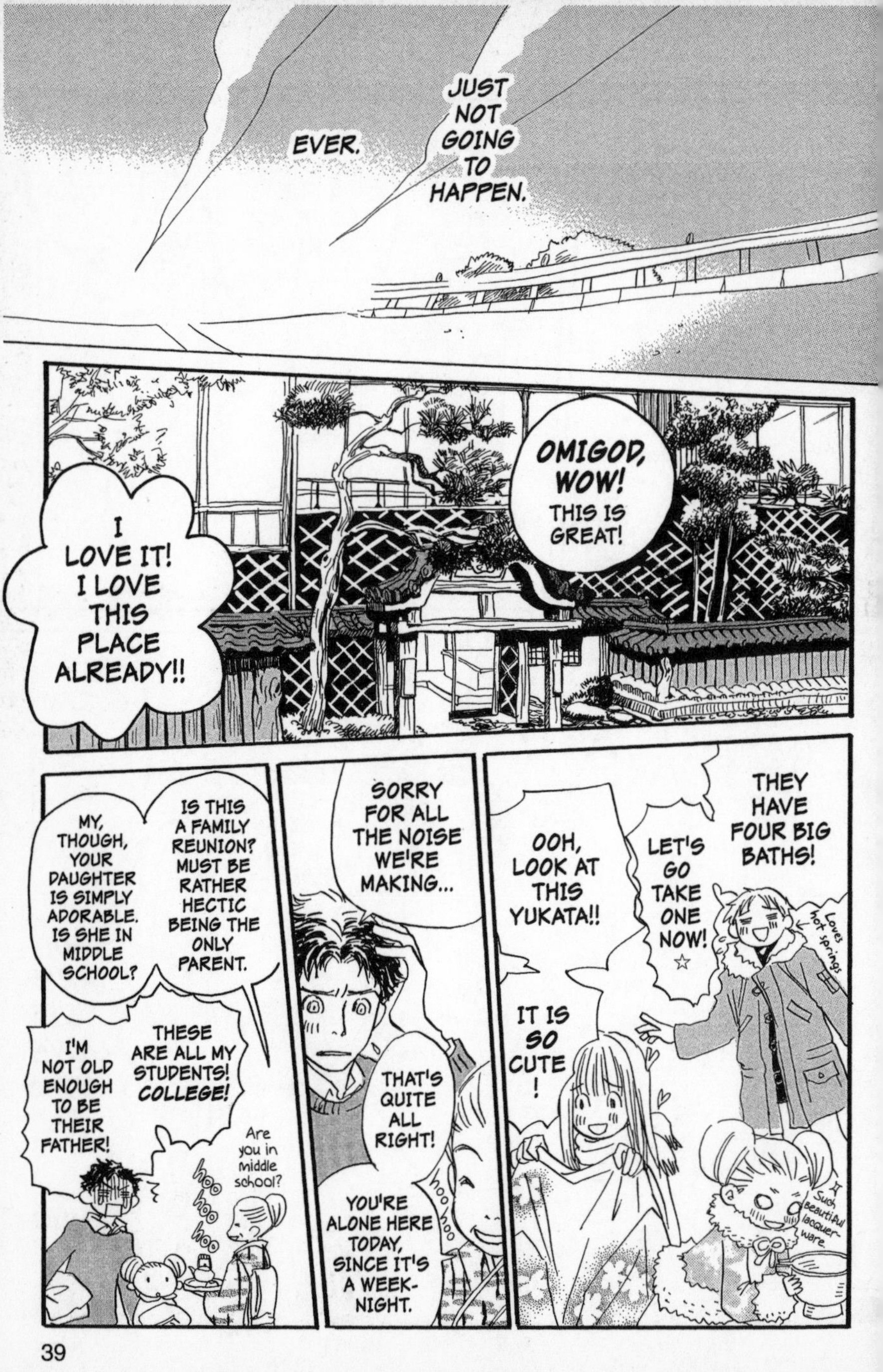
JUST NOT GOING TO HAPPEN.
EVER.
OMIGOD, WOW! THIS IS GREAT!
I LOVE IT! I LOVE THIS PLACE ALREADY!!
THEY HAVE FOUR BIG BATHS!
LET'S GO TAKE ONE NOW! ☆
Loves hot springs
OOH, LOOK AT THIS YUKATA!!
IT IS SO CUTE!
Such beautiful lacquer-ware.
SORRY FOR ALL THE NOISE WE'RE MAKING...
THAT'S QUITE ALL RIGHT!
YOU'RE ALONE HERE TODAY, SINCE IT'S A WEEK-NIGHT.
hoo hoo
IS THIS A FAMILY REUNION? MUST BE RATHER HECTIC BEING THE ONLY PARENT.
MY, THOUGH, YOUR DAUGHTER IS SIMPLY ADORABLE. IS SHE IN MIDDLE SCHOOL?
THESE ARE ALL MY STUDENTS! COLLEGE!
I'M NOT OLD ENOUGH TO BE THEIR FATHER!
Are you in middle school?
hoo hoo hoo

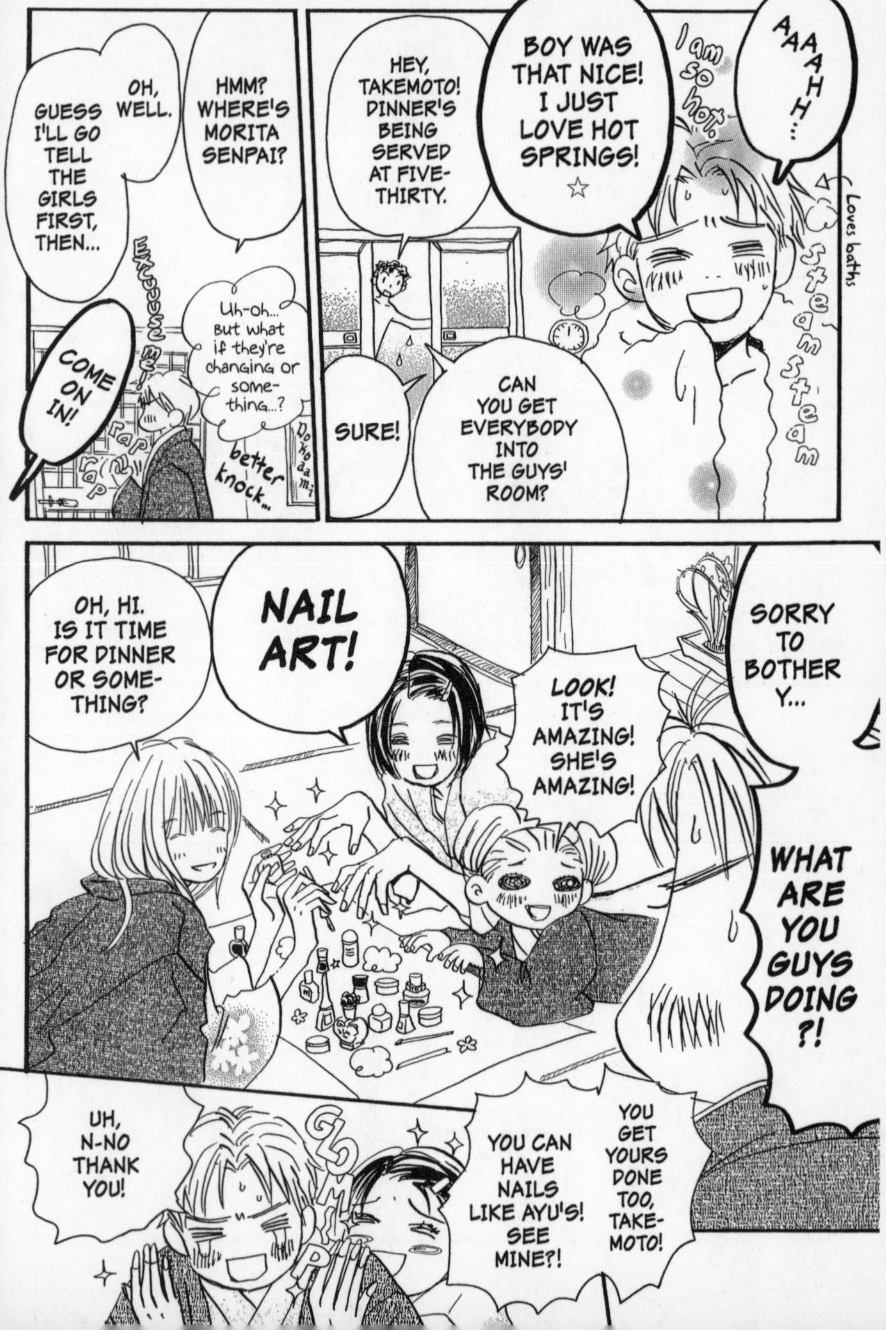
AAAAHH...
Loves baths
Steam Steam
I am so hot.
BOY WAS THAT NICE! I JUST LOVE HOT SPRINGS! ☆
HEY, TAKEMOTO! DINNER'S BEING SERVED AT FIVE-THIRTY.
CAN YOU GET EVERYBODY INTO THE GUYS' ROOM?
SURE!
HMM? WHERE'S MORITA SENPAI?
OH, WELL. GUESS I'LL GO TELL THE GIRLS FIRST, THEN...
Uh-oh... But what if they're changing or some-thing...?
better knock...
rap rap
Excuse me!
COME ON IN!
SORRY TO BOTHER Y...
WHAT ARE YOU GUYS DOING?!
LOOK! IT'S AMAZING! SHE'S AMAZING!
NAIL ART!
OH, HI. IS IT TIME FOR DINNER OR SOME-THING?
YOU GET YOURS DONE TOO, TAKE-MOTO!
YOU CAN HAVE NAILS LIKE AYU'S! SEE MINE?!
GLOMP
UH, N-NO THANK YOU!

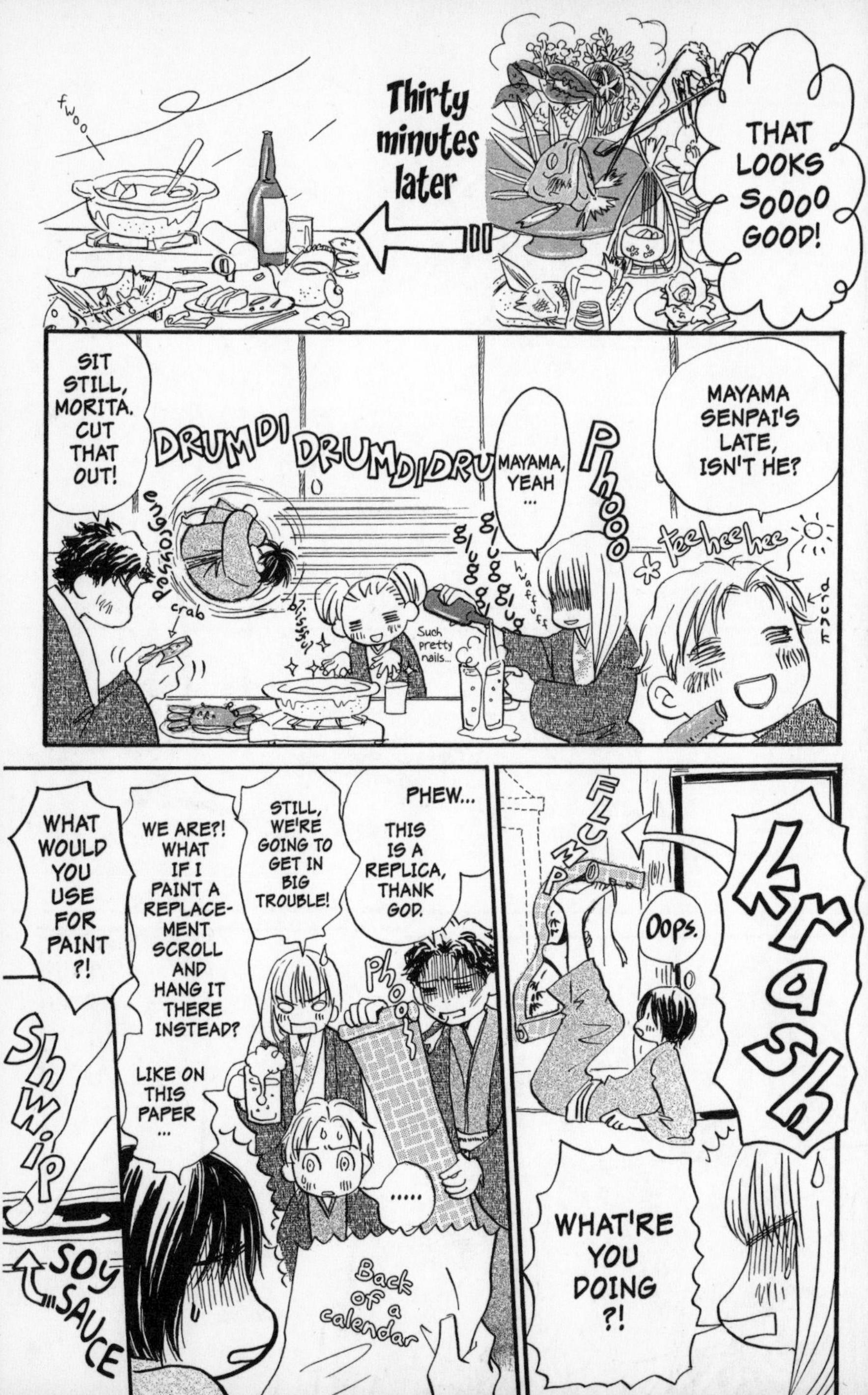
THAT LOOKS SOOOO GOOD!
Thirty minutes later
fwoo
MAYAMA SENPAI'S LATE, ISN'T HE?
teeheehee
drunk
Phoooo
MAYAMA, YEAH ...
glug glug glug glug glug
hwaffuff
Such pretty nails...
blissful
DRUMDIDRUMDIDRU
SIT STILL, MORITA. CUT THAT OUT!
engrossed
crab
krash
FLUMP
Oops.
WHAT'RE YOU DOING ?!
PHEW...
THIS IS A REPLICA, THANK GOD.
STILL, WE'RE GOING TO GET IN BIG TROUBLE!
WE ARE?! WHAT IF I PAINT A REPLACEMENT SCROLL AND HANG IT THERE INSTEAD?
WHAT WOULD YOU USE FOR PAINT ?!
Phooo
LIKE ON THIS PAPER ...
.....
Back of a calendar
Shwip
SOY SAUCE

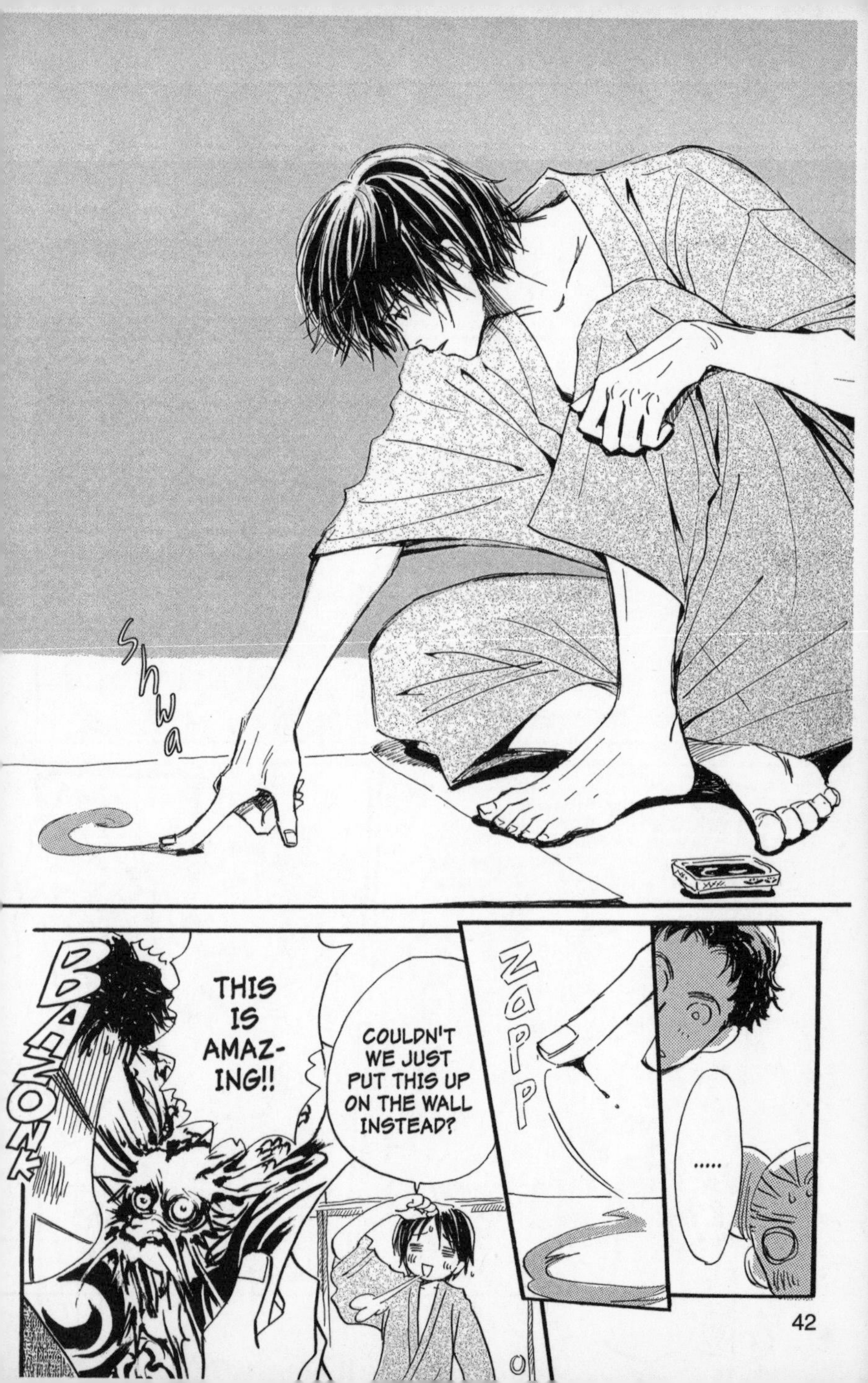

Shwa
Zapp
......
BAAZONK
THIS IS AMAZ-ING!!
COULDN'T WE JUST PUT THIS UP ON THE WALL INSTEAD?

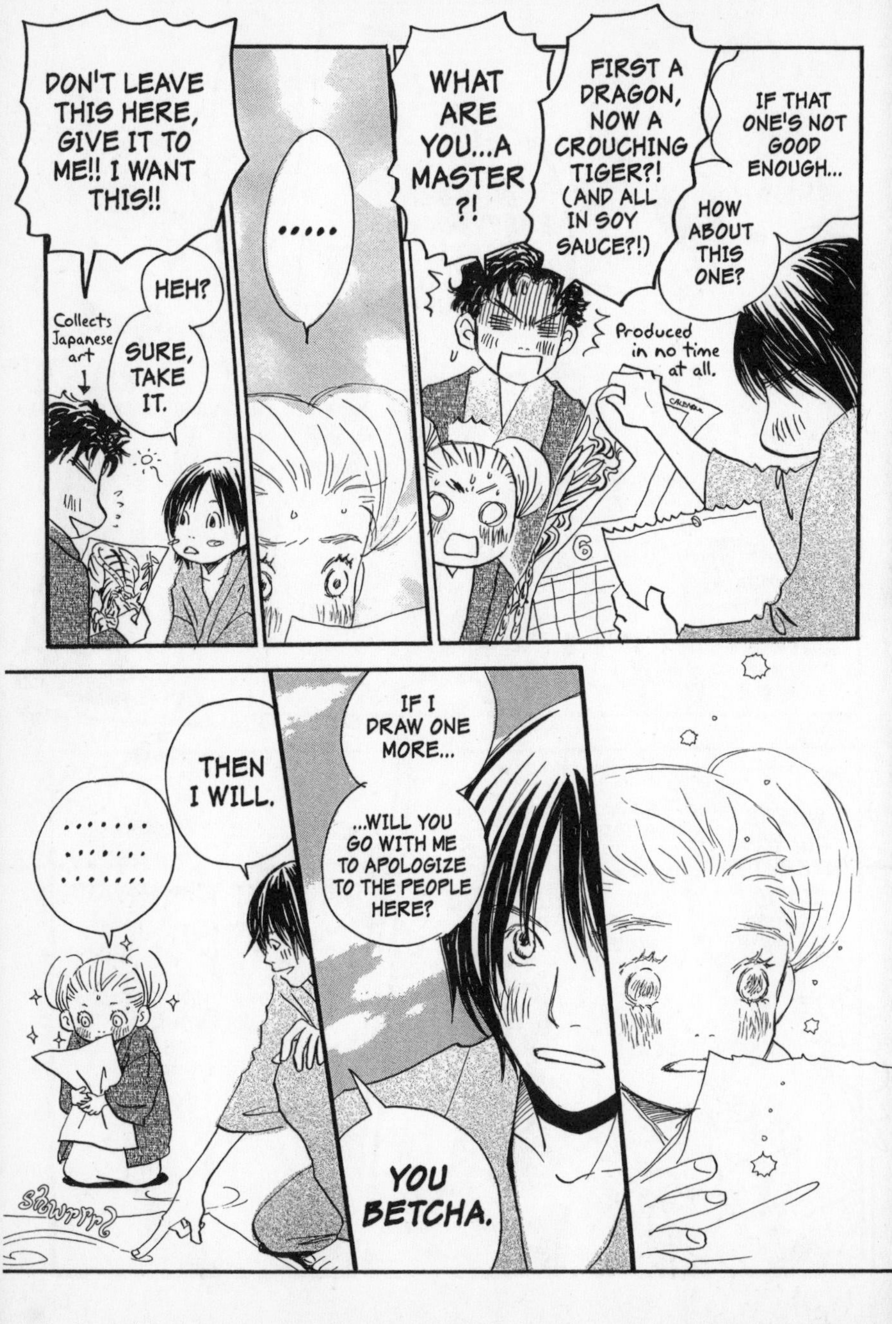
IF THAT ONE'S NOT GOOD ENOUGH...
HOW ABOUT THIS ONE?
Produced in no time at all.
FIRST A DRAGON, NOW A CROUCHING TIGER?! (AND ALL IN SOY SAUCE?!)
WHAT ARE YOU...A MASTER?!
.....
DON'T LEAVE THIS HERE, GIVE IT TO ME!! I WANT THIS!!
HEH?
SURE, TAKE IT.
Collects Japanese art
IF I DRAW ONE MORE...
...WILL YOU GO WITH ME TO APOLOGIZE TO THE PEOPLE HERE?
YOU BETCHA.
THEN I WILL.
....

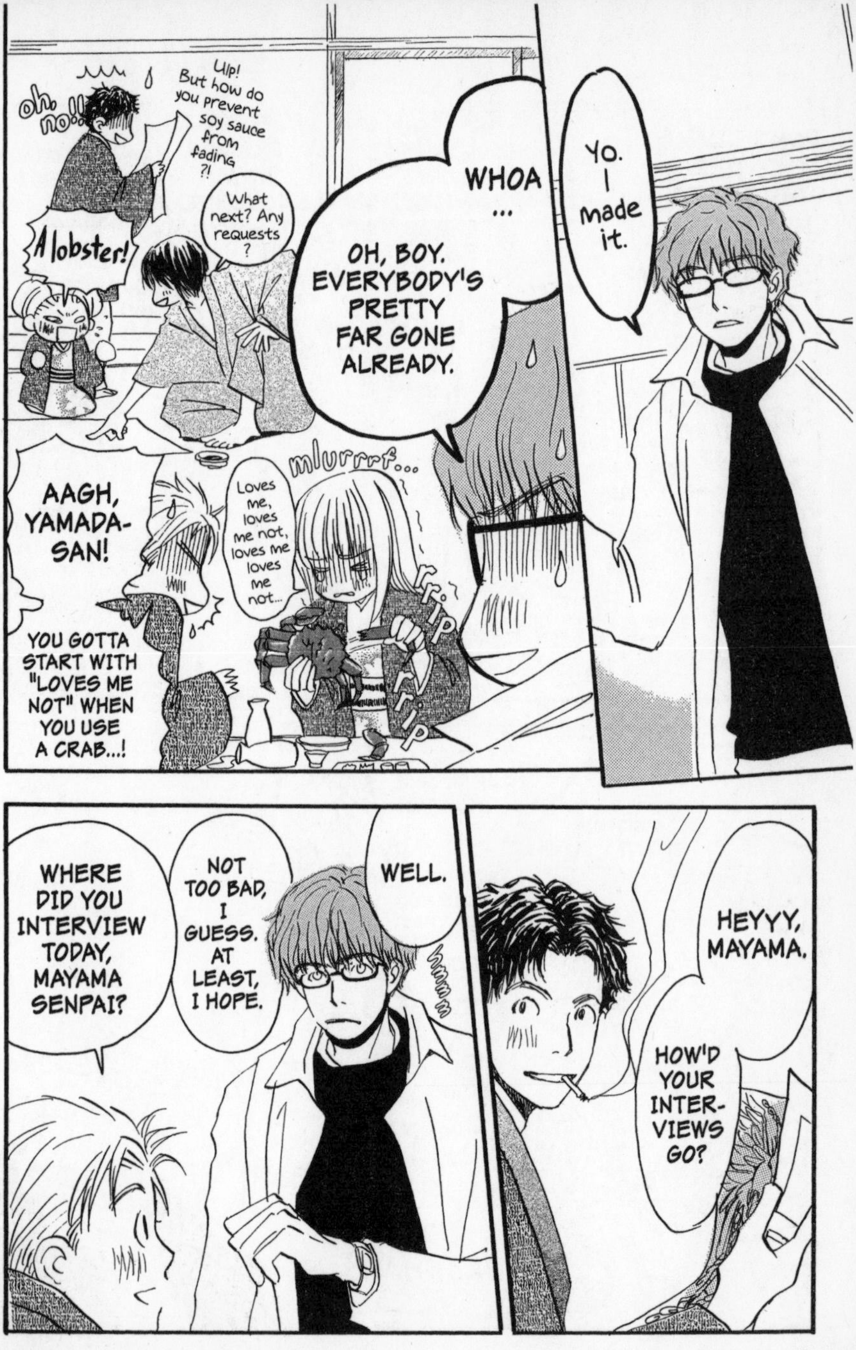

Yo. I made it.
WHOA...
OH, BOY. EVERYBODY'S PRETTY FAR GONE ALREADY.
Ulp! But how do you prevent soy sauce from fading?!
oh no!!
What next? Any requests?
A lobster!
mlurrrf...
Loves me, loves me not, loves me loves me not...
AAGH, YAMADA-SAN!
rrip rrip
YOU GOTTA START WITH "LOVES ME NOT" WHEN YOU USE A CRAB...!
HEYYY, MAYAMA.
HOW'D YOUR INTER-VIEWS GO?
WELL.
hmmm
NOT TOO BAD, I GUESS. AT LEAST, I HOPE.
WHERE DID YOU INTERVIEW TODAY, MAYAMA SENPAI?

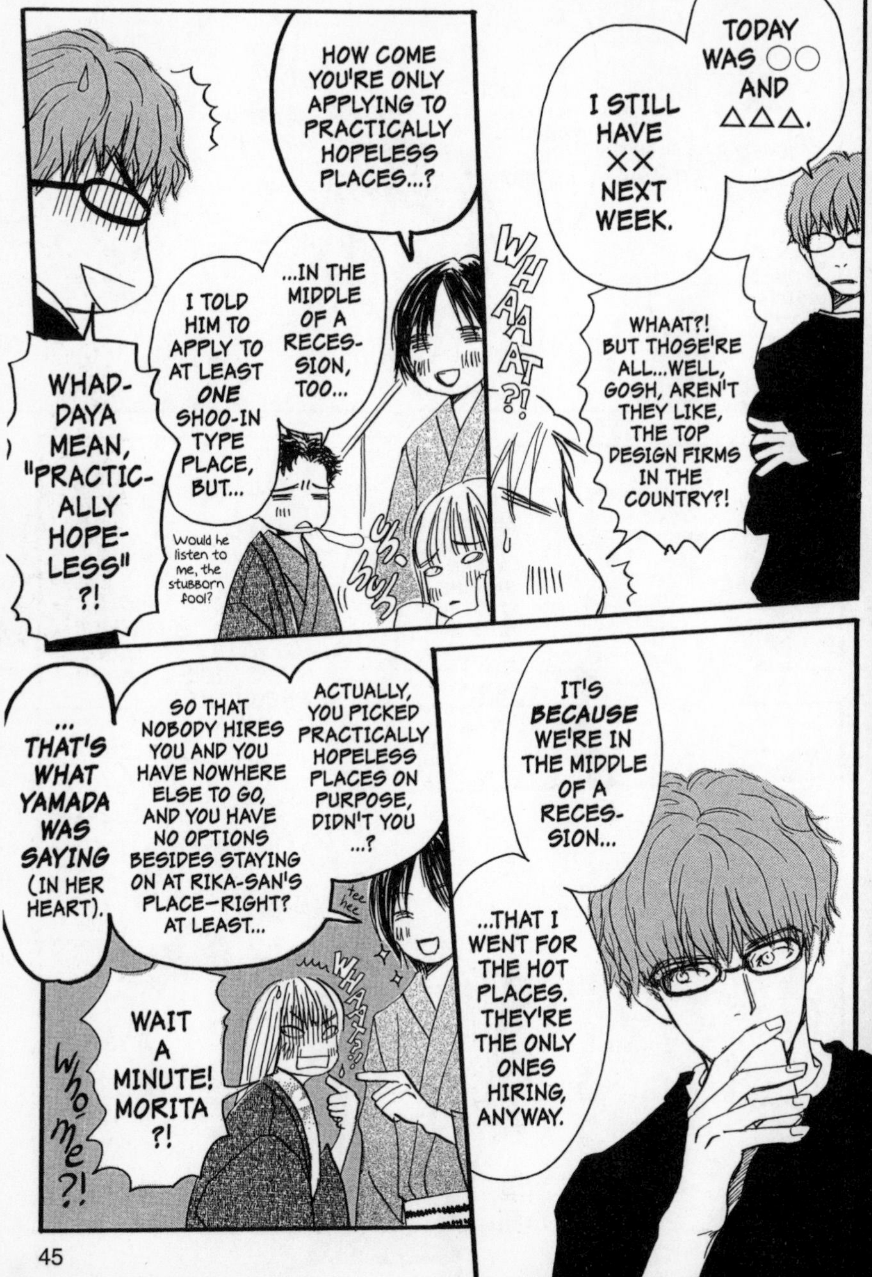
TODAY WAS ○○ AND △△△.
I STILL HAVE ×× NEXT WEEK.
WHAAAT?!
WHAAT?! BUT THOSE'RE ALL...WELL, GOSH, AREN'T THEY LIKE, THE TOP DESIGN FIRMS IN THE COUNTRY?!
HOW COME YOU'RE ONLY APPLYING TO PRACTICALLY HOPELESS PLACES...?
...IN THE MIDDLE OF A RECES-SION, TOO...
I TOLD HIM TO APPLY TO AT LEAST ONE SHOO-IN TYPE PLACE, BUT...
Would he listen to me, the stubborn fool?
WHAD-DAYA MEAN, "PRACTIC-ALLY HOPE-LESS"?!
IT'S BECAUSE WE'RE IN THE MIDDLE OF A RECES-SION...
...THAT I WENT FOR THE HOT PLACES. THEY'RE THE ONLY ONES HIRING, ANYWAY.
ACTUALLY, YOU PICKED PRACTICALLY HOPELESS PLACES ON PURPOSE, DIDN'T YOU ...?
SO THAT NOBODY HIRES YOU AND YOU HAVE NOWHERE ELSE TO GO, AND YOU HAVE NO OPTIONS BESIDES STAYING ON AT RIKA-SAN'S PLACE—RIGHT? AT LEAST...
tee hee
... THAT'S WHAT YAMADA WAS SAYING (IN HER HEART).
WHAAAT?!
WAIT A MINUTE! MORITA ?!
Who, me?!

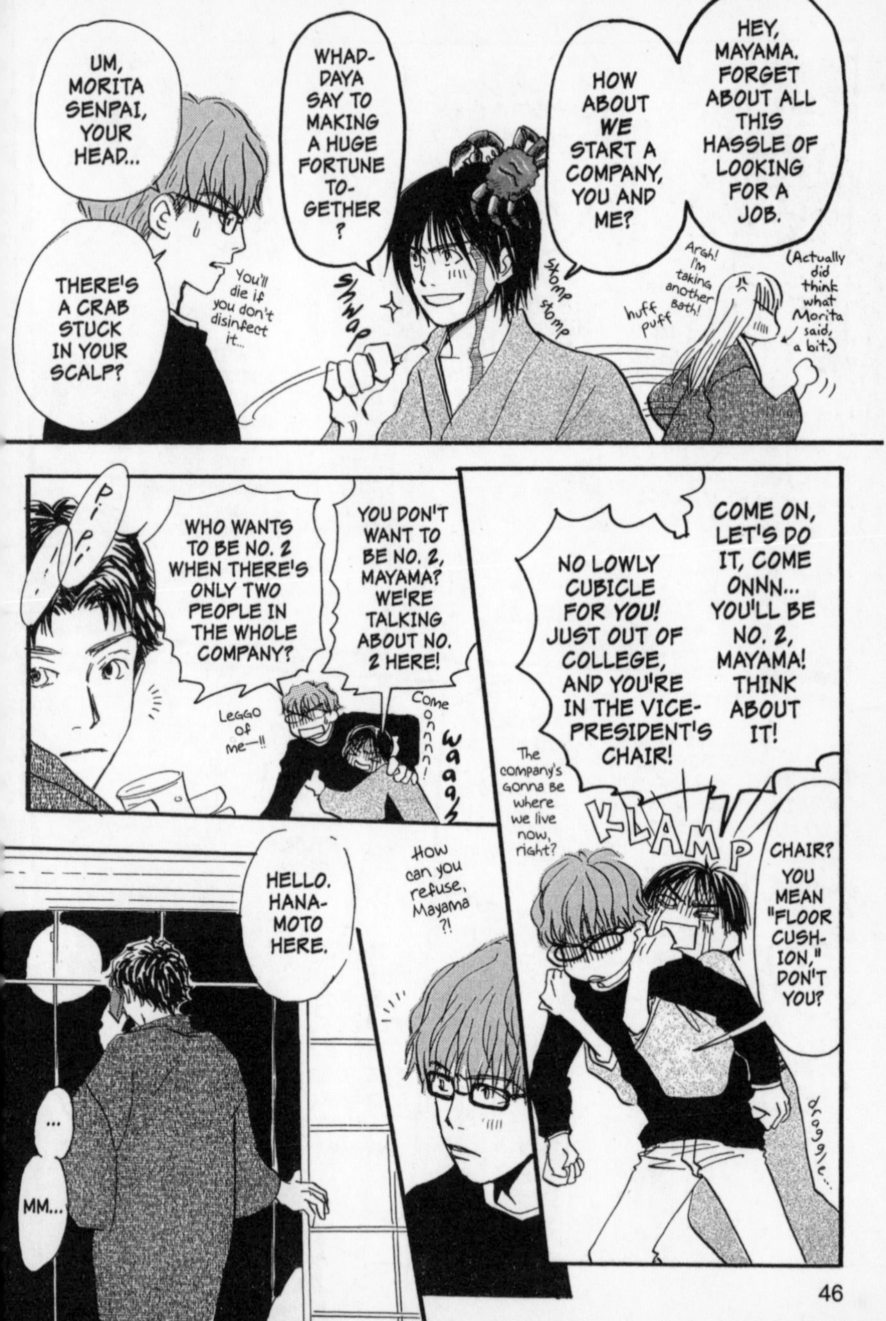
HEY, MAYAMA. FORGET ABOUT ALL THIS HASSLE OF LOOKING FOR A JOB.
HOW ABOUT WE START A COMPANY, YOU AND ME?
(Actually did think what Morita said, a bit.)
Argh! I'm taking another bath!
huff puff
stomp stomp
WHADDAYA SAY TO MAKING A HUGE FORTUNE TOGETHER?
SHWAP
UM, MORITA SENPAI, YOUR HEAD...
You'll die if you don't disinfect it...
THERE'S A CRAB STUCK IN YOUR SCALP?
COME ON, LET'S DO IT, COME ONNN... YOU'LL BE NO. 2, MAYAMA! THINK ABOUT IT!
NO LOWLY CUBICLE FOR YOU! JUST OUT OF COLLEGE, AND YOU'RE IN THE VICE-PRESIDENT'S CHAIR!
The company's gonna be where we live now, right?
YOU DON'T WANT TO BE NO. 2, MAYAMA? WE'RE TALKING ABOUT NO. 2 HERE!
Come onnnn!
Waaah
WHO WANTS TO BE NO. 2 WHEN THERE'S ONLY TWO PEOPLE IN THE WHOLE COMPANY?
Leggo of me—!!
Pi Pi
KLAMP
CHAIR? YOU MEAN "FLOOR CUSHION," DON'T YOU?
draggle...
How can you refuse, Mayama?!
HELLO. HANAMOTO HERE.
...
MM...

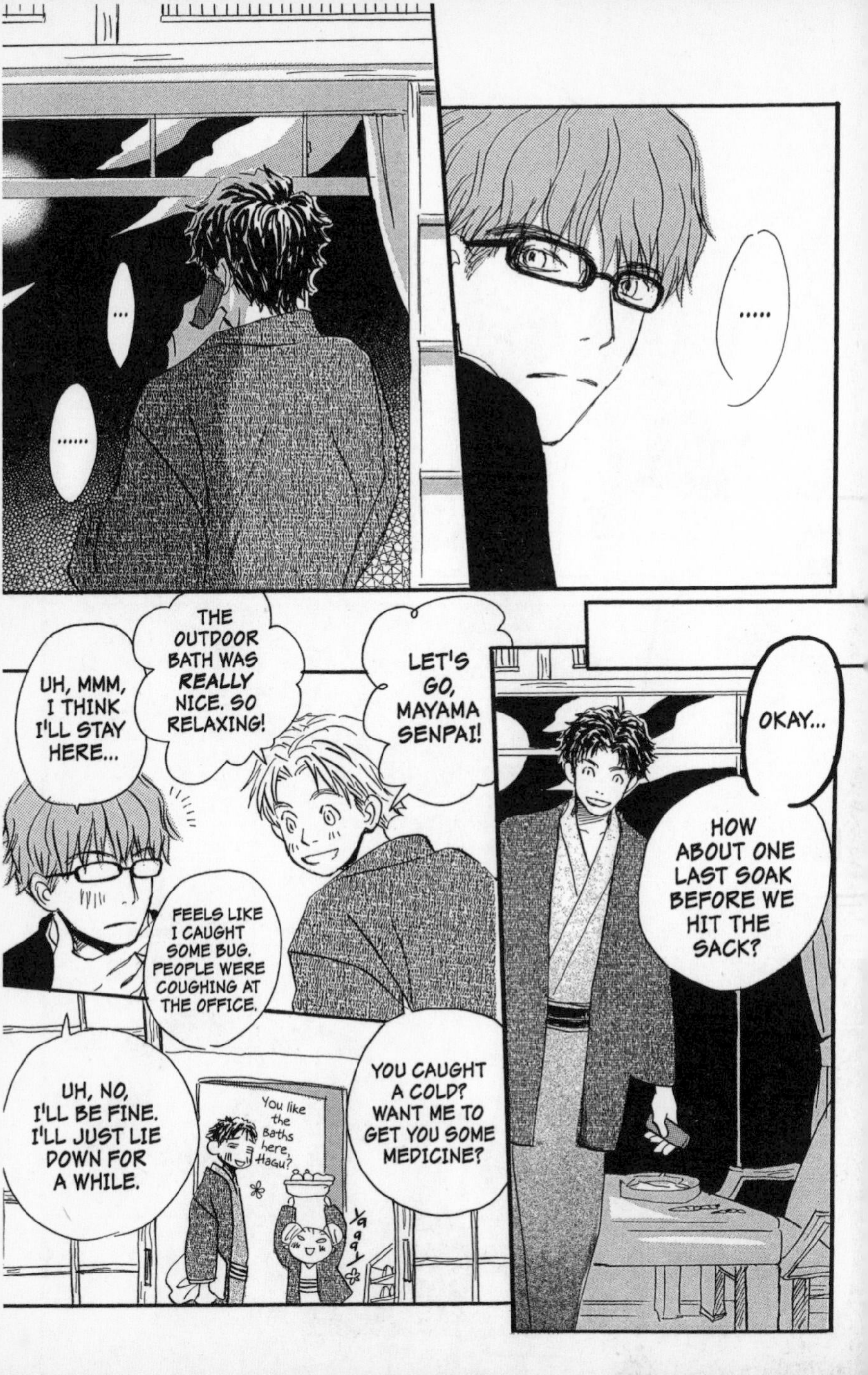
.....
...
......
OKAY...
HOW ABOUT ONE LAST SOAK BEFORE WE HIT THE SACK?
LET'S GO, MAYAMA SENPAI!
THE OUTDOOR BATH WAS REALLY NICE. SO RELAXING!
UH, MMM, I THINK I'LL STAY HERE...
FEELS LIKE I CAUGHT SOME BUG. PEOPLE WERE COUGHING AT THE OFFICE.
YOU CAUGHT A COLD? WANT ME TO GET YOU SOME MEDICINE?
You like the Baths here, Hagu?
Yay!
UH, NO, I'LL BE FINE. I'LL JUST LIE DOWN FOR A WHILE.

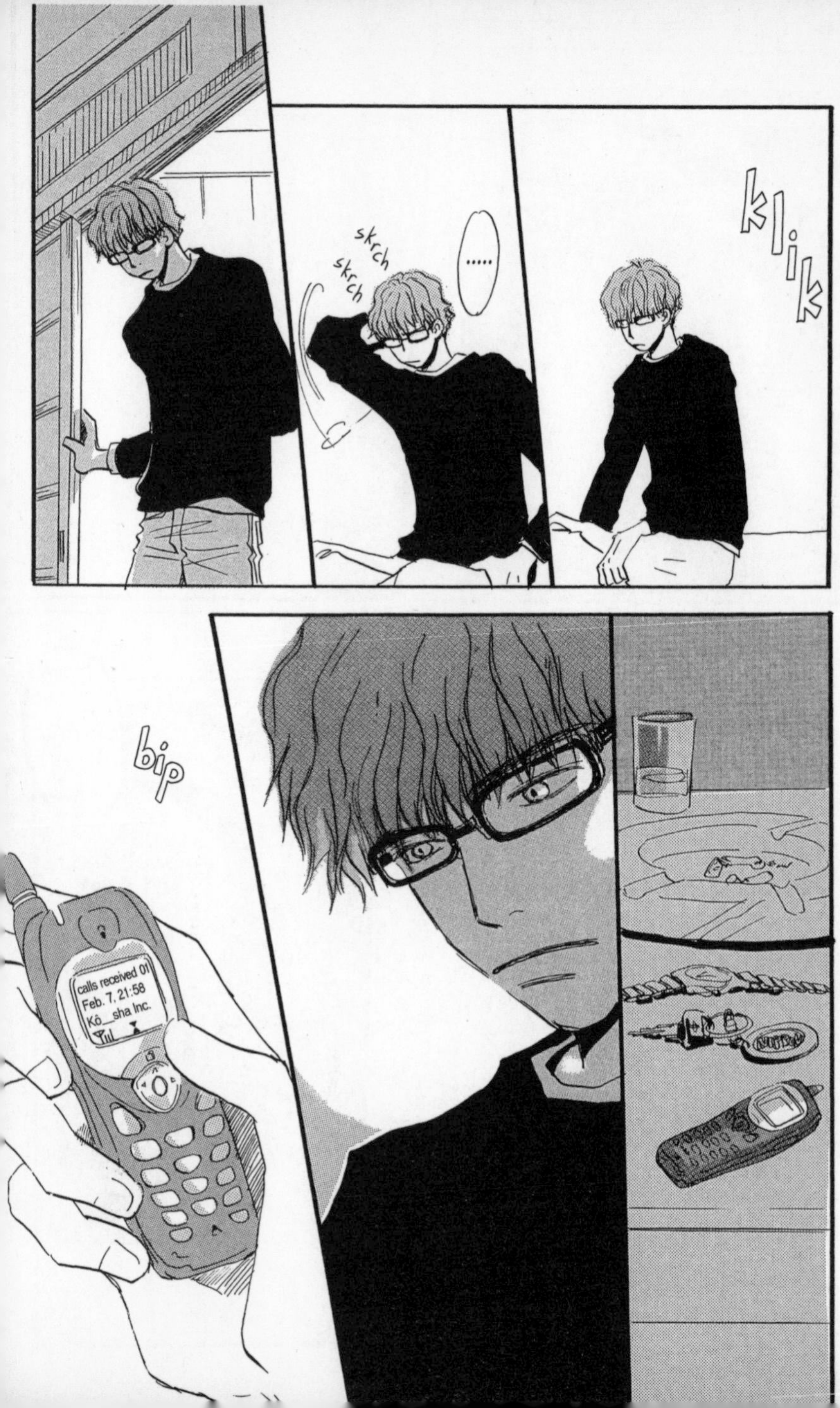
klik
......
skrch skrch
bip
calls received 01
Feb. 7, 21:58
Kô__sha Inc.

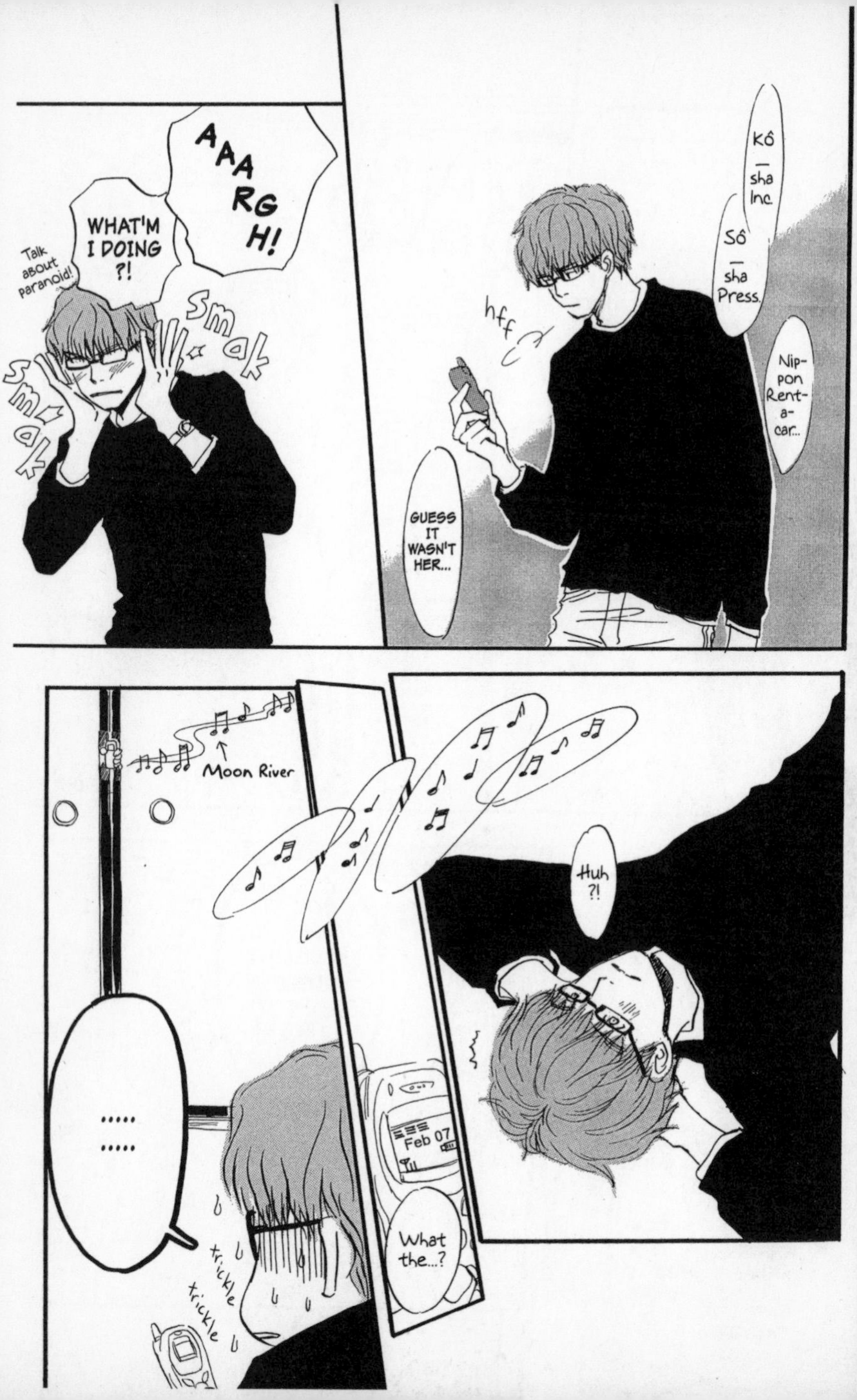
Kô—sha Inc.
Sô—sha Press.
Nippon Rent-a-car...
hff
GUESS IT WASN'T HER...
AAARGH!
WHAT'M I DOING ?!
Talk about paranoid!
Smak
Smak
Huh ?!
Moon River
Feb 07
What the...?
......
......
trickle
trickle

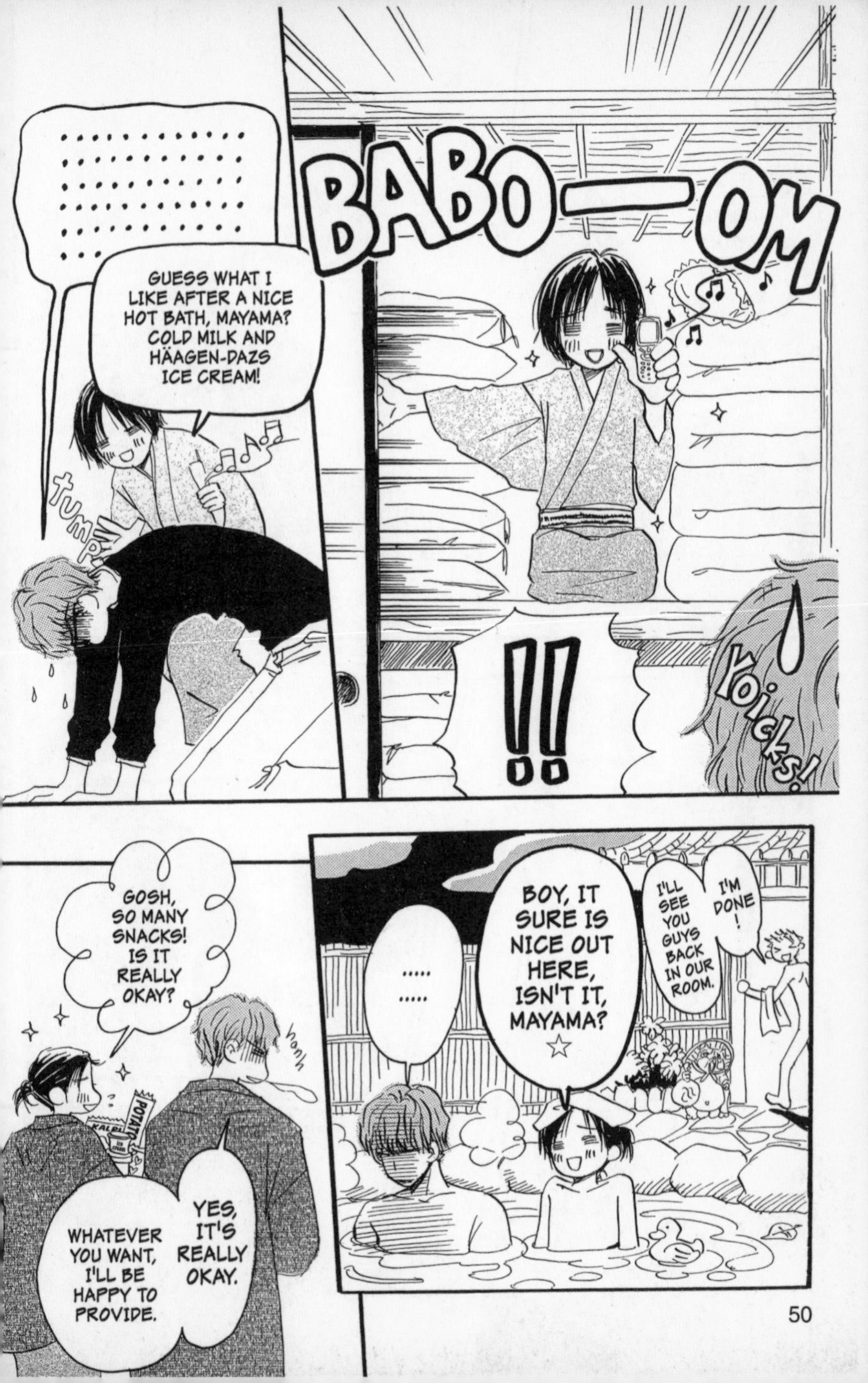
BABO—OM
Yoicks!
!!
GUESS WHAT I LIKE AFTER A NICE HOT BATH, MAYAMA? COLD MILK AND HÄAGEN-DAZS ICE CREAM!
....
tump
I'M DONE!
I'LL SEE YOU GUYS BACK IN OUR ROOM.
BOY, IT SURE IS NICE OUT HERE, ISN'T IT, MAYAMA? ☆
.....
.....
GOSH, SO MANY SNACKS! IS IT REALLY OKAY?
honk
YES, IT'S REALLY OKAY.
WHATEVER YOU WANT, I'LL BE HAPPY TO PROVIDE.

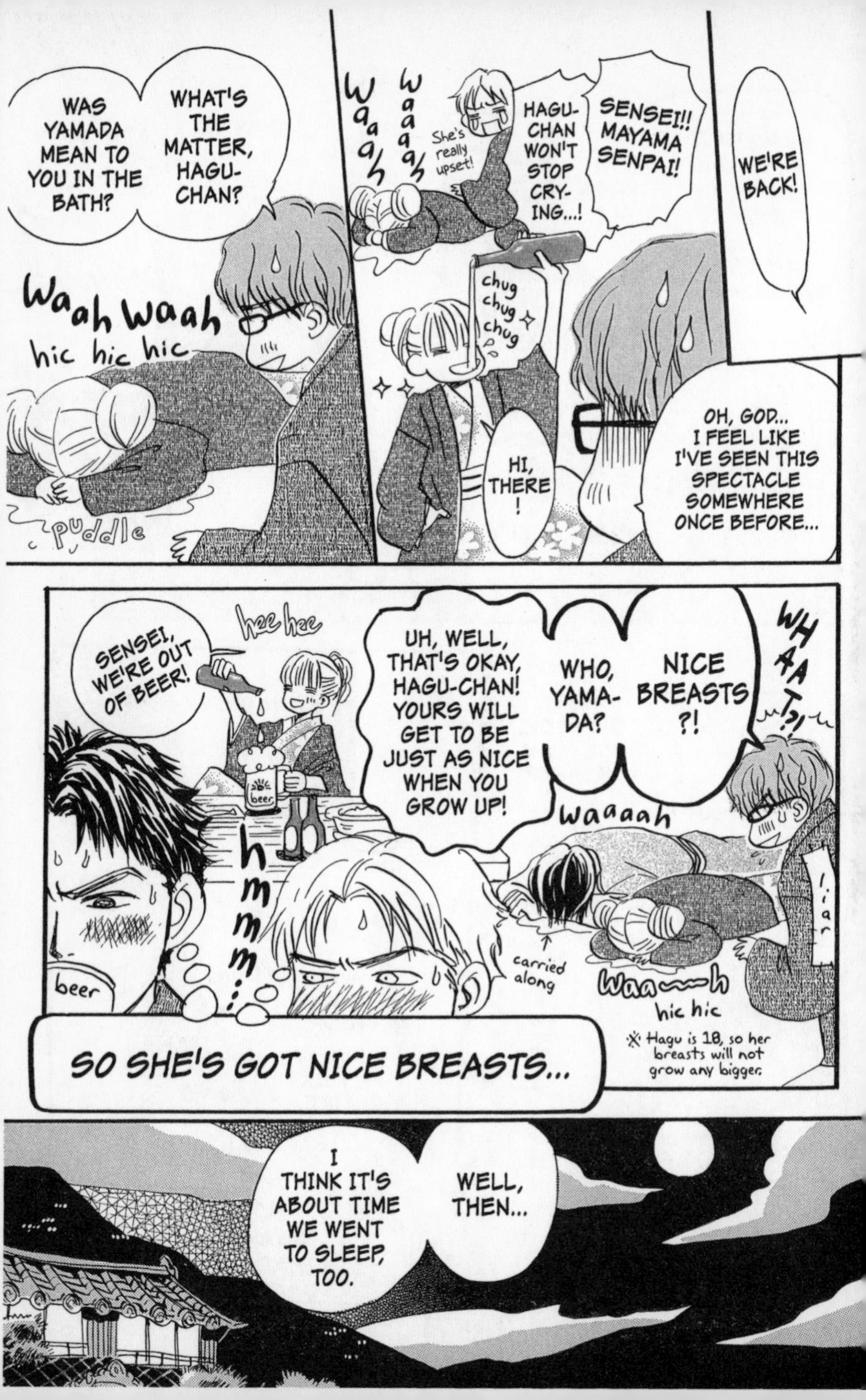
WE'RE BACK!
SENSEI!! MAYAMA SENPAI!
HAGU-CHAN WON'T STOP CRY-ING...!
She's really upset!
Waaaaah
Waaaah
chug chug chug
HI, THERE!
OH, GOD... I FEEL LIKE I'VE SEEN THIS SPECTACLE SOMEWHERE ONCE BEFORE...
WHAT'S THE MATTER, HAGU-CHAN?
WAS YAMADA MEAN TO YOU IN THE BATH?
Waah Waah
hic hic hic
puddle
WHAAT?!
NICE BREASTS?!
WHO, YAMADA?
UH, WELL, THAT'S OKAY, HAGU-CHAN! YOURS WILL GET TO BE JUST AS NICE WHEN YOU GROW UP!
hee hee
SENSEI, WE'RE OUT OF BEER!
beer
waaaah
liar
carried along
Waa—h
hic hic
hmmmm...
beer
SO SHE'S GOT NICE BREASTS...
※ Hagu is 18, so her breasts will not grow any bigger.
WELL, THEN...
I THINK IT'S ABOUT TIME WE WENT TO SLEEP, TOO.

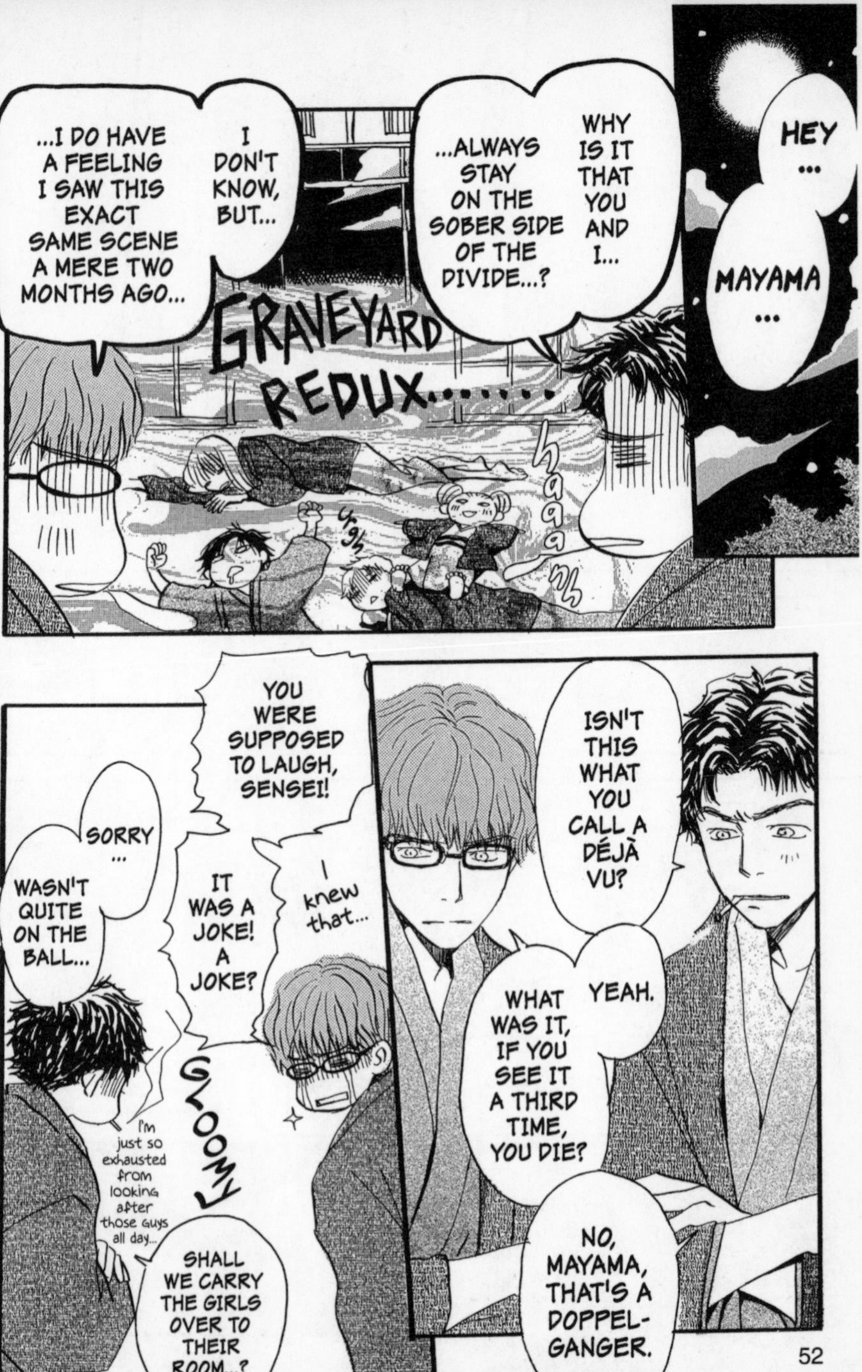
HEY ... MAYAMA ...
WHY IS IT THAT YOU AND I...
...ALWAYS STAY ON THE SOBER SIDE OF THE DIVIDE...?
I DON'T KNOW, BUT...
...I DO HAVE A FEELING I SAW THIS EXACT SAME SCENE A MERE TWO MONTHS AGO...
GRAVEYARD REDUX......
haaaanh
urgh
ISN'T THIS WHAT YOU CALL A DÉJÀ VU?
YEAH.
WHAT WAS IT, IF YOU SEE IT A THIRD TIME, YOU DIE?
NO, MAYAMA, THAT'S A DOPPEL-GANGER.
YOU WERE SUPPOSED TO LAUGH, SENSEI!
I knew that...
IT WAS A JOKE! A JOKE?
SORRY ... WASN'T QUITE ON THE BALL...
GLOOMY
I'm just so exhausted from looking after those guys all day...
SHALL WE CARRY THE GIRLS OVER TO THEIR ROOM...?

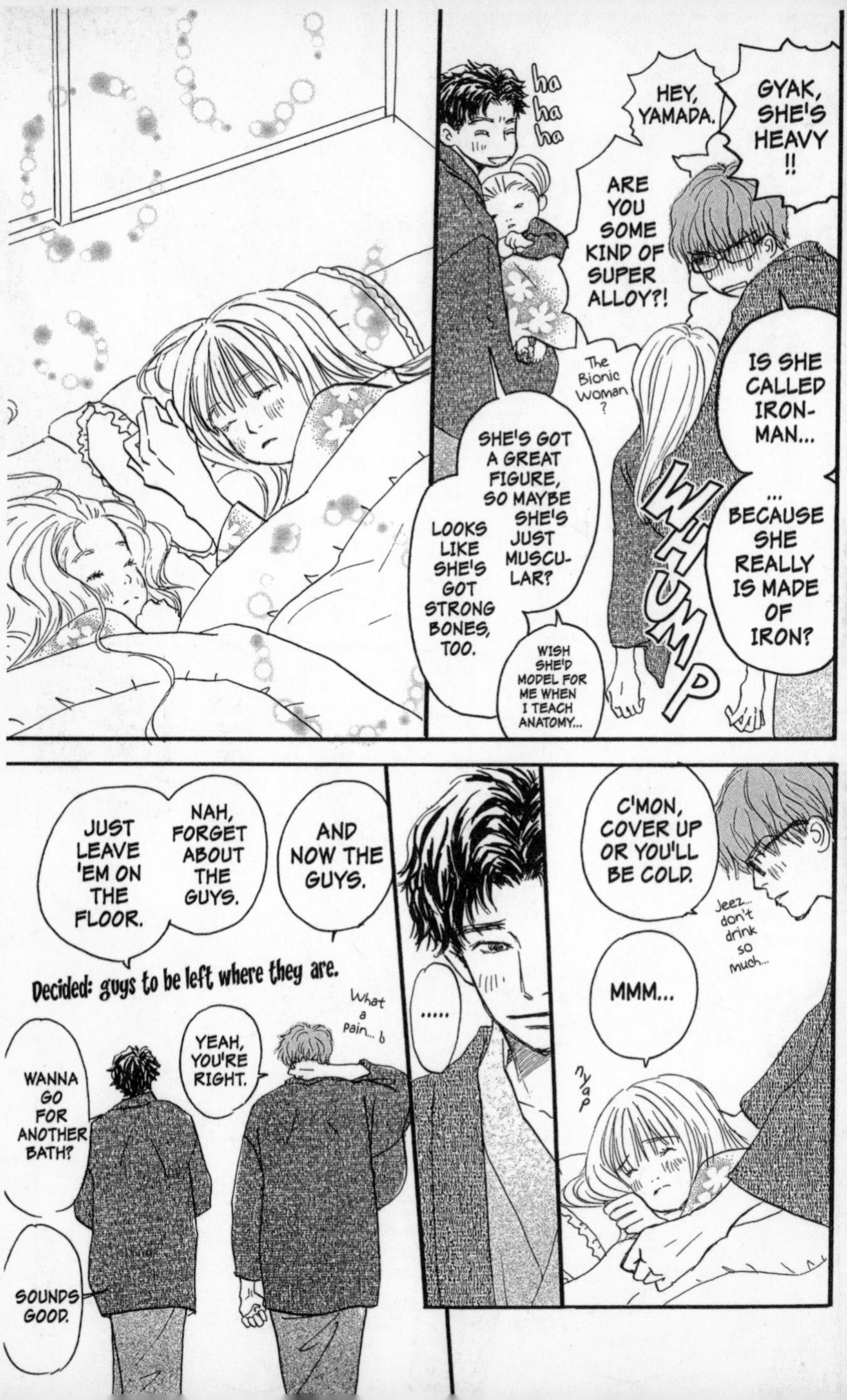
GYAK, SHE'S HEAVY !!
HEY, YAMADA.
ha ha ha
ARE YOU SOME KIND OF SUPER ALLOY?!
IS SHE CALLED IRON-MAN...
... BECAUSE SHE REALLY IS MADE OF IRON?
WHUMP
The Bionic Woman ?
SHE'S GOT A GREAT FIGURE, SO MAYBE SHE'S JUST MUSCULAR?
LOOKS LIKE SHE'S GOT STRONG BONES, TOO.
WISH SHE'D MODEL FOR ME WHEN I TEACH ANATOMY...
C'MON, COVER UP OR YOU'LL BE COLD.
Jeez... don't drink so much...
MMM...
nyap
.....
AND NOW THE GUYS.
NAH, FORGET ABOUT THE GUYS.
JUST LEAVE 'EM ON THE FLOOR.
Decided: guys to be left where they are.
What a pain...
YEAH, YOU'RE RIGHT.
WANNA GO FOR ANOTHER BATH?
SOUNDS GOOD.

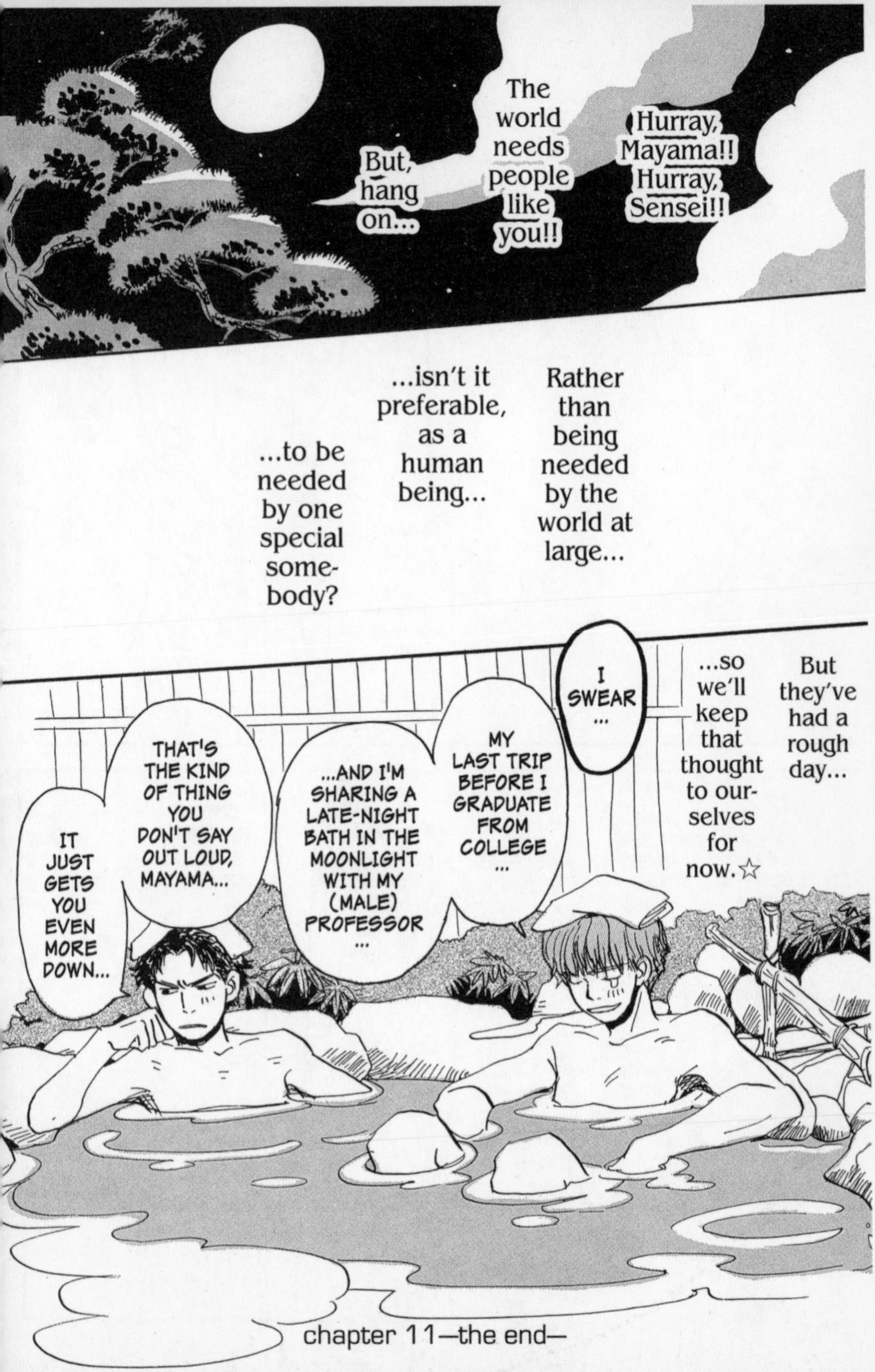
Hurray, Mayama!! Hurray, Sensei!!
The world needs people like you!!
But, hang on...
Rather than being needed by the world at large...
...isn't it preferable, as a human being...
...to be needed by one special somebody?
But they've had a rough day...
...so we'll keep that thought to ourselves for now.☆
I SWEAR...
MY LAST TRIP BEFORE I GRADUATE FROM COLLEGE...
...AND I'M SHARING A LATE-NIGHT BATH IN THE MOONLIGHT WITH MY (MALE) PROFESSOR...
THAT'S THE KIND OF THING YOU DON'T SAY OUT LOUD, MAYAMA...
IT JUST GETS YOU EVEN MORE DOWN...
chapter 11—the end—

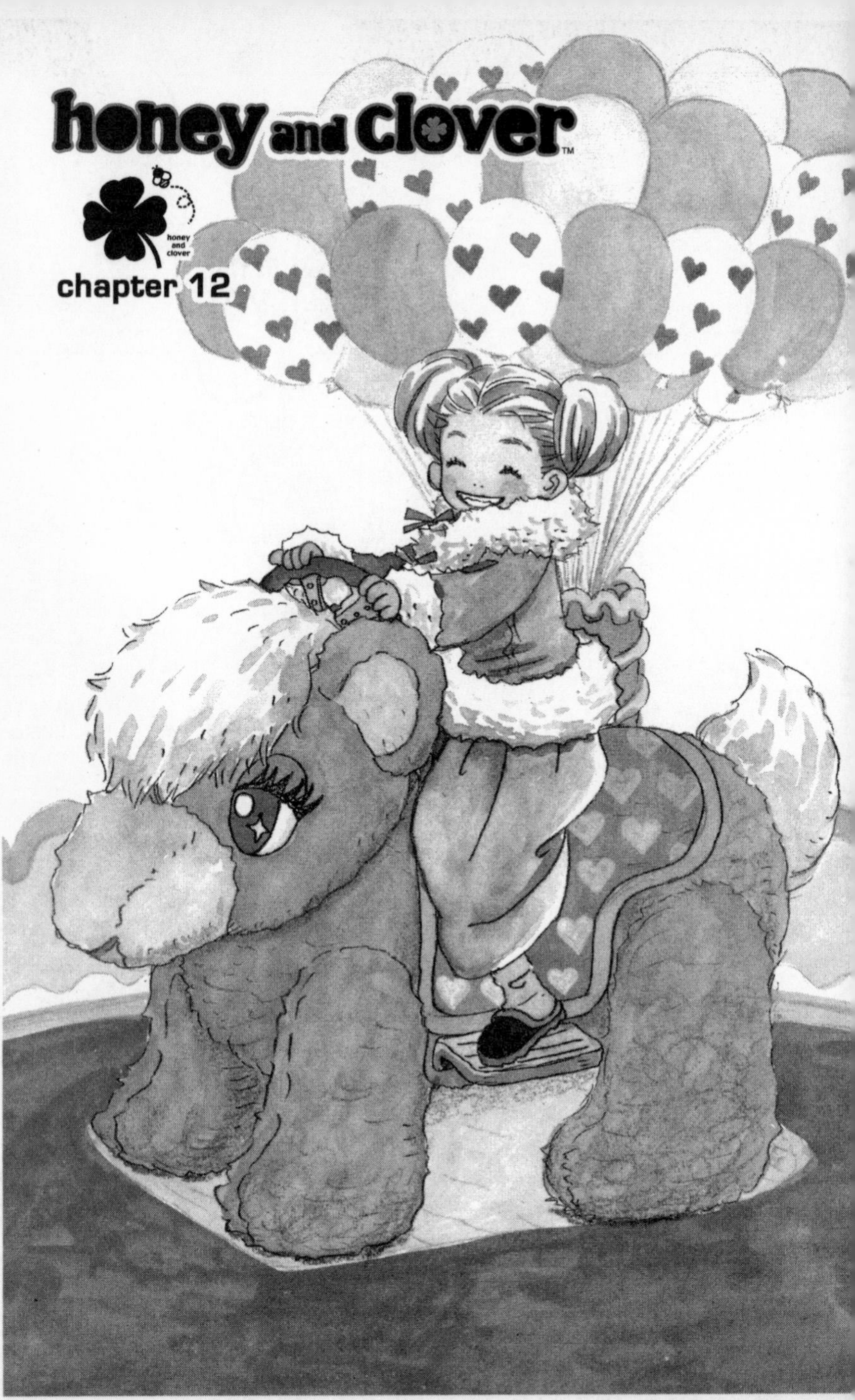
honey and clover
chapter 12

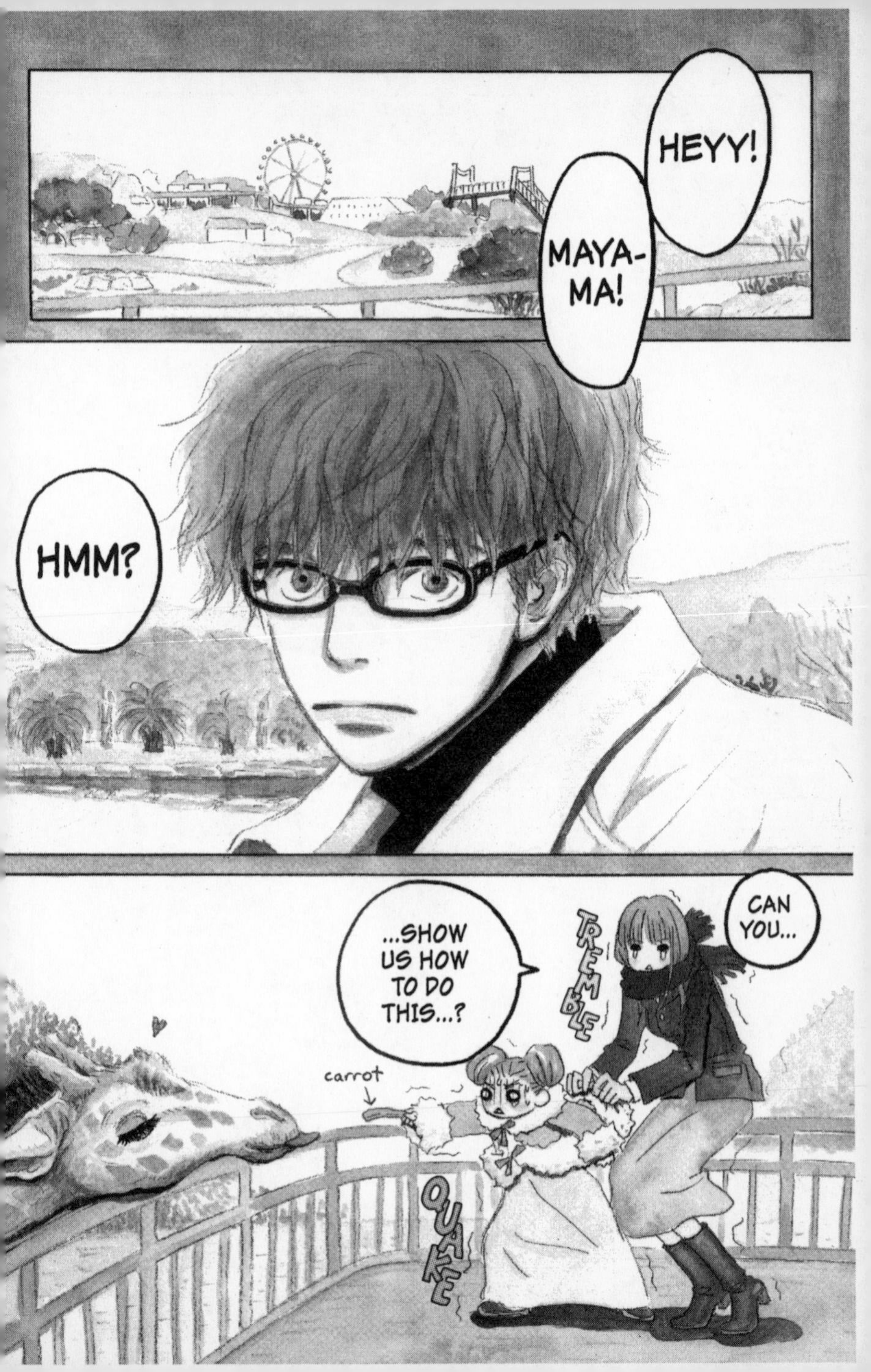
HEYY!
MAYA-MA!
HMM?
CAN YOU...
...SHOW US HOW TO DO THIS...?
TREMBLE
carrot
QUAKE

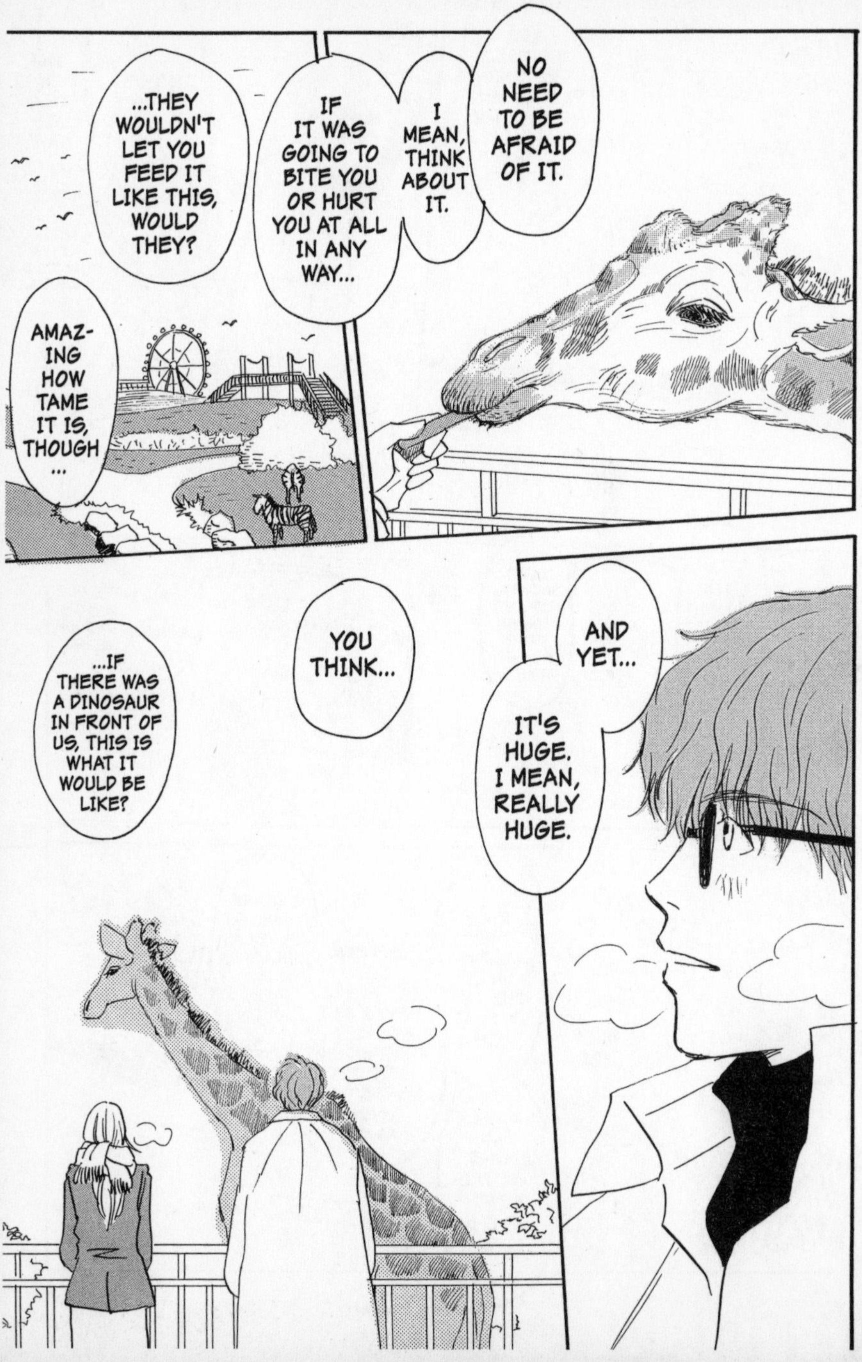
NO NEED TO BE AFRAID OF IT.
I MEAN, THINK ABOUT IT.
IF IT WAS GOING TO BITE YOU OR HURT YOU AT ALL IN ANY WAY...
...THEY WOULDN'T LET YOU FEED IT LIKE THIS, WOULD THEY?
AMAZ-ING HOW TAME IT IS, THOUGH...
AND YET...
IT'S HUGE. I MEAN, REALLY HUGE.
YOU THINK...
...IF THERE WAS A DINOSAUR IN FRONT OF US, THIS IS WHAT IT WOULD BE LIKE?

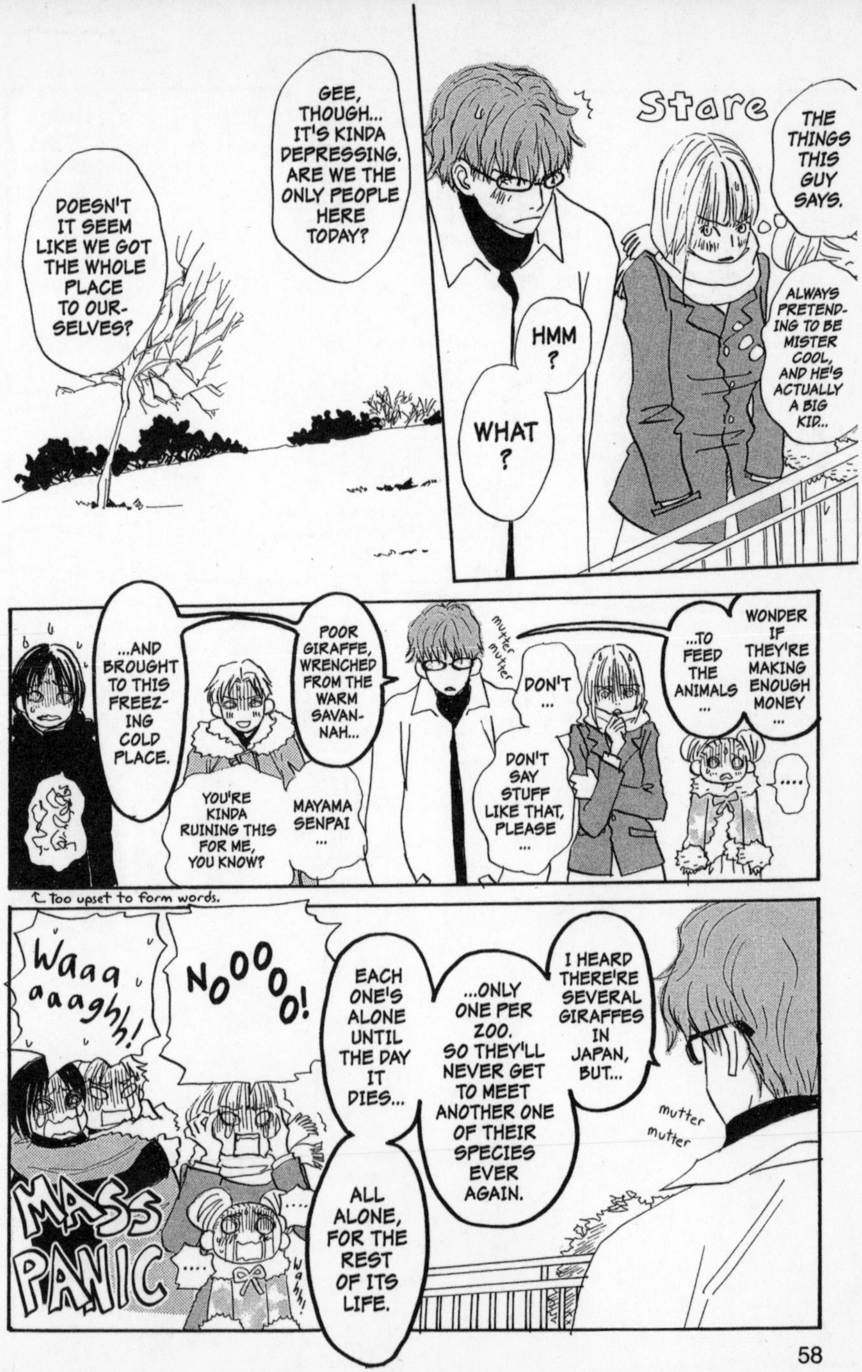
Stare
THE THINGS THIS GUY SAYS.
ALWAYS PRETENDING TO BE MISTER COOL, AND HE'S ACTUALLY A BIG KID...
HMM?
WHAT?
GEE, THOUGH... IT'S KINDA DEPRESSING. ARE WE THE ONLY PEOPLE HERE TODAY?
DOESN'T IT SEEM LIKE WE GOT THE WHOLE PLACE TO OURSELVES?
WONDER IF THEY'RE MAKING ENOUGH MONEY...
...TO FEED THE ANIMALS...
....
mutter mutter
DON'T...
DON'T SAY STUFF LIKE THAT, PLEASE...
POOR GIRAFFE, WRENCHED FROM THE WARM SAVANNAH...
...AND BROUGHT TO THIS FREEZING COLD PLACE.
MAYAMA SENPAI...
YOU'RE KINDA RUINING THIS FOR ME, YOU KNOW?
↰ too upset to form words.
I HEARD THERE'RE SEVERAL GIRAFFES IN JAPAN, BUT...
...ONLY ONE PER ZOO. SO THEY'LL NEVER GET TO MEET ANOTHER ONE OF THEIR SPECIES EVER AGAIN.
mutter mutter
EACH ONE'S ALONE UNTIL THE DAY IT DIES...
ALL ALONE, FOR THE REST OF ITS LIFE.
NOOOOO!
Waaaaaaghhh!
MASS PANIC
....
....
Wahh!

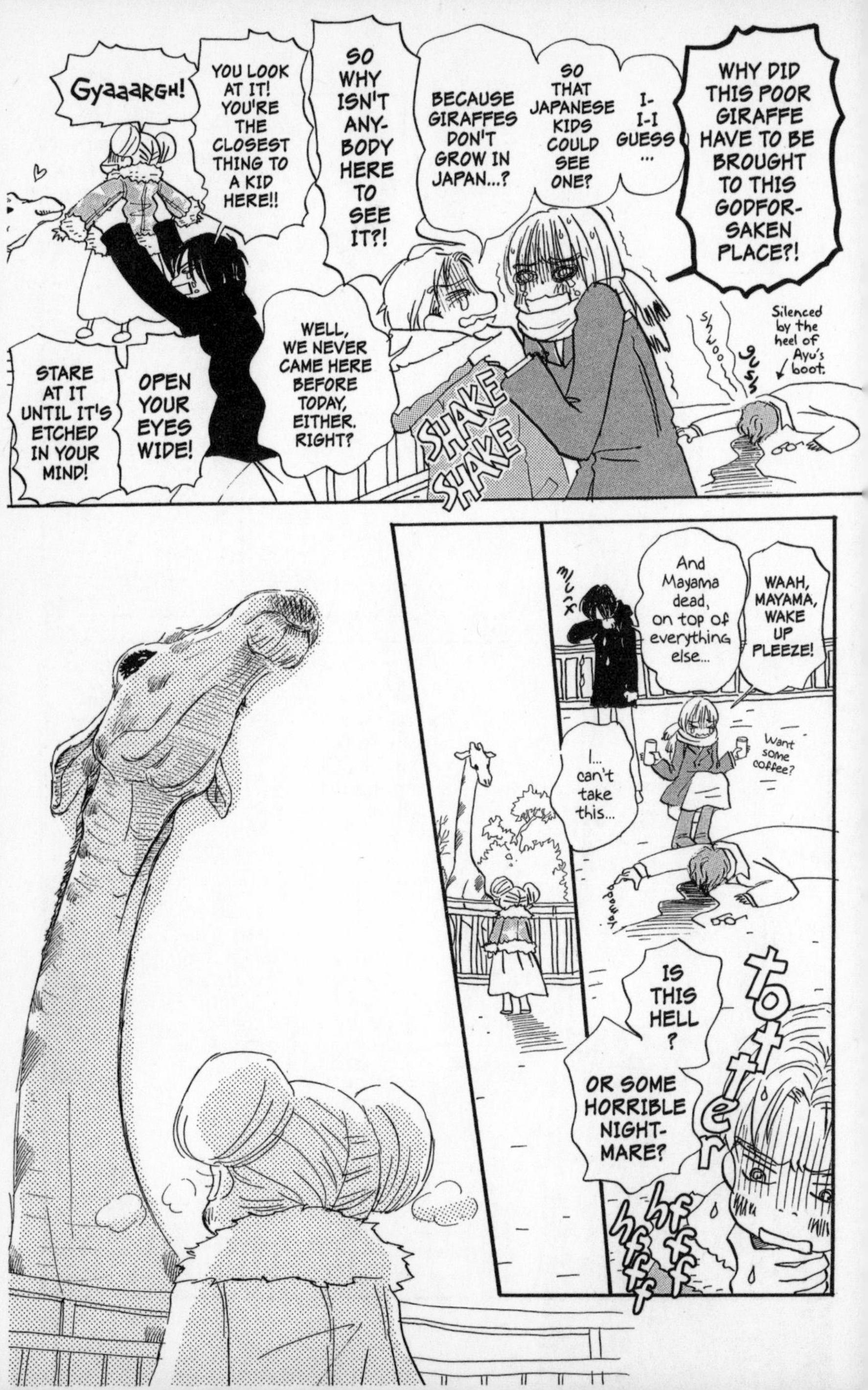
WHY DID THIS POOR GIRAFFE HAVE TO BE BROUGHT TO THIS GODFORSAKEN PLACE?!
I- I-I GUESS...
SO THAT JAPANESE KIDS COULD SEE ONE?
BECAUSE GIRAFFES DON'T GROW IN JAPAN...?
SO WHY ISN'T ANYBODY HERE TO SEE IT?!
YOU LOOK AT IT! YOU'RE THE CLOSEST THING TO A KID HERE!!
Gyaaargh!
Silenced by the heel of Ayu's boot.
shwoo
gush
SHAKE SHAKE
WELL, WE NEVER CAME HERE BEFORE TODAY, EITHER. RIGHT?
OPEN YOUR EYES WIDE!
STARE AT IT UNTIL IT'S ETCHED IN YOUR MIND!
WAAH, MAYAMA, WAKE UP PLEEZE!
And Mayama dead, on top of everything else...
Want some coffee?
I... can't take this...
totter
IS THIS HELL?
OR SOME HORRIBLE NIGHTMARE?
hff hff

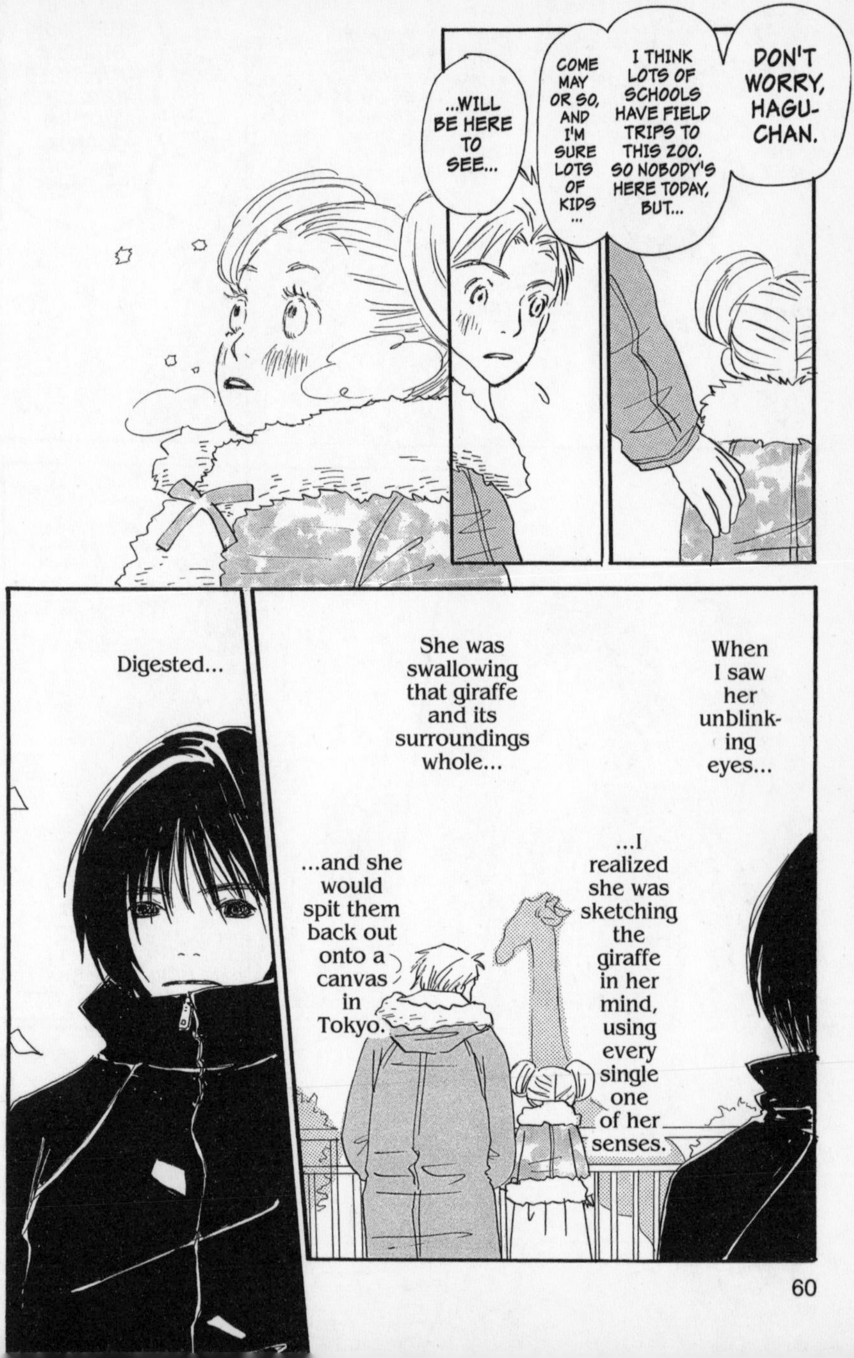

DON'T WORRY, HAGU-CHAN.
I THINK LOTS OF SCHOOLS HAVE FIELD TRIPS TO THIS ZOO. SO NOBODY'S HERE TODAY, BUT...
COME MAY OR SO, AND I'M SURE LOTS OF KIDS ...
...WILL BE HERE TO SEE...
When I saw her unblink-ing eyes...
She was swallowing that giraffe and its surroundings whole...
...I realized she was sketching the giraffe in her mind, using every single one of her senses.
...and she would spit them back out onto a canvas in Tokyo.
Digested...

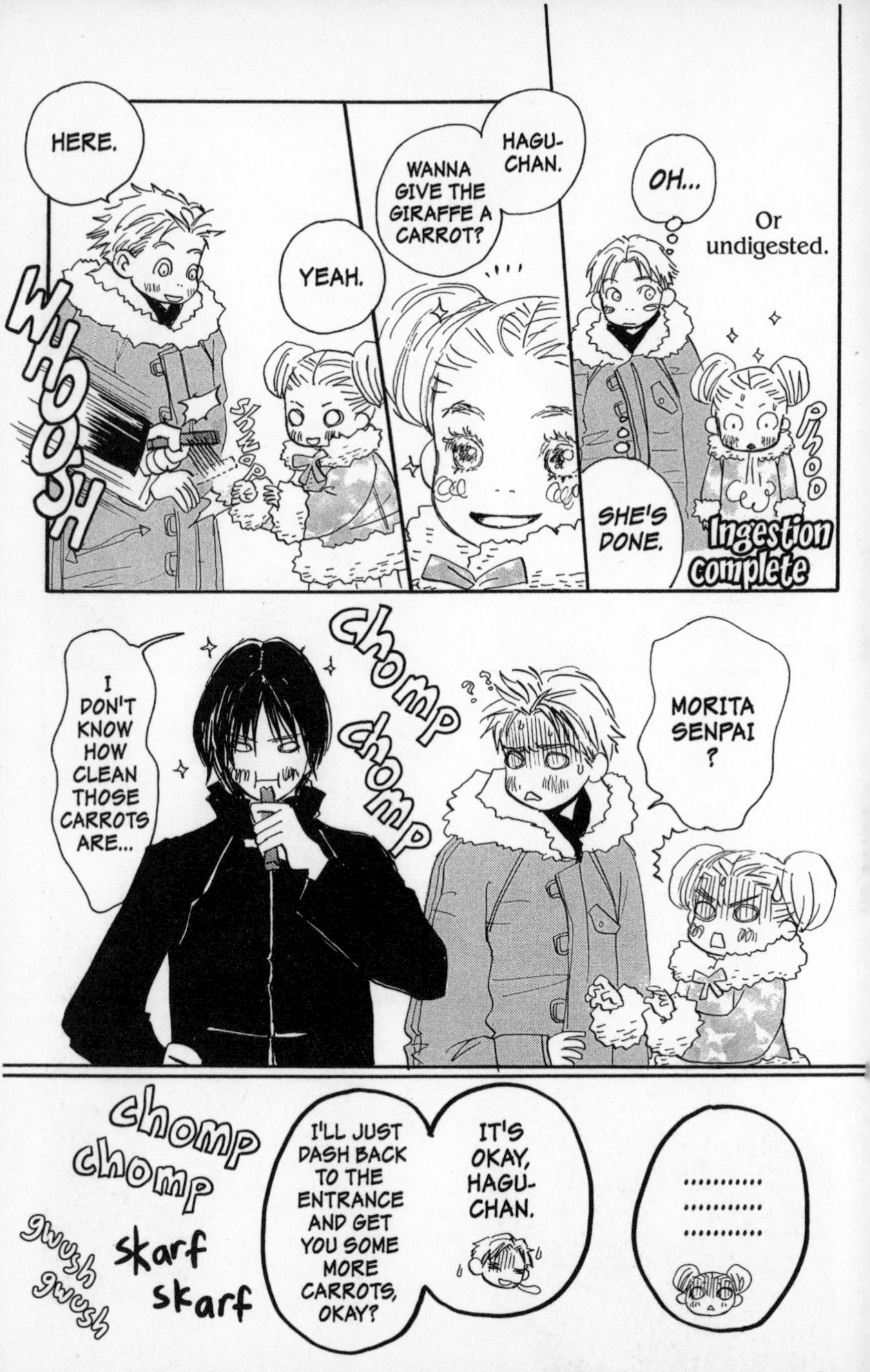
Or undigested.
OH...
phoo
Ingestion complete
SHE'S DONE.
HAGU-CHAN.
WANNA GIVE THE GIRAFFE A CARROT?
YEAH.
HERE.
SHWOOP
WHOOSH
MORITA SENPAI ?
chomp chomp
I DON'T KNOW HOW CLEAN THOSE CARROTS ARE...
....
....
....
IT'S OKAY, HAGU-CHAN.
I'LL JUST DASH BACK TO THE ENTRANCE AND GET YOU SOME MORE CARROTS, OKAY?
chomp chomp
skarf skarf
gwush gwush

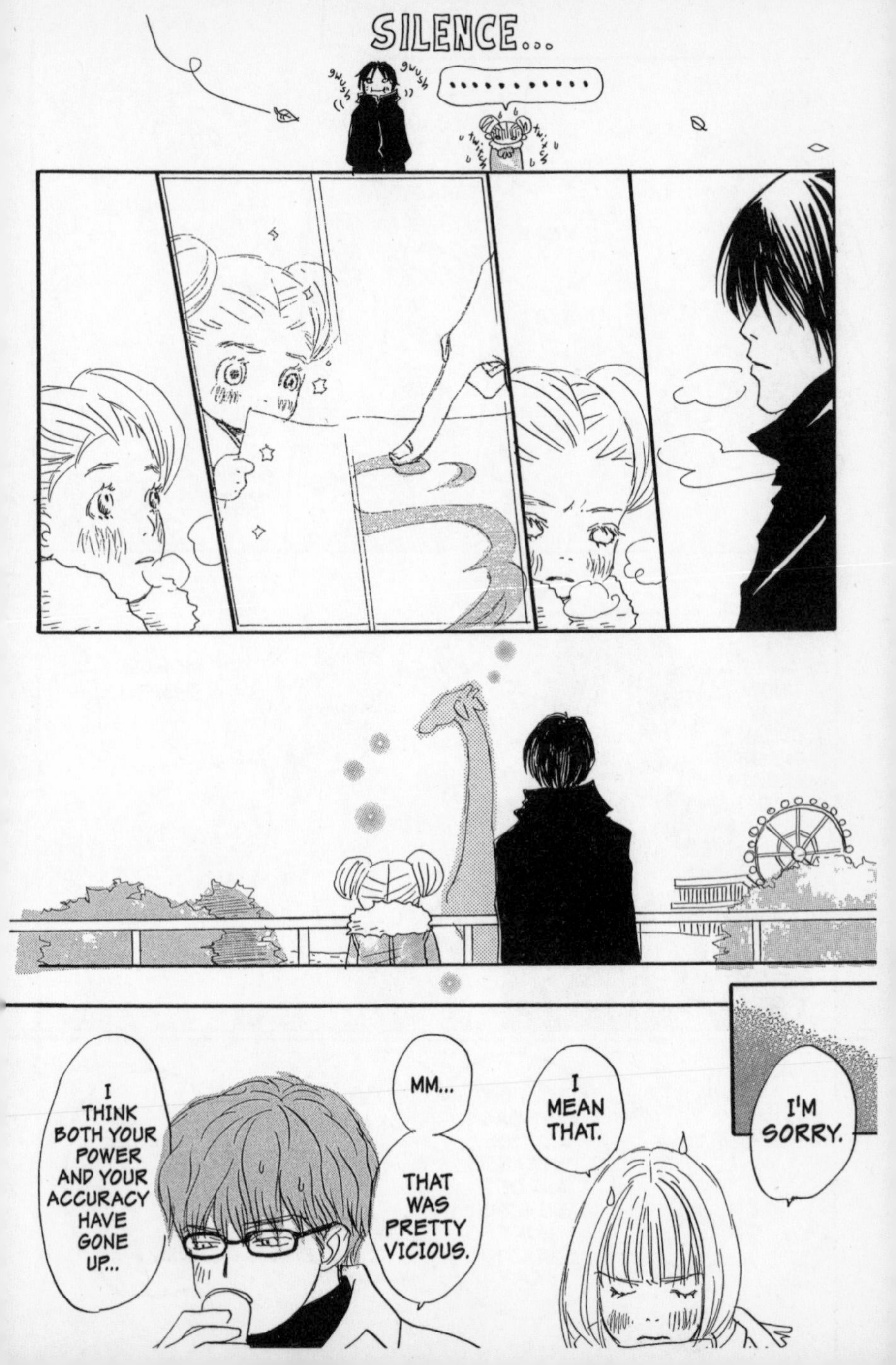
SILENCE...
twitch
....
twitch
gwush
gwush
I'M SORRY.
I MEAN THAT.
MM...
THAT WAS PRETTY VICIOUS.
I THINK BOTH YOUR POWER AND YOUR ACCURACY HAVE GONE UP...

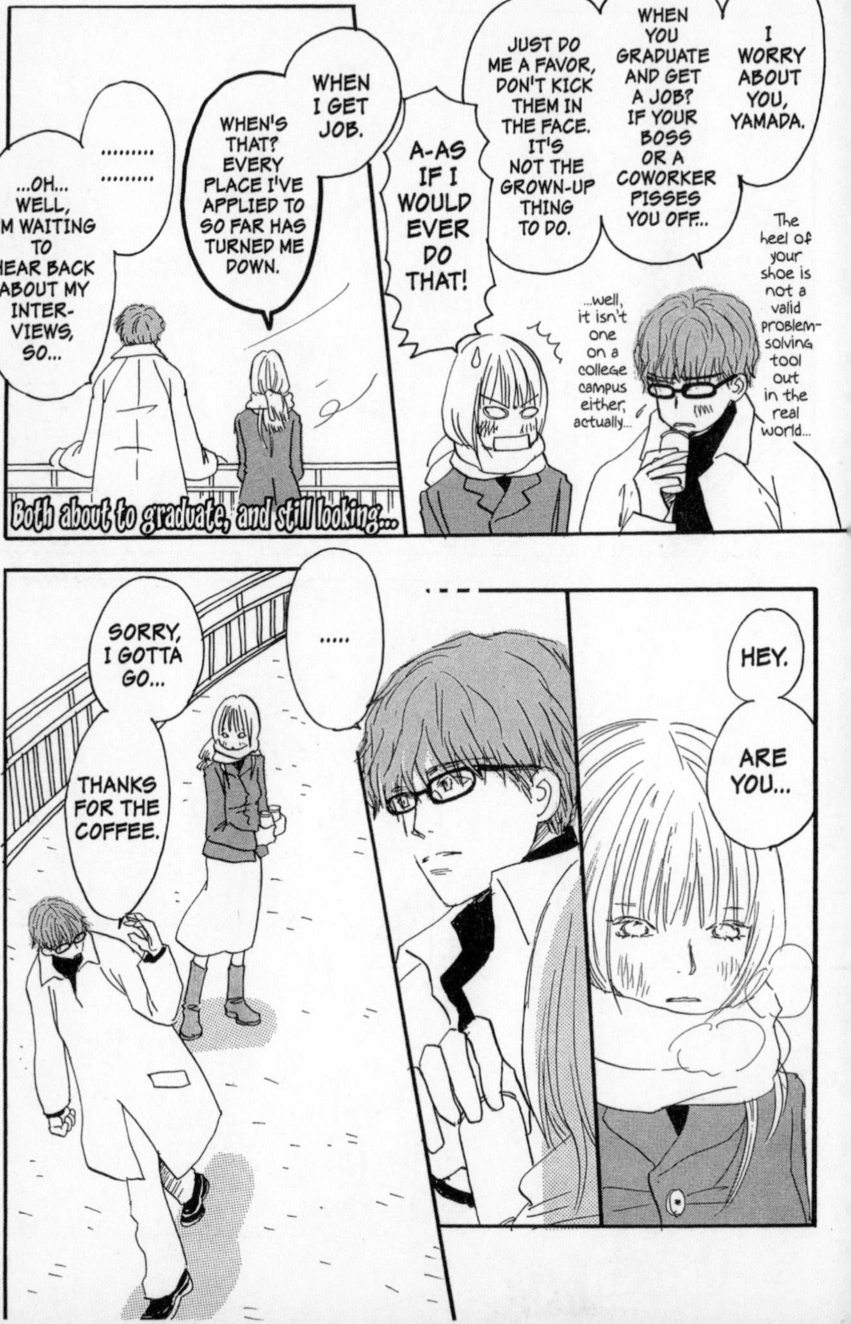
I WORRY ABOUT YOU, YAMADA.
WHEN YOU GRADUATE AND GET A JOB? IF YOUR BOSS OR A COWORKER PISSES YOU OFF...
JUST DO ME A FAVOR, DON'T KICK THEM IN THE FACE. IT'S NOT THE GROWN-UP THING TO DO.
The heel of your shoe is not a valid problem-solving tool out in the real world...
A-AS IF I WOULD EVER DO THAT!
...well, it isn't one on a college campus either, actually...
WHEN I GET JOB.
WHEN'S THAT? EVERY PLACE I'VE APPLIED TO SO FAR HAS TURNED ME DOWN.
....
....
...OH... WELL, I'M WAITING TO HEAR BACK ABOUT MY INTER-VIEWS, SO...
Both about to graduate, and still looking...
HEY.
ARE YOU...
.....
SORRY, I GOTTA GO...
THANKS FOR THE COFFEE.

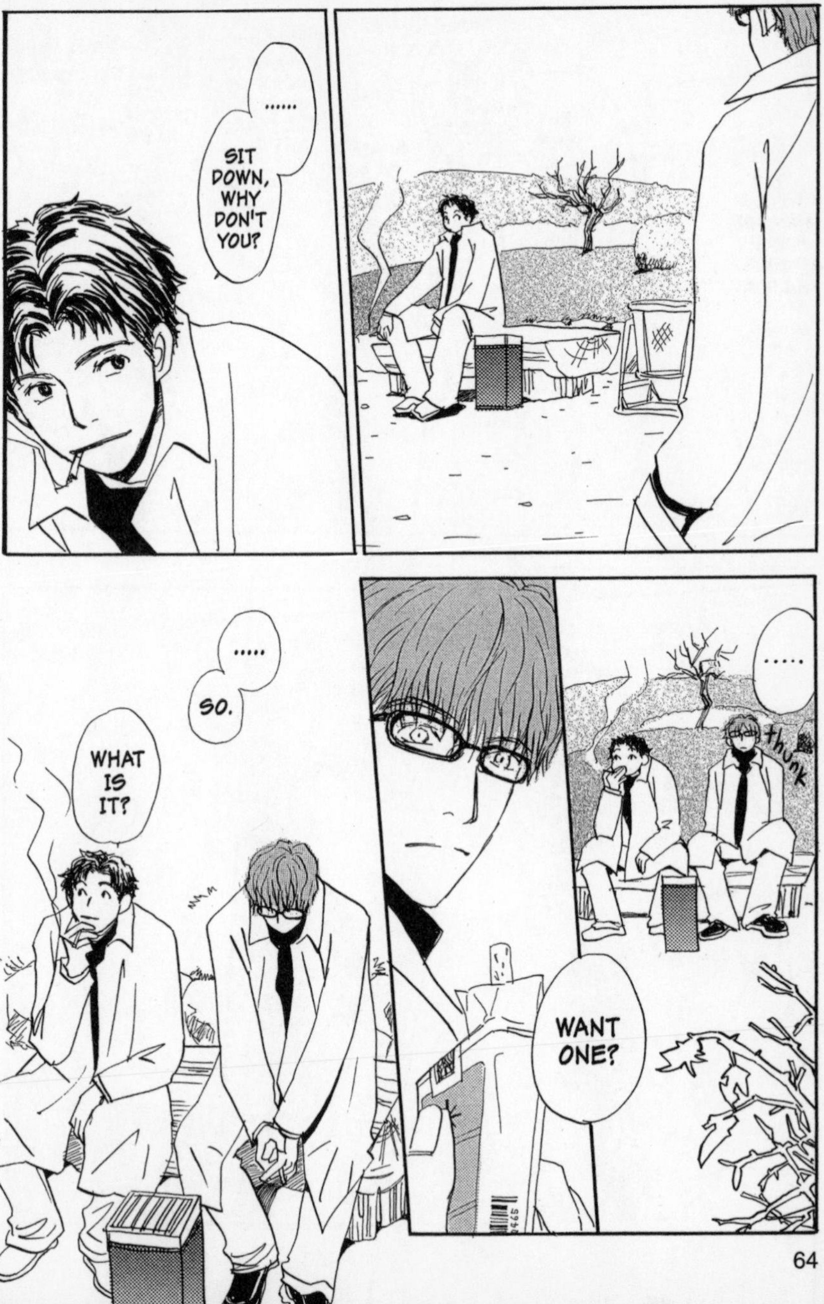
......
SIT DOWN, WHY DON'T YOU?
.....
thunk
WANT ONE?
......
SO.
WHAT IS IT?

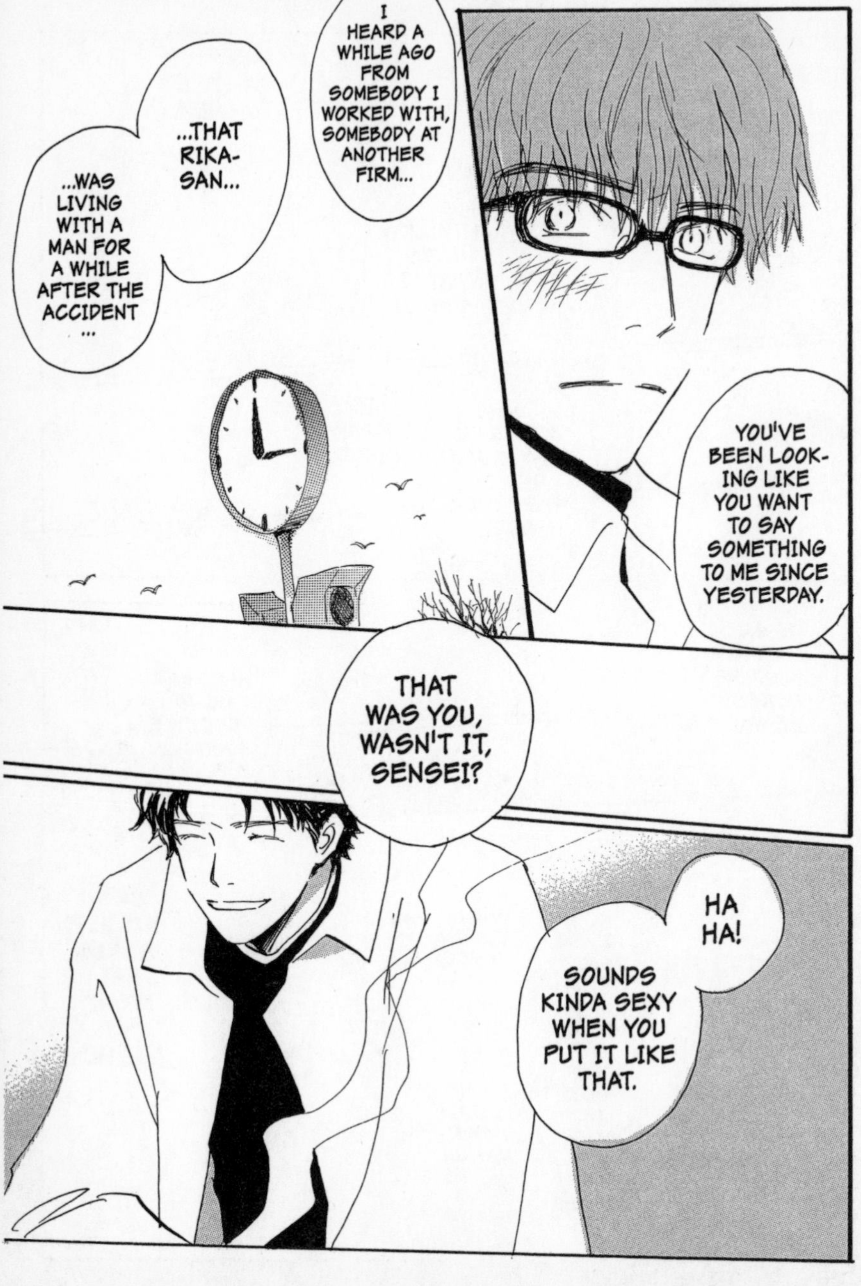
YOU'VE BEEN LOOK-ING LIKE YOU WANT TO SAY SOMETHING TO ME SINCE YESTERDAY.
I HEARD A WHILE AGO FROM SOMEBODY I WORKED WITH, SOMEBODY AT ANOTHER FIRM...
...THAT RIKA-SAN...
...WAS LIVING WITH A MAN FOR A WHILE AFTER THE ACCIDENT ...
THAT WAS YOU, WASN'T IT, SENSEI?
HA HA!
SOUNDS KINDA SEXY WHEN YOU PUT IT LIKE THAT.

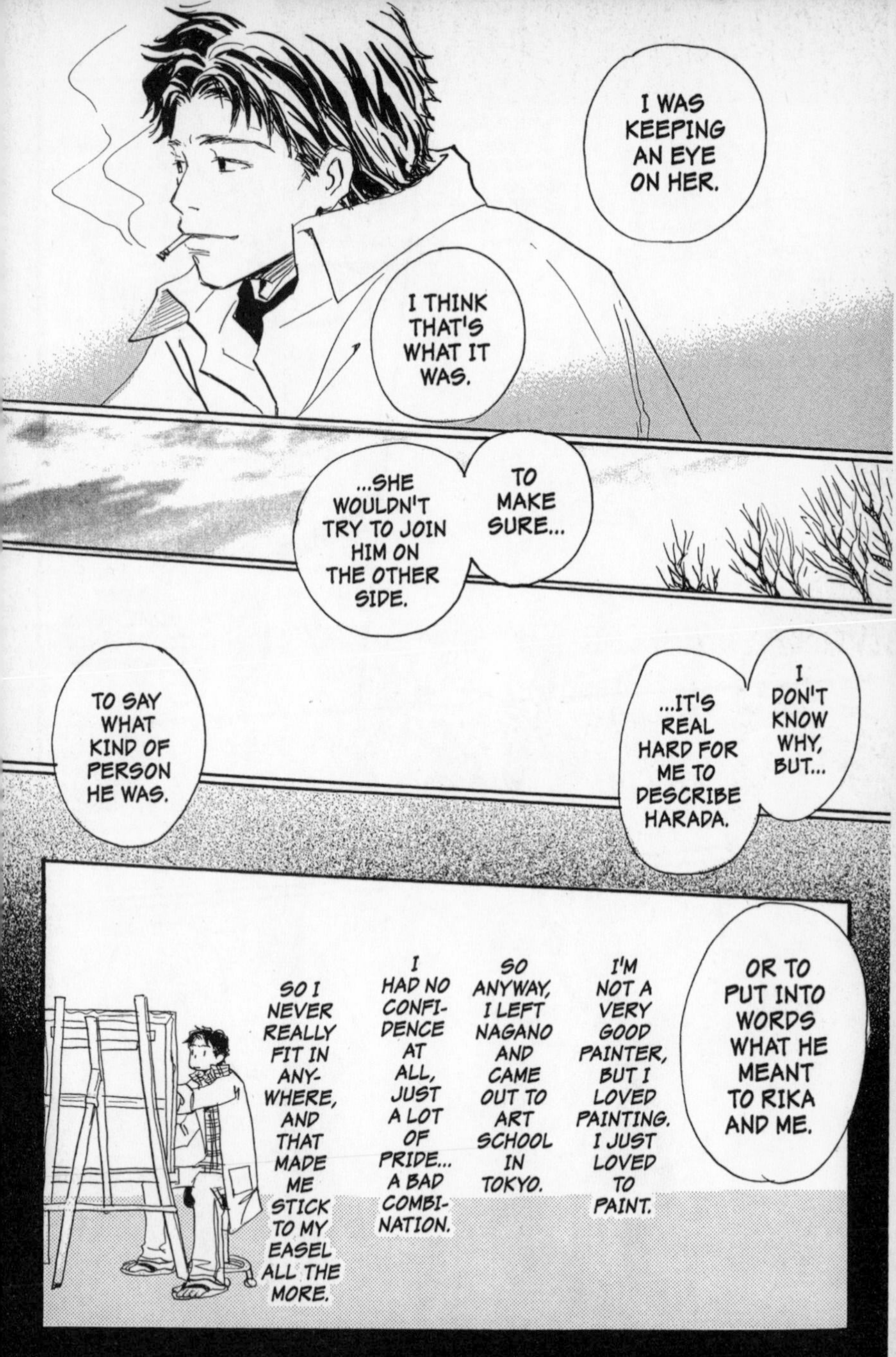
I WAS KEEPING AN EYE ON HER.
I THINK THAT'S WHAT IT WAS.
TO MAKE SURE...
...SHE WOULDN'T TRY TO JOIN HIM ON THE OTHER SIDE.
I DON'T KNOW WHY, BUT...
...IT'S REAL HARD FOR ME TO DESCRIBE HARADA.
TO SAY WHAT KIND OF PERSON HE WAS.
OR TO PUT INTO WORDS WHAT HE MEANT TO RIKA AND ME.
I'M NOT A VERY GOOD PAINTER, BUT I LOVED PAINTING. I JUST LOVED TO PAINT.
SO ANYWAY, I LEFT NAGANO AND CAME OUT TO ART SCHOOL IN TOKYO.
I HAD NO CONFIDENCE AT ALL, JUST A LOT OF PRIDE... A BAD COMBINATION.
SO I NEVER REALLY FIT IN ANYWHERE, AND THAT MADE ME STICK TO MY EASEL ALL THE MORE.

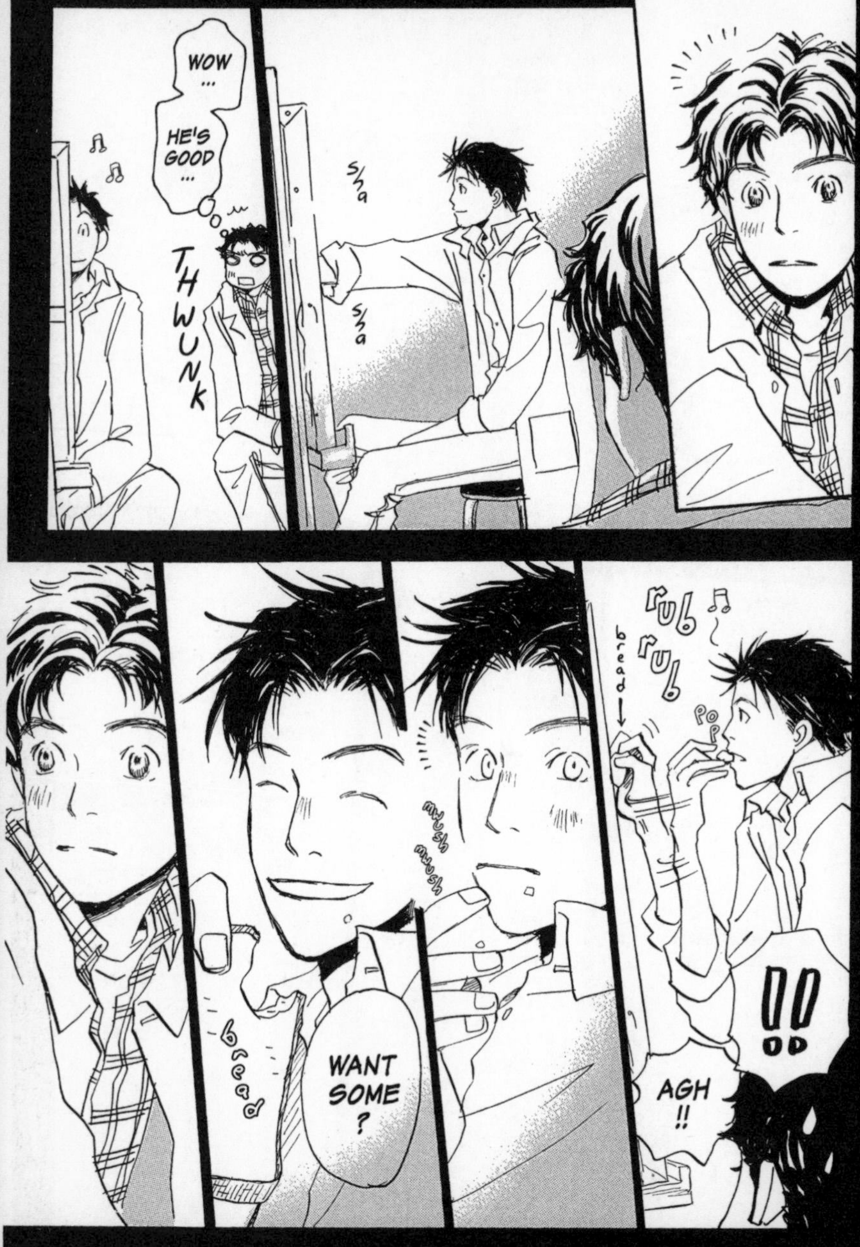

s/ha
s/ha
WOW... HE'S GOOD...
THWUNK
rub rub
bread
pop
!!
AGH!!
mwush mwush
bread
WANT SOME?

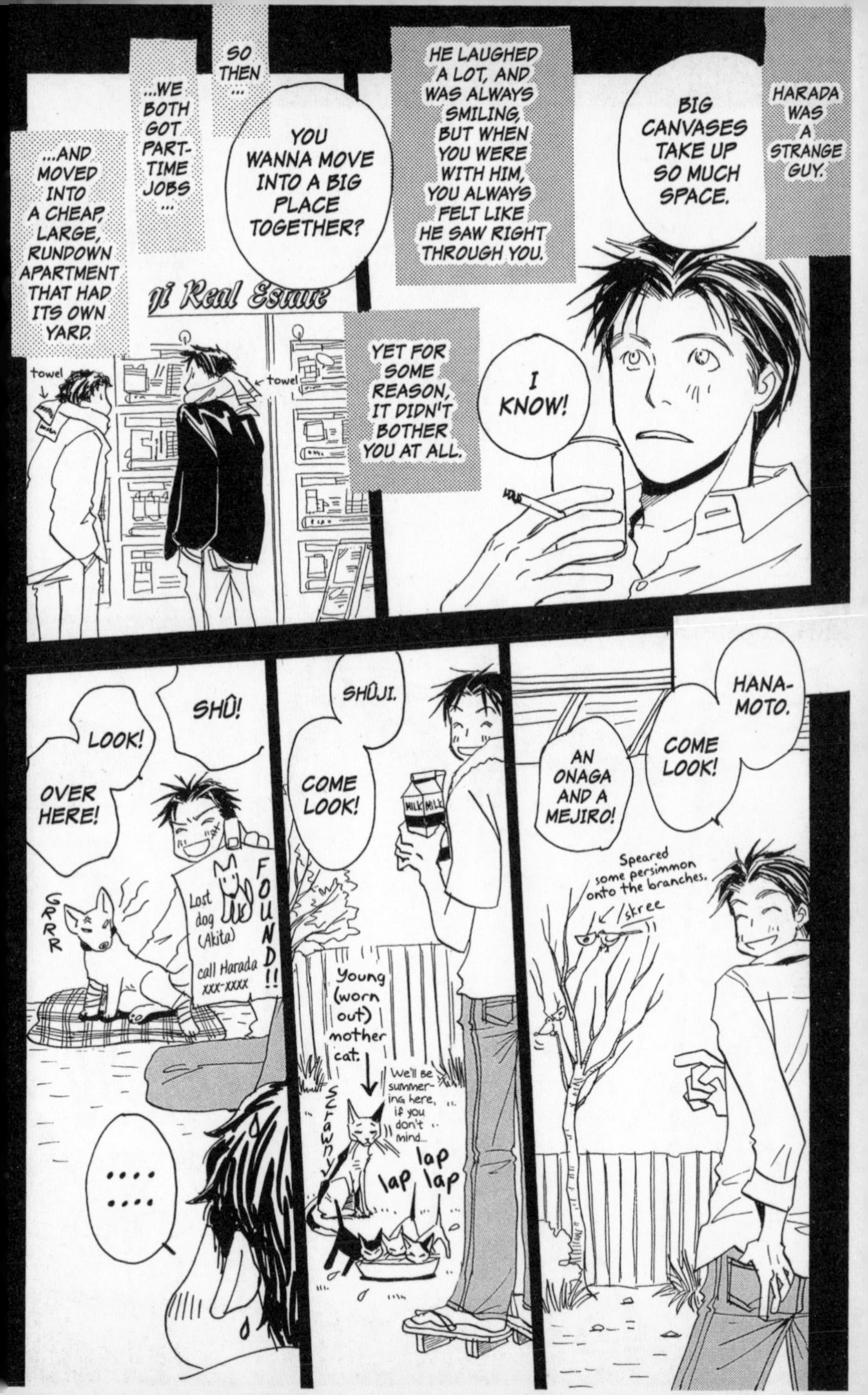
HARADA WAS A STRANGE GUY.
BIG CANVASES TAKE UP SO MUCH SPACE.
HE LAUGHED A LOT, AND WAS ALWAYS SMILING, BUT WHEN YOU WERE WITH HIM, YOU ALWAYS FELT LIKE HE SAW RIGHT THROUGH YOU.
I KNOW!
YET FOR SOME REASON, IT DIDN'T BOTHER YOU AT ALL.
YOU WANNA MOVE INTO A BIG PLACE TOGETHER?
SO THEN ...
...WE BOTH GOT PART-TIME JOBS ...
...AND MOVED INTO A CHEAP, LARGE, RUNDOWN APARTMENT THAT HAD ITS OWN YARD.
gi Real Estate
towel
towel
HANA-MOTO.
COME LOOK!
AN ONAGA AND A MEJIRO!
Speared some persimmon onto the branches.
skree
SHÛJI.
COME LOOK!
MILK MILK
Young (worn out) mother cat.
SCRAWNY
We'll be summering here, if you don't mind...
lap lap lap
SHÛ!
LOOK!
OVER HERE!
GRRR
Lost dog (Akita) call Harada xxx-xxxx
FOUND!!
....
....

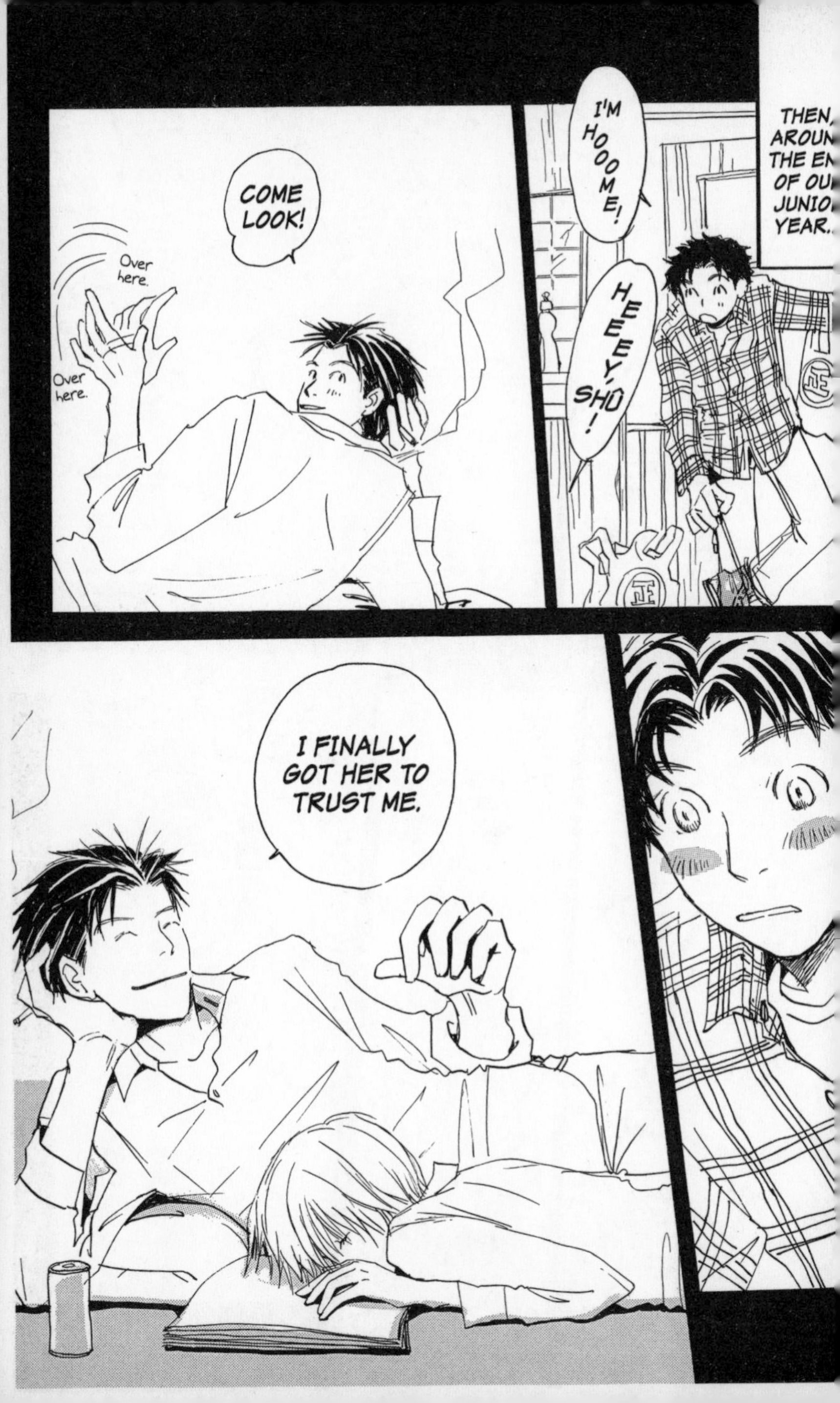
THEN, AROUN THE EN OF OU JUNIO YEAR..
I'M HOOOME!
HEEEY, SHÛ!
COME LOOK!
Over here.
Over here.
I FINALLY GOT HER TO TRUST ME.

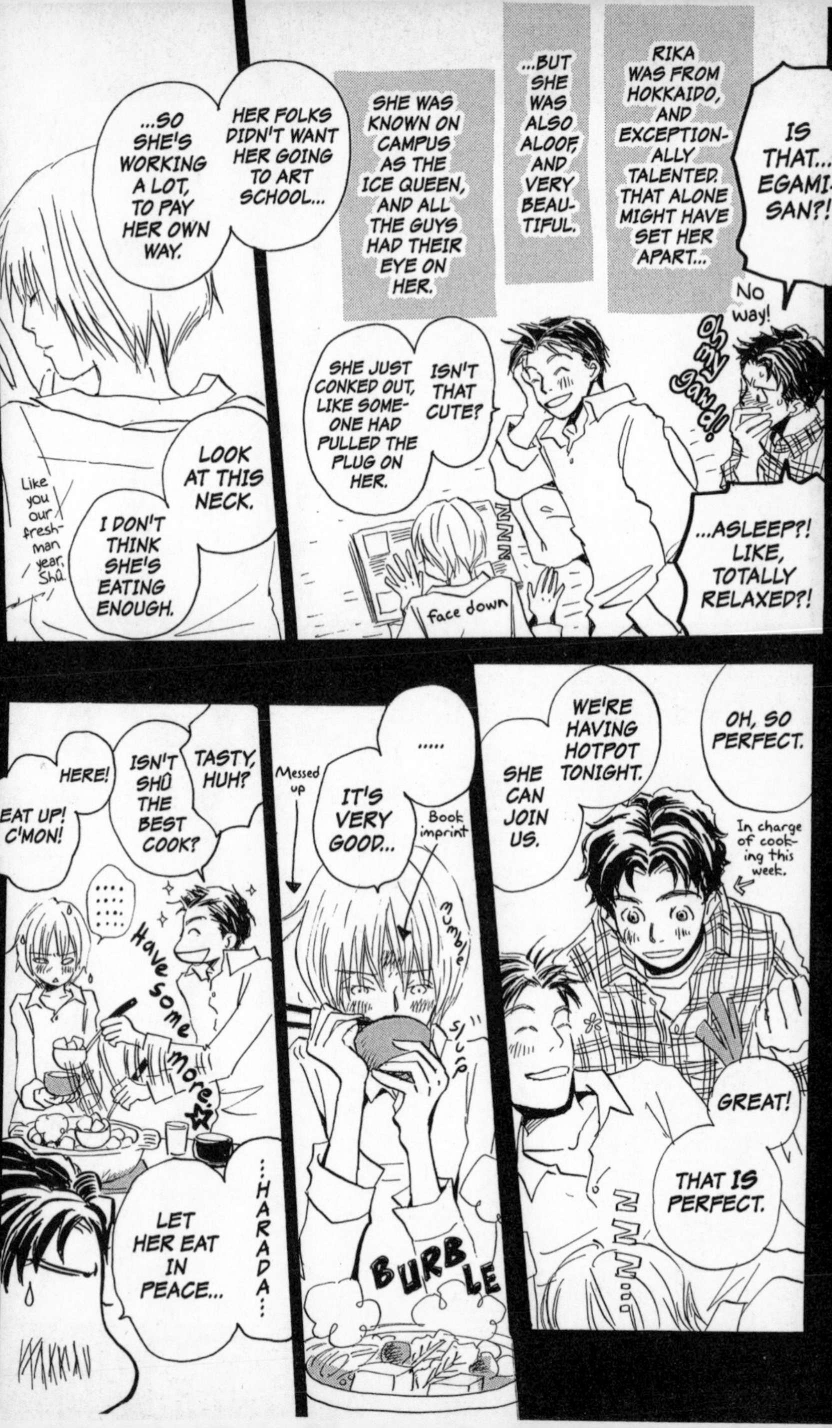
IS THAT... EGAMI-SAN?!
No way!
Oh my gawd!
RIKA WAS FROM HOKKAIDO, AND EXCEPTION-ALLY TALENTED. THAT ALONE MIGHT HAVE SET HER APART...
...BUT SHE WAS ALSO ALOOF, AND VERY BEAU-TIFUL.
SHE WAS KNOWN ON CAMPUS AS THE ICE QUEEN, AND ALL THE GUYS HAD THEIR EYE ON HER.
...ASLEEP?! LIKE, TOTALLY RELAXED?!
ISN'T THAT CUTE?
SHE JUST CONKED OUT, LIKE SOME-ONE HAD PULLED THE PLUG ON HER.
NNN
face down
HER FOLKS DIDN'T WANT HER GOING TO ART SCHOOL...
...SO SHE'S WORKING A LOT, TO PAY HER OWN WAY.
LOOK AT THIS NECK.
I DON'T THINK SHE'S EATING ENOUGH.
Like you our fresh-man year, Shû.
OH, SO PERFECT.
WE'RE HAVING HOTPOT TONIGHT.
SHE CAN JOIN US.
In charge of cook-ing this week.
GREAT!
THAT IS PERFECT.
NNN...
.....
IT'S VERY GOOD...
Messed up
Book imprint
mumble
slurp
BURBLE
TASTY, HUH?
ISN'T SHÛ THE BEST COOK?
HERE!
EAT UP! C'MON!
Have some more☆
...HARADA...
LET HER EAT IN PEACE...

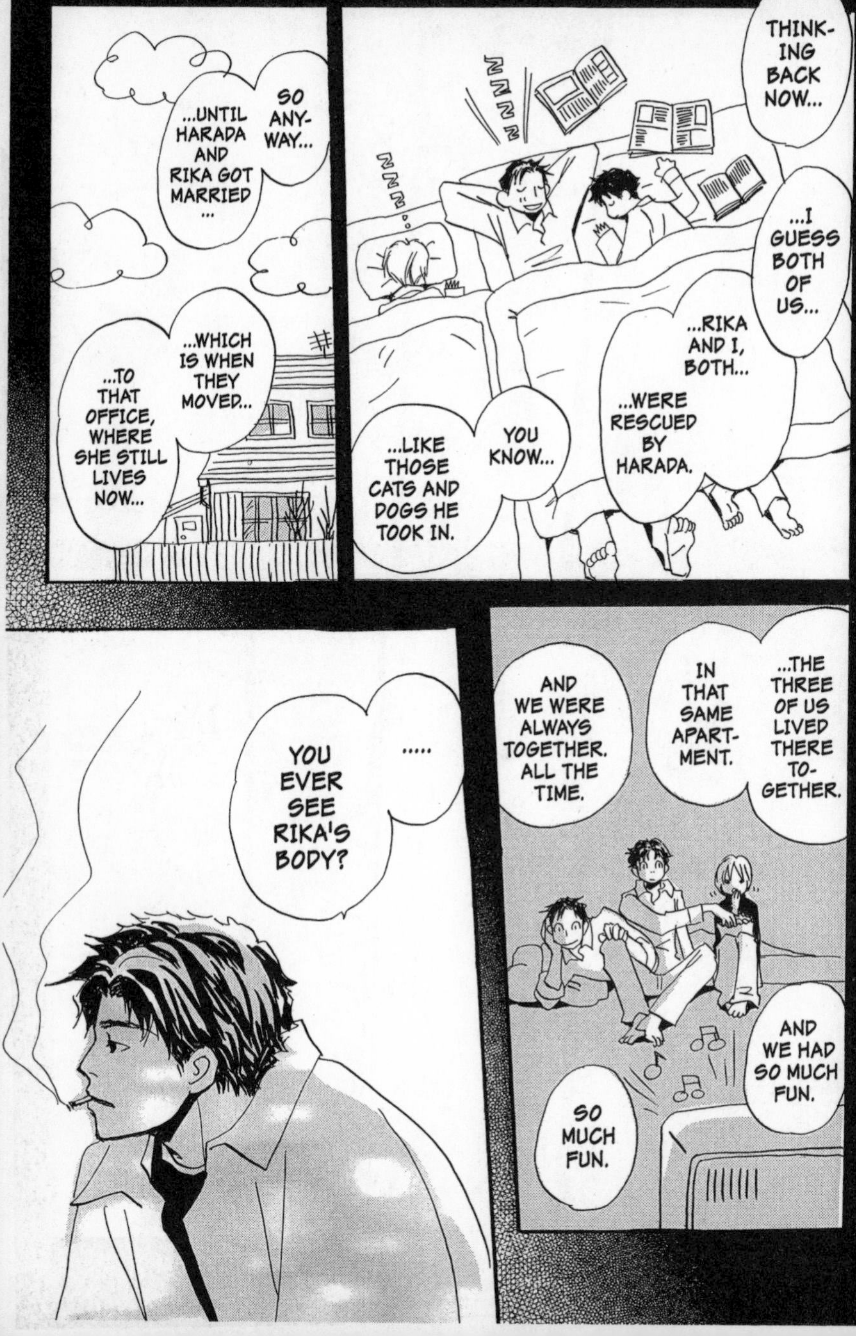
THINKING BACK NOW...
...I GUESS BOTH OF US...
...RIKA AND I, BOTH...
...WERE RESCUED BY HARADA.
YOU KNOW...
...LIKE THOSE CATS AND DOGS HE TOOK IN.
SO ANYWAY...
...UNTIL HARADA AND RIKA GOT MARRIED...
...WHICH IS WHEN THEY MOVED...
...TO THAT OFFICE, WHERE SHE STILL LIVES NOW...
...THE THREE OF US LIVED THERE TOGETHER.
IN THAT SAME APARTMENT.
AND WE WERE ALWAYS TOGETHER. ALL THE TIME.
AND WE HAD SO MUCH FUN.
SO MUCH FUN.
.....
YOU EVER SEE RIKA'S BODY?

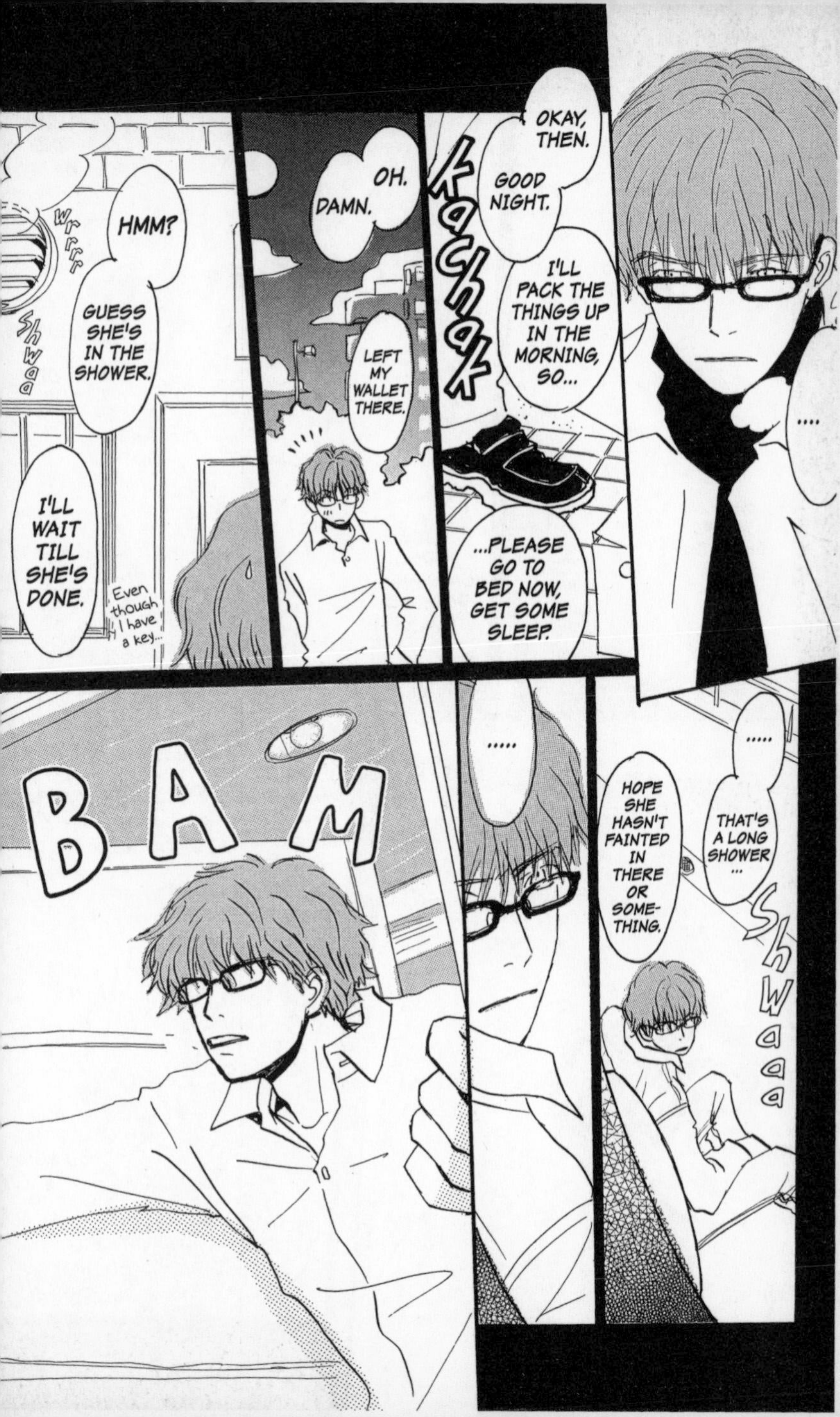
....
OKAY, THEN.
GOOD NIGHT.
I'LL PACK THE THINGS UP IN THE MORNING, SO...
Kachak
...PLEASE GO TO BED NOW, GET SOME SLEEP.
OH. DAMN.
LEFT MY WALLET THERE.
HMM?
wrrrr
Shwaa
GUESS SHE'S IN THE SHOWER.
I'LL WAIT TILL SHE'S DONE.
Even though I have a key...
.....
THAT'S A LONG SHOWER...
HOPE SHE HASN'T FAINTED IN THERE OR SOMETHING.
Shwaaa
.....
BAM

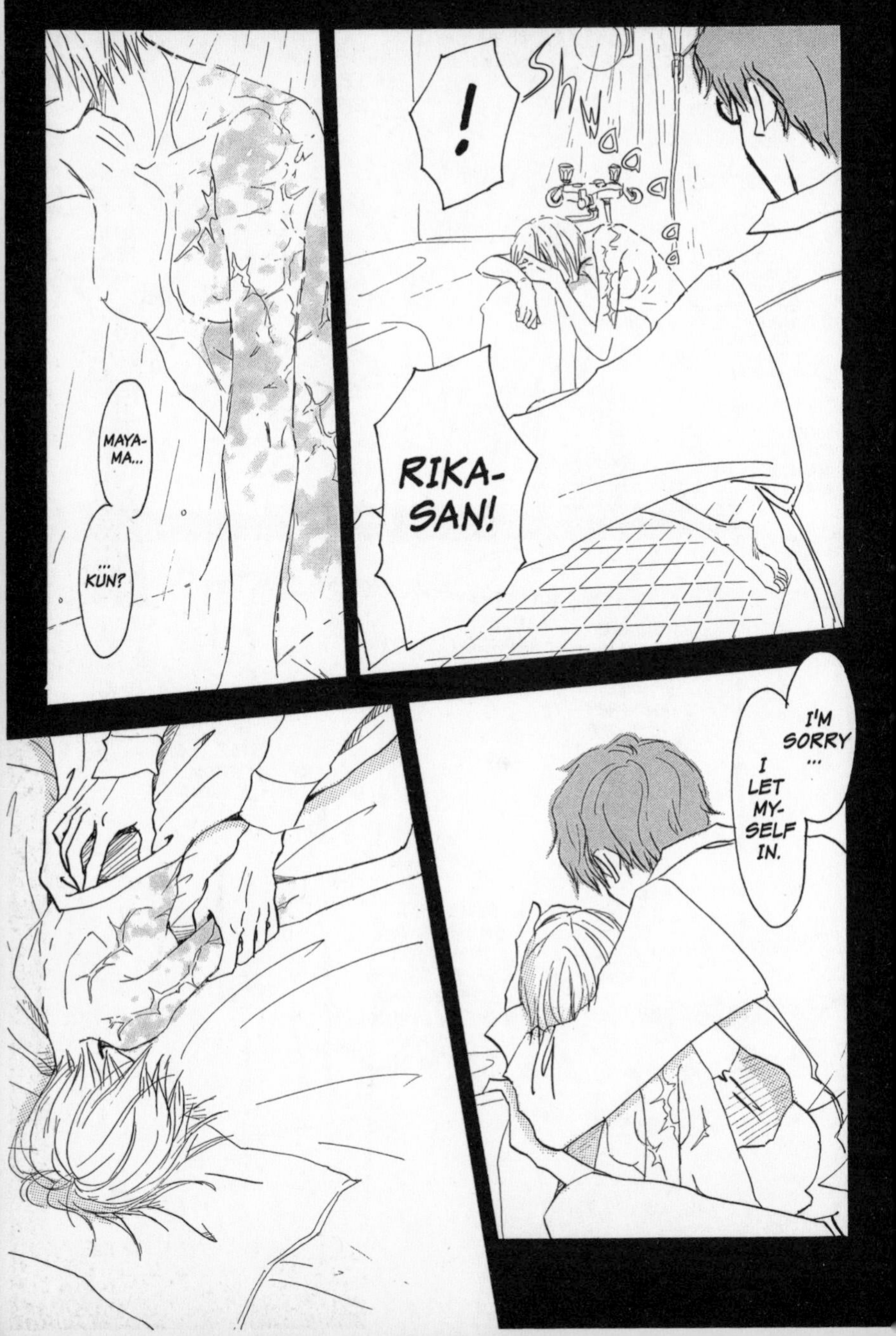
!
ShWaaaaa
RIKA-SAN!
MAYAMA...
...KUN?
I'M SORRY...
I LET MYSELF IN.

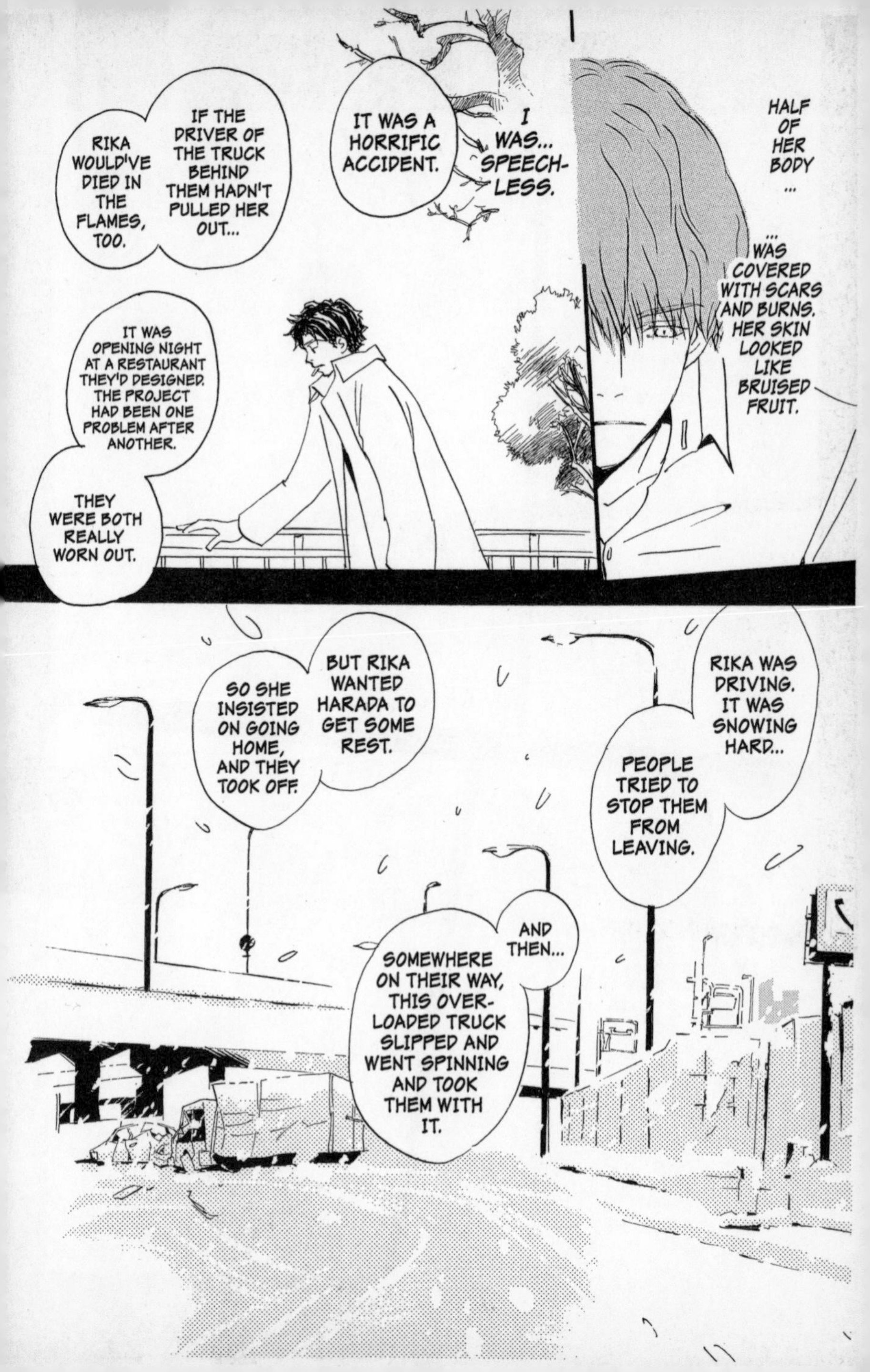
HALF OF HER BODY ...
... WAS COVERED WITH SCARS AND BURNS. HER SKIN LOOKED LIKE BRUISED FRUIT.
I WAS... SPEECHLESS.
IT WAS A HORRIFIC ACCIDENT.
IF THE DRIVER OF THE TRUCK BEHIND THEM HADN'T PULLED HER OUT...
RIKA WOULD'VE DIED IN THE FLAMES, TOO.
IT WAS OPENING NIGHT AT A RESTAURANT THEY'D DESIGNED. THE PROJECT HAD BEEN ONE PROBLEM AFTER ANOTHER.
THEY WERE BOTH REALLY WORN OUT.
RIKA WAS DRIVING. IT WAS SNOWING HARD...
PEOPLE TRIED TO STOP THEM FROM LEAVING.
BUT RIKA WANTED HARADA TO GET SOME REST.
SO SHE INSISTED ON GOING HOME, AND THEY TOOK OFF.
AND THEN...
SOMEWHERE ON THEIR WAY, THIS OVER-LOADED TRUCK SLIPPED AND WENT SPINNING AND TOOK THEM WITH IT.

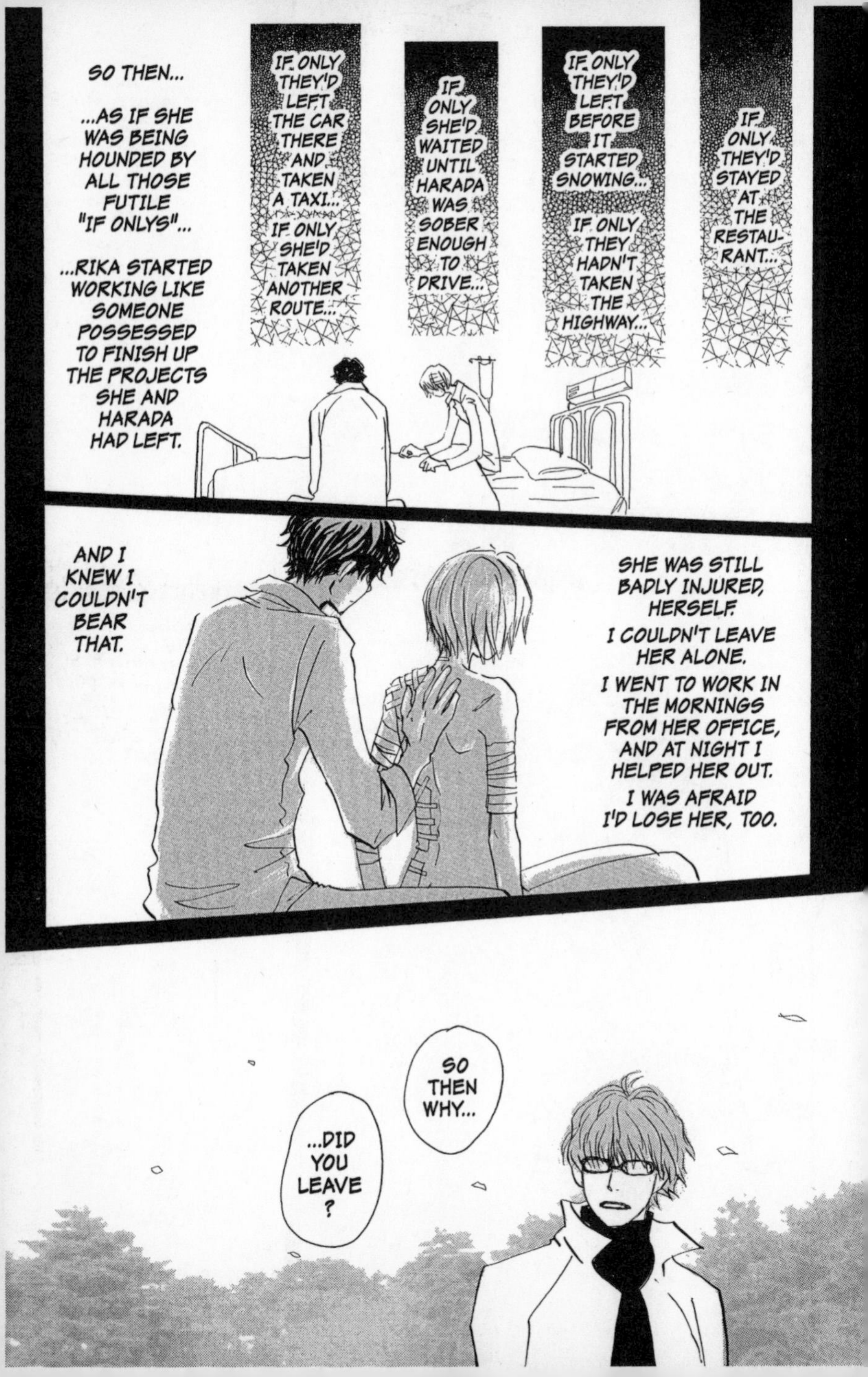
IF ONLY THEY'D STAYED AT THE RESTAURANT...
IF ONLY THEY'D LEFT BEFORE IT STARTED SNOWING...
IF ONLY THEY HADN'T TAKEN THE HIGHWAY...
IF ONLY SHE'D WAITED UNTIL HARADA WAS SOBER ENOUGH TO DRIVE...
IF ONLY THEY'D LEFT THE CAR THERE AND TAKEN A TAXI...
IF ONLY SHE'D TAKEN ANOTHER ROUTE...
SO THEN...
...AS IF SHE WAS BEING HOUNDED BY ALL THOSE FUTILE "IF ONLYS"...
...RIKA STARTED WORKING LIKE SOMEONE POSSESSED TO FINISH UP THE PROJECTS SHE AND HARADA HAD LEFT.
SHE WAS STILL BADLY INJURED, HERSELF.
I COULDN'T LEAVE HER ALONE.
I WENT TO WORK IN THE MORNINGS FROM HER OFFICE, AND AT NIGHT I HELPED HER OUT.
I WAS AFRAID I'D LOSE HER, TOO.
AND I KNEW I COULDN'T BEAR THAT.
SO THEN WHY...
...DID YOU LEAVE?

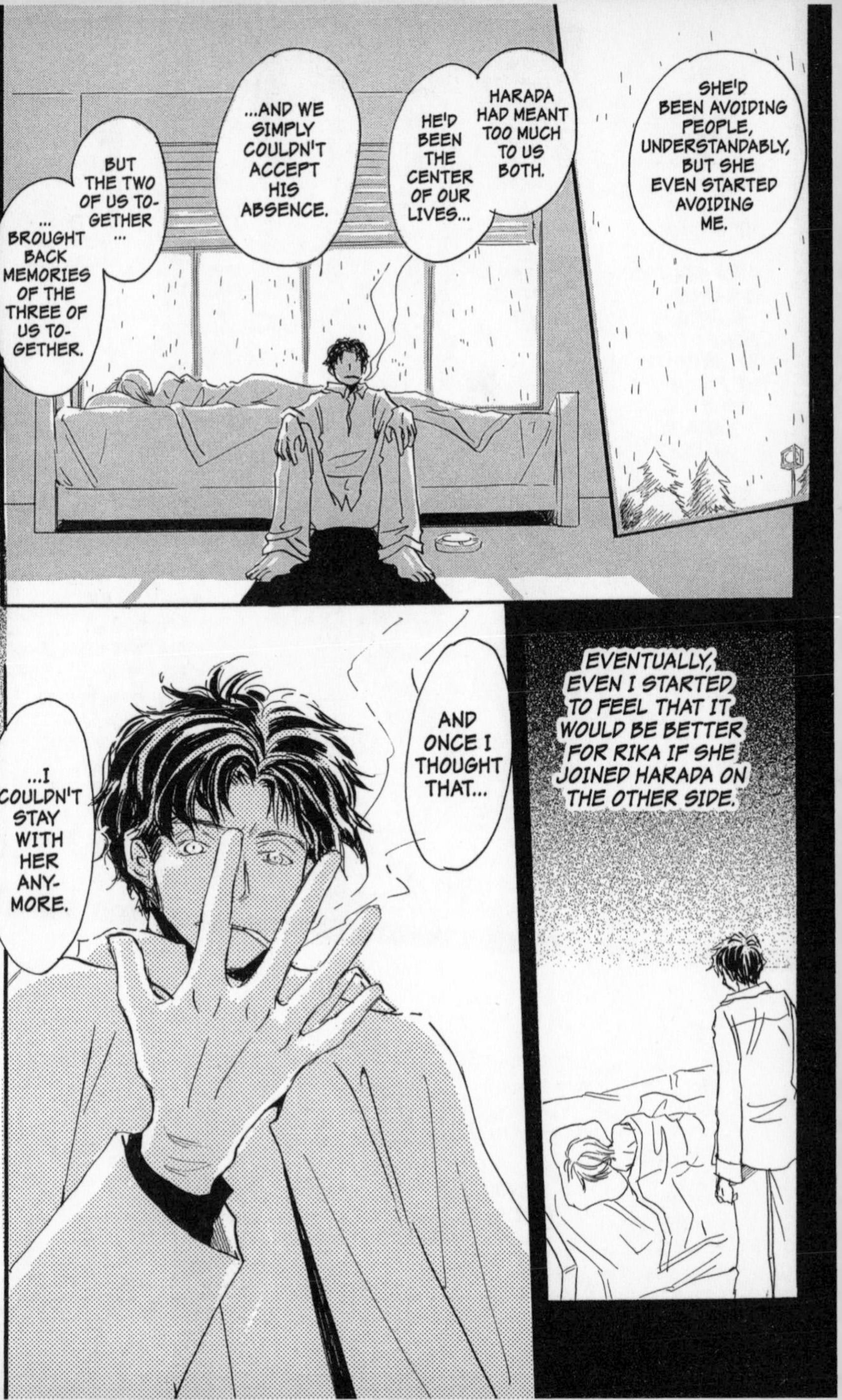
SHE'D BEEN AVOIDING PEOPLE, UNDERSTANDABLY, BUT SHE EVEN STARTED AVOIDING ME.
HARADA HAD MEANT TOO MUCH TO US BOTH.
HE'D BEEN THE CENTER OF OUR LIVES...
...AND WE SIMPLY COULDN'T ACCEPT HIS ABSENCE.
BUT THE TWO OF US TO-GETHER ...
... BROUGHT BACK MEMORIES OF THE THREE OF US TO-GETHER.
EVENTUALLY, EVEN I STARTED TO FEEL THAT IT WOULD BE BETTER FOR RIKA IF SHE JOINED HARADA ON THE OTHER SIDE.
AND ONCE I THOUGHT THAT...
...I COULDN'T STAY WITH HER ANY-MORE.

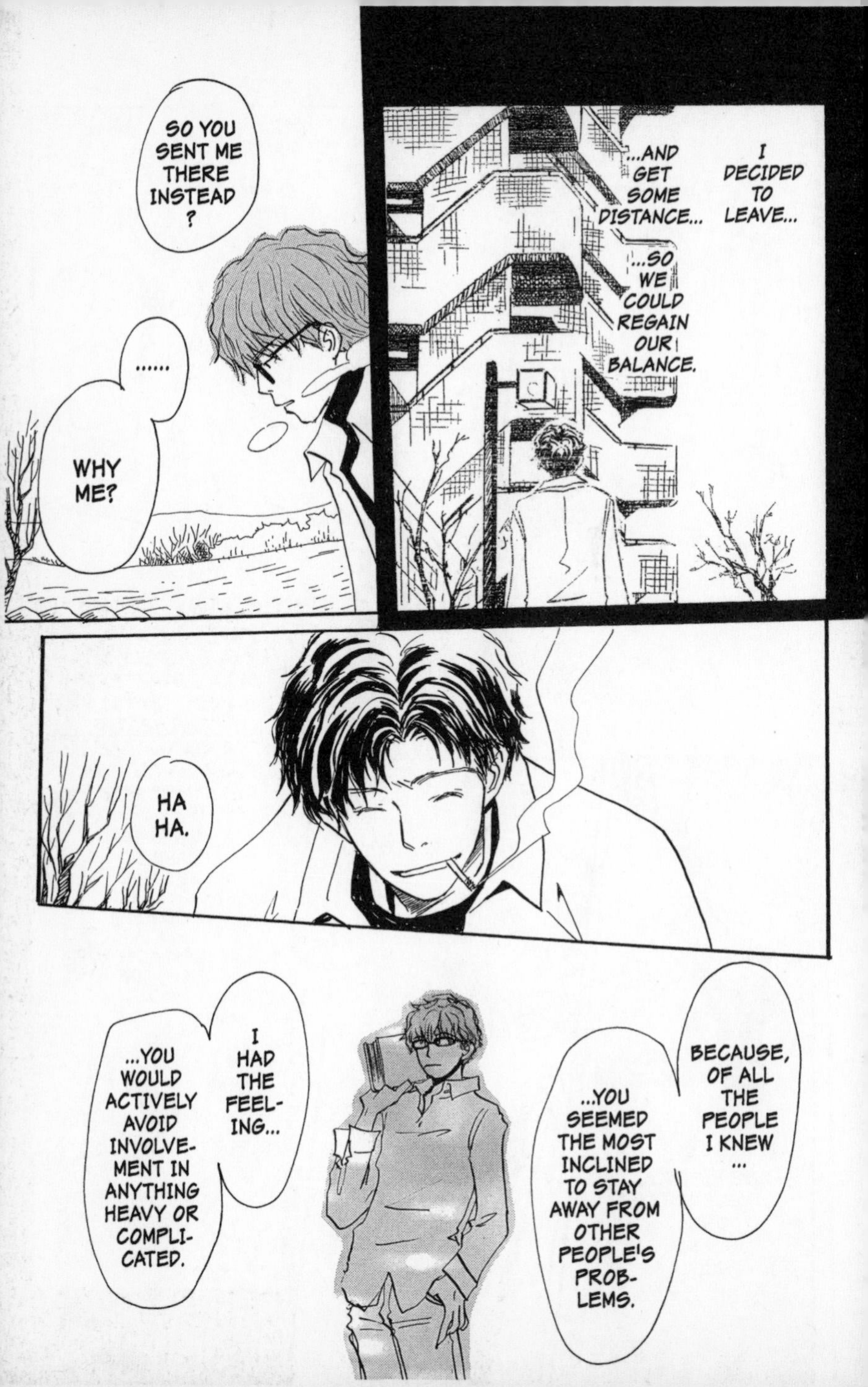
I DECIDED TO LEAVE...
...AND GET SOME DISTANCE...
...SO WE COULD REGAIN OUR BALANCE.
SO YOU SENT ME THERE INSTEAD?
......
WHY ME?
HA HA.
BECAUSE, OF ALL THE PEOPLE I KNEW...
...YOU SEEMED THE MOST INCLINED TO STAY AWAY FROM OTHER PEOPLE'S PROB-LEMS.
I HAD THE FEEL-ING...
...YOU WOULD ACTIVELY AVOID INVOLVE-MENT IN ANYTHING HEAVY OR COMPLI-CATED.

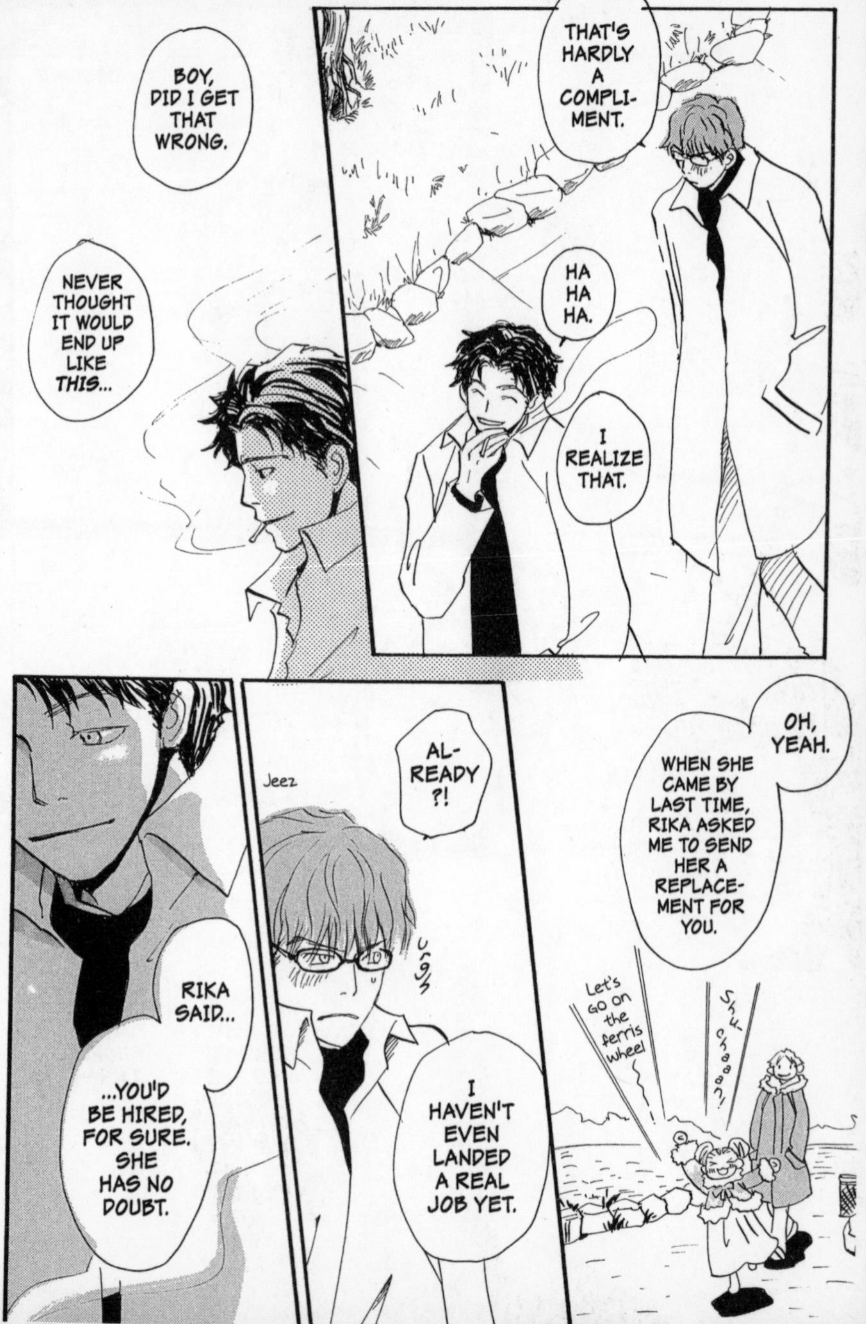

THAT'S HARDLY A COMPLIMENT.
HA HA HA.
I REALIZE THAT.
BOY, DID I GET THAT WRONG.
NEVER THOUGHT IT WOULD END UP LIKE THIS...
OH, YEAH.
WHEN SHE CAME BY LAST TIME, RIKA ASKED ME TO SEND HER A REPLACEMENT FOR YOU.
Let's go on the ferris wheel
Shu-chaaan!
AL-READY?!
Jeez
urgh
I HAVEN'T EVEN LANDED A REAL JOB YET.
RIKA SAID...
...YOU'D BE HIRED, FOR SURE. SHE HAS NO DOUBT.

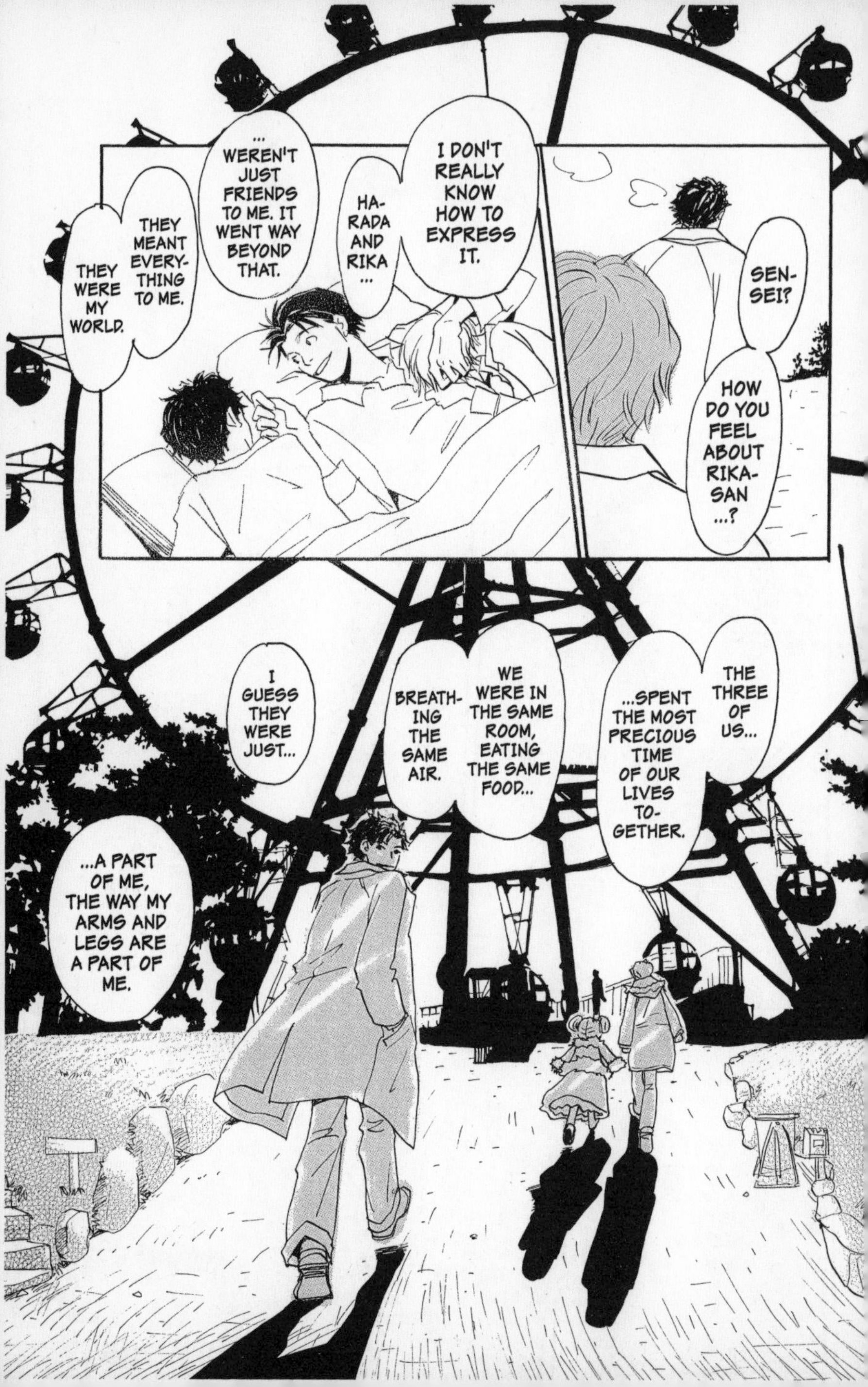
SEN-SEI?
HOW DO YOU FEEL ABOUT RIKA-SAN ...?
I DON'T REALLY KNOW HOW TO EXPRESS IT.
HA-RADA AND RIKA ...
... WEREN'T JUST FRIENDS TO ME. IT WENT WAY BEYOND THAT.
THEY MEANT EVERY-THING TO ME.
THEY WERE MY WORLD.
THE THREE OF US...
...SPENT THE MOST PRECIOUS TIME OF OUR LIVES TO-GETHER.
WE WERE IN THE SAME ROOM, EATING THE SAME FOOD...
BREATH-ING THE SAME AIR.
I GUESS THEY WERE JUST...
...A PART OF ME, THE WAY MY ARMS AND LEGS ARE A PART OF ME.

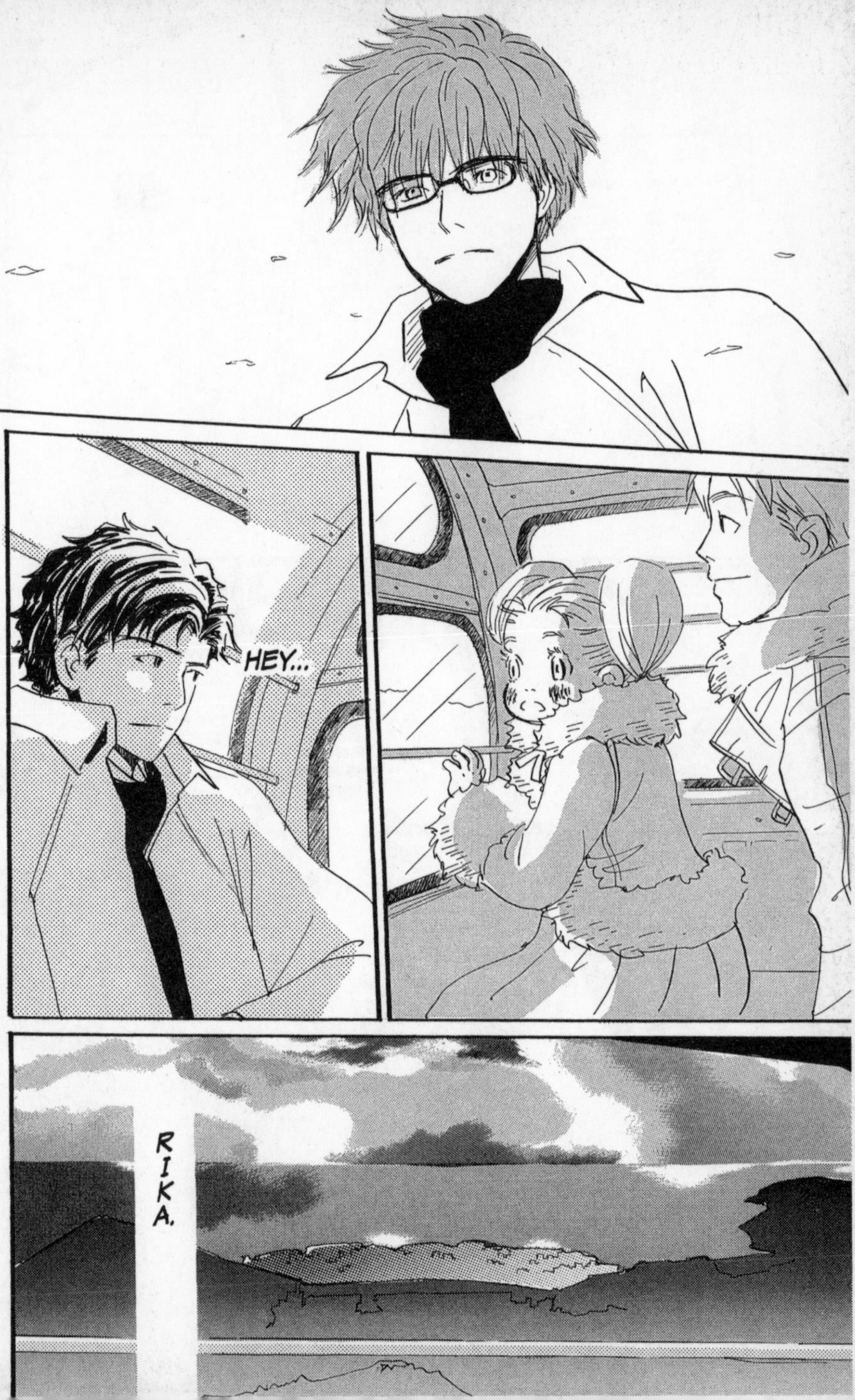
HEY...
RIKA.

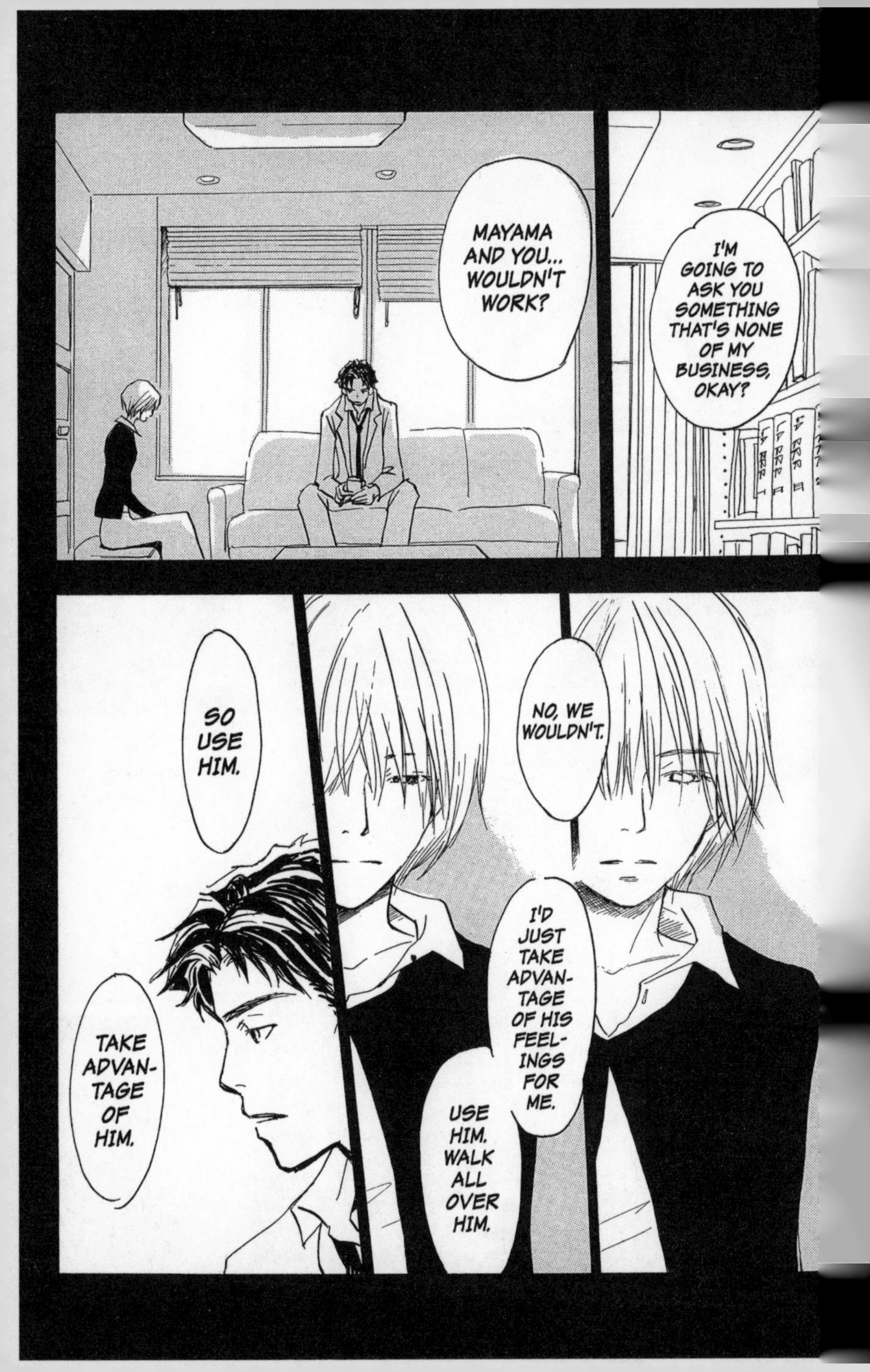
I'M GOING TO ASK YOU SOMETHING THAT'S NONE OF MY BUSINESS, OKAY?
MAYAMA AND YOU... WOULDN'T WORK?
NO, WE WOULDN'T.
I'D JUST TAKE ADVANTAGE OF HIS FEELINGS FOR ME.
USE HIM. WALK ALL OVER HIM.
SO USE HIM.
TAKE ADVANTAGE OF HIM.

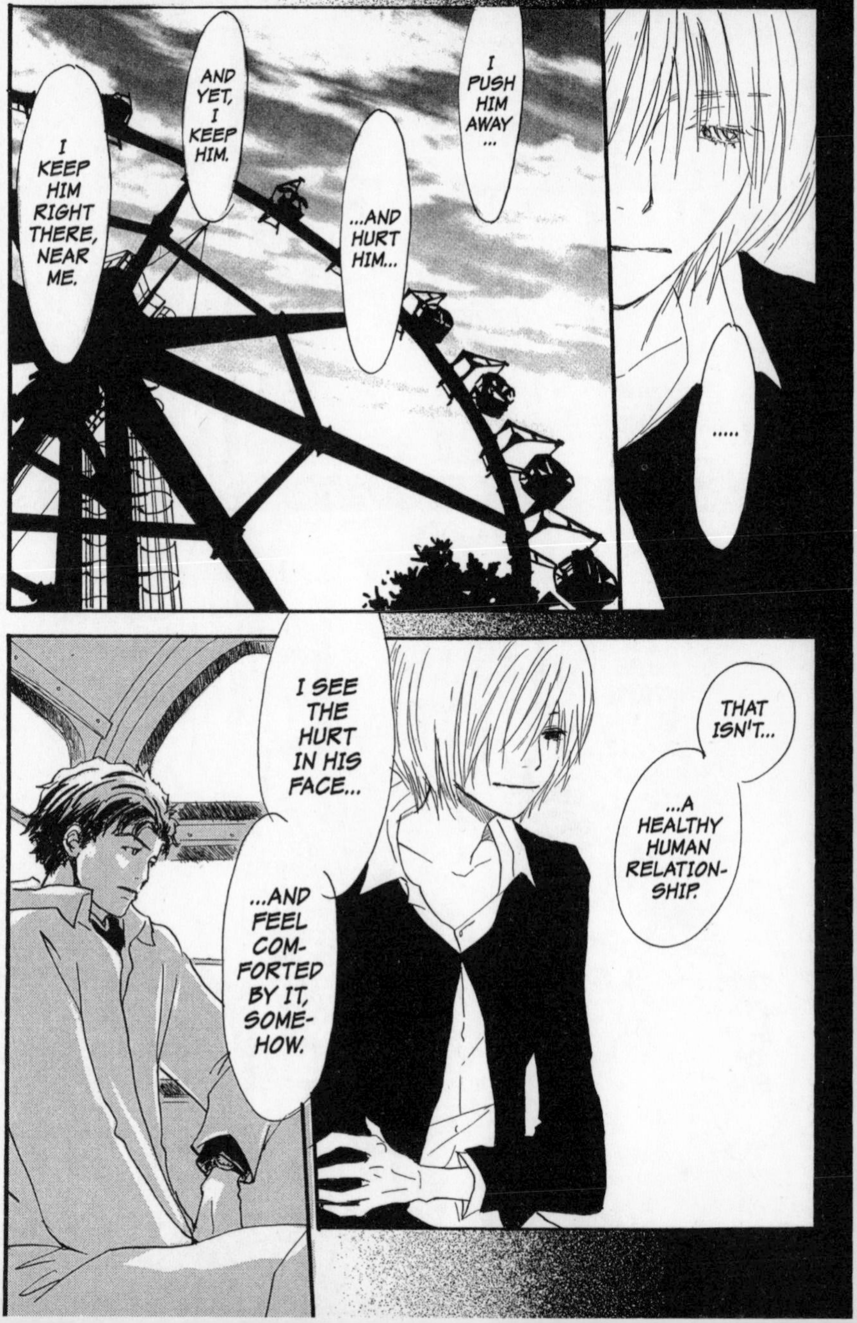
.....
I PUSH HIM AWAY...
...AND HURT HIM...
AND YET, I KEEP HIM.
I KEEP HIM RIGHT THERE, NEAR ME.
THAT ISN'T...
...A HEALTHY HUMAN RELATIONSHIP.
I SEE THE HURT IN HIS FACE...
...AND FEEL COMFORTED BY IT, SOMEHOW.

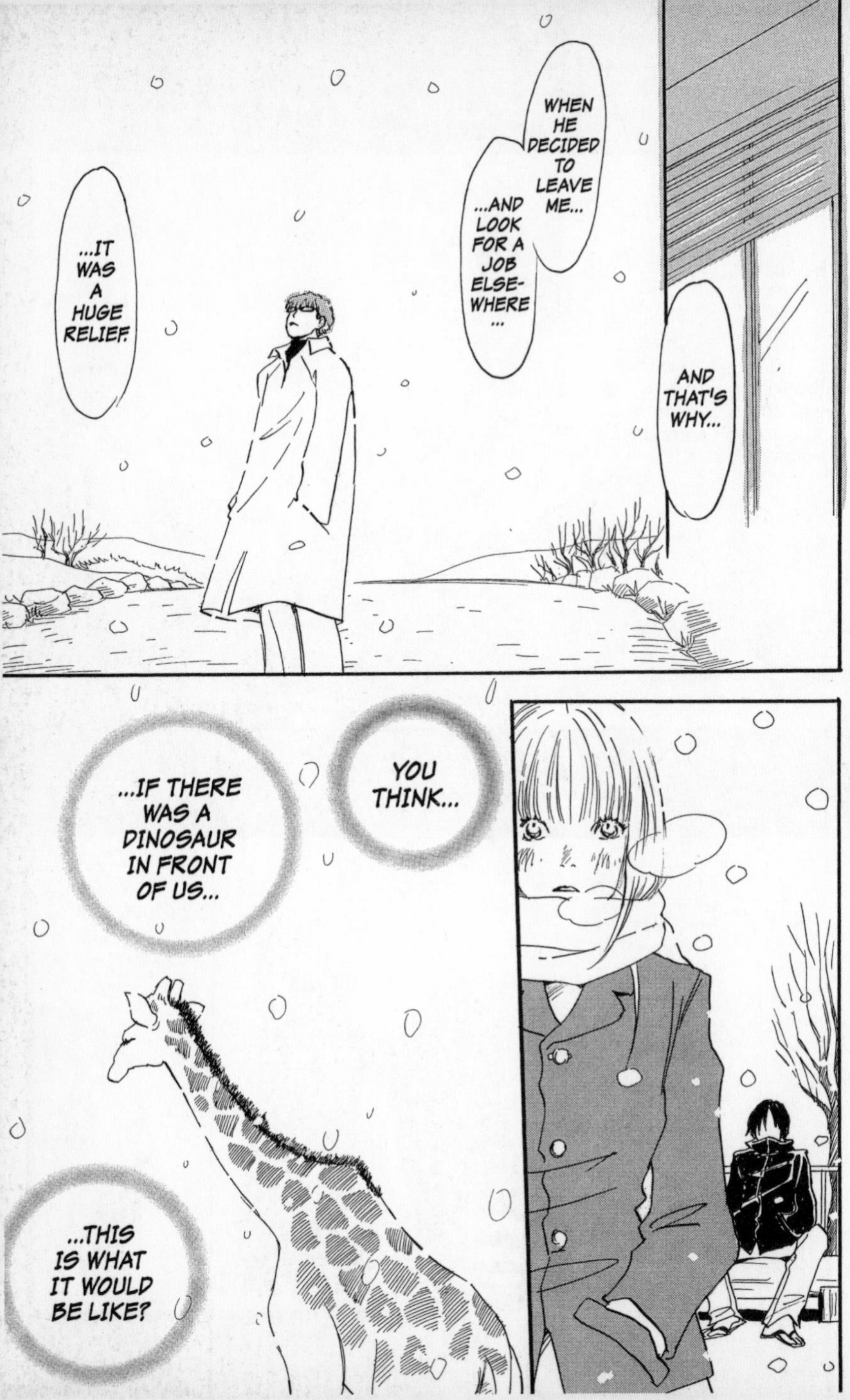
WHEN HE DECIDED TO LEAVE ME...
...AND LOOK FOR A JOB ELSEWHERE...
...IT WAS A HUGE RELIEF.
AND THAT'S WHY...
YOU THINK...
...IF THERE WAS A DINOSAUR IN FRONT OF US...
...THIS IS WHAT IT WOULD BE LIKE?

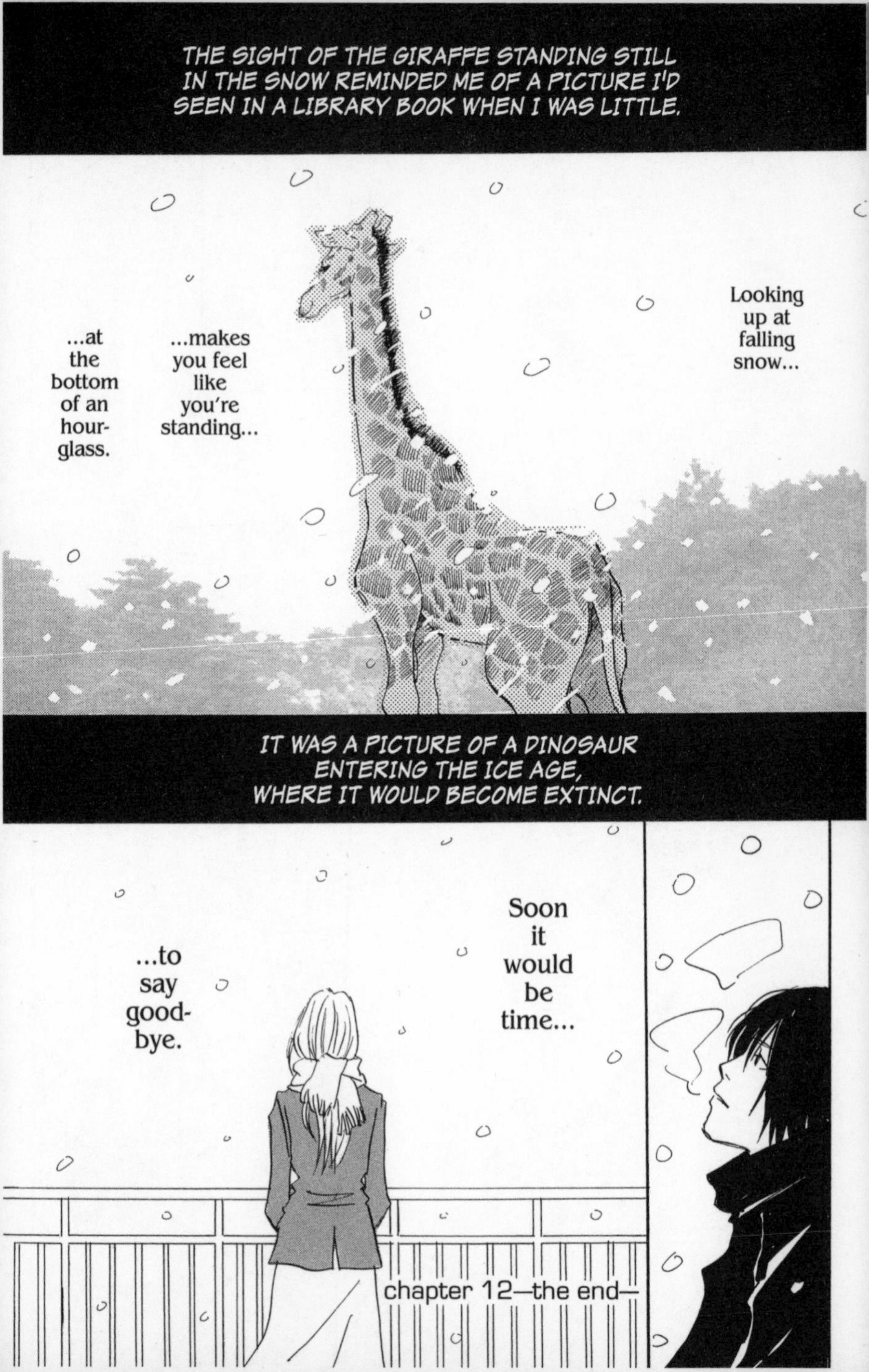
THE SIGHT OF THE GIRAFFE STANDING STILL IN THE SNOW REMINDED ME OF A PICTURE I'D SEEN IN A LIBRARY BOOK WHEN I WAS LITTLE.
Looking up at falling snow...
...makes you feel like you're standing...
...at the bottom of an hour-glass.
IT WAS A PICTURE OF A DINOSAUR ENTERING THE ICE AGE, WHERE IT WOULD BECOME EXTINCT.
Soon it would be time...
...to say good-bye.
chapter 12—the end—

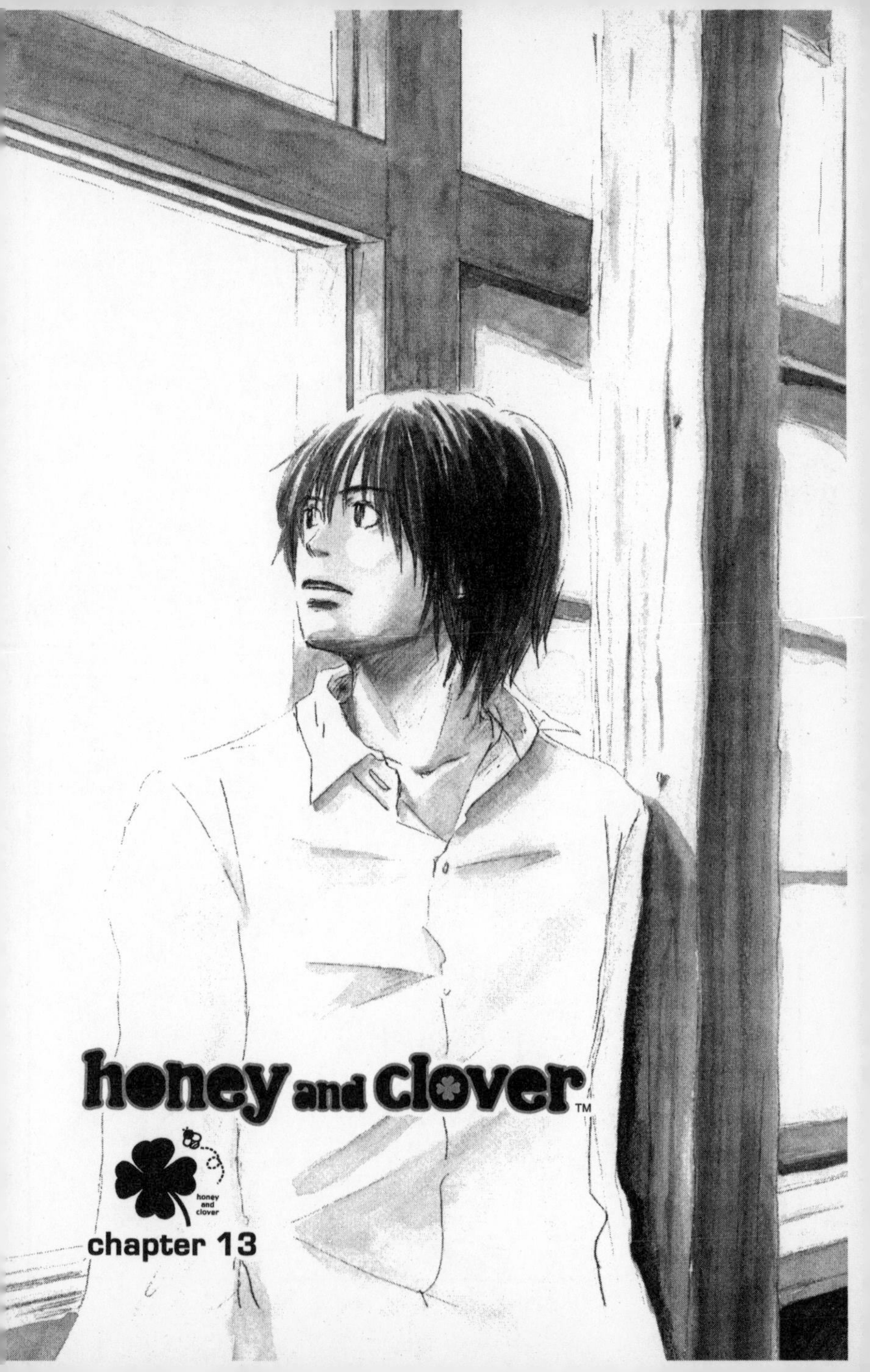
honey and clover™
honey and clover
chapter 13

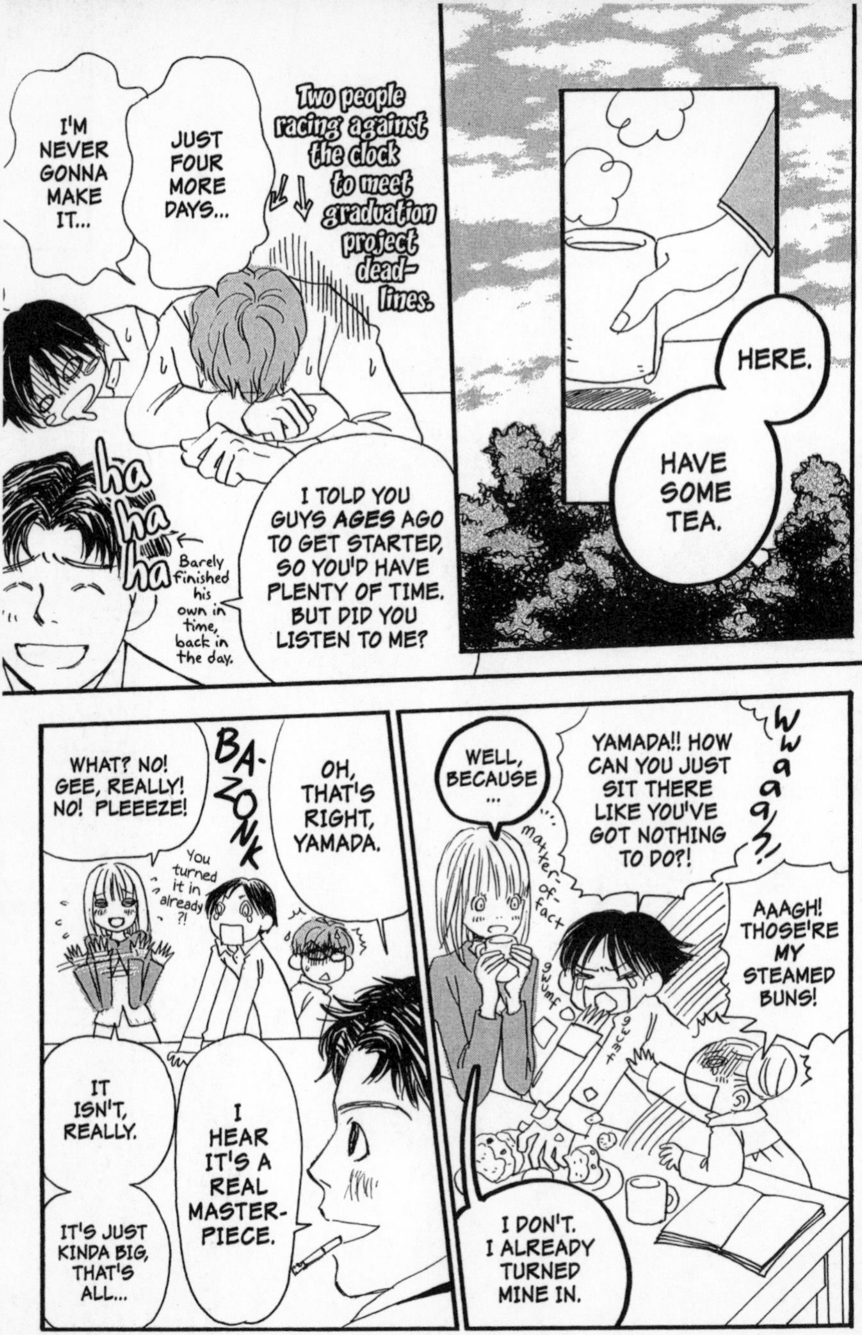
HERE.
HAVE SOME TEA.
Two people racing against the clock to meet graduation project dead-lines.
JUST FOUR MORE DAYS...
I'M NEVER GONNA MAKE IT...
ha ha ha
I TOLD YOU GUYS AGES AGO TO GET STARTED, SO YOU'D HAVE PLENTY OF TIME. BUT DID YOU LISTEN TO ME?
Barely finished his own in time, back in the day.
Wwaaah?!
YAMADA!! HOW CAN YOU JUST SIT THERE LIKE YOU'VE GOT NOTHING TO DO?!
WELL, BECAUSE ...
matter-of-fact
AAAGH! THOSE'RE MY STEAMED BUNS!
gwumf
I DON'T. I ALREADY TURNED MINE IN.
OH, THAT'S RIGHT, YAMADA.
BA-ZONK
WHAT? NO! GEE, REALLY! NO! PLEEEZE!
You turned it in already?!
I HEAR IT'S A REAL MASTERPIECE.
IT ISN'T, REALLY.
IT'S JUST KINDA BIG, THAT'S ALL...

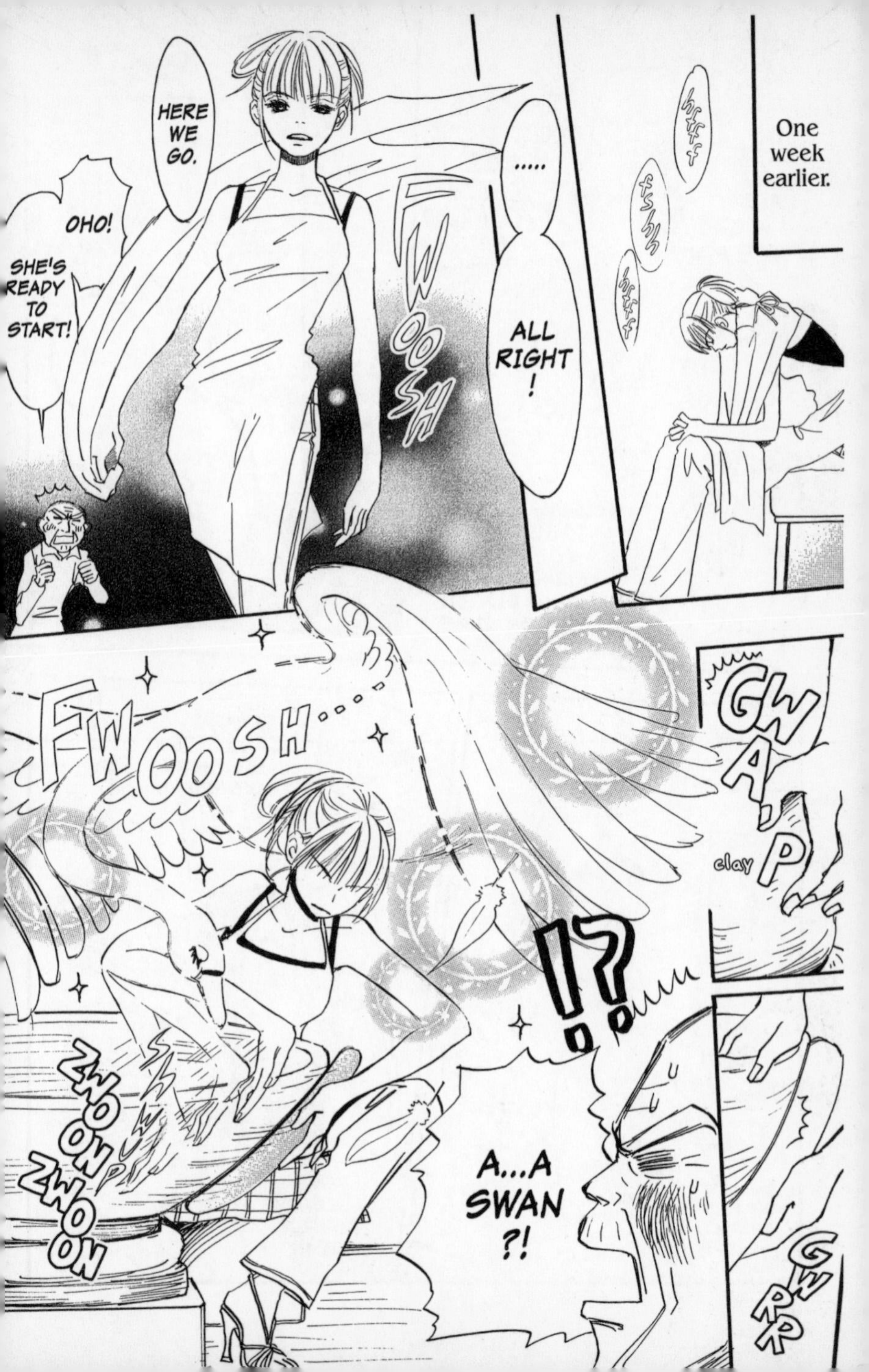
One week earlier.
hfff
fshh
hfff
.....
ALL RIGHT!
FWOOSH
HERE WE GO.
OHO!
SHE'S READY TO START!
GWAP
clay
FWOOSH...
!?
A...A SWAN?!
ZWOON ZWOON
GWRR

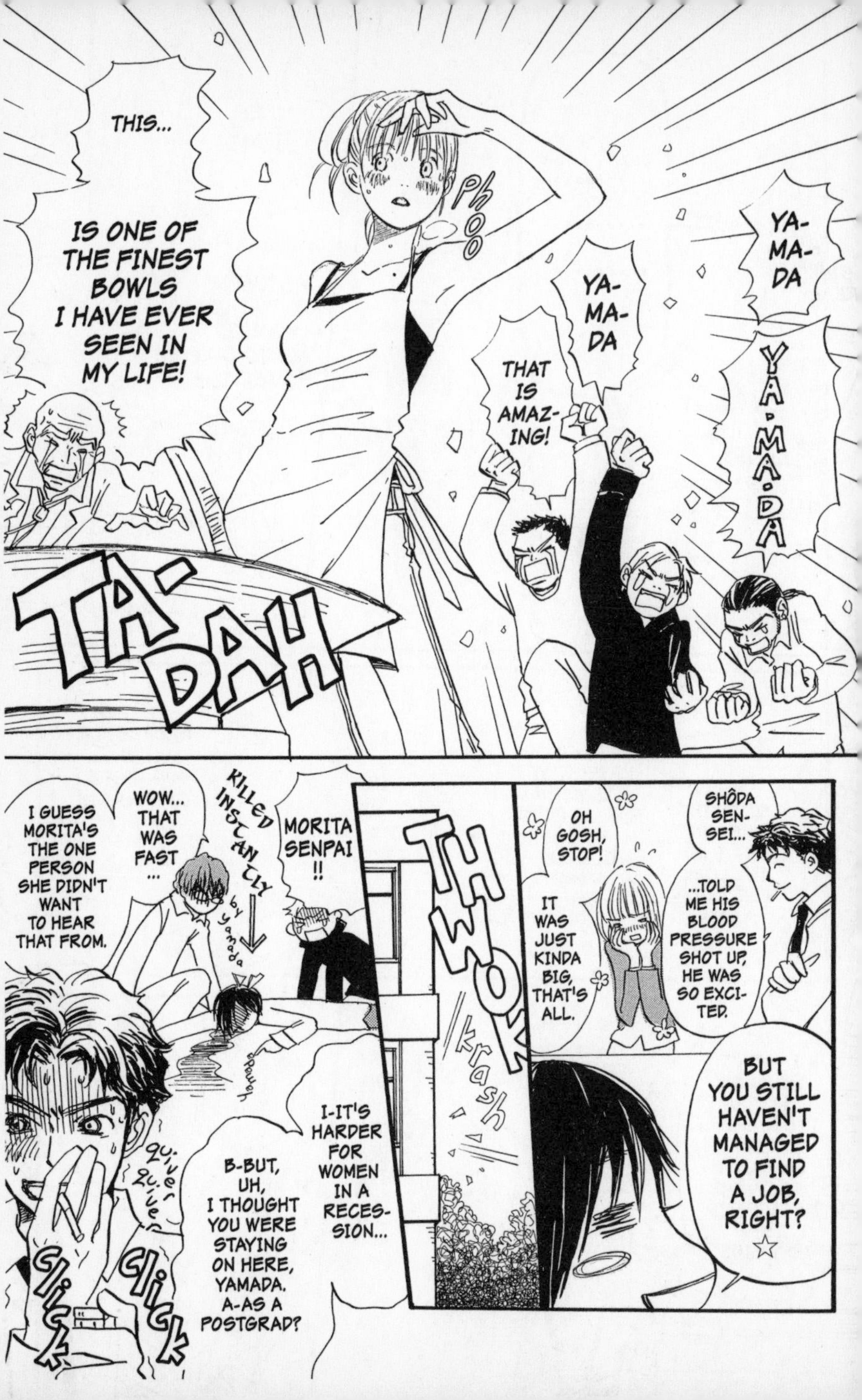
YA-MA-DA
YA-MA-DA
YA-MA-DA
THAT IS AMAZ-ING!
Phooo
THIS...
IS ONE OF THE FINEST BOWLS I HAVE EVER SEEN IN MY LIFE!
TA-DAH
SHÔDA SENSEI...
...TOLD ME HIS BLOOD PRESSURE SHOT UP, HE WAS SO EXCI-TED.
OH GOSH, STOP!
IT WAS JUST KINDA BIG, THAT'S ALL.
BUT YOU STILL HAVEN'T MANAGED TO FIND A JOB, RIGHT? ☆
THWOK
krash
MORITA SENPAI !!
KILLED INSTANTLY
by Yamada
WOW... THAT WAS FAST ...
I GUESS MORITA'S THE ONE PERSON SHE DIDN'T WANT TO HEAR THAT FROM.
I-IT'S HARDER FOR WOMEN IN A RECES-SION...
B-BUT, UH, I THOUGHT YOU WERE STAYING ON HERE, YAMADA. A-AS A POSTGRAD?
quiver quiver
click click

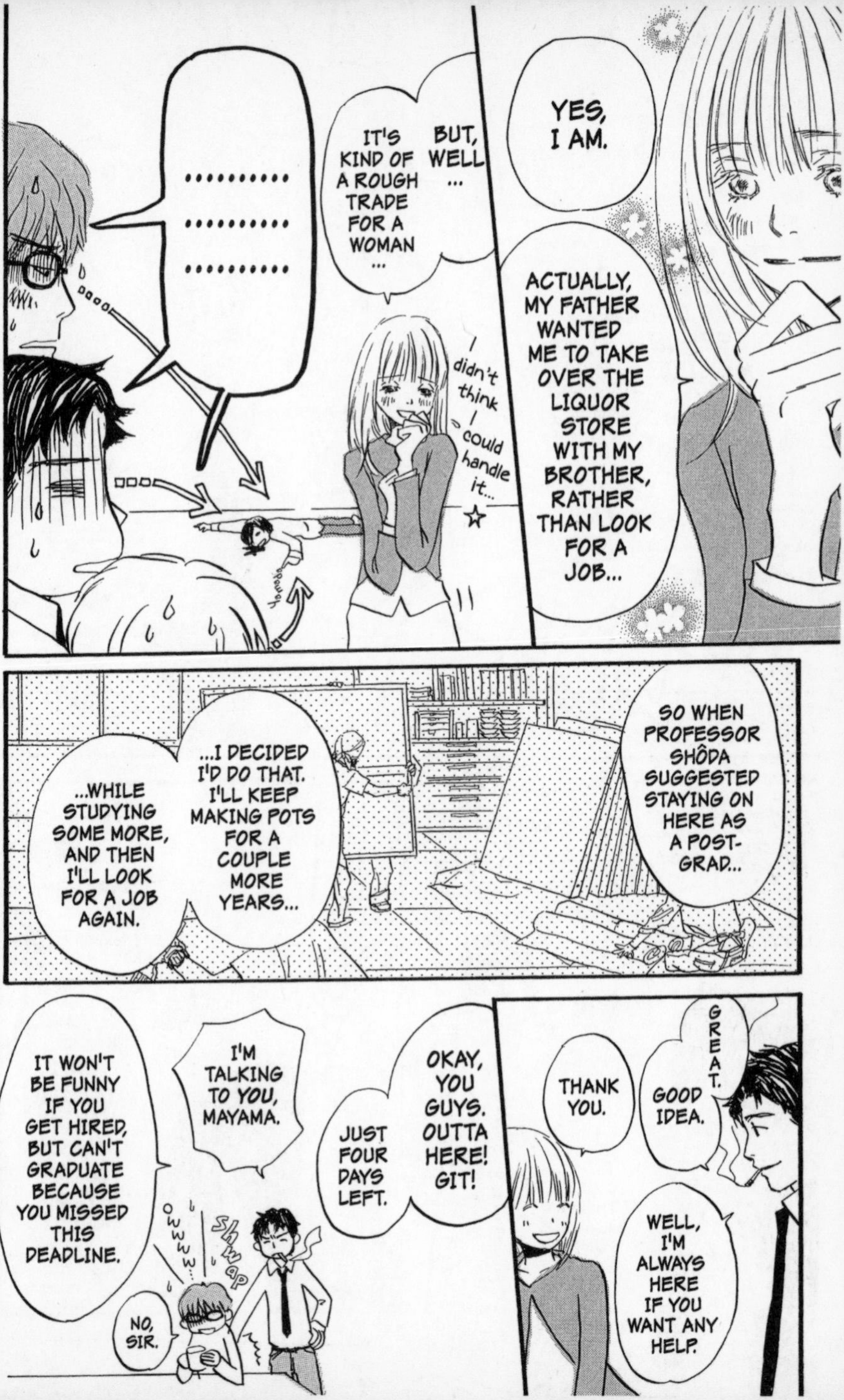
YES, I AM.
ACTUALLY, MY FATHER WANTED ME TO TAKE OVER THE LIQUOR STORE WITH MY BROTHER, RATHER THAN LOOK FOR A JOB...
BUT, WELL ...
IT'S KIND OF A ROUGH TRADE FOR A WOMAN ...
I didn't think I could handle it... ☆
....
....
....
SO WHEN PROFESSOR SHÔDA SUGGESTED STAYING ON HERE AS A POST-GRAD...
...I DECIDED I'D DO THAT. I'LL KEEP MAKING POTS FOR A COUPLE MORE YEARS...
...WHILE STUDYING SOME MORE, AND THEN I'LL LOOK FOR A JOB AGAIN.
GREAT.
GOOD IDEA.
THANK YOU.
WELL, I'M ALWAYS HERE IF YOU WANT ANY HELP.
OKAY, YOU GUYS. OUTTA HERE! GIT!
JUST FOUR DAYS LEFT.
I'M TALKING TO YOU, MAYAMA.
IT WON'T BE FUNNY IF YOU GET HIRED, BUT CAN'T GRADUATE BECAUSE YOU MISSED THIS DEADLINE.
Shwap
OWWW...
NO, SIR.

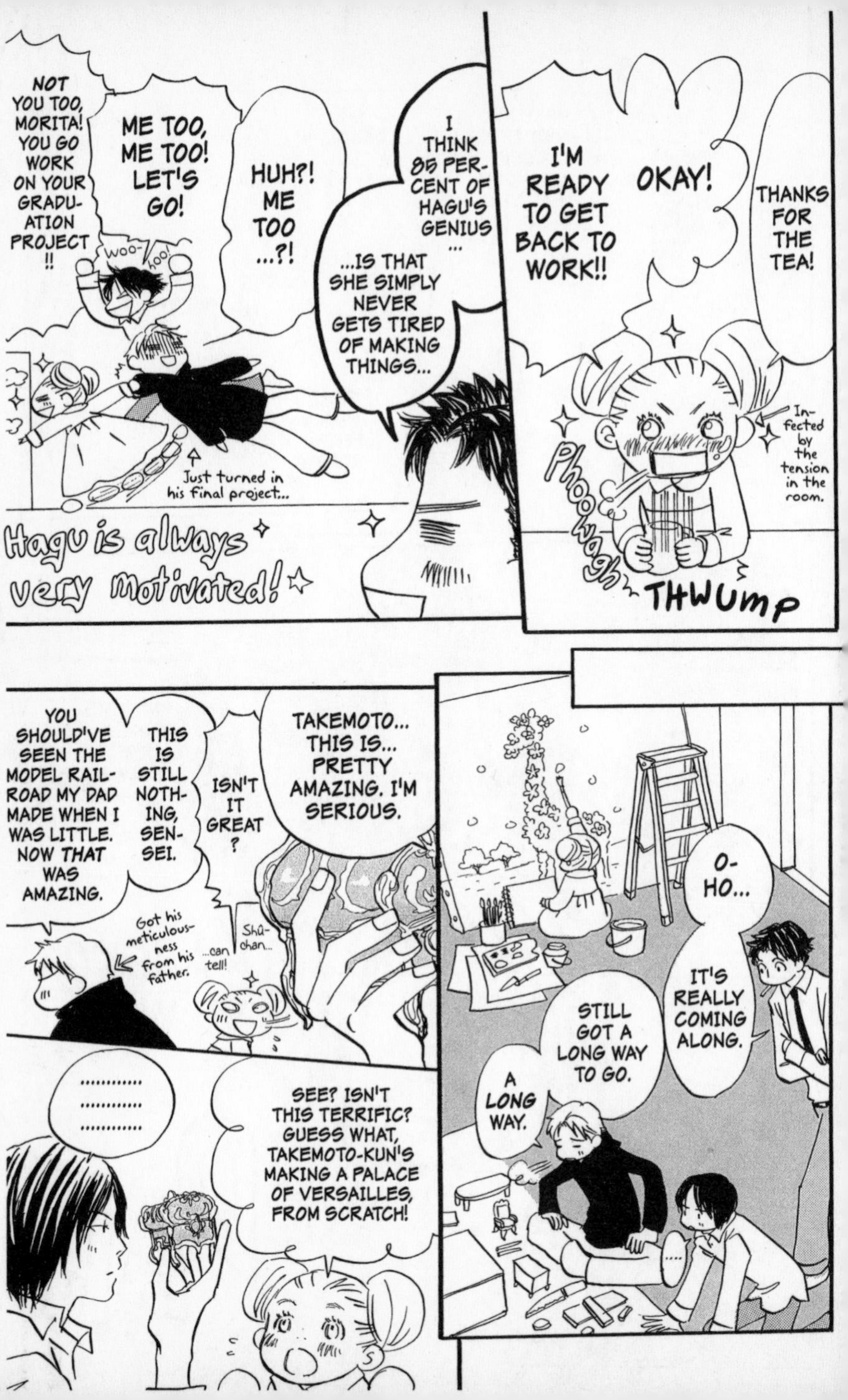
THANKS FOR THE TEA!
OKAY!
I'M READY TO GET BACK TO WORK!!
Infected by the tension in the room.
Phoowagh
THWUMP
I THINK 85 PERCENT OF HAGU'S GENIUS ...
...IS THAT SHE SIMPLY NEVER GETS TIRED OF MAKING THINGS...
HUH?! ME TOO ...?!
ME TOO, ME TOO! LET'S GO!
NOT YOU TOO, MORITA! YOU GO WORK ON YOUR GRADUATION PROJECT !!
Woo-hoo!
Just turned in his final project...
Hagu is always very motivated!
O-HO...
IT'S REALLY COMING ALONG.
STILL GOT A LONG WAY TO GO.
A LONG WAY.
....
TAKEMOTO... THIS IS... PRETTY AMAZING. I'M SERIOUS.
ISN'T IT GREAT?
THIS IS STILL NOTHING, SENSEI.
YOU SHOULD'VE SEEN THE MODEL RAILROAD MY DAD MADE WHEN I WAS LITTLE. NOW THAT WAS AMAZING.
Shû-chan...
...can tell!
Got his meticulousness from his father.
SEE? ISN'T THIS TERRIFIC? GUESS WHAT, TAKEMOTO-KUN'S MAKING A PALACE OF VERSAILLES, FROM SCRATCH!
....
....
....

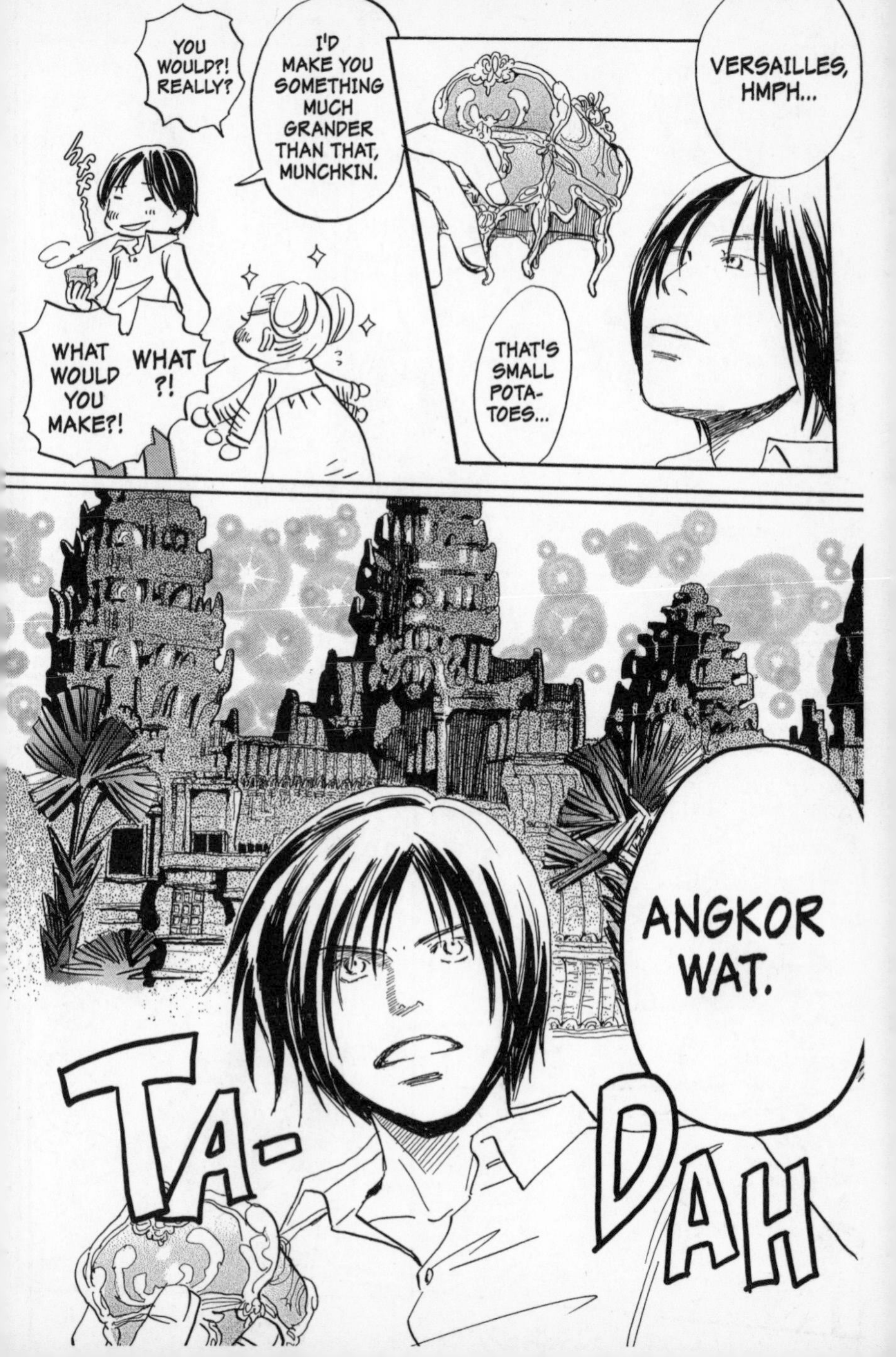
VERSAILLES, HMPH...
THAT'S SMALL POTA-TOES...
I'D MAKE YOU SOMETHING MUCH GRANDER THAN THAT, MUNCHKIN.
YOU WOULD?! REALLY?
WHAT?!
WHAT WOULD YOU MAKE?!
ANGKOR WAT.
TA-DAH

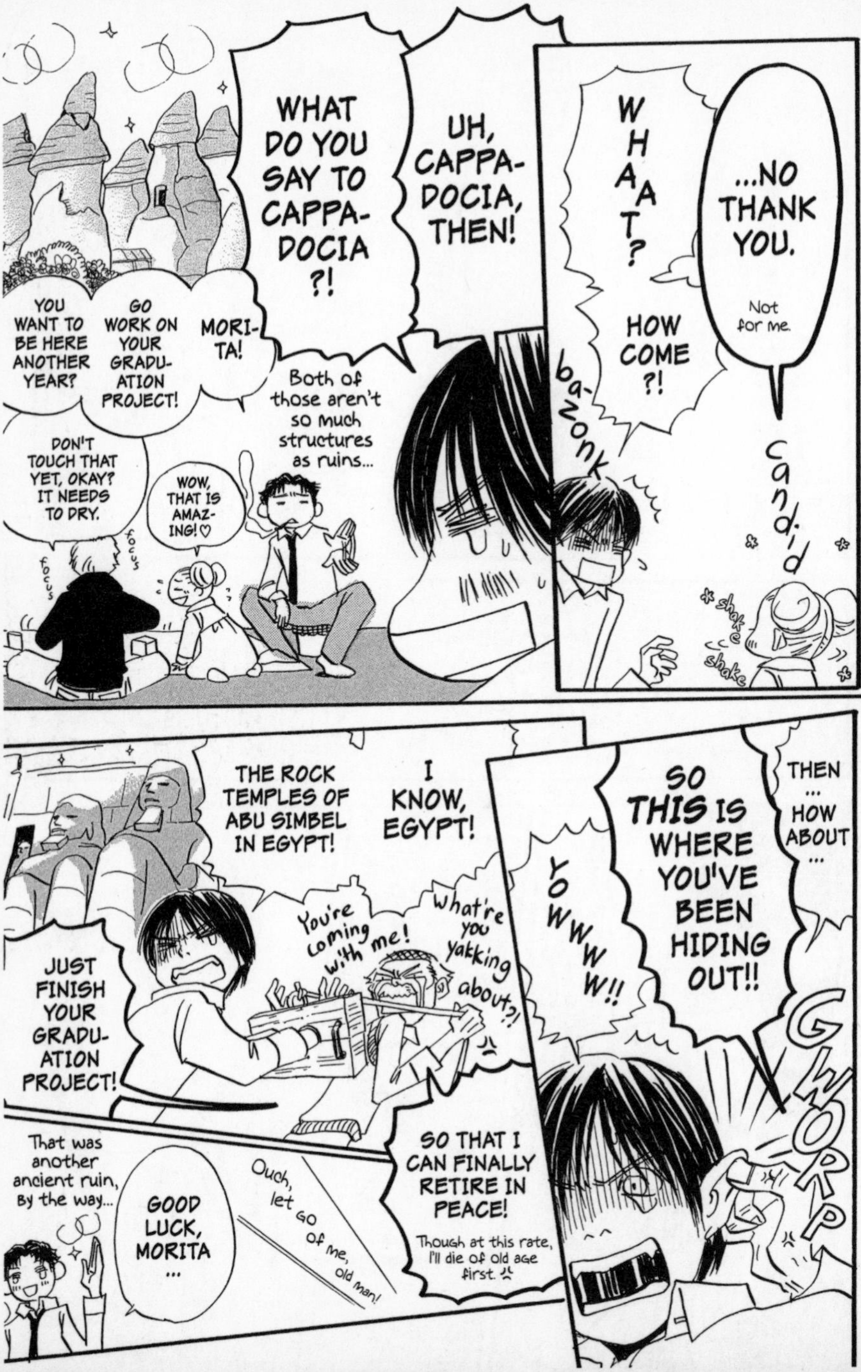
...NO THANK YOU.
Not for me.
candid
shake shake
WHAAT?
HOW COME?!
ba-zonk
UH, CAPPA-DOCIA, THEN!
WHAT DO YOU SAY TO CAPPA-DOCIA?!
Both of those aren't so much structures as ruins...
MORI-TA!
GO WORK ON YOUR GRADU-ATION PROJECT!
YOU WANT TO BE HERE ANOTHER YEAR?
DON'T TOUCH THAT YET, OKAY? IT NEEDS TO DRY.
WOW, THAT IS AMAZ-ING!♡
focus focus
THEN ... HOW ABOUT ...
SO THIS IS WHERE YOU'VE BEEN HIDING OUT!!
YOWWWWW!!
GWORP
I KNOW, EGYPT!
THE ROCK TEMPLES OF ABU SIMBEL IN EGYPT!
What're you yakking about?!
You're coming with me!
JUST FINISH YOUR GRADU-ATION PROJECT!
SO THAT I CAN FINALLY RETIRE IN PEACE!
Though at this rate, I'll die of old age first.
Ouch, let go of me, old man!
GOOD LUCK, MORITA ...
That was another ancient ruin, by the way...

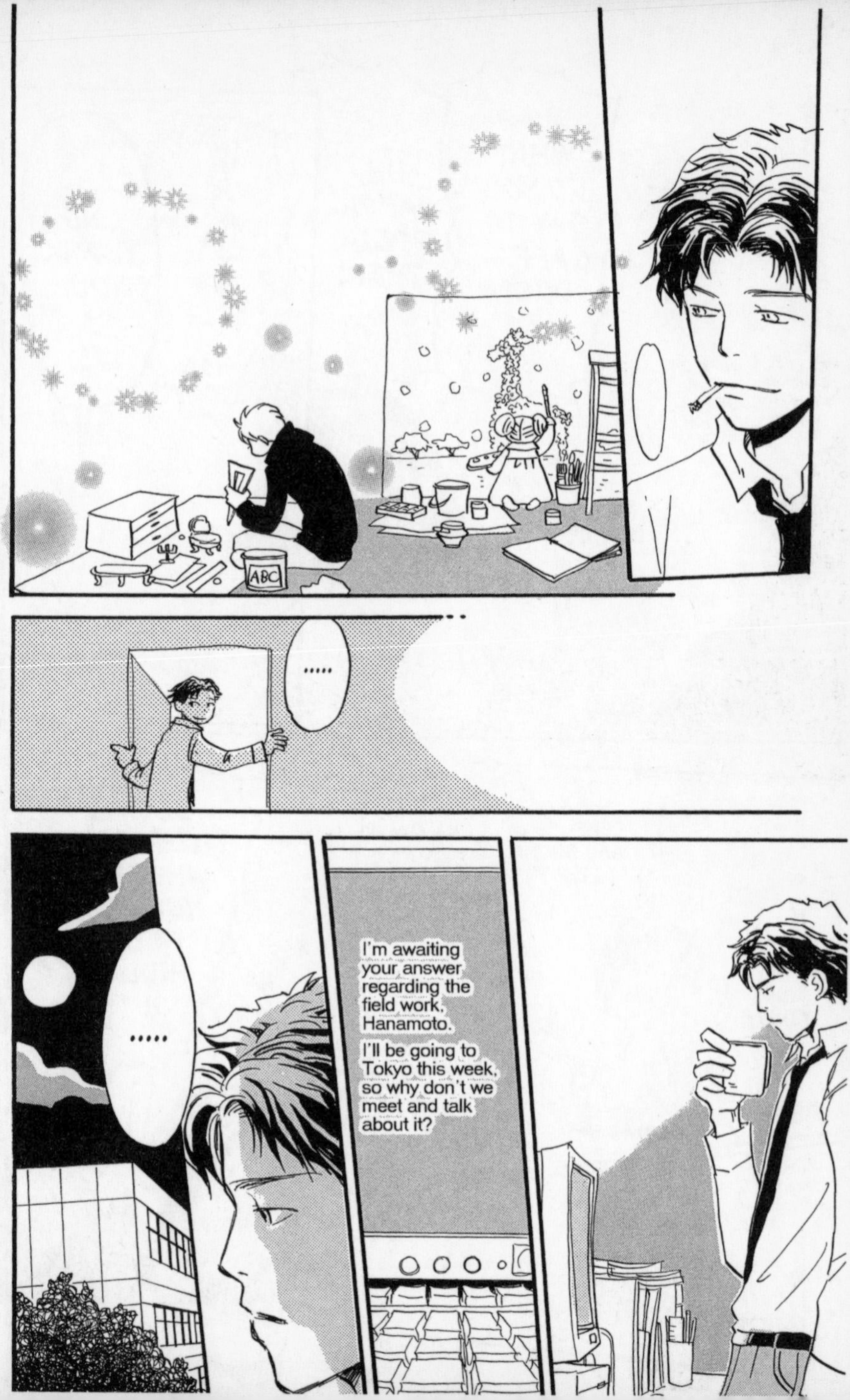
.....
I'm awaiting your answer regarding the field work, Hanamoto.
I'll be going to Tokyo this week, so why don't we meet and talk about it?
.....

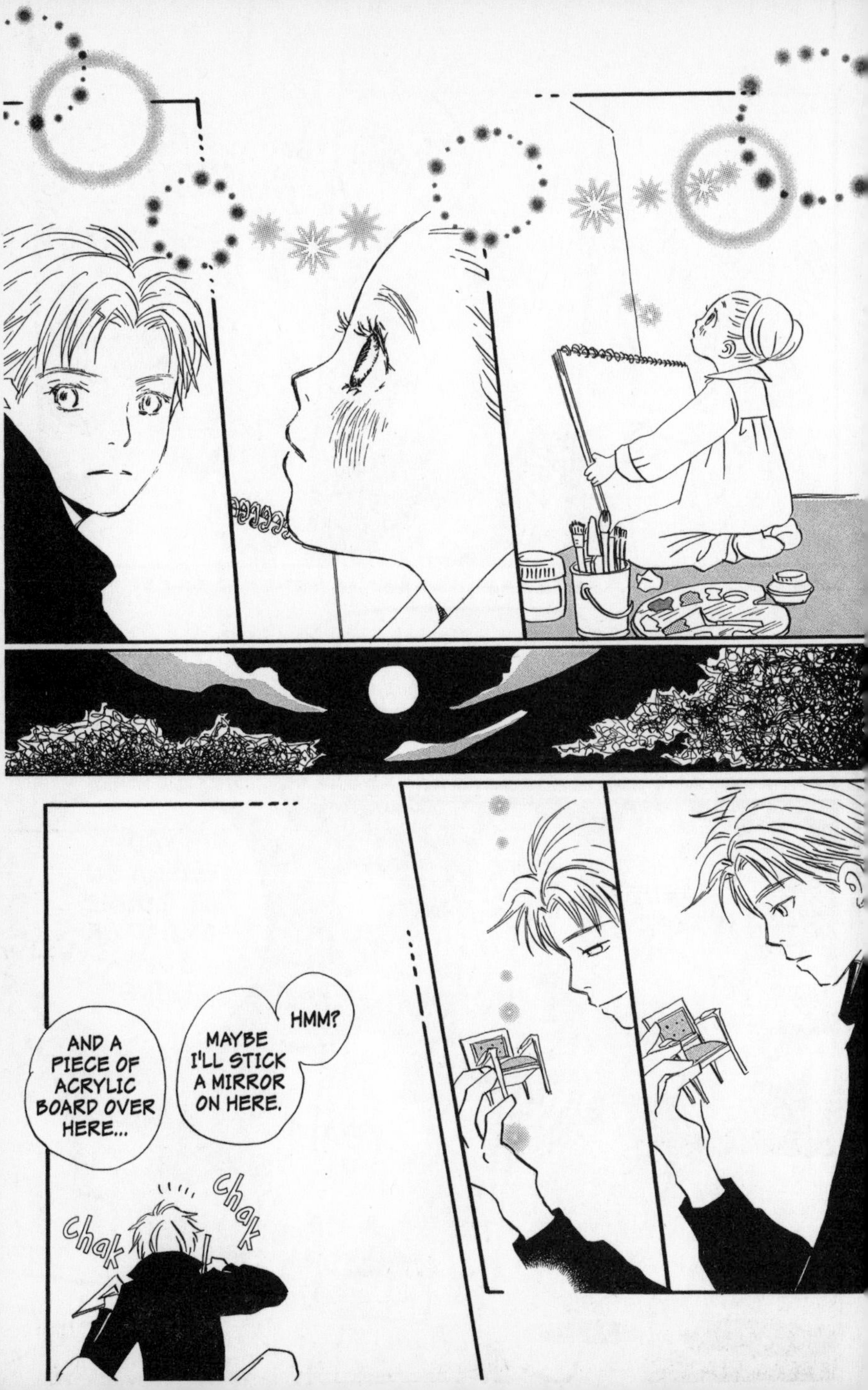
HMM?
MAYBE I'LL STICK A MIRROR ON HERE.
AND A PIECE OF ACRYLIC BOARD OVER HERE...
Chak
Chak

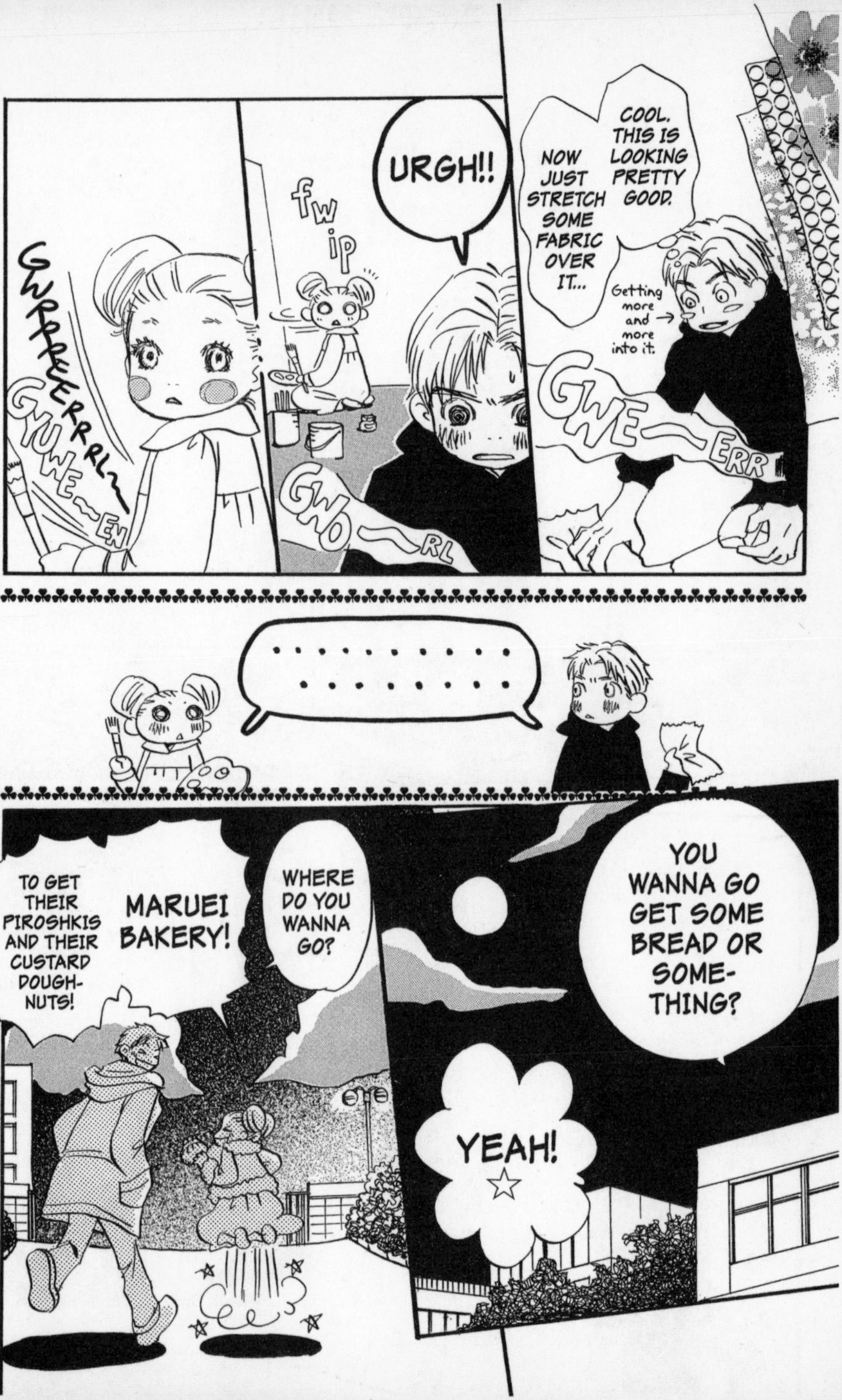
COOL. THIS IS LOOKING PRETTY GOOD.
NOW JUST STRETCH SOME FABRIC OVER IT...
Getting more and more into it.
GWE—ERR
URGH!!
fwip
GWO—RL
GYUWE—EN
....
....
YOU WANNA GO GET SOME BREAD OR SOME-THING?
YEAH! ☆
WHERE DO YOU WANNA GO?
MARUEI BAKERY!
TO GET THEIR PIROSHKIS AND THEIR CUSTARD DOUGH-NUTS!

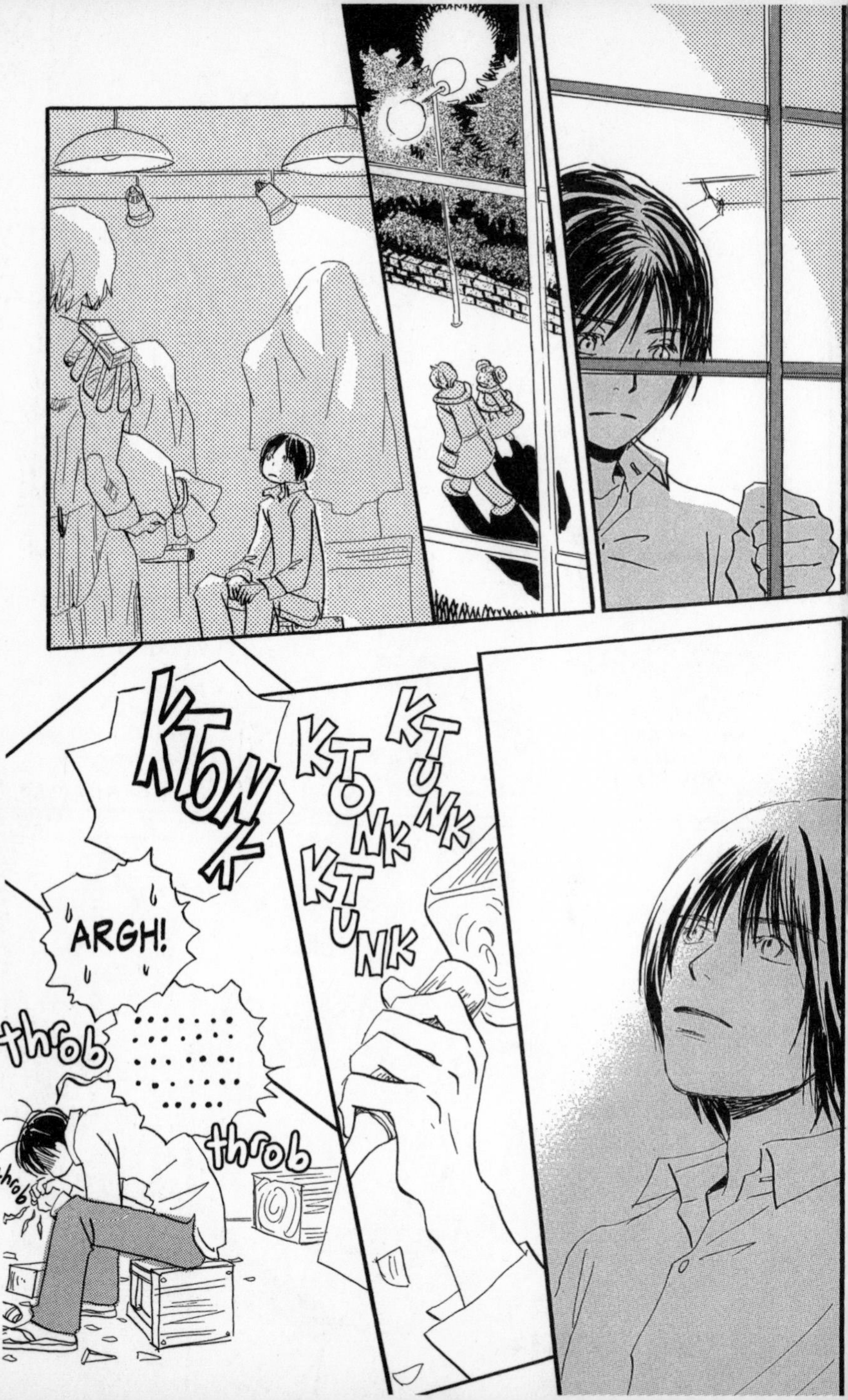
KTUNK
KTONK
KTUNK
KTONK
ARGH!
throb
......
throb
throb

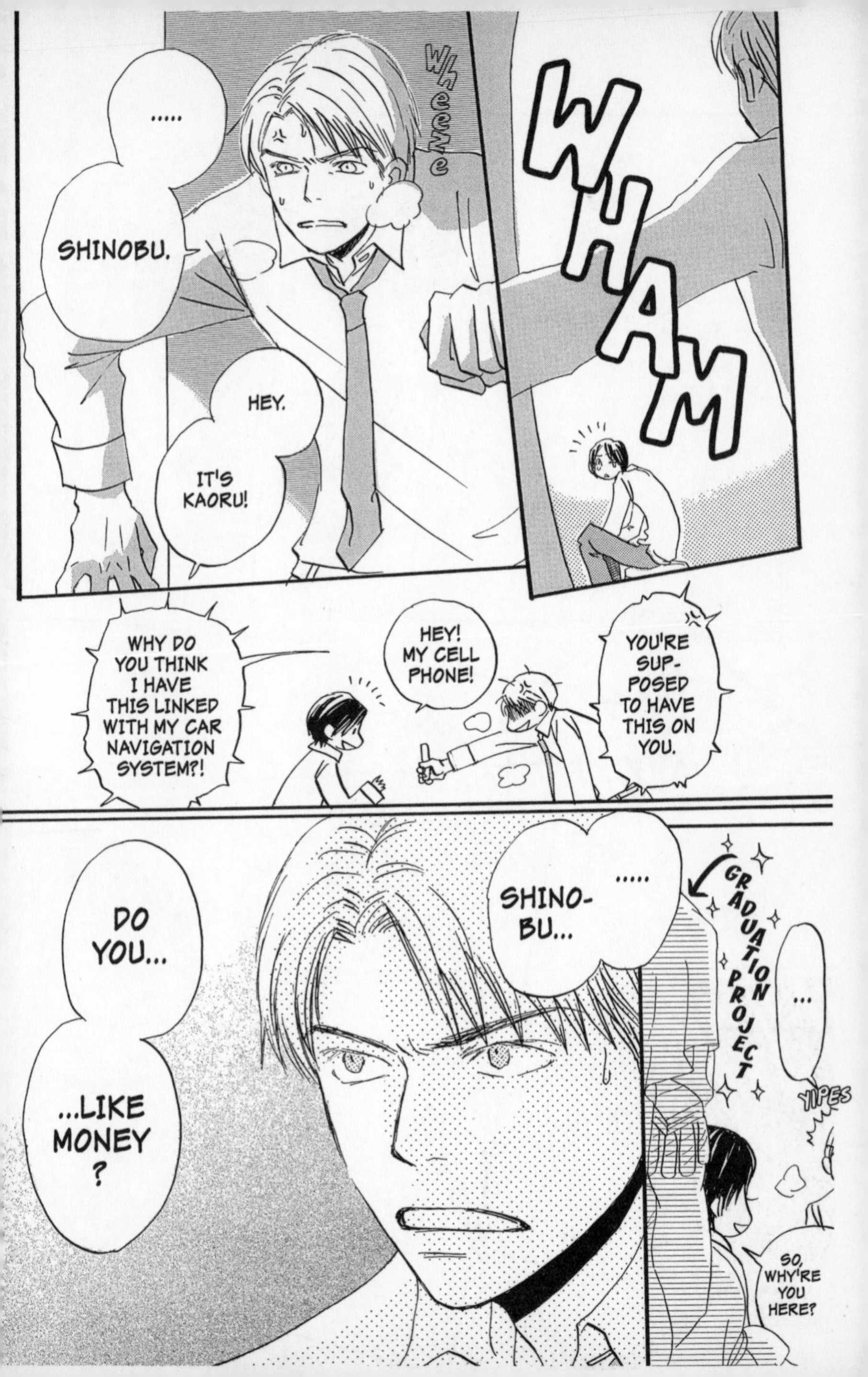
WHAM
Wheeze
..... SHINOBU.
HEY. IT'S KAORU!
YOU'RE SUP-POSED TO HAVE THIS ON YOU.
HEY! MY CELL PHONE!
WHY DO YOU THINK I HAVE THIS LINKED WITH MY CAR NAVIGATION SYSTEM?!
GRADUATION PROJECT
...
YIPES
SO, WHY'RE YOU HERE?
..... SHINO-BU...
DO YOU... ...LIKE MONEY?

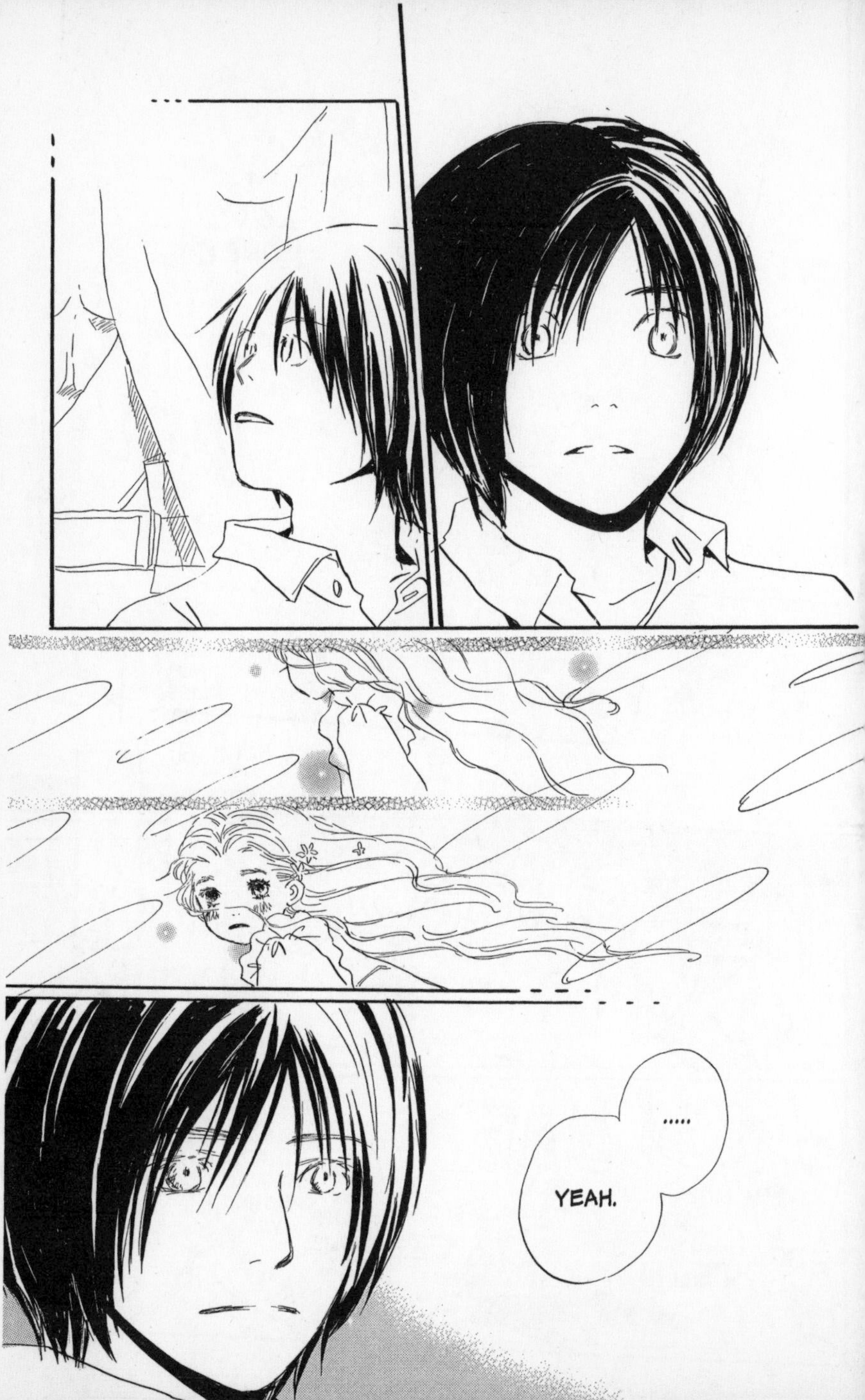
......
YEAH.

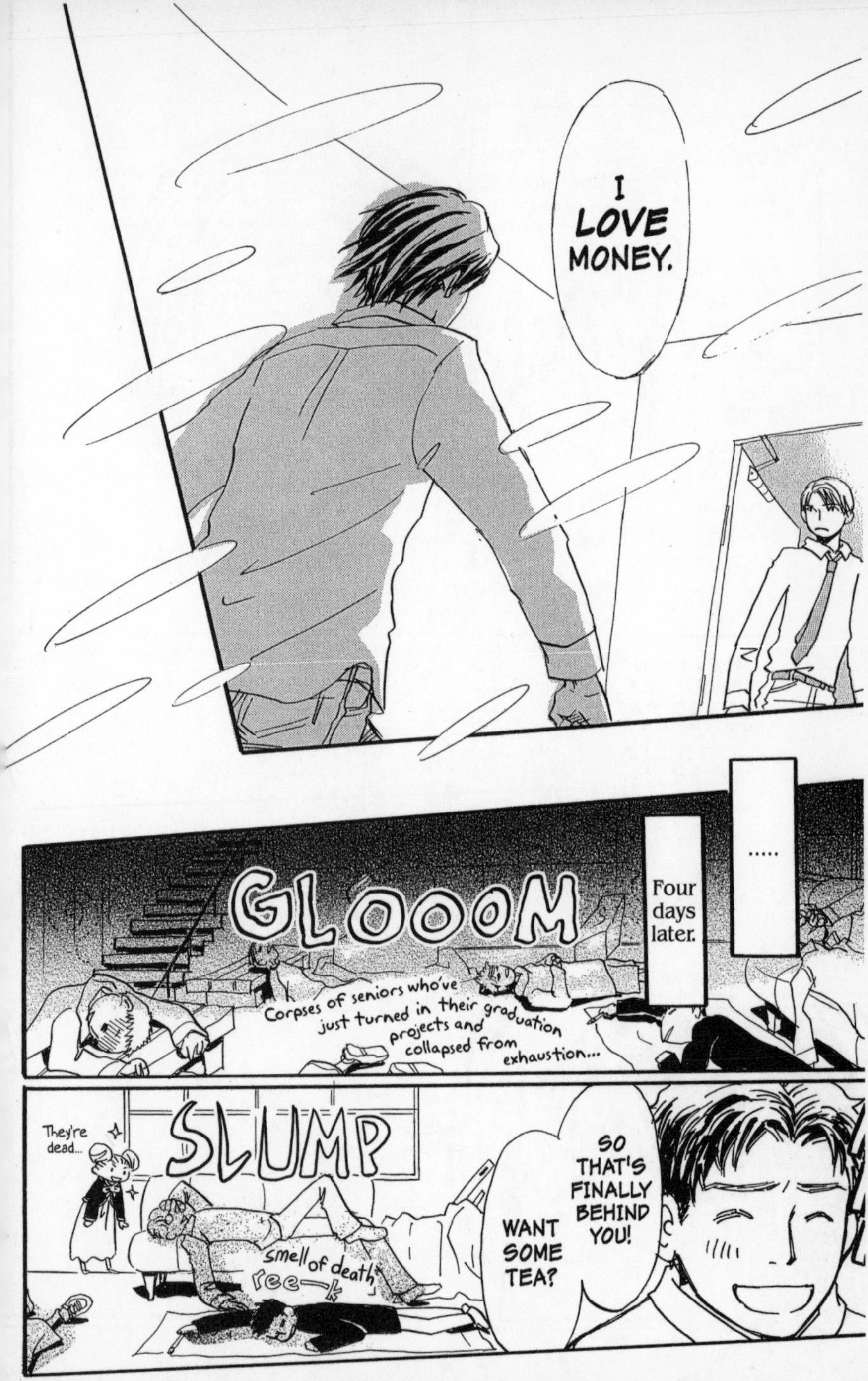
I LOVE MONEY.
.....
Four days later.
GLOOOM
Corpses of seniors who've just turned in their graduation projects and collapsed from exhaustion...
SO THAT'S FINALLY BEHIND YOU!
WANT SOME TEA?
SLUMP
smell of death
ree—k
They're dead...

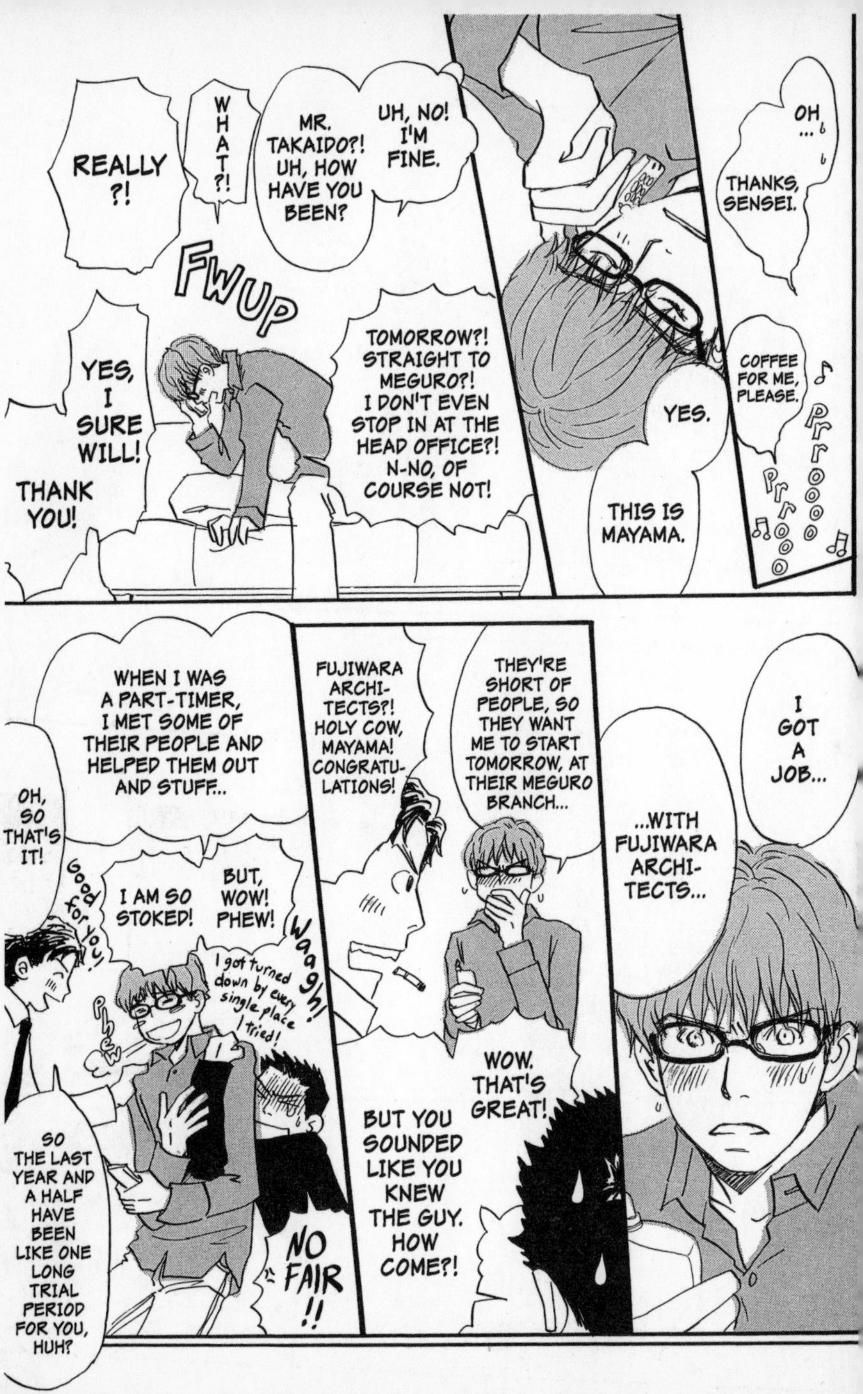
OH... THANKS, SENSEI.
COFFEE FOR ME, PLEASE.
Prrrooo
Prrrooo
YES.
THIS IS MAYAMA.
MR. TAKAIDO?! UH, HOW HAVE YOU BEEN?
UH, NO! I'M FINE.
WHAT?!
REALLY?!
FWUP
TOMORROW?! STRAIGHT TO MEGURO?! I DON'T EVEN STOP IN AT THE HEAD OFFICE?! N-NO, OF COURSE NOT!
YES, I SURE WILL!
THANK YOU!
I GOT A JOB...
...WITH FUJIWARA ARCHITECTS...
THEY'RE SHORT OF PEOPLE, SO THEY WANT ME TO START TOMORROW, AT THEIR MEGURO BRANCH...
FUJIWARA ARCHITECTS?! HOLY COW, MAYAMA! CONGRATULATIONS!
WOW. THAT'S GREAT!
BUT YOU SOUNDED LIKE YOU KNEW THE GUY. HOW COME?!
WHEN I WAS A PART-TIMER, I MET SOME OF THEIR PEOPLE AND HELPED THEM OUT AND STUFF...
OH, SO THAT'S IT!
BUT, WOW! PHEW!
I AM SO STOKED!
Waagh!
I got turned down by every single place I tried!
Good for you!
Phew
NO FAIR!!
SO THE LAST YEAR AND A HALF HAVE BEEN LIKE ONE LONG TRIAL PERIOD FOR YOU, HUH?

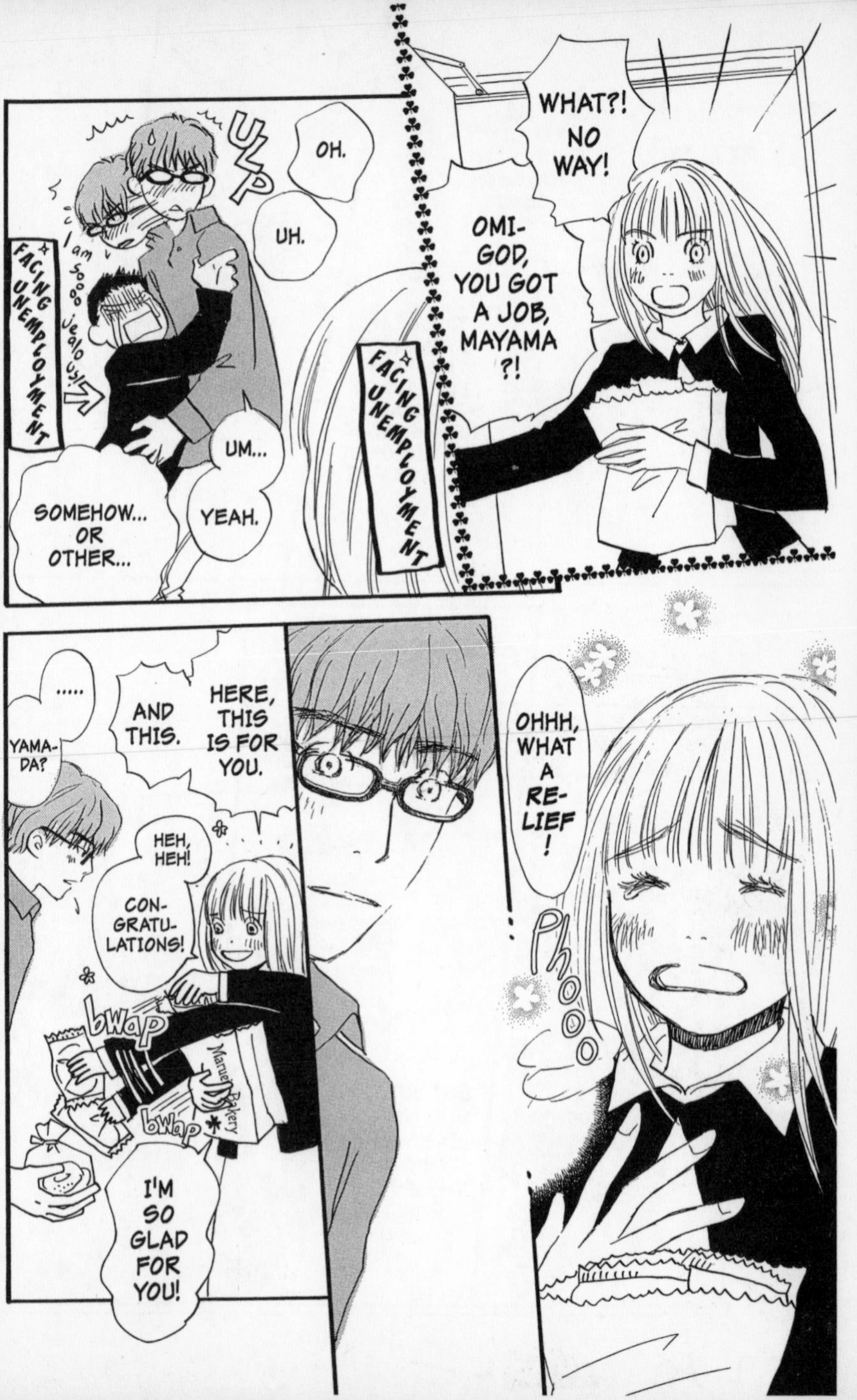
WHAT?! NO WAY!
OMI-GOD, YOU GOT A JOB, MAYAMA?!
FACING UNEMPLOYMENT
OH.
ULP
UH.
FACING UNEMPLOYMENT
I am soooo jealous!
UM...
YEAH.
SOMEHOW... OR OTHER...
OHHH, WHAT A RE-LIEF!
Phoooo
HERE, THIS IS FOR YOU.
AND THIS.
.....
YAMA-DA?
HEH, HEH!
CON-GRATU-LATIONS!
bwap
bwap
I'M SO GLAD FOR YOU!

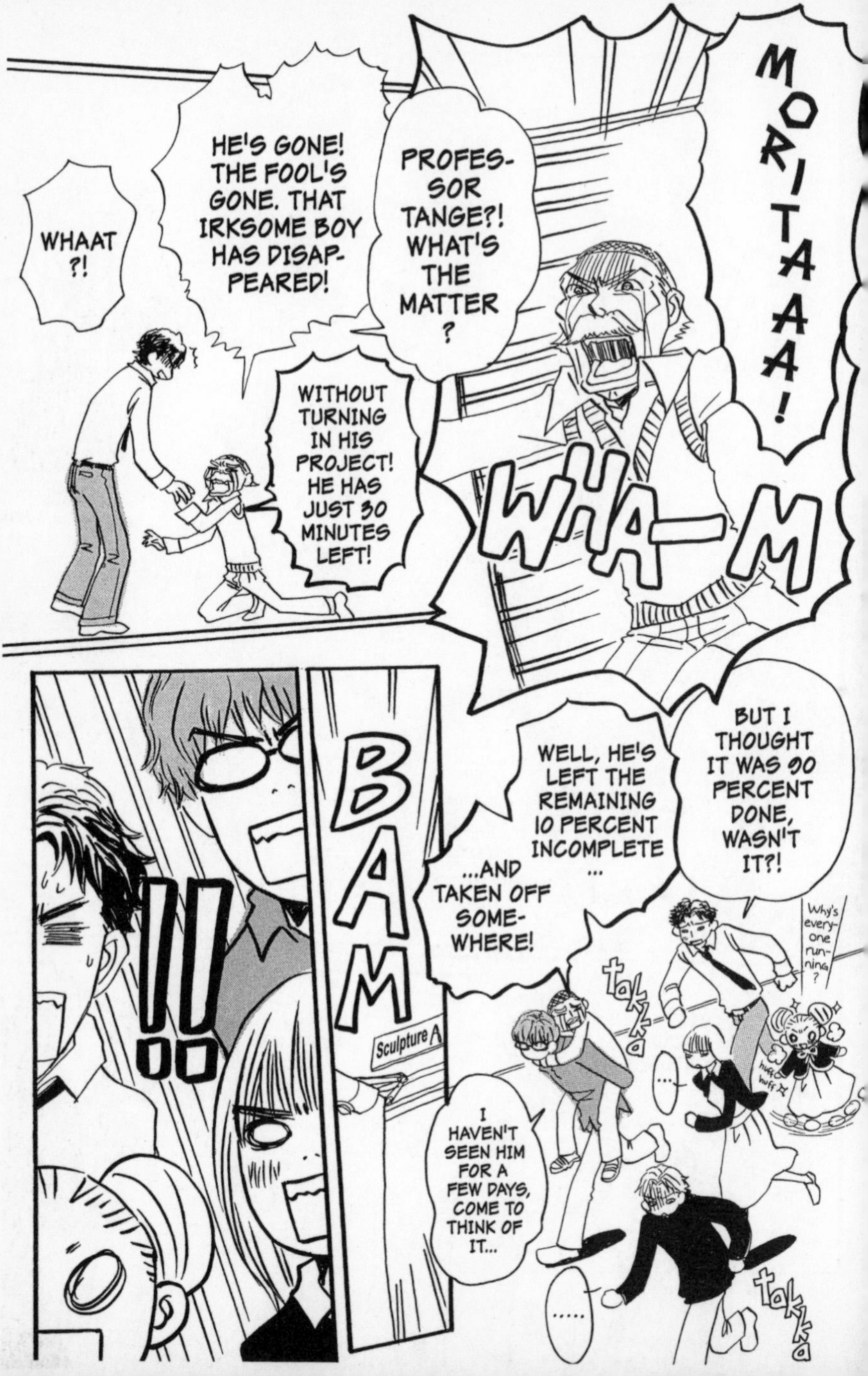
MORITAAAA!
WHA-M
PROFES-SOR TANGE?! WHAT'S THE MATTER?
HE'S GONE! THE FOOL'S GONE. THAT IRKSOME BOY HAS DISAP-PEARED!
WITHOUT TURNING IN HIS PROJECT! HE HAS JUST 30 MINUTES LEFT!
WHAAT?!
BUT I THOUGHT IT WAS 90 PERCENT DONE, WASN'T IT?!
WELL, HE'S LEFT THE REMAINING 10 PERCENT INCOMPLETE...
...AND TAKEN OFF SOME-WHERE!
Why's every-one run-ning?
takka
huff huff
....
I HAVEN'T SEEN HIM FOR A FEW DAYS, COME TO THINK OF IT...
.....
takka
BAM
Sculpture A
!!

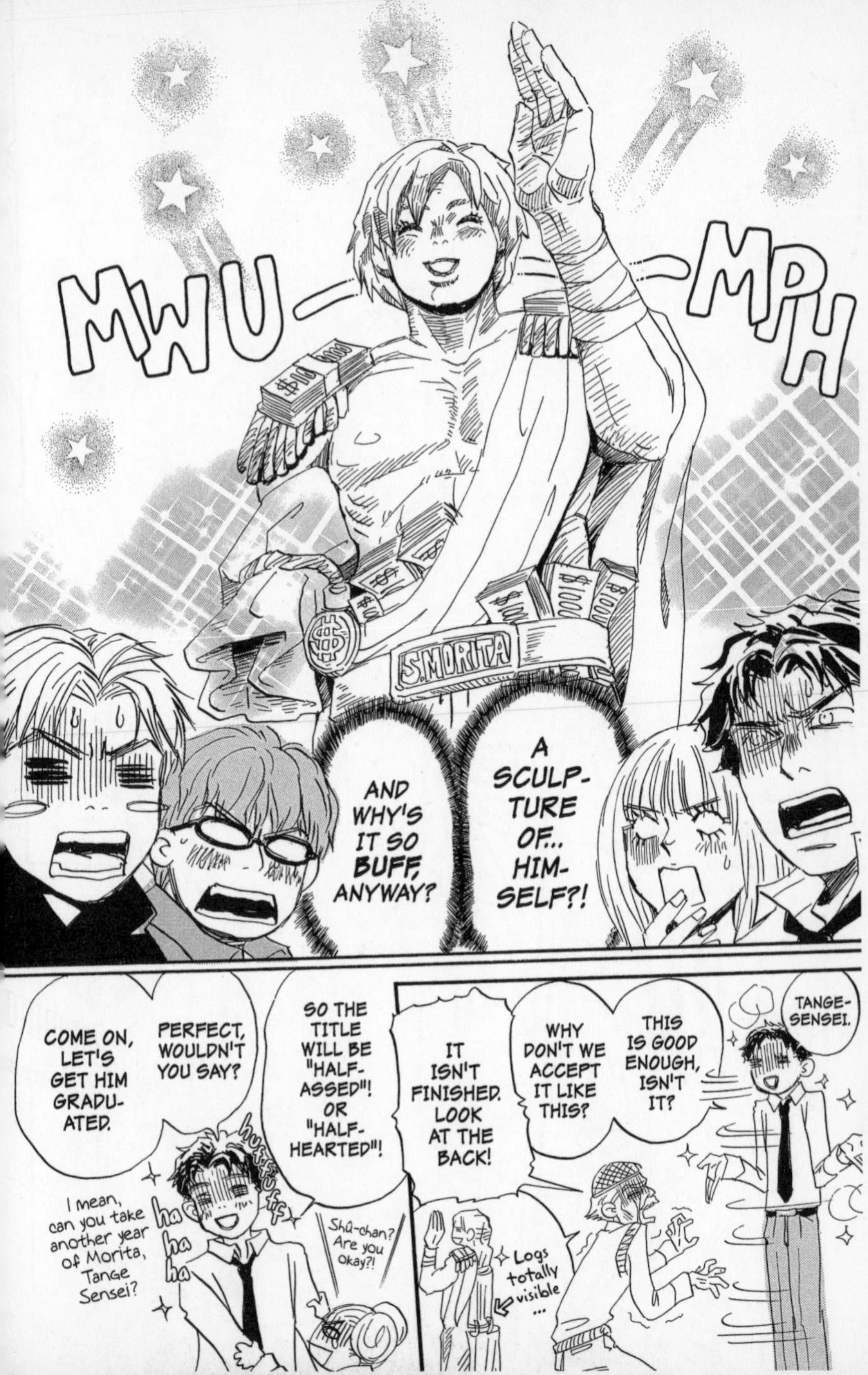
MWU—
—MPH
A SCULPTURE OF... HIMSELF?!
AND WHY'S IT SO BUFF, ANYWAY?
TANGE-SENSEI.
THIS IS GOOD ENOUGH, ISN'T IT?
WHY DON'T WE ACCEPT IT LIKE THIS?
IT ISN'T FINISHED. LOOK AT THE BACK!
Logs totally visible ...
SO THE TITLE WILL BE "HALF-ASSED"! OR "HALF-HEARTED"!
PERFECT, WOULDN'T YOU SAY?
COME ON, LET'S GET HIM GRADUATED.
hufufuff
Shû-chan? Are you okay?!
ha ha ha
I mean, can you take another year of Morita, Tange Sensei?

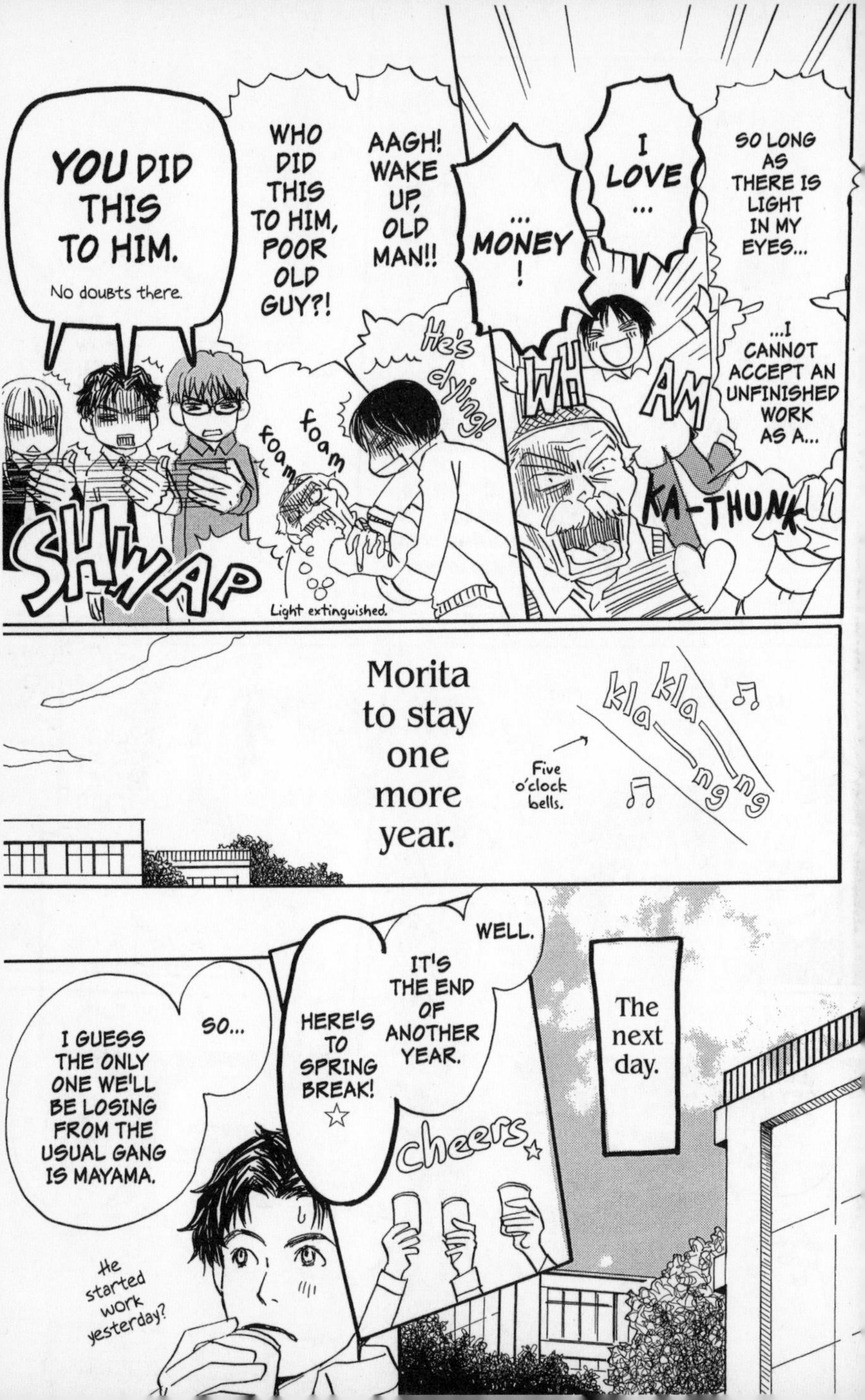
SO LONG AS THERE IS LIGHT IN MY EYES...
...I CANNOT ACCEPT AN UNFINISHED WORK AS A...
I LOVE ...
... MONEY !
WHAM
KA-THUNK
AAGH! WAKE UP, OLD MAN!!
He's dying!
WHO DID THIS TO HIM, POOR OLD GUY?!
foam foam
YOU DID THIS TO HIM.
No doubts there.
SHWAP
Light extinguished.
kla—ng kla—ng
Five o'clock bells.
Morita to stay one more year.
The next day.
WELL.
IT'S THE END OF ANOTHER YEAR.
HERE'S TO SPRING BREAK! ☆
cheers☆
SO...
I GUESS THE ONLY ONE WE'LL BE LOSING FROM THE USUAL GANG IS MAYAMA.
He started work yesterday?

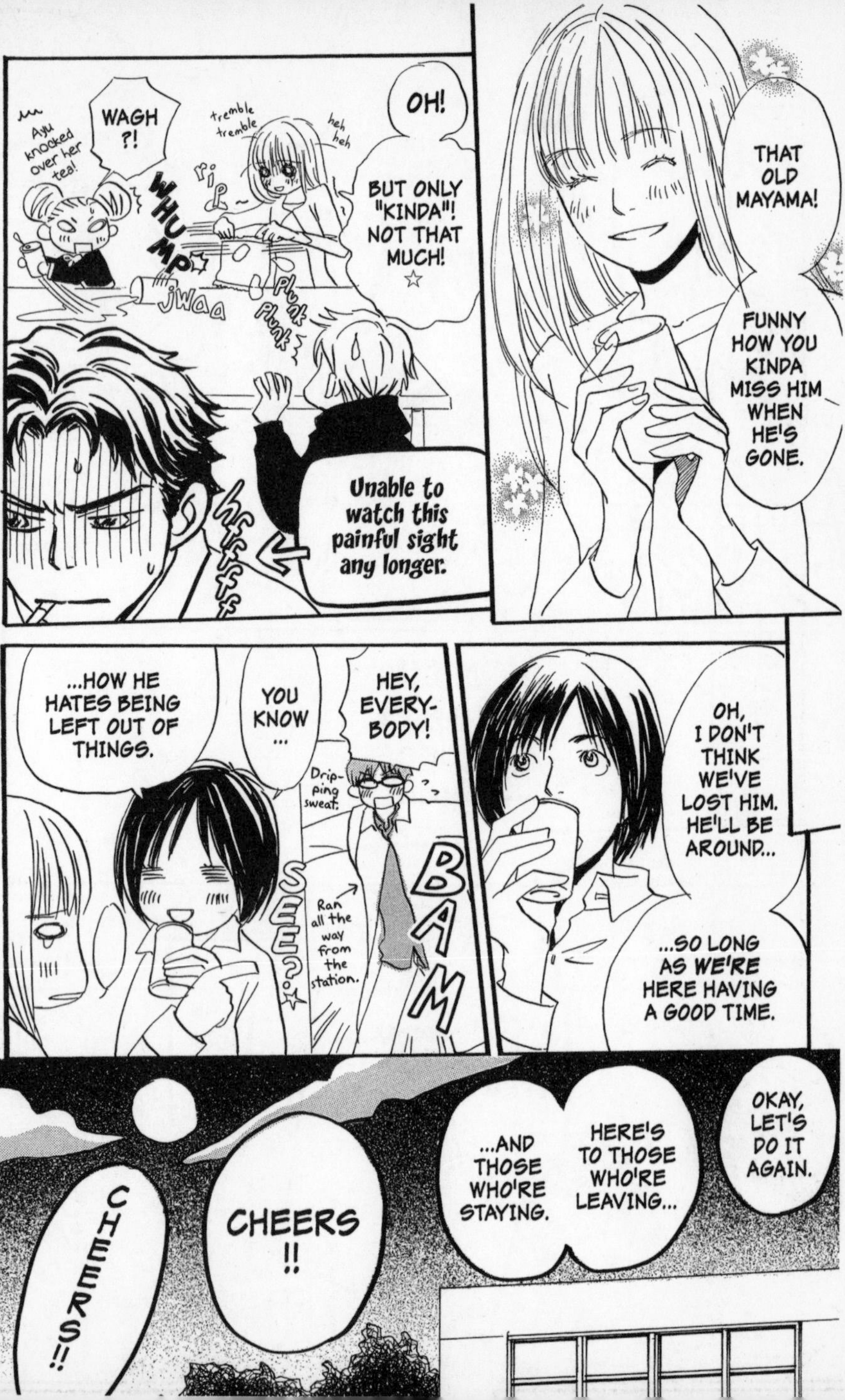
THAT OLD MAYAMA!
FUNNY HOW YOU KINDA MISS HIM WHEN HE'S GONE.
OH!
BUT ONLY "KINDA"! NOT THAT MUCH! ☆
heh heh
tremble tremble
WAGH ?!
Ayu knocked over her tea!
rip
WHUMP
jwaa
Plunk Plunk
Unable to watch this painful sight any longer.
hfffff
OH, I DON'T THINK WE'VE LOST HIM. HE'LL BE AROUND...
...SO LONG AS WE'RE HERE HAVING A GOOD TIME.
HEY, EVERY-BODY!
BAM
Drip-ping sweat.
Ran all the way from the station.
YOU KNOW...
...HOW HE HATES BEING LEFT OUT OF THINGS.
SEE?☆
OKAY, LET'S DO IT AGAIN.
HERE'S TO THOSE WHO'RE LEAVING...
...AND THOSE WHO'RE STAYING.
CHEERS !!
CHEERS!!

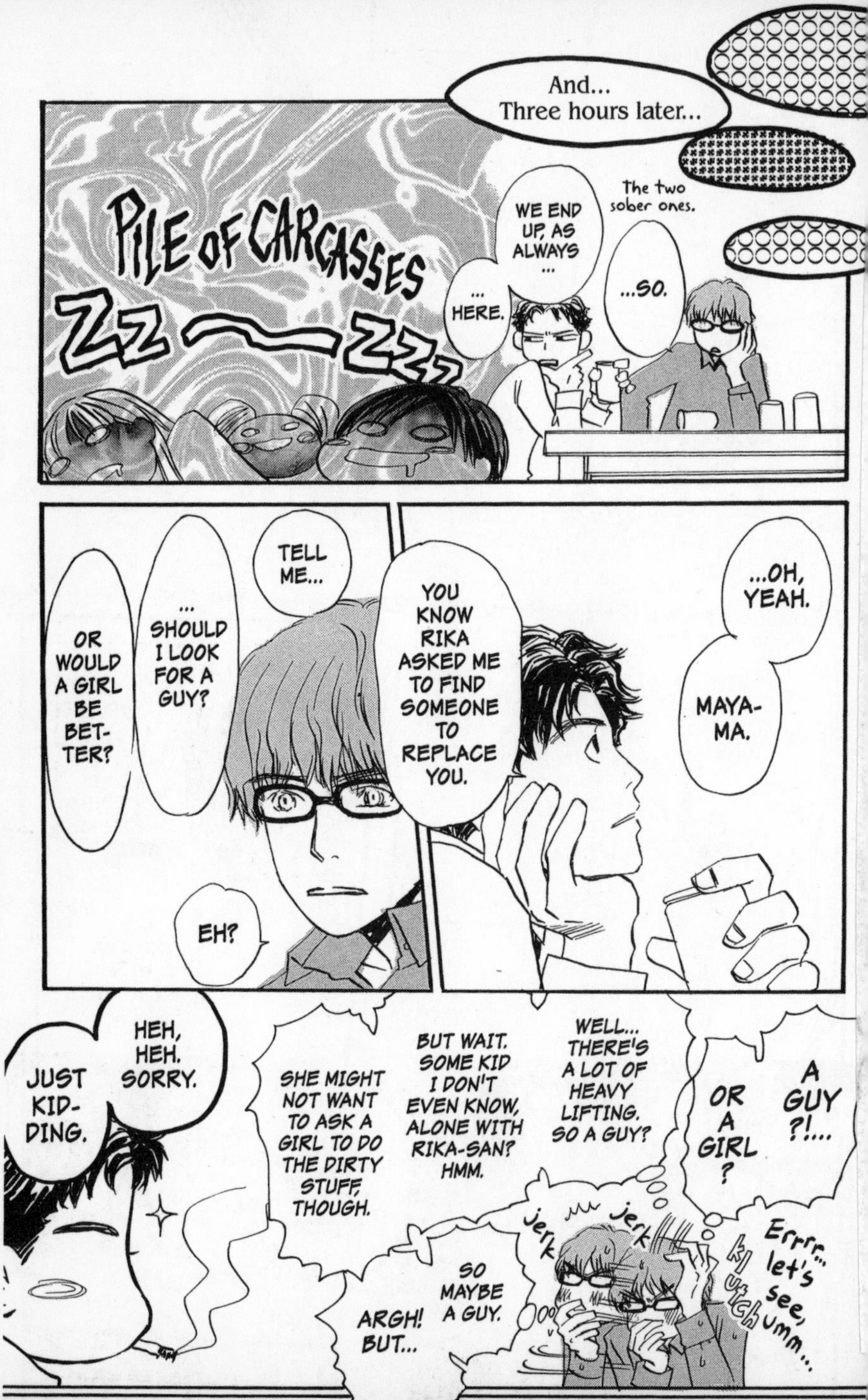
And... Three hours later...
The two sober ones.
...SO.
WE END UP, AS ALWAYS ...
... HERE.
PILE OF CARCASSES
Zz—Zzz
...OH, YEAH.
MAYA-MA.
YOU KNOW RIKA ASKED ME TO FIND SOMEONE TO REPLACE YOU.
TELL ME...
... SHOULD I LOOK FOR A GUY?
OR WOULD A GIRL BE BET-TER?
EH?
A GUY?!....
OR A GIRL?
WELL... THERE'S A LOT OF HEAVY LIFTING. SO A GUY?
BUT WAIT. SOME KID I DON'T EVEN KNOW, ALONE WITH RIKA-SAN? HMM.
SHE MIGHT NOT WANT TO ASK A GIRL TO DO THE DIRTY STUFF, THOUGH.
SO MAYBE A GUY.
ARGH! BUT...
Errrr... let's see, umm...
klutch
jerk jerk
HEH, HEH. SORRY.
JUST KID-DING.

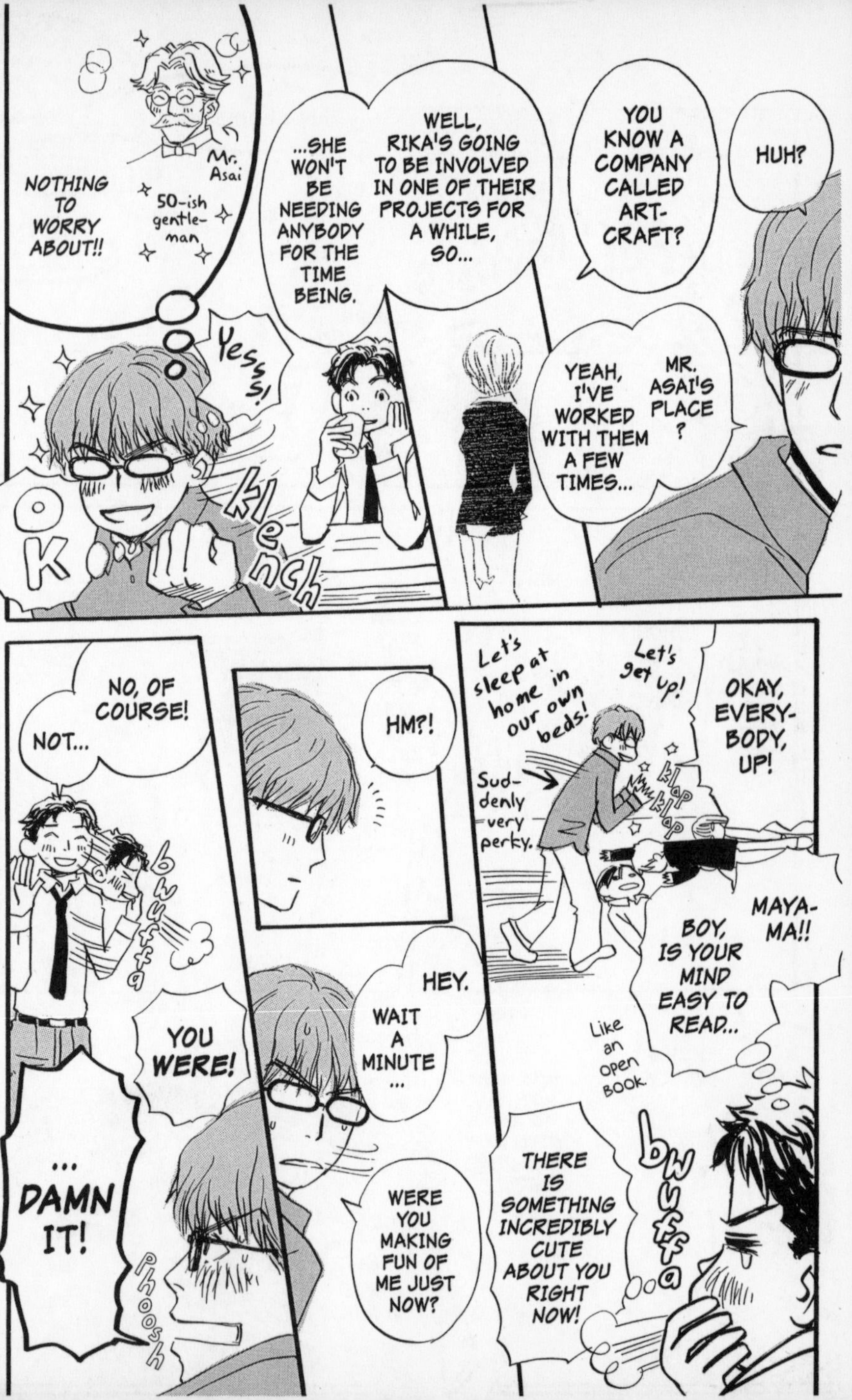
HUH?
YOU KNOW A COMPANY CALLED ART-CRAFT?
MR. ASAI'S PLACE?
YEAH, I'VE WORKED WITH THEM A FEW TIMES...
WELL, RIKA'S GOING TO BE INVOLVED IN ONE OF THEIR PROJECTS FOR A WHILE, SO...
...SHE WON'T BE NEEDING ANYBODY FOR THE TIME BEING.
NOTHING TO WORRY ABOUT!!
Mr. Asai
50-ish gentleman
Yessss!
OK
klench
OKAY, EVERYBODY, UP!
Let's get up!
Let's sleep at home in our own beds!
klap klap
Suddenly very perky.
MAYAMA!!
BOY, IS YOUR MIND EASY TO READ...
Like an open book.
bwuffa
THERE IS SOMETHING INCREDIBLY CUTE ABOUT YOU RIGHT NOW!
HM?!
HEY.
WAIT A MINUTE...
WERE YOU MAKING FUN OF ME JUST NOW?
phoosh
NO, OF COURSE!
NOT...
bwuffa
YOU WERE!
...DAMN IT!

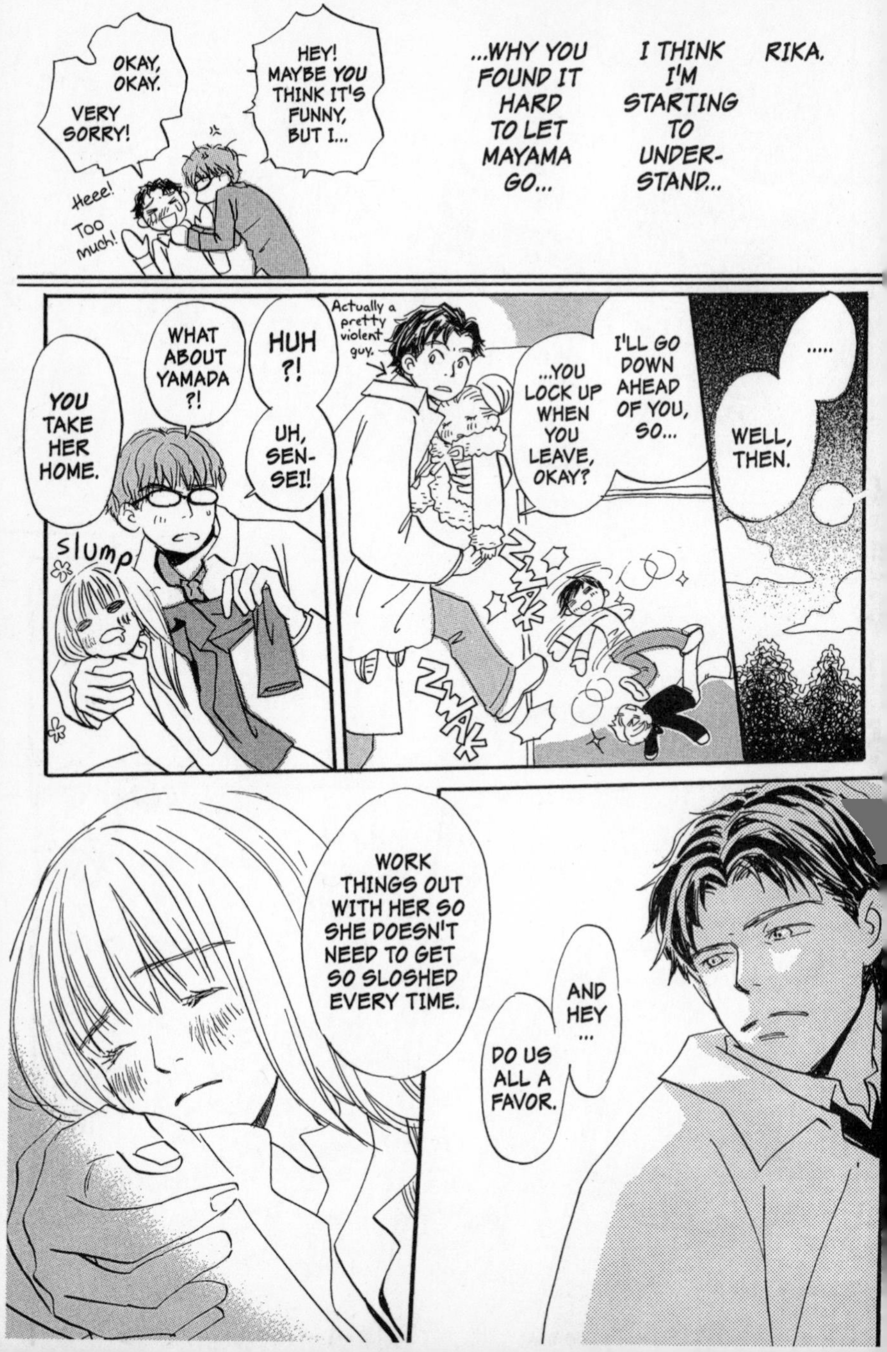
RIKA.
I THINK I'M STARTING TO UNDERSTAND...
...WHY YOU FOUND IT HARD TO LET MAYAMA GO...
HEY! MAYBE YOU THINK IT'S FUNNY, BUT I...
OKAY, OKAY. VERY SORRY!
Heee! Too much!
.....
WELL, THEN.
I'LL GO DOWN AHEAD OF YOU, SO...
...YOU LOCK UP WHEN YOU LEAVE, OKAY?
ZWAK
ZWAK
Actually a pretty violent guy.
HUH?!
UH, SEN-SEI!
WHAT ABOUT YAMADA?!
YOU TAKE HER HOME.
slump
AND HEY...
DO US ALL A FAVOR.
WORK THINGS OUT WITH HER SO SHE DOESN'T NEED TO GET SO SLOSHED EVERY TIME.

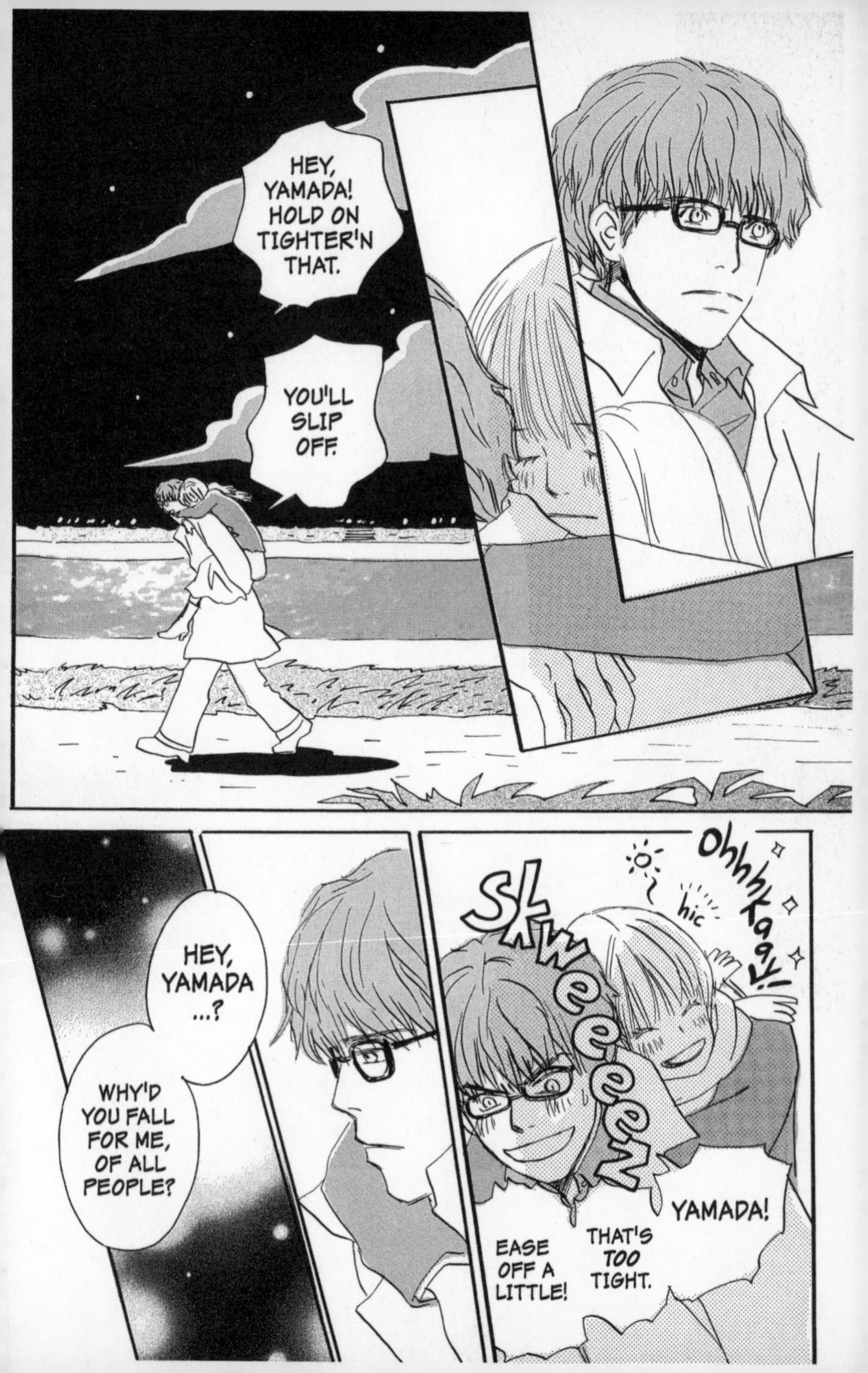
HEY, YAMADA! HOLD ON TIGHTER'N THAT.
YOU'LL SLIP OFF.
Ohhhkaay!
hic
SKWEEEEN
YAMADA!
THAT'S TOO TIGHT.
EASE OFF A LITTLE!
HEY, YAMADA...?
WHY'D YOU FALL FOR ME, OF ALL PEOPLE?

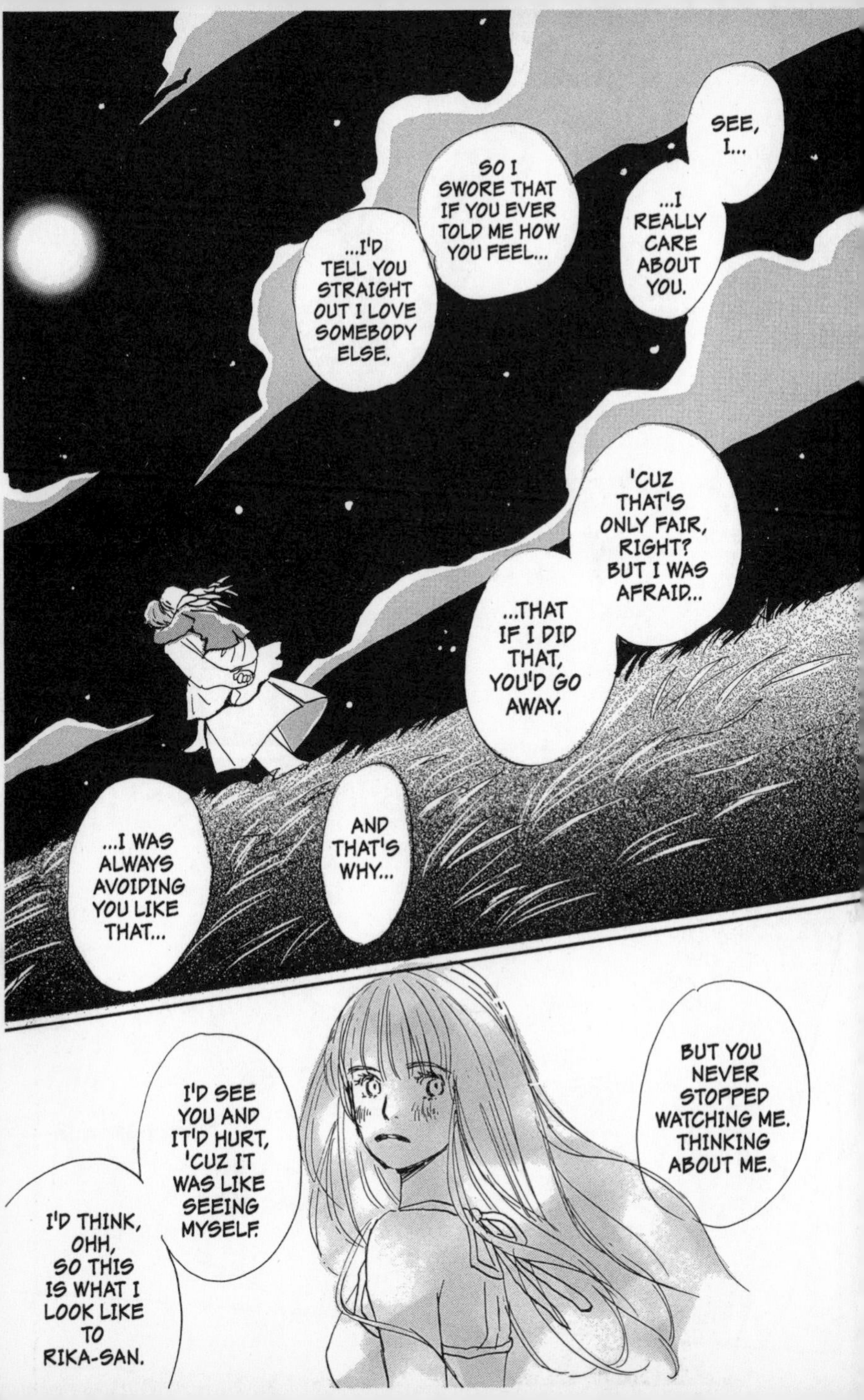
SEE, I...
...I REALLY CARE ABOUT YOU.
SO I SWORE THAT IF YOU EVER TOLD ME HOW YOU FEEL...
...I'D TELL YOU STRAIGHT OUT I LOVE SOMEBODY ELSE.
'CUZ THAT'S ONLY FAIR, RIGHT? BUT I WAS AFRAID...
...THAT IF I DID THAT, YOU'D GO AWAY.
AND THAT'S WHY...
...I WAS ALWAYS AVOIDING YOU LIKE THAT...
BUT YOU NEVER STOPPED WATCHING ME. THINKING ABOUT ME.
I'D SEE YOU AND IT'D HURT, 'CUZ IT WAS LIKE SEEING MYSELF.
I'D THINK, OHH, SO THIS IS WHAT I LOOK LIKE TO RIKA-SAN.

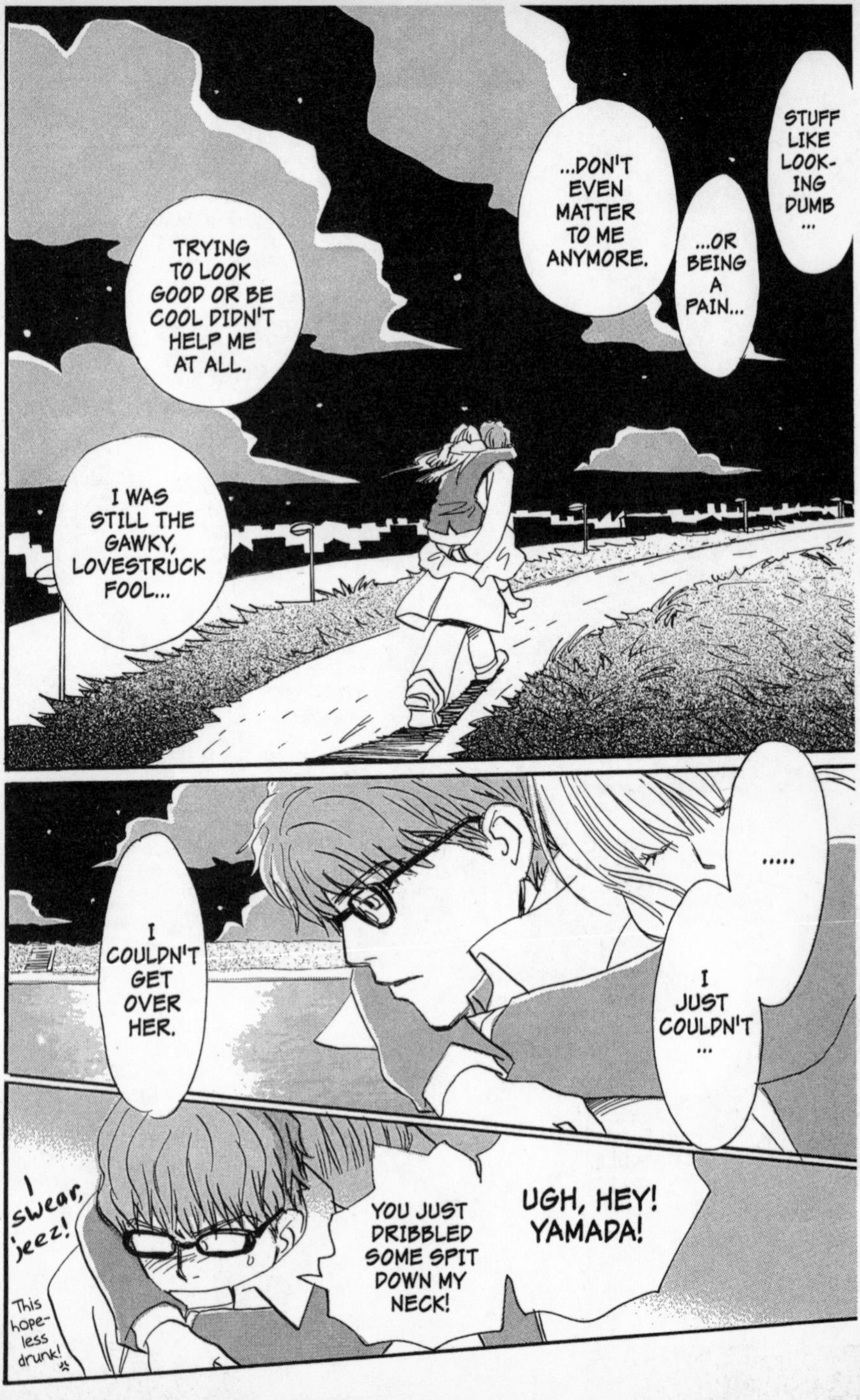
STUFF LIKE LOOK-ING DUMB ...
...OR BEING A PAIN...
...DON'T EVEN MATTER TO ME ANYMORE.
TRYING TO LOOK GOOD OR BE COOL DIDN'T HELP ME AT ALL.
I WAS STILL THE GAWKY, LOVESTRUCK FOOL...
.....
I JUST COULDN'T ...
I COULDN'T GET OVER HER.
UGH, HEY! YAMADA!
YOU JUST DRIBBLED SOME SPIT DOWN MY NECK!
I swear, jeez!
This hope-less drunk!

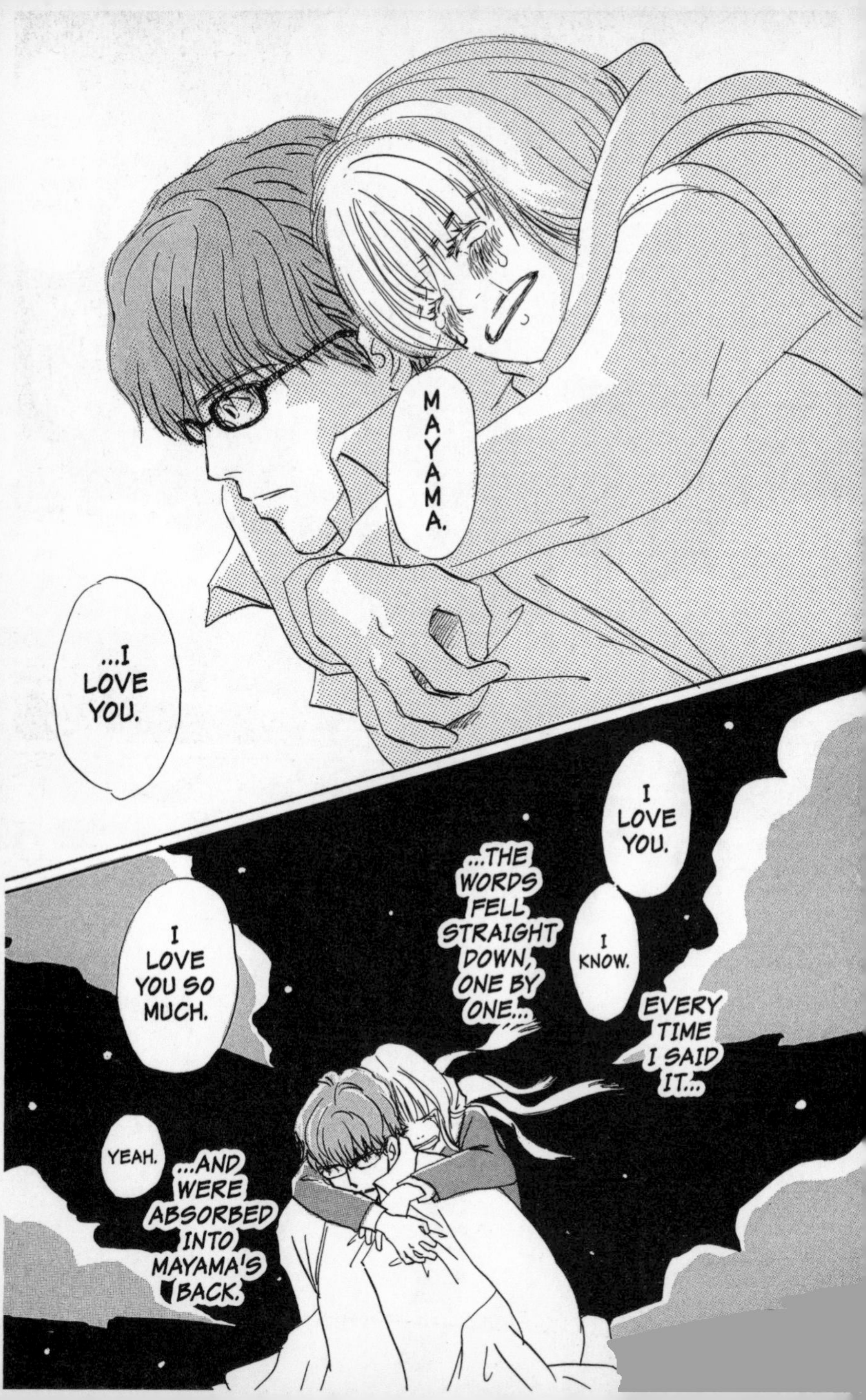
MAYAMA.
...I LOVE YOU.
I LOVE YOU.
I KNOW.
EVERY TIME I SAID IT...
...THE WORDS FELL STRAIGHT DOWN, ONE BY ONE...
I LOVE YOU SO MUCH.
YEAH.
...AND WERE ABSORBED INTO MAYAMA'S BACK.

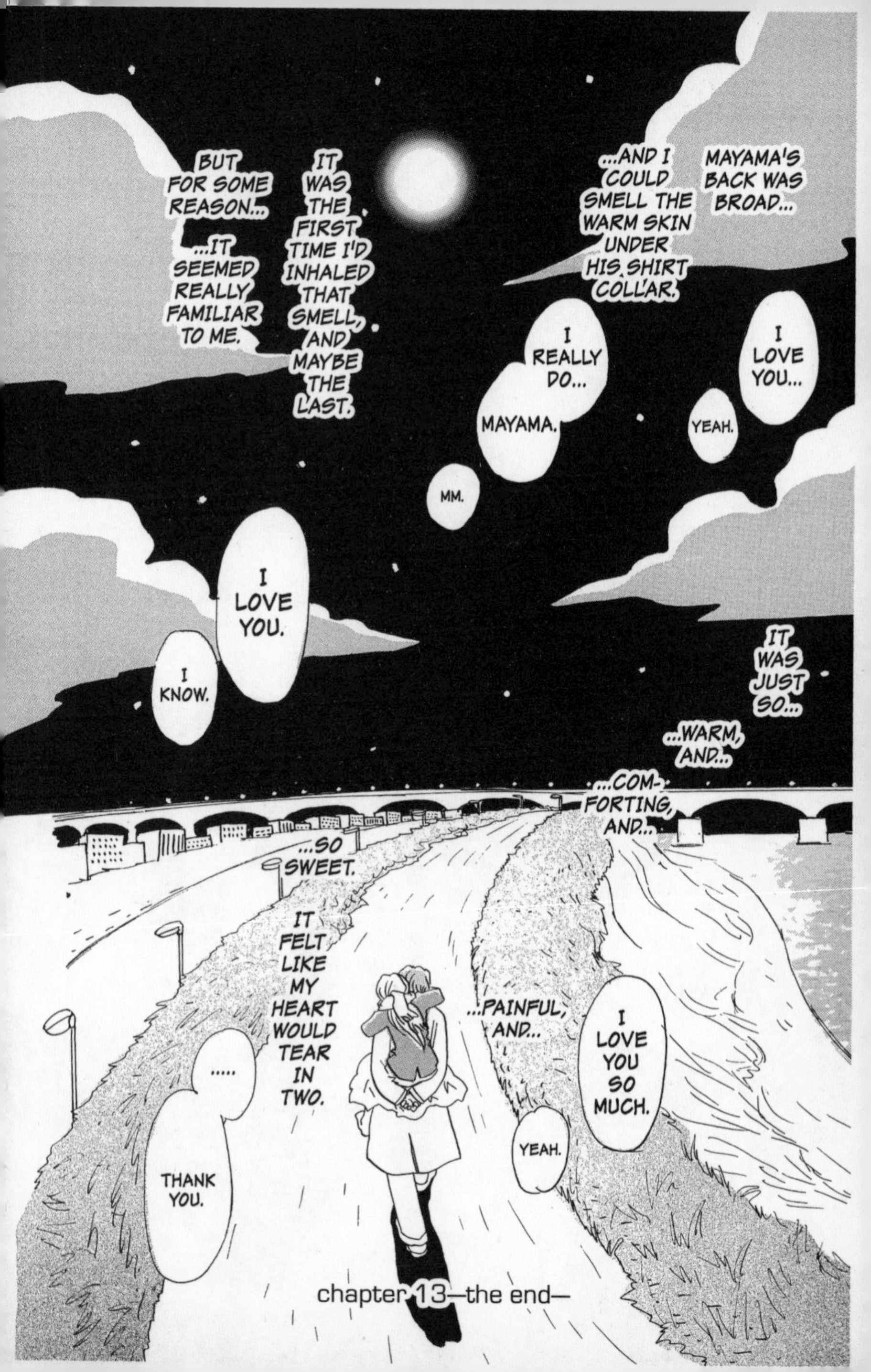
MAYAMA'S BACK WAS BROAD...
...AND I COULD SMELL THE WARM SKIN UNDER HIS SHIRT COLLAR.
IT WAS THE FIRST TIME I'D INHALED THAT SMELL, AND MAYBE THE LAST.
BUT FOR SOME REASON...
...IT SEEMED REALLY FAMILIAR TO ME.
I LOVE YOU...
YEAH.
I REALLY DO...
MAYAMA.
MM.
I LOVE YOU.
I KNOW.
IT WAS JUST SO...
...WARM, AND...
...COM-FORTING, AND...
...SO SWEET.
I LOVE YOU SO MUCH.
YEAH.
...PAINFUL, AND...
IT FELT LIKE MY HEART WOULD TEAR IN TWO.
.....
THANK YOU.
chapter 13—the end—

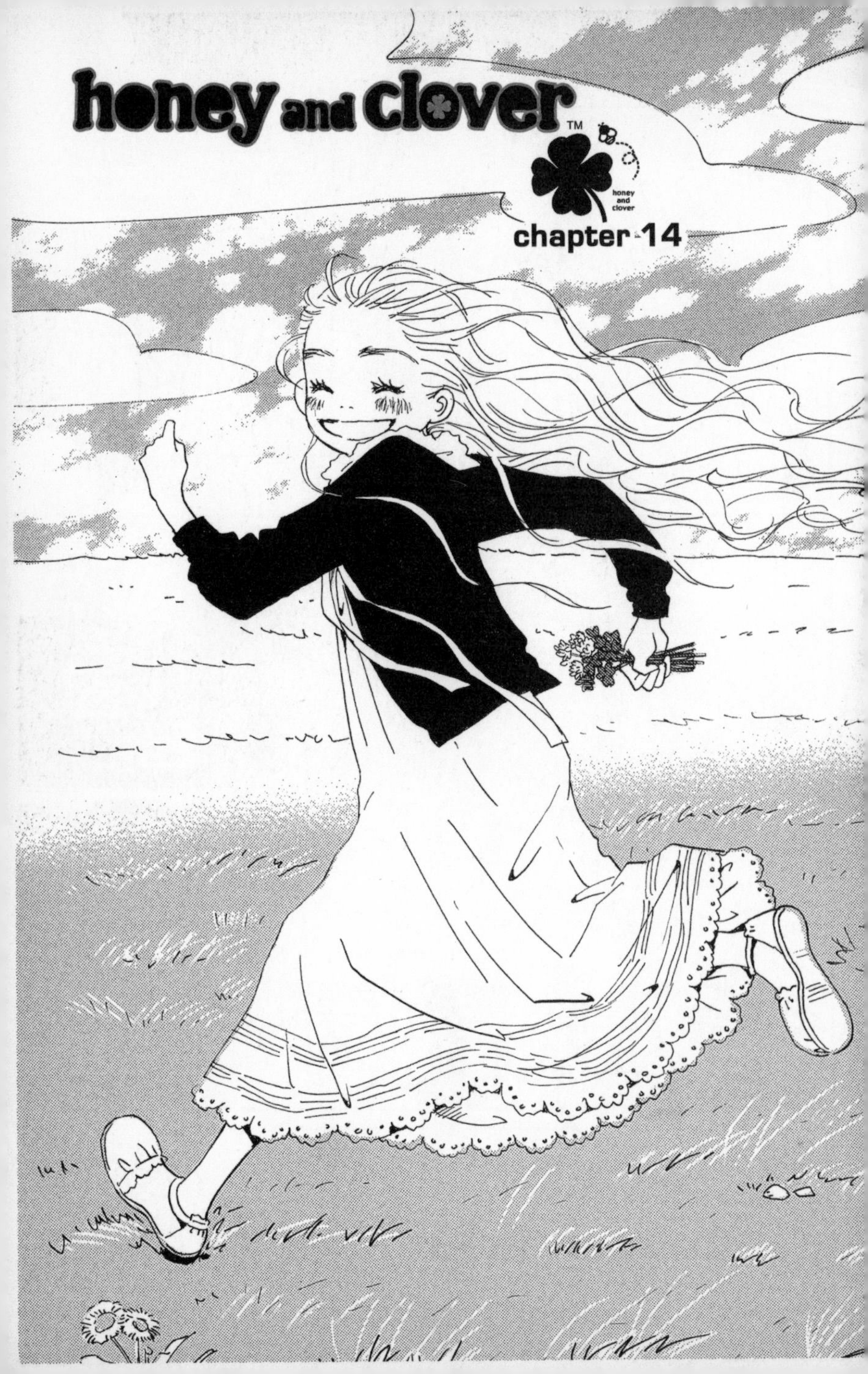
honey and clover™
honey and clover
chapter 14

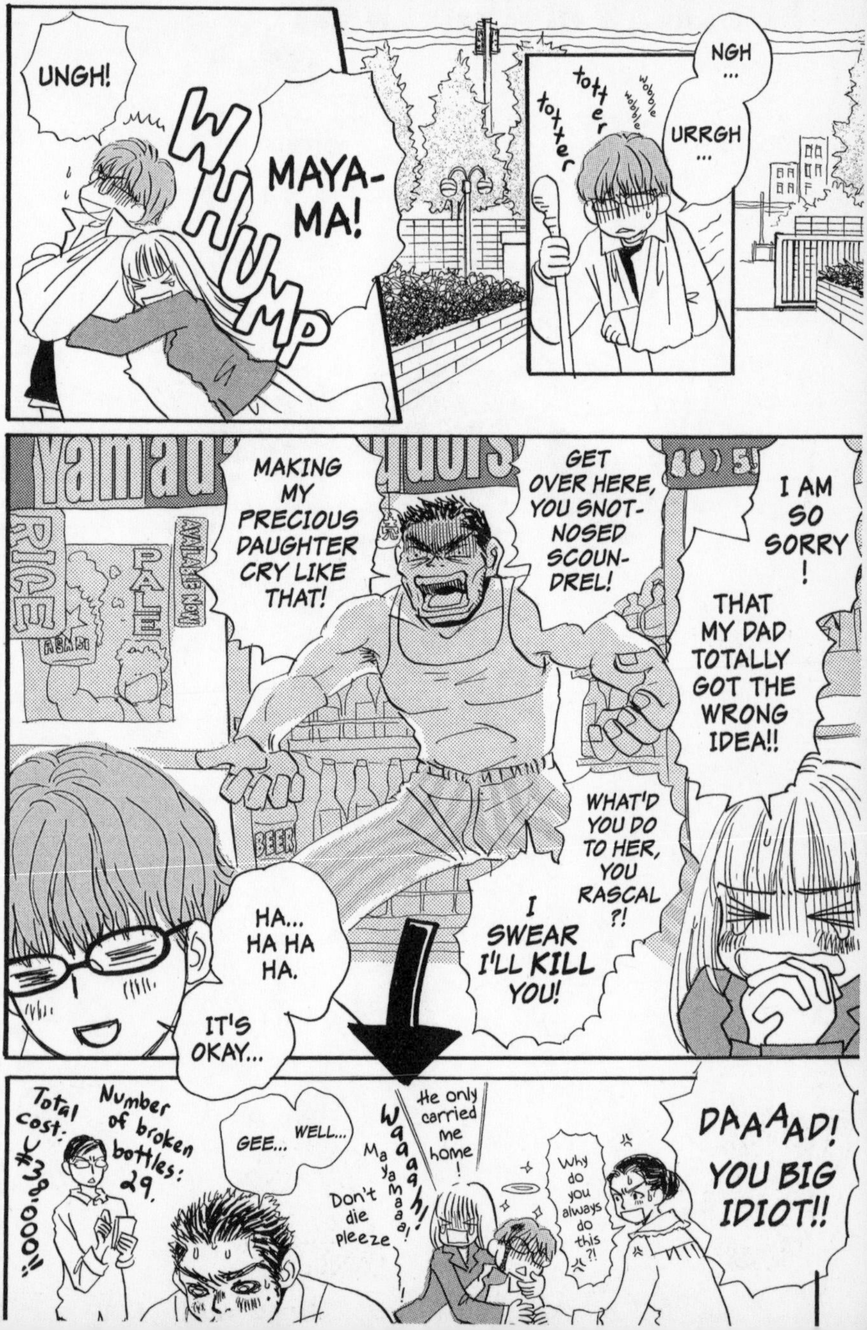
NGH ...
URRGH ...
totter totter
wobble wobble
MAYA-MA!
WHUMP
UNGH!
I AM SO SORRY!
THAT MY DAD TOTALLY GOT THE WRONG IDEA!!
GET OVER HERE, YOU SNOT-NOSED SCOUN-DREL!
MAKING MY PRECIOUS DAUGHTER CRY LIKE THAT!
RICE
PALE
BEER
WHAT'D YOU DO TO HER, YOU RASCAL?!
I SWEAR I'LL KILL YOU!
HA... HA HA HA.
IT'S OKAY...
DAAAAD! YOU BIG IDIOT!!
Why do you always do this?!
He only carried me home!
Waaaaah! Mayamaaa!
Don't die pleeze
GEE... WELL...
Number of broken bottles: 29.
Total cost: ¥38,000!!

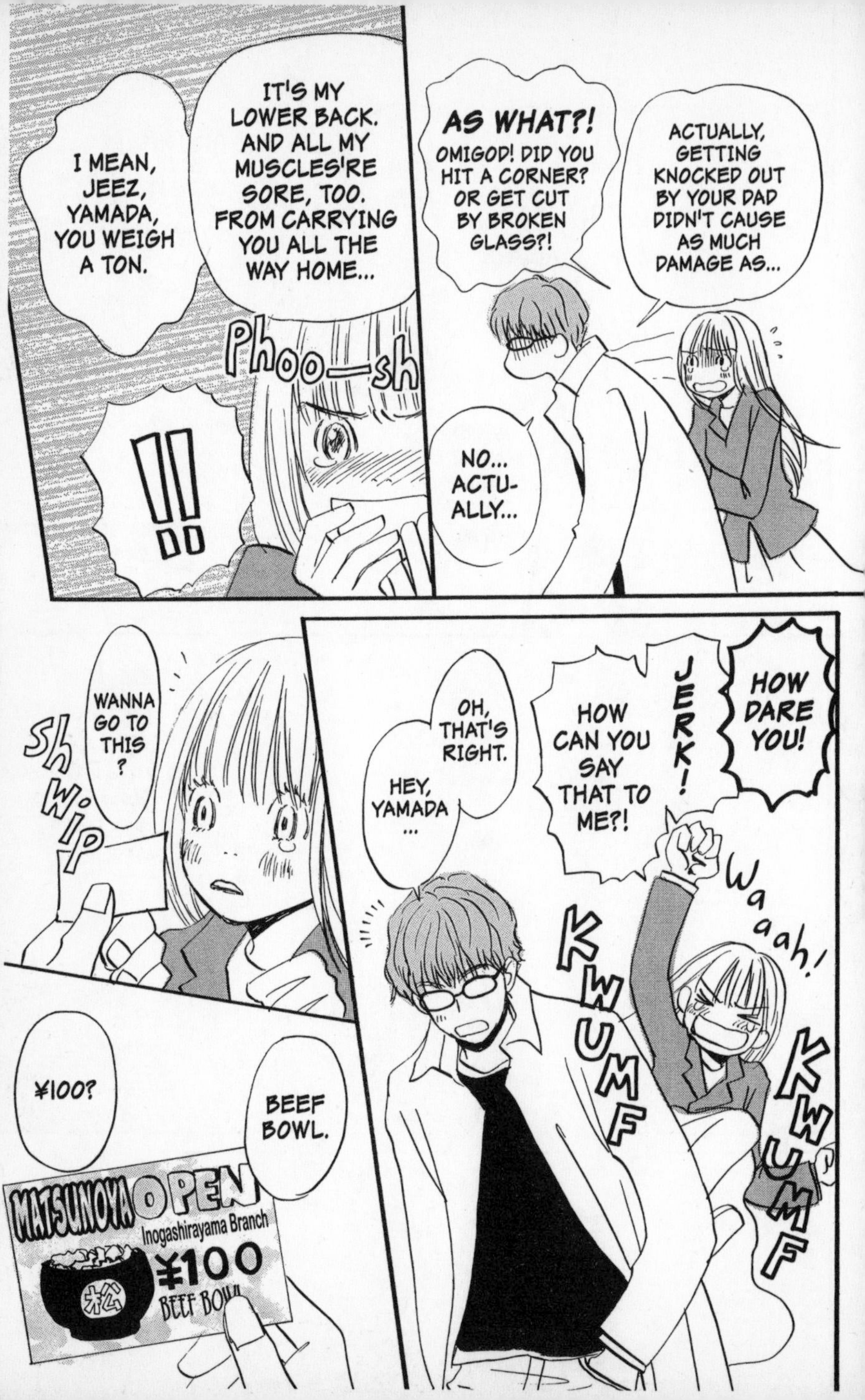
ACTUALLY, GETTING KNOCKED OUT BY YOUR DAD DIDN'T CAUSE AS MUCH DAMAGE AS...
AS WHAT?! OMIGOD! DID YOU HIT A CORNER? OR GET CUT BY BROKEN GLASS?!
NO... ACTU-ALLY...
IT'S MY LOWER BACK. AND ALL MY MUSCLES'RE SORE, TOO. FROM CARRYING YOU ALL THE WAY HOME...
I MEAN, JEEZ, YAMADA, YOU WEIGH A TON.
Phoo—sh
!!
HOW DARE YOU!
JERK!
HOW CAN YOU SAY THAT TO ME?!
OH, THAT'S RIGHT.
HEY, YAMADA ...
Waaah!
KWUMF
KWUMF
WANNA GO TO THIS ?
Shwip
BEEF BOWL.
¥100?
MATSUNOYA OPEN
Inogashirayama Branch
¥100
BEEF BOWL

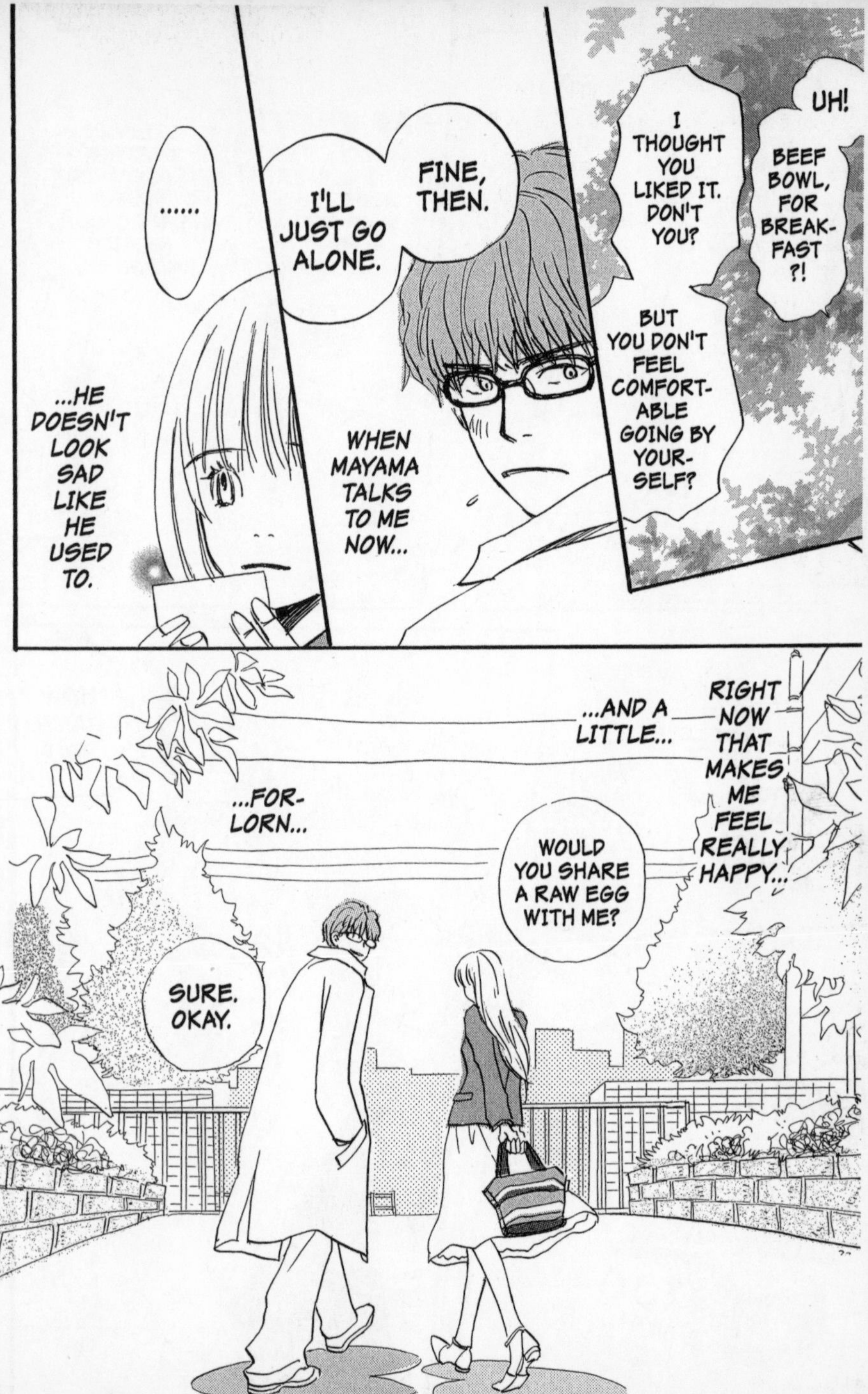
UH!
BEEF BOWL, FOR BREAK-FAST?!
I THOUGHT YOU LIKED IT. DON'T YOU?
BUT YOU DON'T FEEL COMFORT-ABLE GOING BY YOUR-SELF?
FINE, THEN.
I'LL JUST GO ALONE.
WHEN MAYAMA TALKS TO ME NOW...
......
...HE DOESN'T LOOK SAD LIKE HE USED TO.
RIGHT NOW THAT MAKES ME FEEL REALLY HAPPY...
...AND A LITTLE...
...FOR-LORN...
WOULD YOU SHARE A RAW EGG WITH ME?
SURE. OKAY.

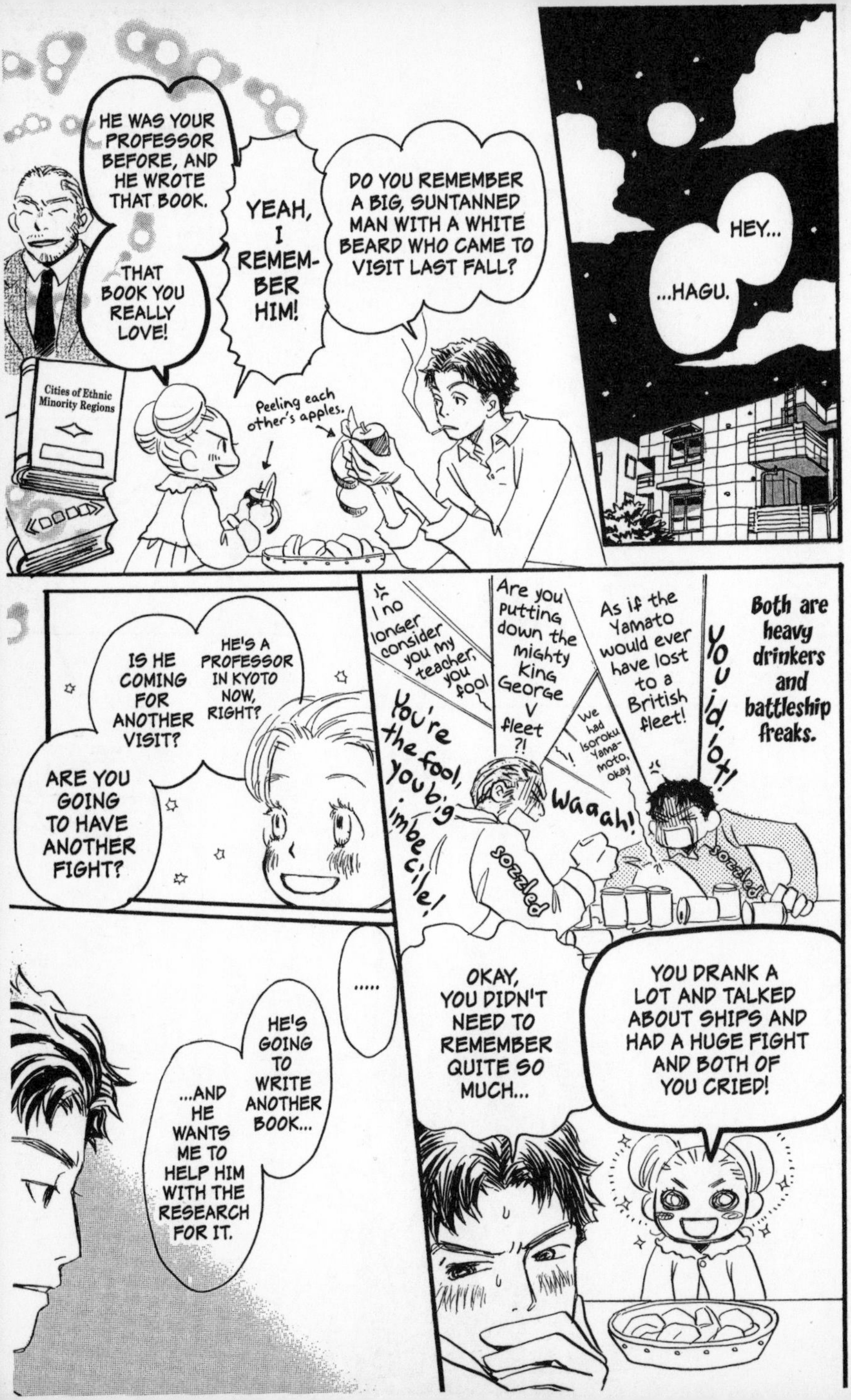
HEY...
...HAGU.
DO YOU REMEMBER A BIG, SUNTANNED MAN WITH A WHITE BEARD WHO CAME TO VISIT LAST FALL?
YEAH, I REMEMBER HIM!
HE WAS YOUR PROFESSOR BEFORE, AND HE WROTE THAT BOOK.
THAT BOOK YOU REALLY LOVE!
Cities of Ethnic Minority Regions
Peeling each other's apples.
Both are heavy drinkers and battleship freaks.
You idiot!
As if the Yamato would ever have lost to a British fleet!
We had Isoroku Yamamoto, okay
Are you putting down the mighty King George V fleet?!
I no longer consider you my teacher, you fool!
You're the fool, you big imbecile!
Waaah!
sozzled
sozzled
HE'S A PROFESSOR IN KYOTO NOW, RIGHT?
IS HE COMING FOR ANOTHER VISIT?
ARE YOU GOING TO HAVE ANOTHER FIGHT?
YOU DRANK A LOT AND TALKED ABOUT SHIPS AND HAD A HUGE FIGHT AND BOTH OF YOU CRIED!
OKAY, YOU DIDN'T NEED TO REMEMBER QUITE SO MUCH...
.....
HE'S GOING TO WRITE ANOTHER BOOK...
...AND HE WANTS ME TO HELP HIM WITH THE RESEARCH FOR IT.

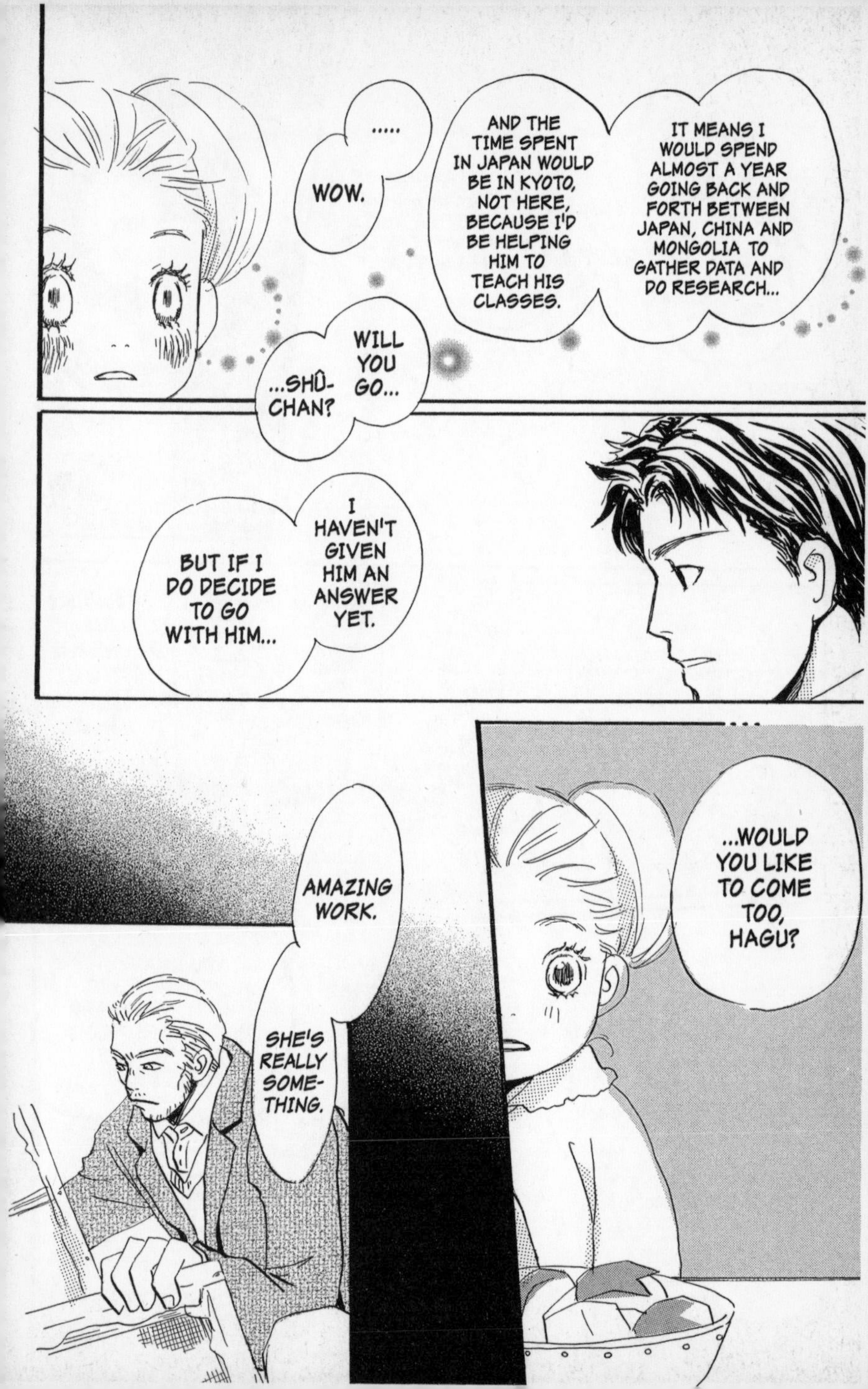
IT MEANS I WOULD SPEND ALMOST A YEAR GOING BACK AND FORTH BETWEEN JAPAN, CHINA AND MONGOLIA TO GATHER DATA AND DO RESEARCH...
AND THE TIME SPENT IN JAPAN WOULD BE IN KYOTO, NOT HERE, BECAUSE I'D BE HELPING HIM TO TEACH HIS CLASSES.
.....
WOW.
WILL YOU GO...
...SHÛ-CHAN?
I HAVEN'T GIVEN HIM AN ANSWER YET.
BUT IF I DO DECIDE TO GO WITH HIM...
...WOULD YOU LIKE TO COME TOO, HAGU?
AMAZING WORK.
SHE'S REALLY SOME-THING.

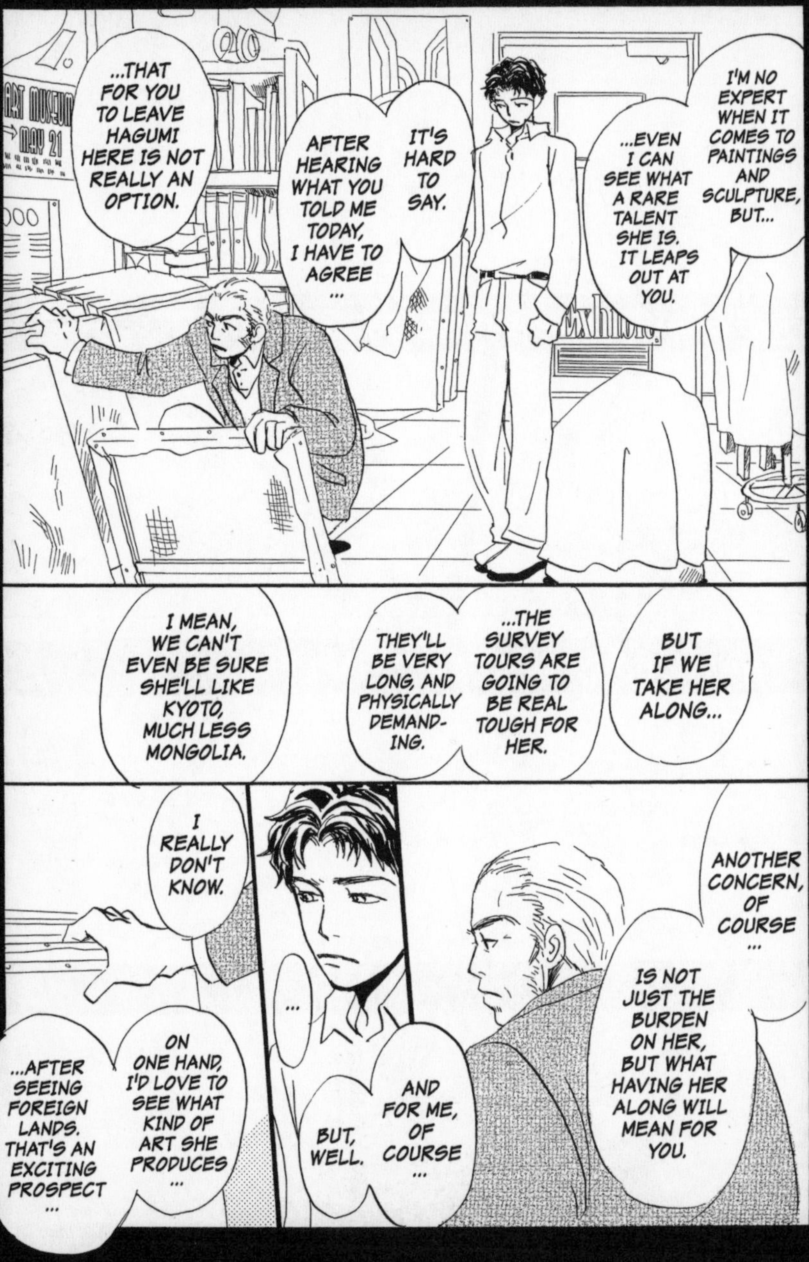
I'M NO EXPERT WHEN IT COMES TO PAINTINGS AND SCULPTURE, BUT...
...EVEN I CAN SEE WHAT A RARE TALENT SHE IS. IT LEAPS OUT AT YOU.
IT'S HARD TO SAY.
AFTER HEARING WHAT YOU TOLD ME TODAY, I HAVE TO AGREE ...
...THAT FOR YOU TO LEAVE HAGUMI HERE IS NOT REALLY AN OPTION.
BUT IF WE TAKE HER ALONG...
...THE SURVEY TOURS ARE GOING TO BE REAL TOUGH FOR HER.
THEY'LL BE VERY LONG, AND PHYSICALLY DEMAND-ING.
I MEAN, WE CAN'T EVEN BE SURE SHE'LL LIKE KYOTO, MUCH LESS MONGOLIA.
ANOTHER CONCERN, OF COURSE ...
IS NOT JUST THE BURDEN ON HER, BUT WHAT HAVING HER ALONG WILL MEAN FOR YOU.
I REALLY DON'T KNOW.
...
AND FOR ME, OF COURSE ...
BUT, WELL.
ON ONE HAND, I'D LOVE TO SEE WHAT KIND OF ART SHE PRODUCES ...
...AFTER SEEING FOREIGN LANDS. THAT'S AN EXCITING PROSPECT ...

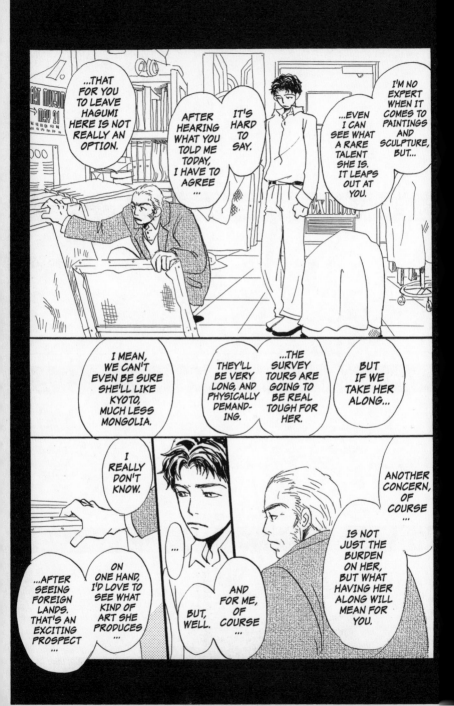

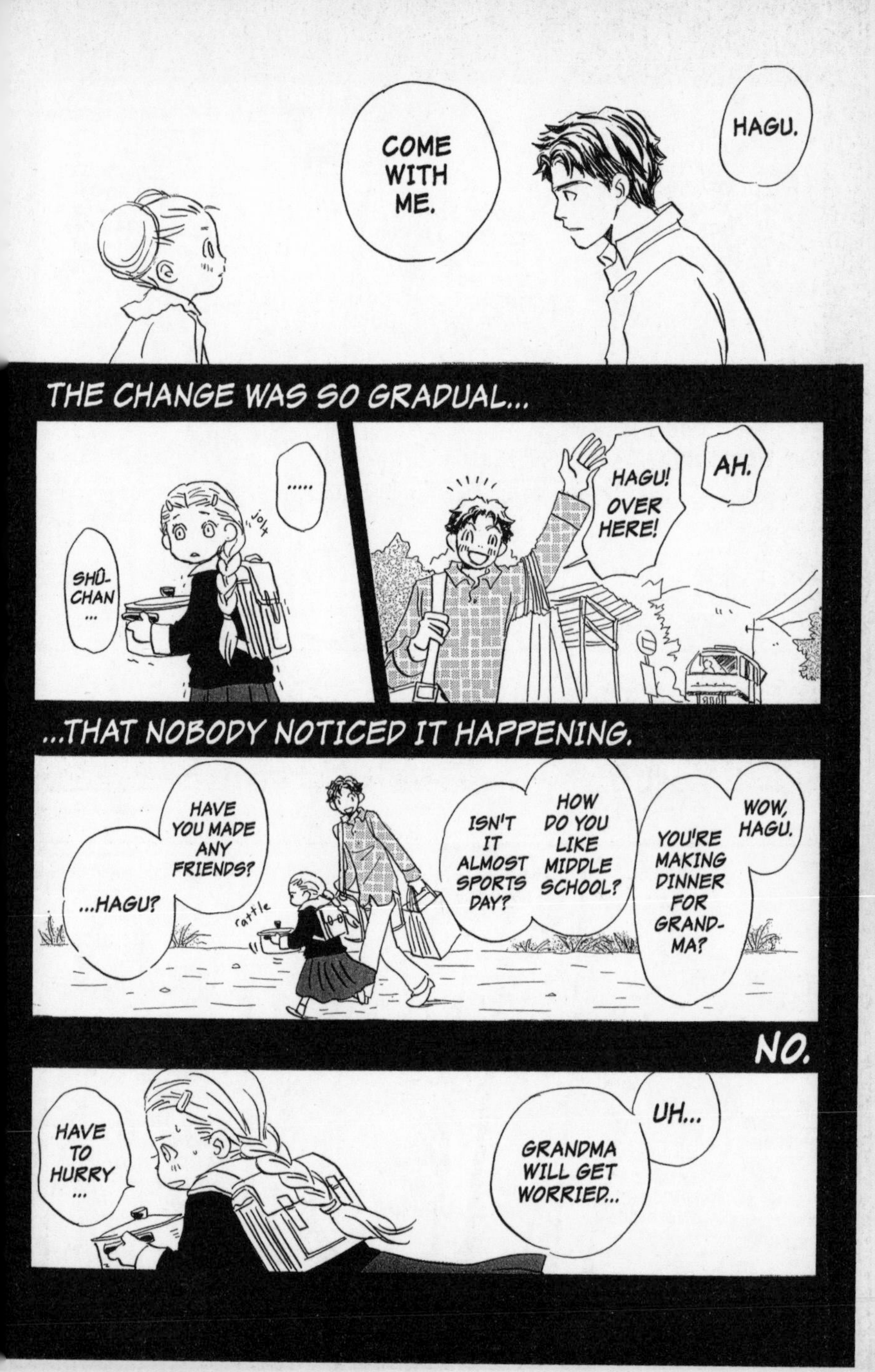
HAGU.
COME WITH ME.
THE CHANGE WAS SO GRADUAL...
AH.
HAGU! OVER HERE!
.....
jolt
SHŪ-CHAN ...
...THAT NOBODY NOTICED IT HAPPENING.
WOW, HAGU.
YOU'RE MAKING DINNER FOR GRAND-MA?
HOW DO YOU LIKE MIDDLE SCHOOL?
ISN'T IT ALMOST SPORTS DAY?
HAVE YOU MADE ANY FRIENDS?
...HAGU?
rattle
NO.
UH...
GRANDMA WILL GET WORRIED...
HAVE TO HURRY ...

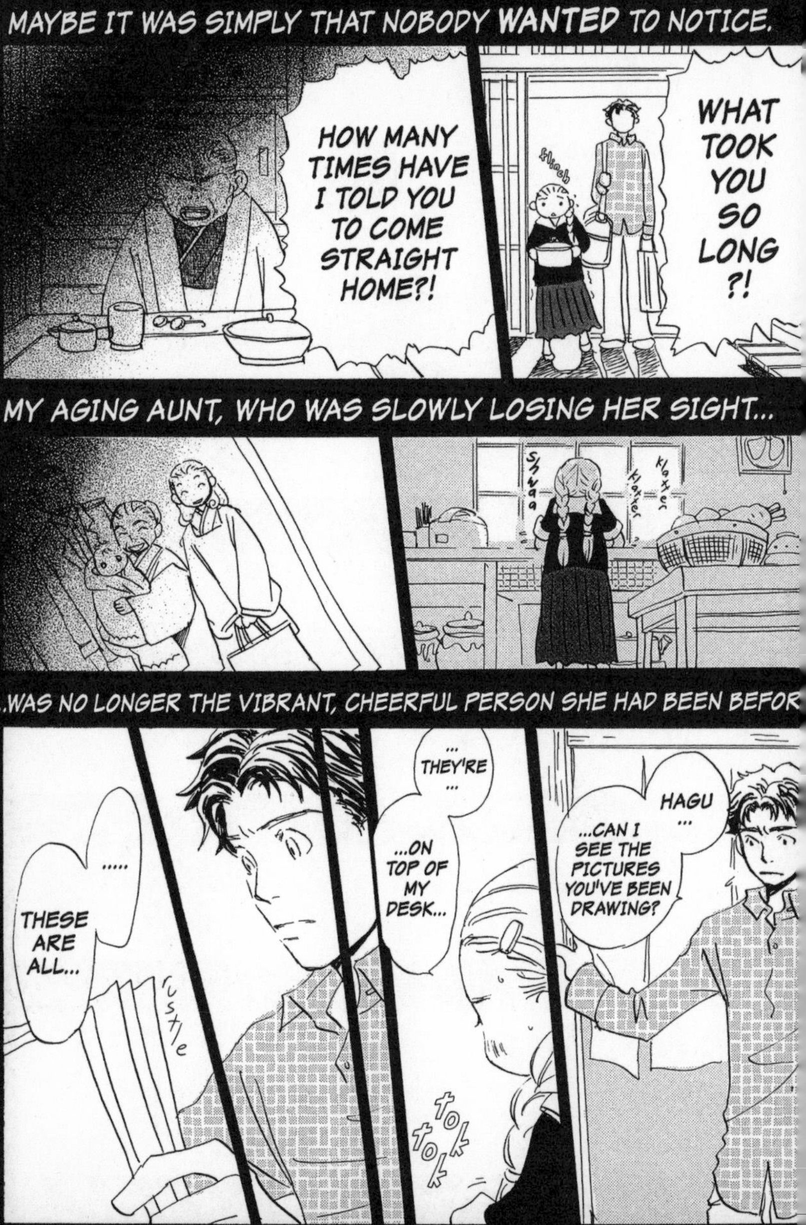
MAYBE IT WAS SIMPLY THAT NOBODY **WANTED** TO NOTICE.
WHAT TOOK YOU SO LONG?!
flinch
HOW MANY TIMES HAVE I TOLD YOU TO COME STRAIGHT HOME?!
MY AGING AUNT, WHO WAS SLOWLY LOSING HER SIGHT...
shwaa
klatter klatter
...WAS NO LONGER THE VIBRANT, CHEERFUL PERSON SHE HAD BEEN BEFOR
HAGU...
...CAN I SEE THE PICTURES YOU'VE BEEN DRAWING?
...THEY'RE...
...ON TOP OF MY DESK...
tok tok
.....
THESE ARE ALL...
rustle

THERE WERE PILES AND PILES OF PICTURES, ALL OF THEM LANDSCAPES.

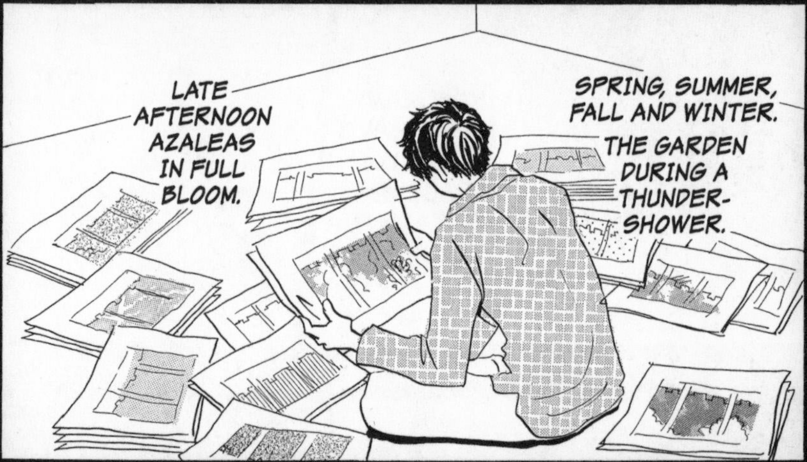
SPRING, SUMMER, FALL AND WINTER.
THE GARDEN DURING A THUNDER-SHOWER.
LATE AFTERNOON AZALEAS IN FULL BLOOM.

ALL OF THEM THE SAME LANDSCAPE.

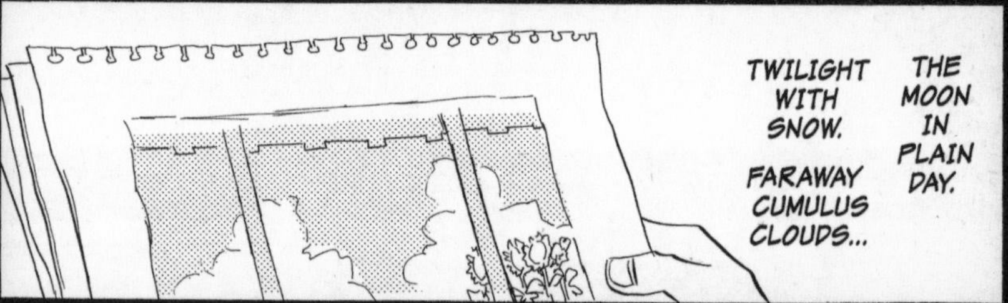
THE MOON IN PLAIN DAY.
TWILIGHT WITH SNOW.
FARAWAY CUMULUS CLOUDS...

THE TWO OF THEM IN THAT BIG OLD HOUSE IN THAT SMALL VILLAGE...

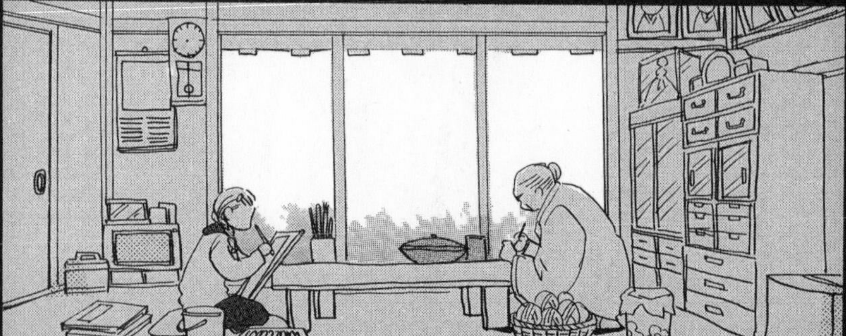

...HAD QUIETLY LOST THEIR WAY OUT, AND BECOME TRAPPED.

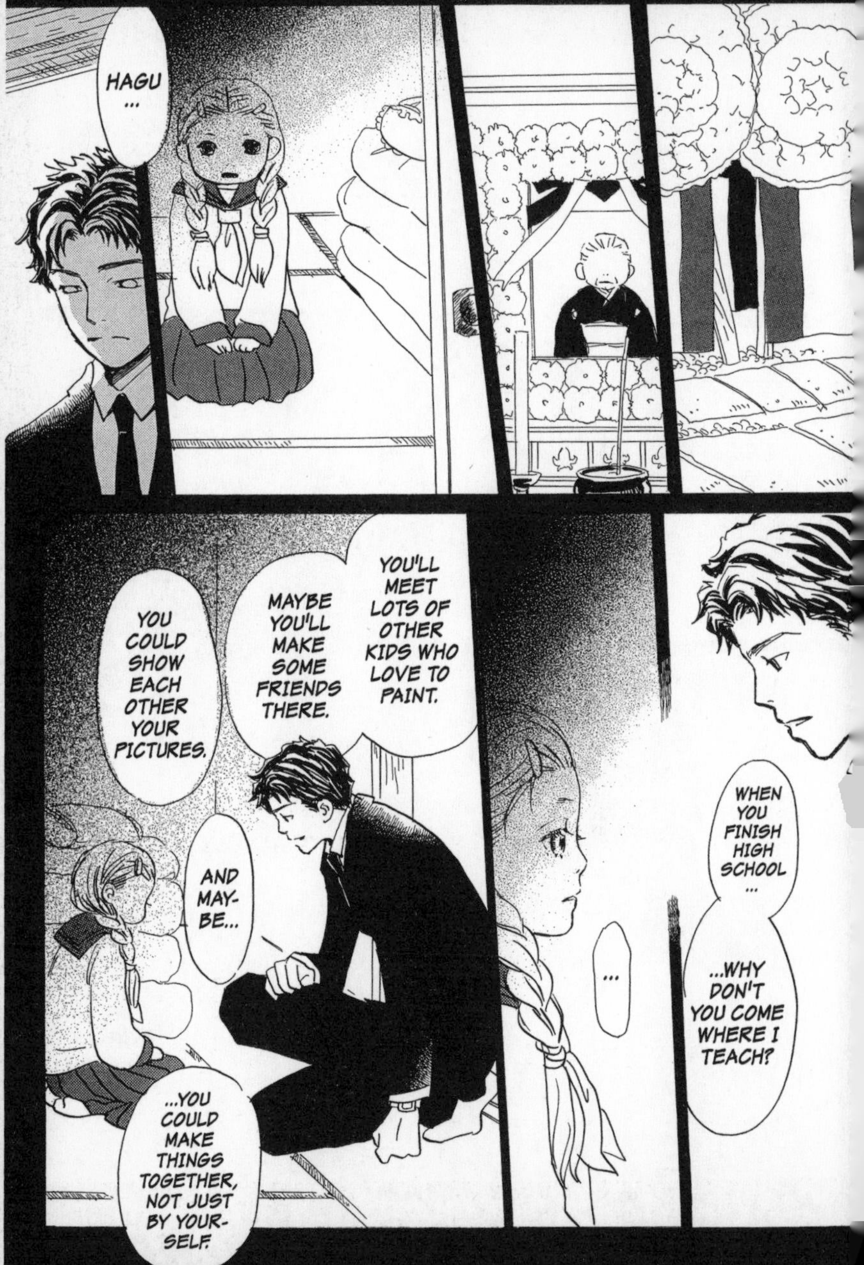
HAGU ...
WHEN YOU FINISH HIGH SCHOOL ...
...WHY DON'T YOU COME WHERE I TEACH?
...
YOU'LL MEET LOTS OF OTHER KIDS WHO LOVE TO PAINT.
MAYBE YOU'LL MAKE SOME FRIENDS THERE.
YOU COULD SHOW EACH OTHER YOUR PICTURES.
AND MAY-BE...
...YOU COULD MAKE THINGS TOGETHER, NOT JUST BY YOUR-SELF.

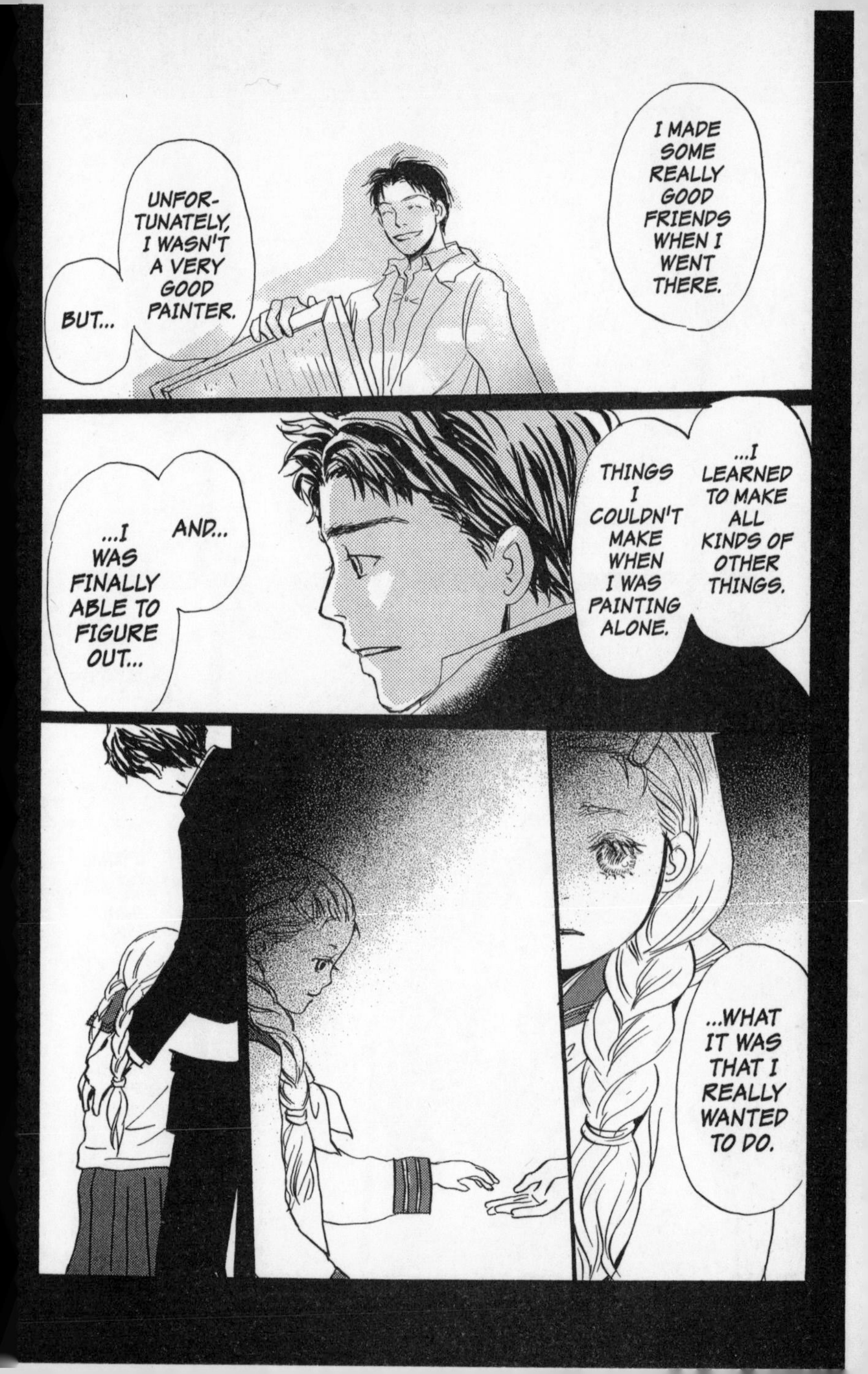
I MADE SOME REALLY GOOD FRIENDS WHEN I WENT THERE.
UNFOR-TUNATELY, I WASN'T A VERY GOOD PAINTER.
BUT...
...I LEARNED TO MAKE ALL KINDS OF OTHER THINGS.
THINGS I COULDN'T MAKE WHEN I WAS PAINTING ALONE.
AND...
...I WAS FINALLY ABLE TO FIGURE OUT...
...WHAT IT WAS THAT I REALLY WANTED TO DO.

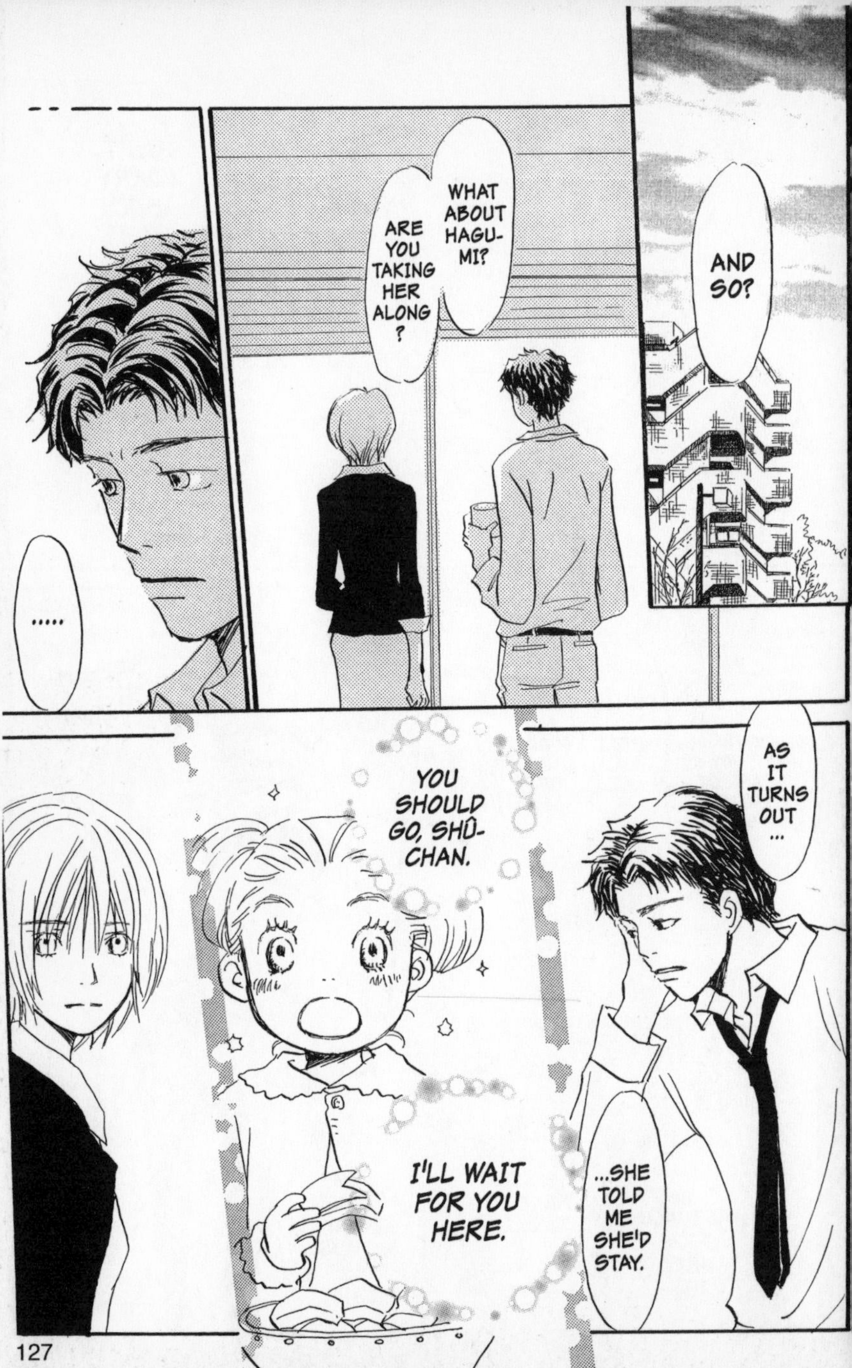
AND SO?
WHAT ABOUT HAGU-MI?
ARE YOU TAKING HER ALONG?
......
AS IT TURNS OUT...
...SHE TOLD ME SHE'D STAY.
YOU SHOULD GO, SHÛ-CHAN.
I'LL WAIT FOR YOU HERE.

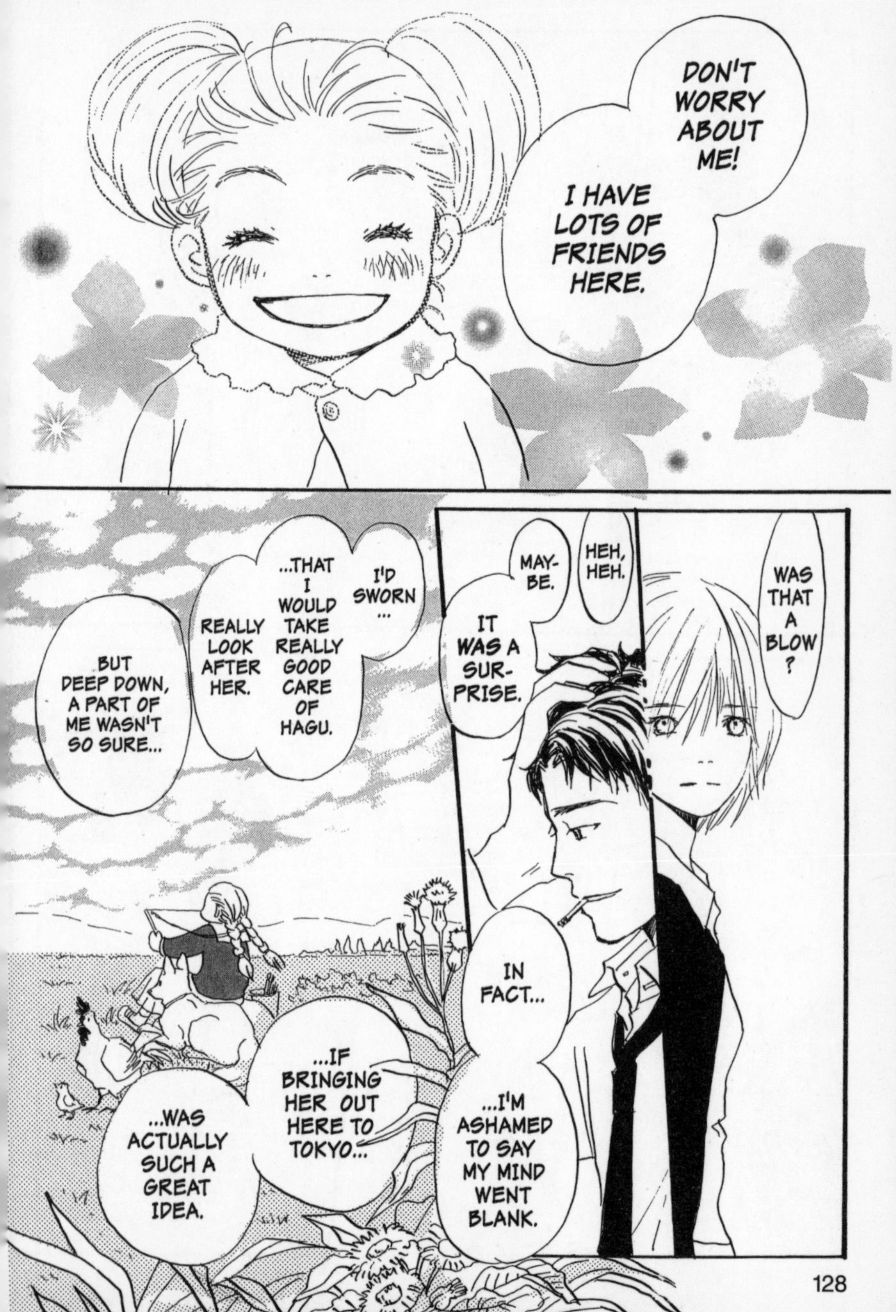
DON'T WORRY ABOUT ME!
I HAVE LOTS OF FRIENDS HERE.
WAS THAT A BLOW?
HEH, HEH.
MAY-BE.
IT WAS A SUR-PRISE.
IN FACT...
...I'M ASHAMED TO SAY MY MIND WENT BLANK.
I'D SWORN...
...THAT I WOULD TAKE REALLY GOOD CARE OF HAGU.
REALLY LOOK AFTER HER.
BUT DEEP DOWN, A PART OF ME WASN'T SO SURE...
...IF BRINGING HER OUT HERE TO TOKYO...
...WAS ACTUALLY SUCH A GREAT IDEA.

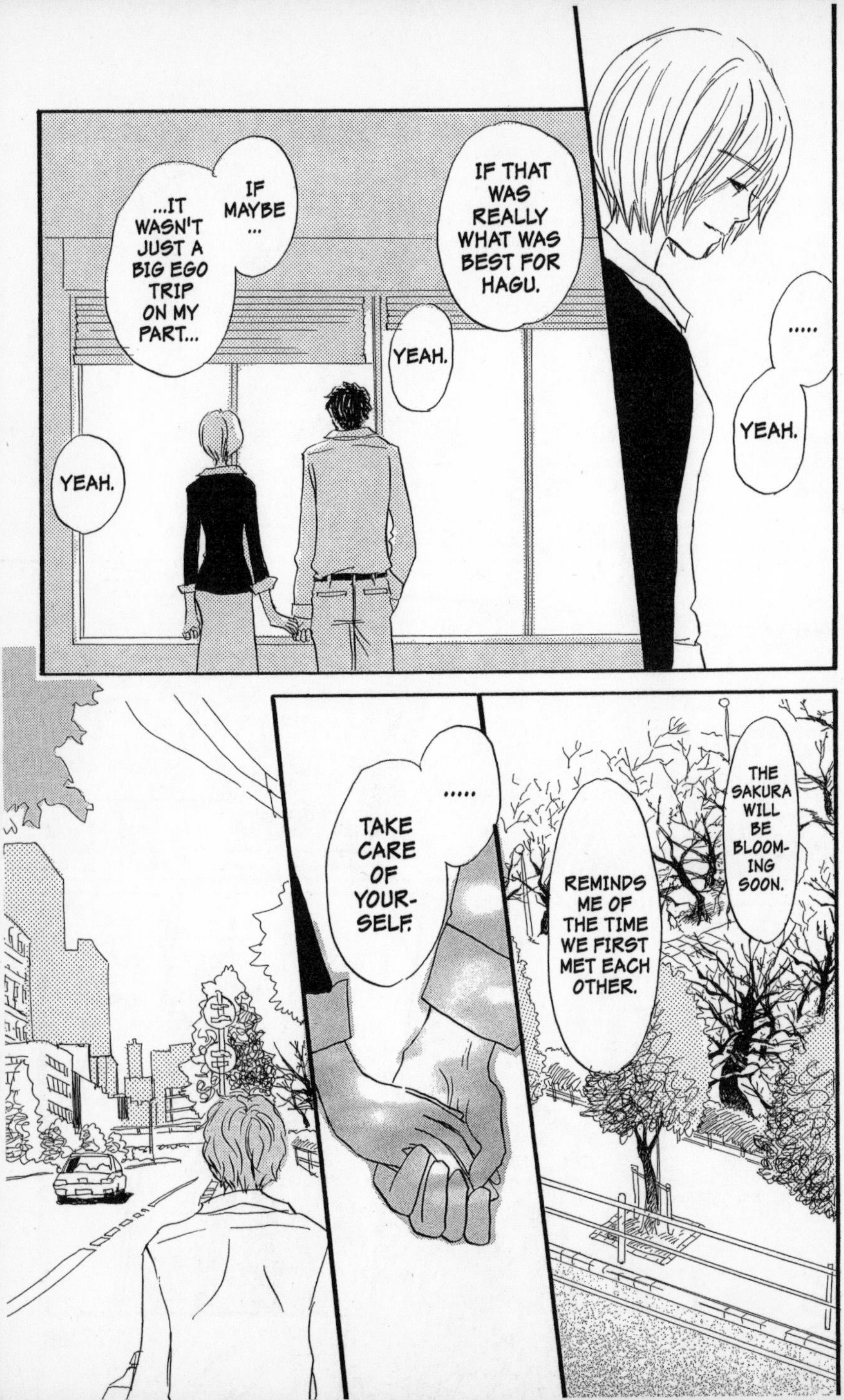
.....
YEAH.
IF THAT WAS REALLY WHAT WAS BEST FOR HAGU.
YEAH.
IF MAYBE ...
...IT WASN'T JUST A BIG EGO TRIP ON MY PART...
YEAH.
THE SAKURA WILL BE BLOOMING SOON.
REMINDS ME OF THE TIME WE FIRST MET EACH OTHER.
.....
TAKE CARE OF YOURSELF.

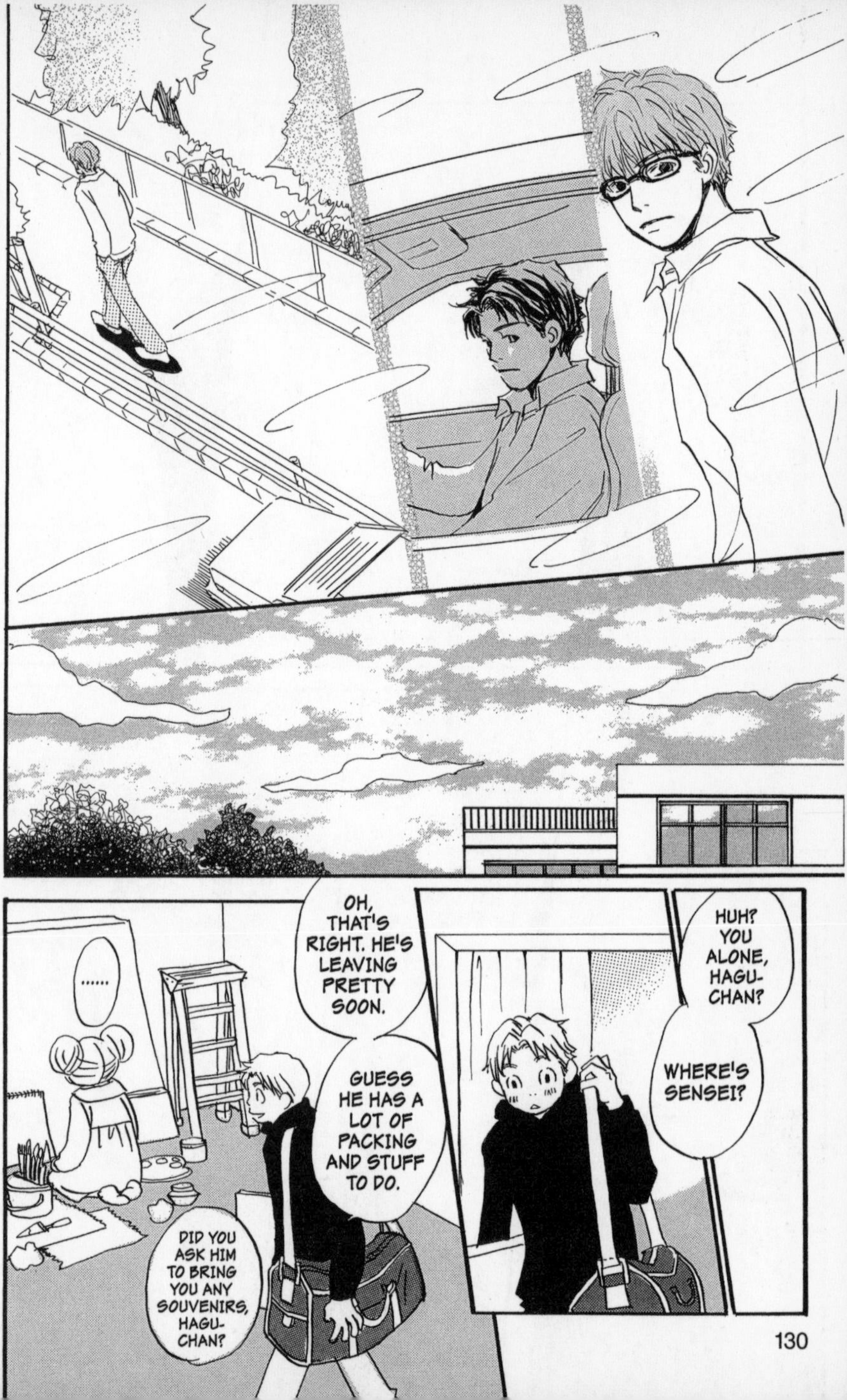
HUH? YOU ALONE, HAGU-CHAN?
WHERE'S SENSEI?
OH, THAT'S RIGHT. HE'S LEAVING PRETTY SOON.
......
GUESS HE HAS A LOT OF PACKING AND STUFF TO DO.
DID YOU ASK HIM TO BRING YOU ANY SOUVENIRS, HAGU-CHAN?

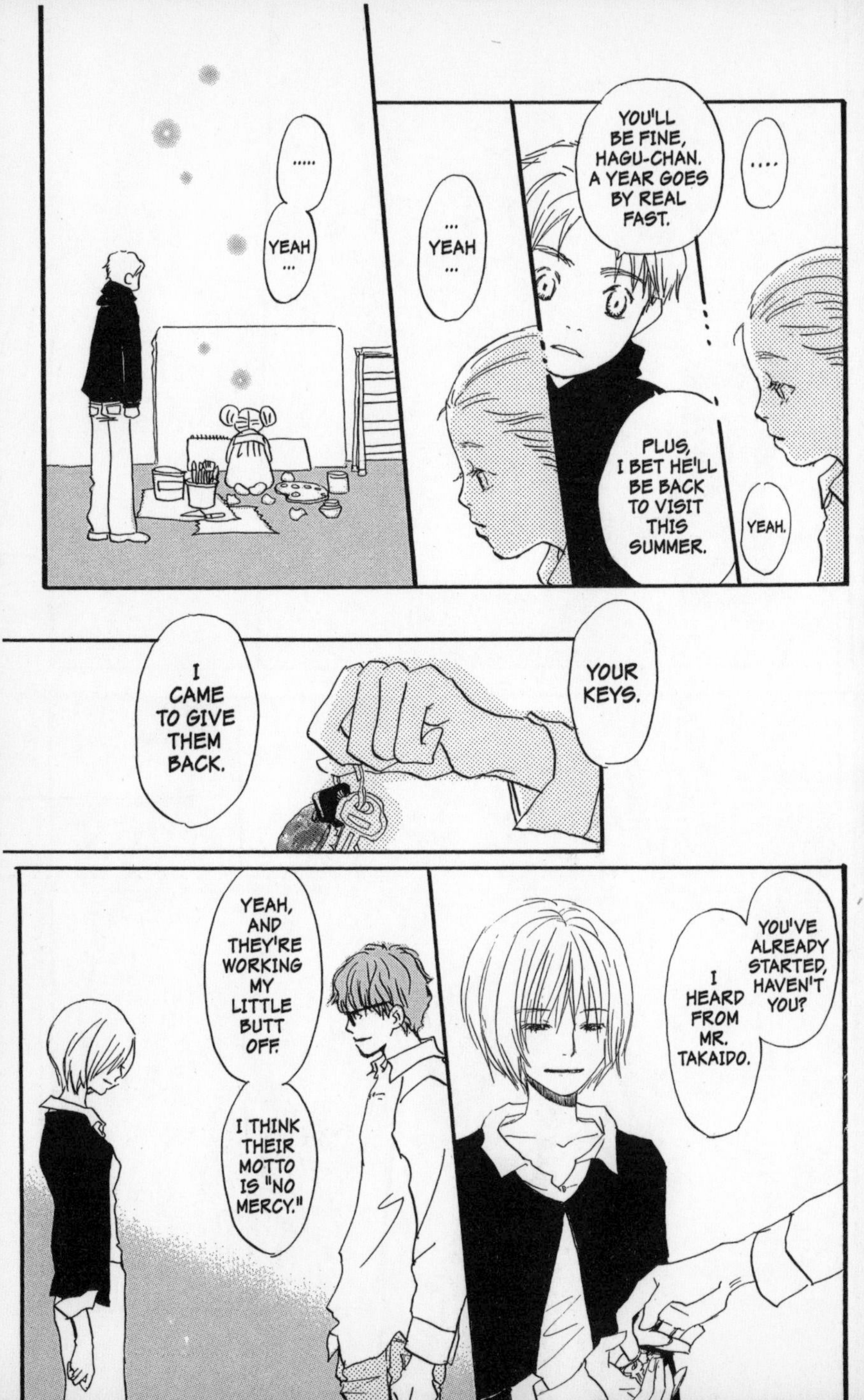
YOU'LL BE FINE, HAGU-CHAN. A YEAR GOES BY REAL FAST.
....
PLUS, I BET HE'LL BE BACK TO VISIT THIS SUMMER.
YEAH.
... YEAH ...
.....
YEAH ...
YOUR KEYS.
I CAME TO GIVE THEM BACK.
YOU'VE ALREADY STARTED, HAVEN'T YOU?
I HEARD FROM MR. TAKAIDO.
YEAH, AND THEY'RE WORKING MY LITTLE BUTT OFF.
I THINK THEIR MOTTO IS "NO MERCY."

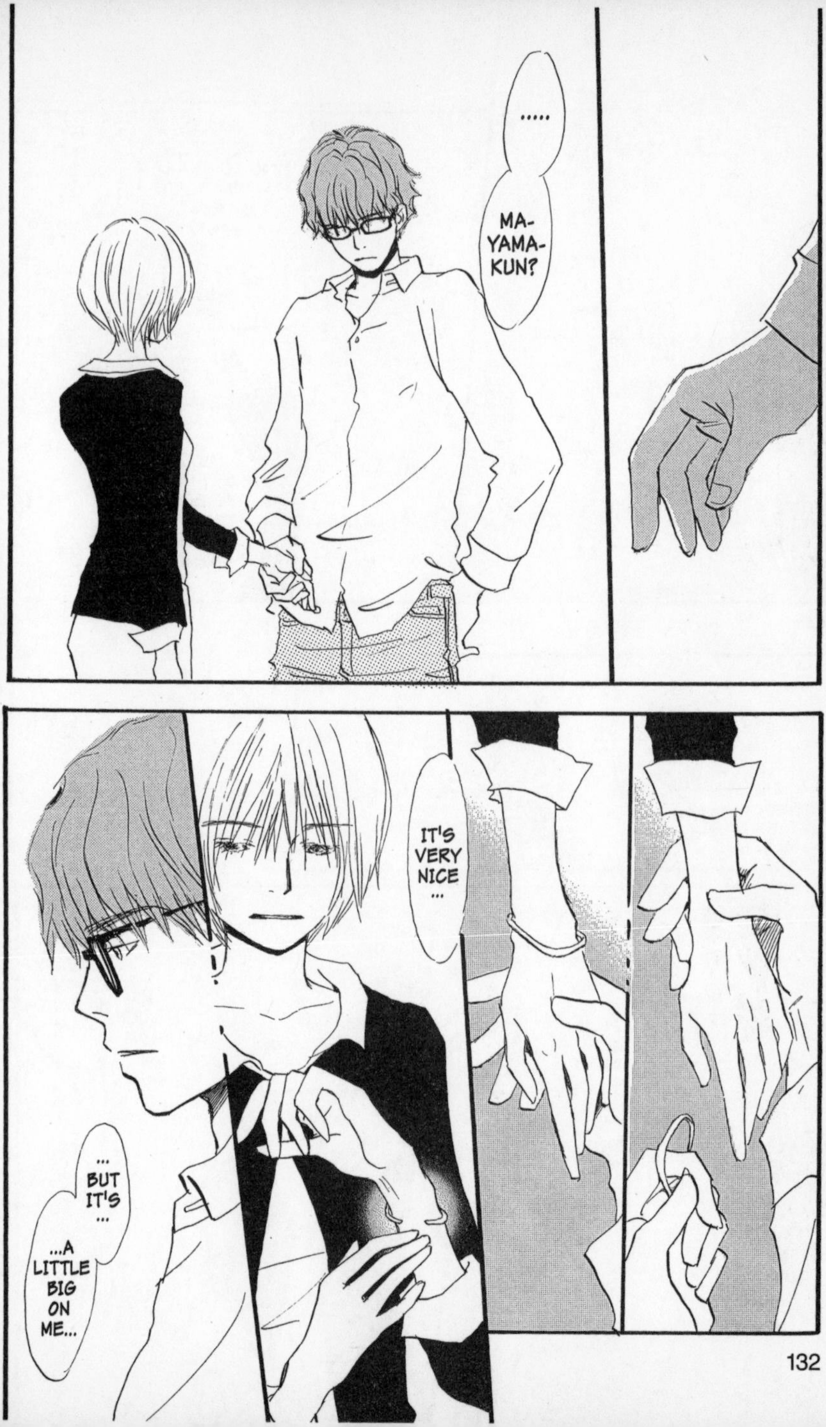
.....
MA-YAMA-KUN?
IT'S VERY NICE ...
... BUT IT'S ...
...A LITTLE BIG ON ME...

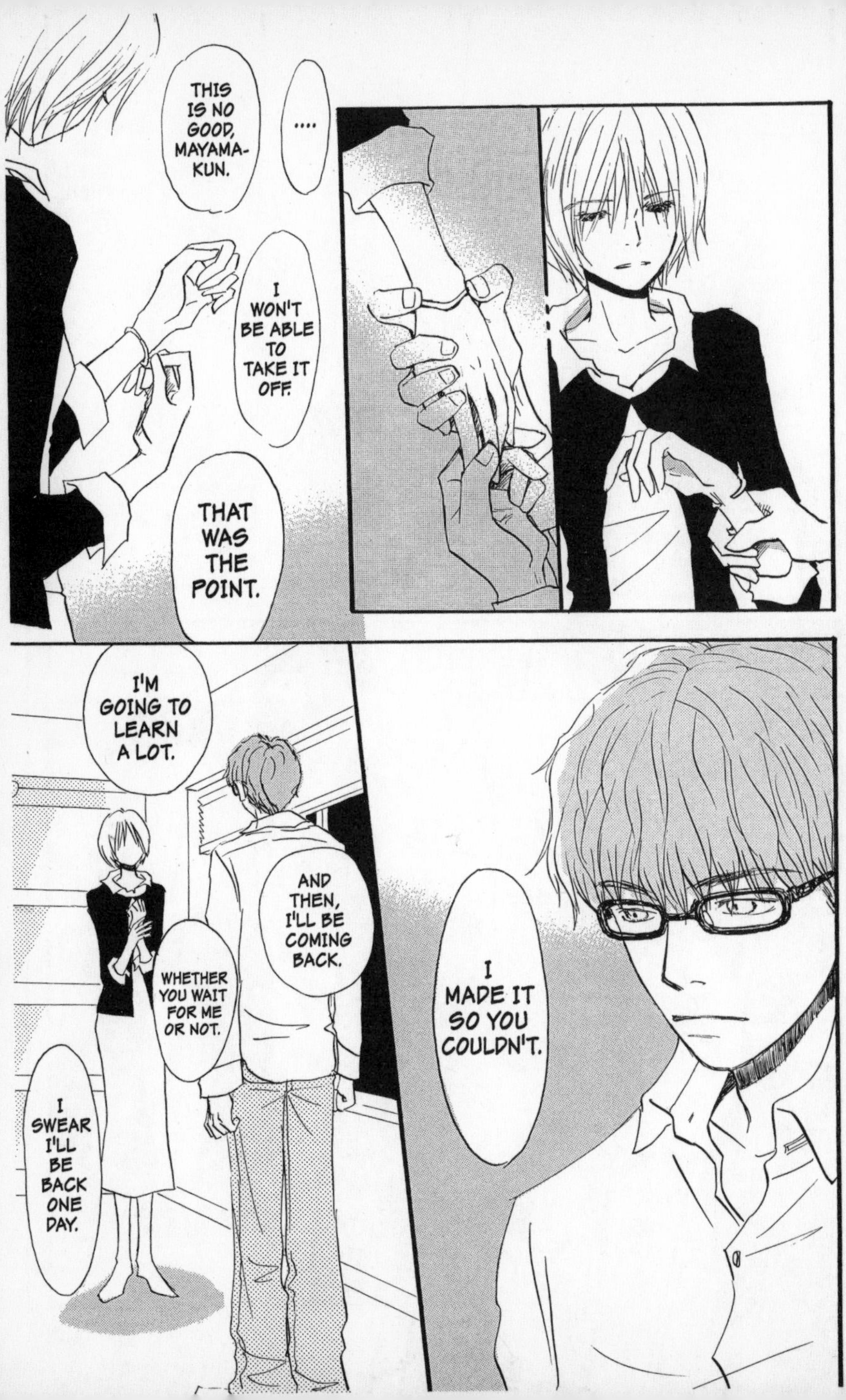
....
THIS IS NO GOOD, MAYAMA-KUN.
I WON'T BE ABLE TO TAKE IT OFF.
THAT WAS THE POINT.
I MADE IT SO YOU COULDN'T.
I'M GOING TO LEARN A LOT.
AND THEN, I'LL BE COMING BACK.
WHETHER YOU WAIT FOR ME OR NOT.
I SWEAR I'LL BE BACK ONE DAY.

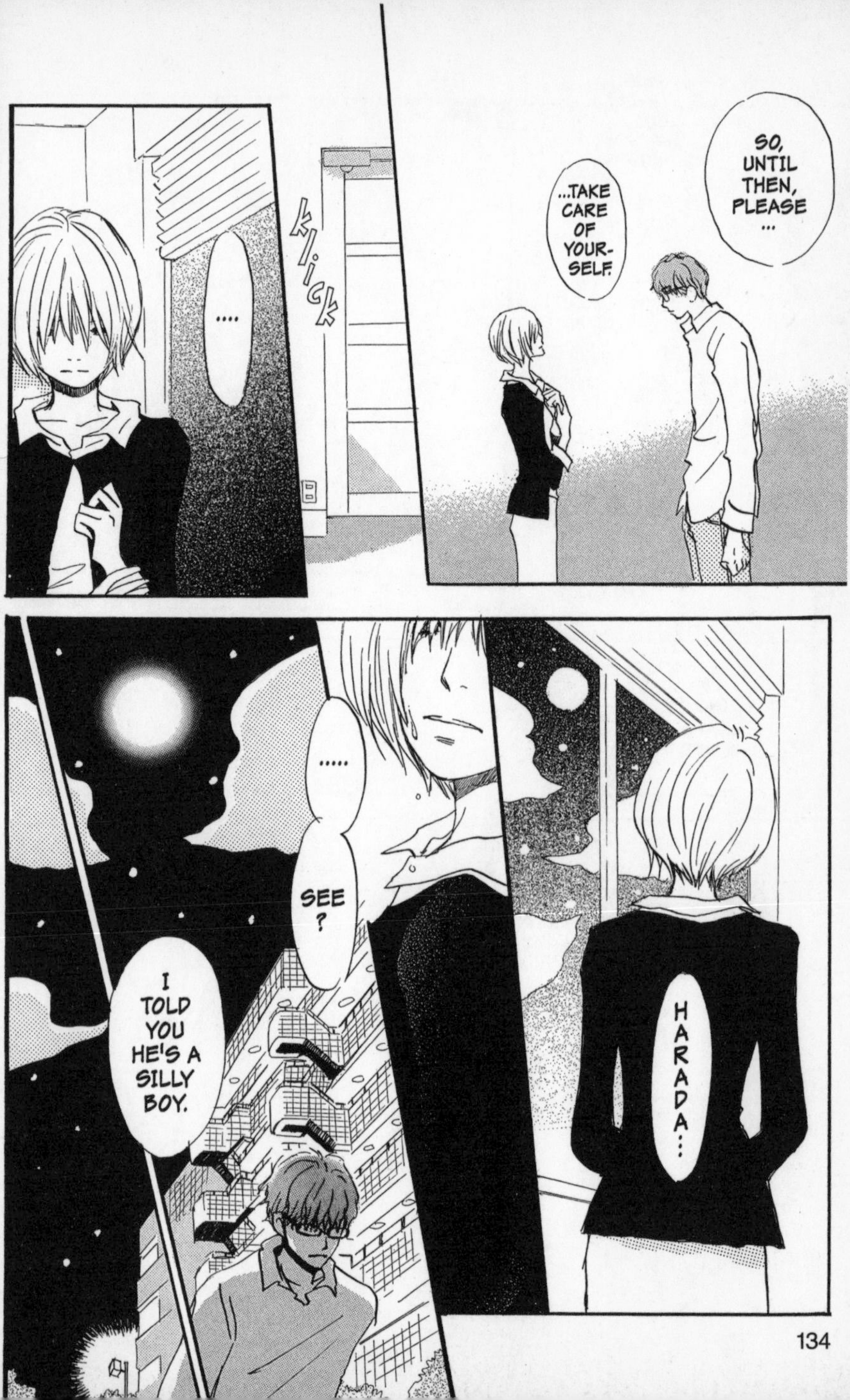
SO, UNTIL THEN, PLEASE ...
...TAKE CARE OF YOURSELF.
KLICK
....
HARADA...
.....
SEE?
I TOLD YOU HE'S A SILLY BOY.

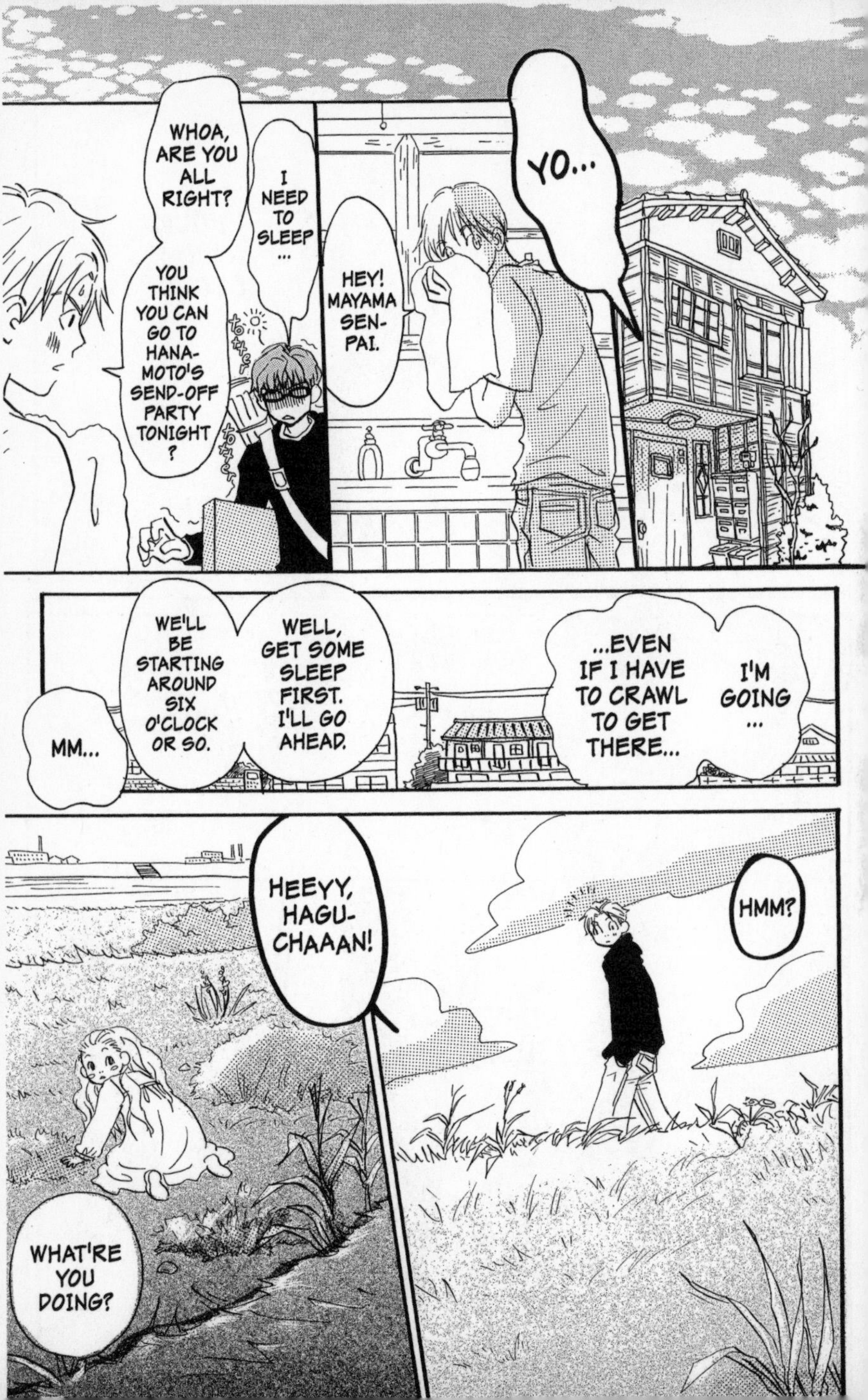
YO...
HEY! MAYAMA SEN-PAI.
WHOA, ARE YOU ALL RIGHT?
I NEED TO SLEEP ...
totter totter
YOU THINK YOU CAN GO TO HANA-MOTO'S SEND-OFF PARTY TONIGHT?
I'M GOING ...
...EVEN IF I HAVE TO CRAWL TO GET THERE...
WELL, GET SOME SLEEP FIRST. I'LL GO AHEAD.
WE'LL BE STARTING AROUND SIX O'CLOCK OR SO.
MM...
HEEYY, HAGU-CHAAAN!
HMM?
WHAT'RE YOU DOING?

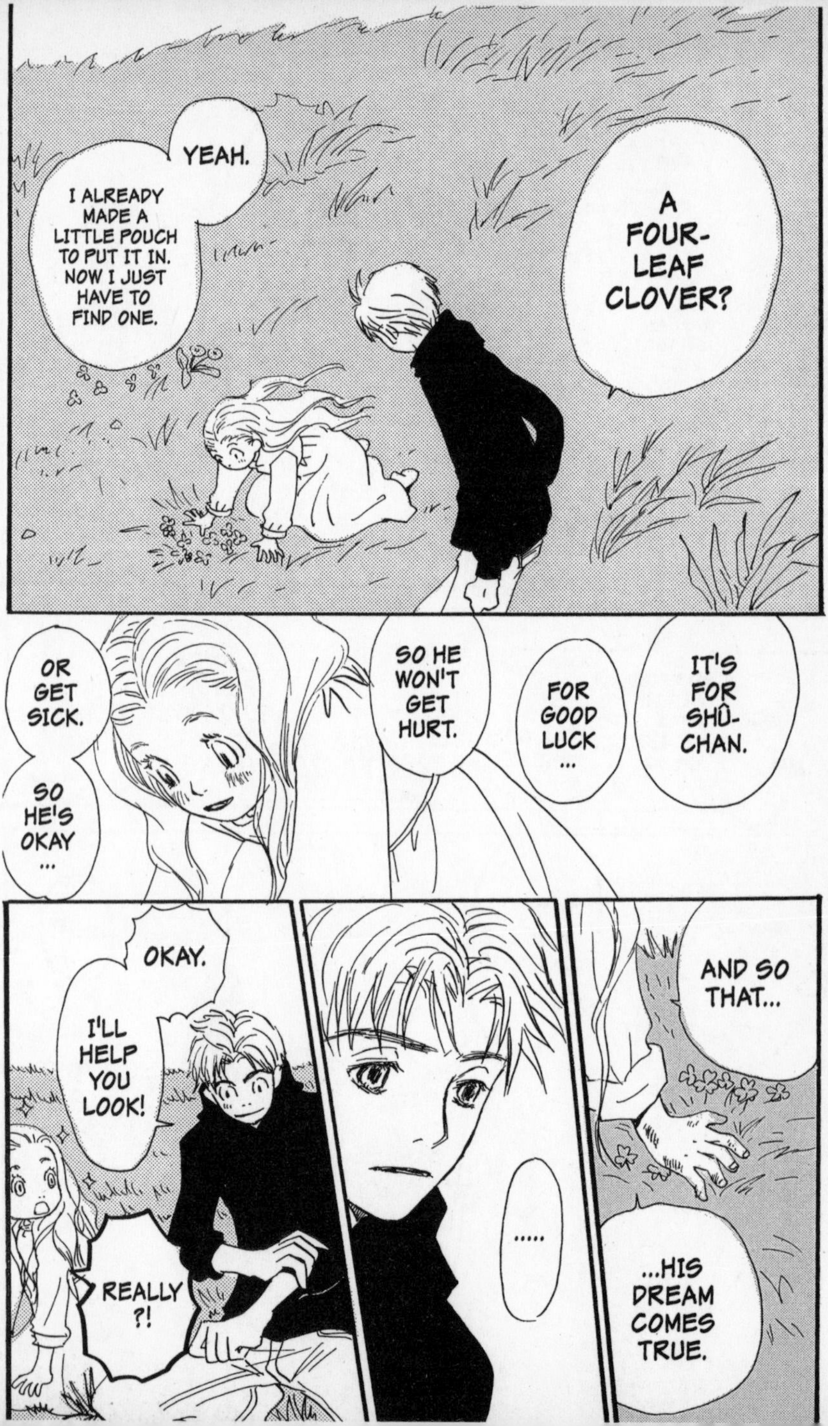
A FOUR-LEAF CLOVER?
YEAH.
I ALREADY MADE A LITTLE POUCH TO PUT IT IN. NOW I JUST HAVE TO FIND ONE.
IT'S FOR SHÛ-CHAN.
FOR GOOD LUCK...
SO HE WON'T GET HURT.
OR GET SICK.
SO HE'S OKAY...
AND SO THAT...
...HIS DREAM COMES TRUE.
.....
OKAY.
I'LL HELP YOU LOOK!
REALLY?!

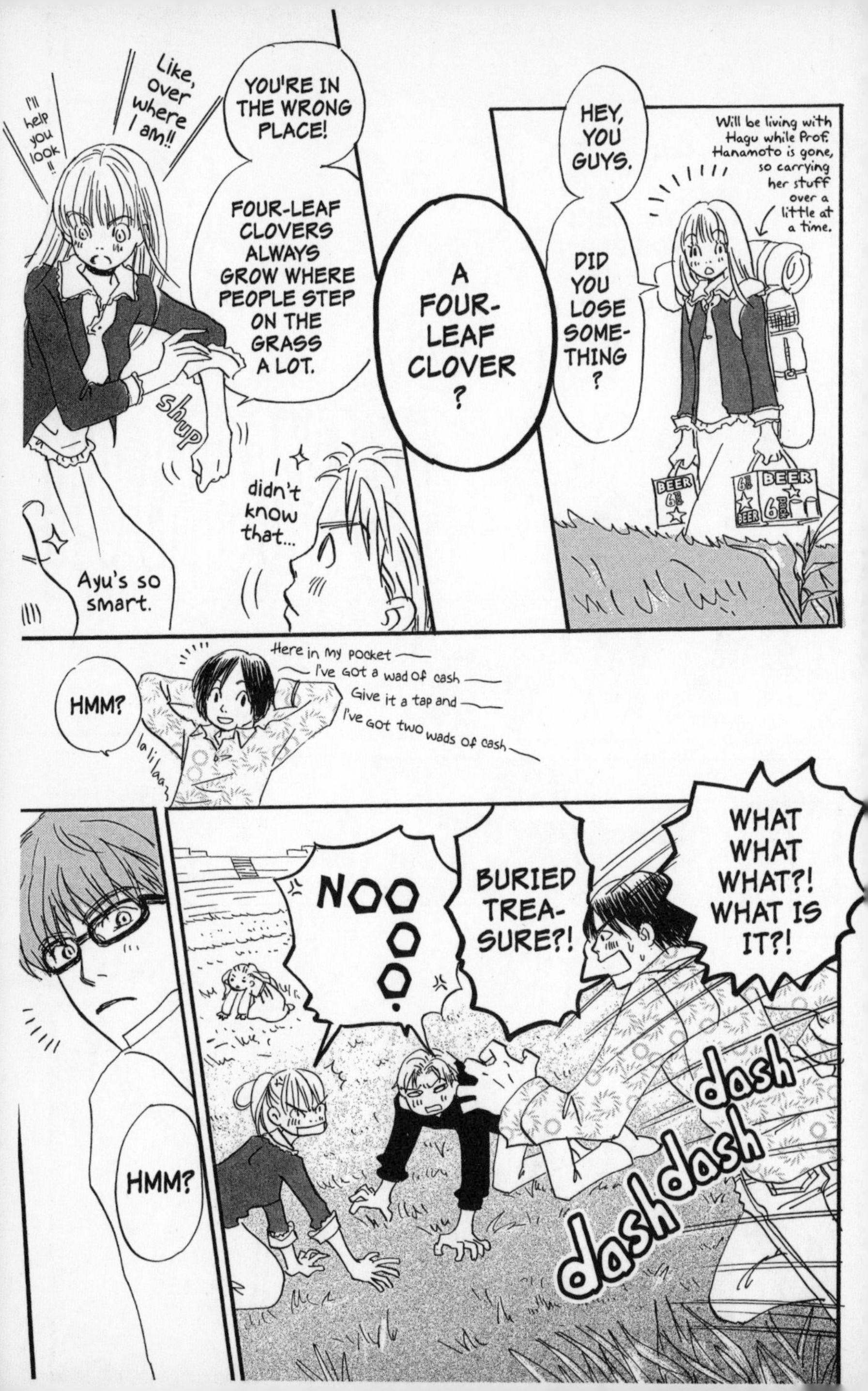
HEY, YOU GUYS.
DID YOU LOSE SOME-THING?
Will be living with Hagu while Prof. Hanamoto is gone, so carrying her stuff over a little at a time.
BEER
A FOUR-LEAF CLOVER?
YOU'RE IN THE WRONG PLACE!
FOUR-LEAF CLOVERS ALWAYS GROW WHERE PEOPLE STEP ON THE GRASS A LOT.
Like, over where I am!!
I'll help you look!!
shup
I didn't know that...
Ayu's so smart.
Here in my pocket
I've got a wad of cash
Give it a tap and
I've got two wads of cash
HMM?
la li laa
WHAT WHAT WHAT?! WHAT IS IT?!
BURIED TREA-SURE?!
NOOOO.
dash dash dash
HMM?

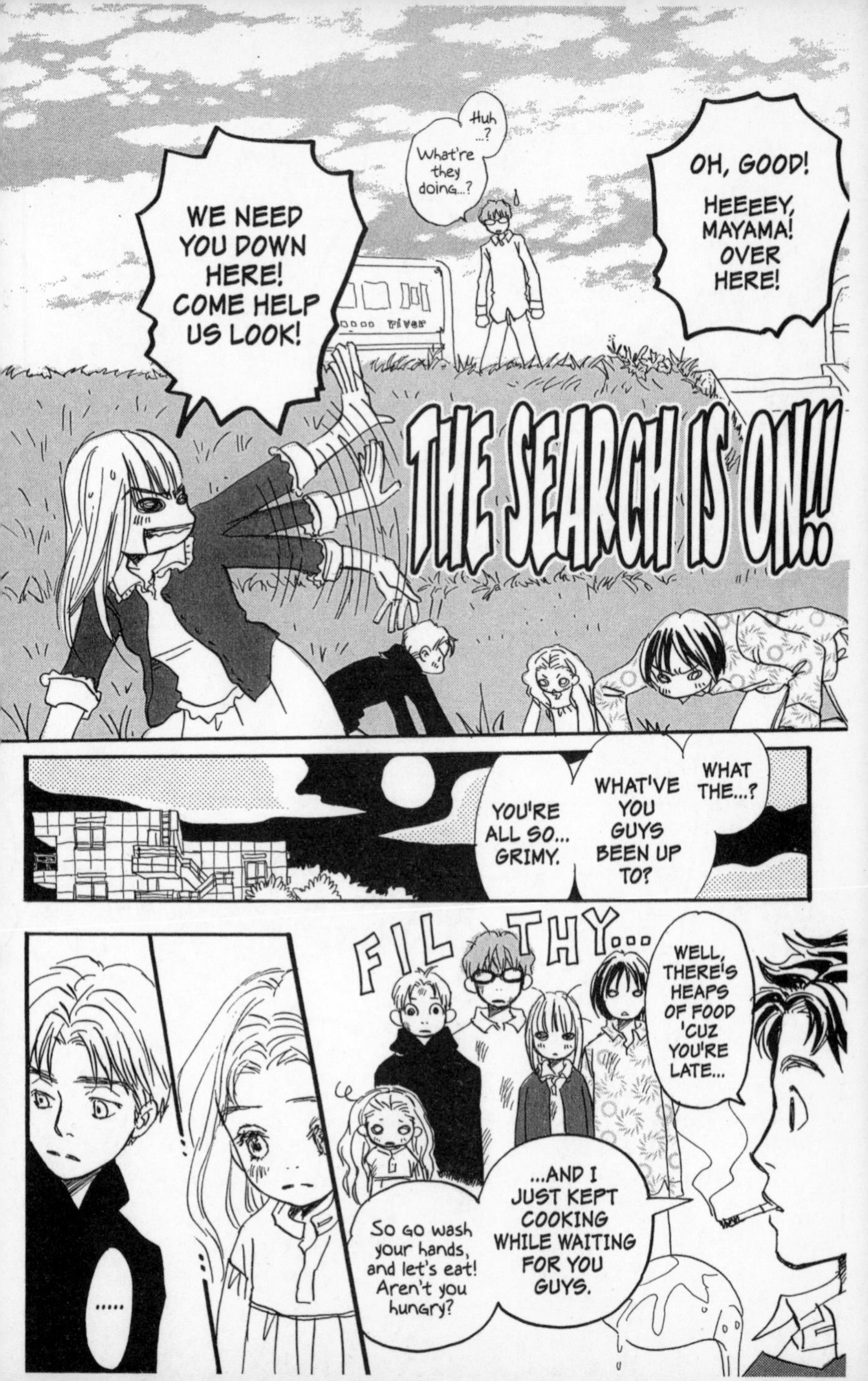
OH, GOOD! HEEEEY, MAYAMA! OVER HERE!
Huh ...? What're they doing...?
WE NEED YOU DOWN HERE! COME HELP US LOOK!
river
THE SEARCH IS ON!!
WHAT THE...?
WHAT'VE YOU GUYS BEEN UP TO?
YOU'RE ALL SO... GRIMY.
FILTHY...
WELL, THERE'S HEAPS OF FOOD 'CUZ YOU'RE LATE...
...AND I JUST KEPT COOKING WHILE WAITING FOR YOU GUYS.
So go wash your hands, and let's eat! Aren't you hungry?
.....

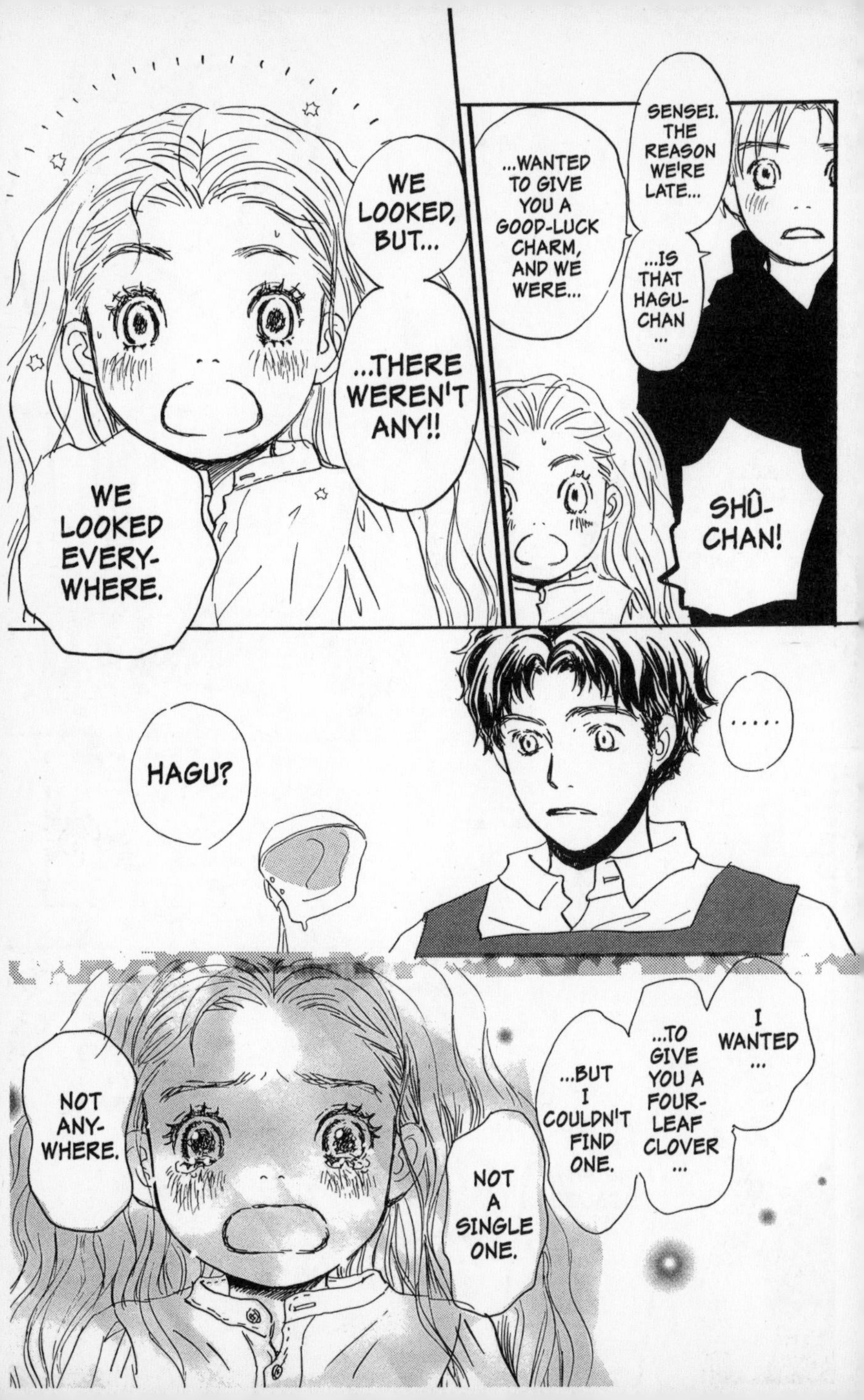
SENSEI. THE REASON WE'RE LATE...
...IS THAT HAGU-CHAN ...
...WANTED TO GIVE YOU A GOOD-LUCK CHARM, AND WE WERE...
SHÛ-CHAN!
WE LOOKED, BUT...
...THERE WEREN'T ANY!!
WE LOOKED EVERY-WHERE.
.....
HAGU?
I WANTED ...
...TO GIVE YOU A FOUR-LEAF CLOVER ...
...BUT I COULDN'T FIND ONE.
NOT A SINGLE ONE.
NOT ANY-WHERE.

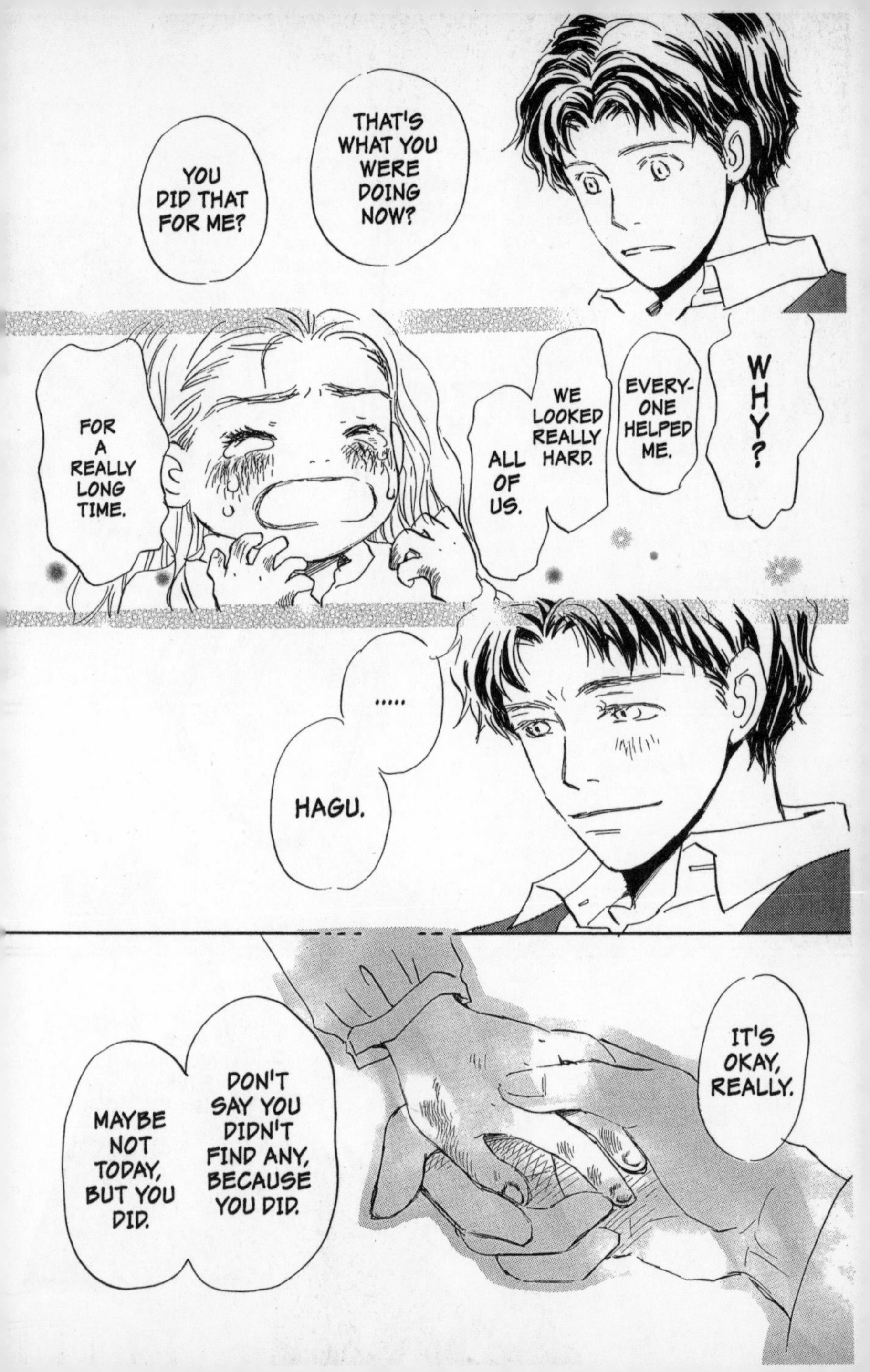
THAT'S WHAT YOU WERE DOING NOW?
YOU DID THAT FOR ME?
WHY?
EVERY-ONE HELPED ME.
WE LOOKED REALLY HARD.
ALL OF US.
FOR A REALLY LONG TIME.
.....
HAGU.
IT'S OKAY, REALLY.
DON'T SAY YOU DIDN'T FIND ANY, BECAUSE YOU DID.
MAYBE NOT TODAY, BUT YOU DID.

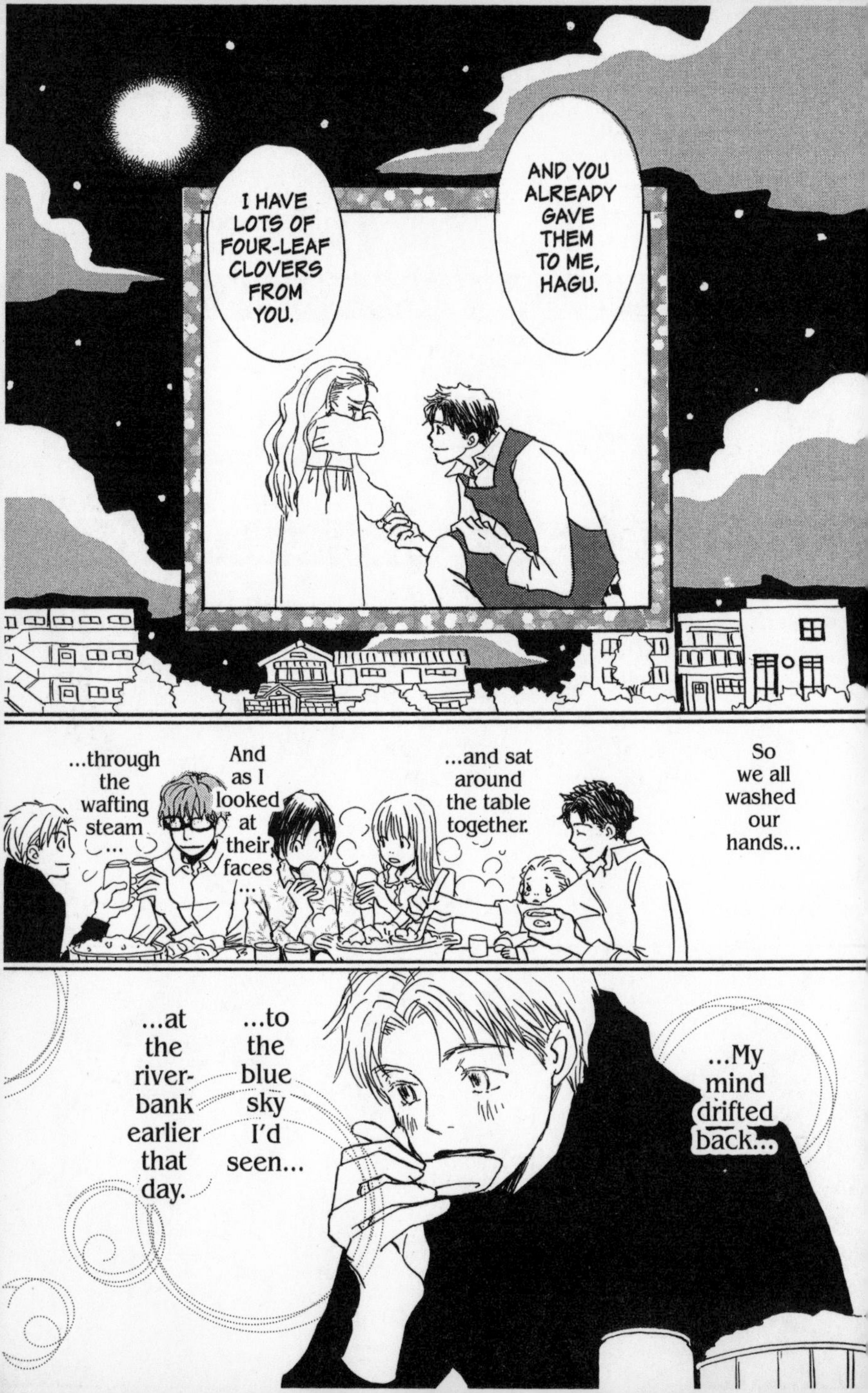
AND YOU ALREADY GAVE THEM TO ME, HAGU.
I HAVE LOTS OF FOUR-LEAF CLOVERS FROM YOU.
So we all washed our hands...
...and sat around the table together.
And as I looked at their faces...
...through the wafting steam...
...My mind drifted back...
...to the blue sky I'd seen...
...at the river-bank earlier that day.

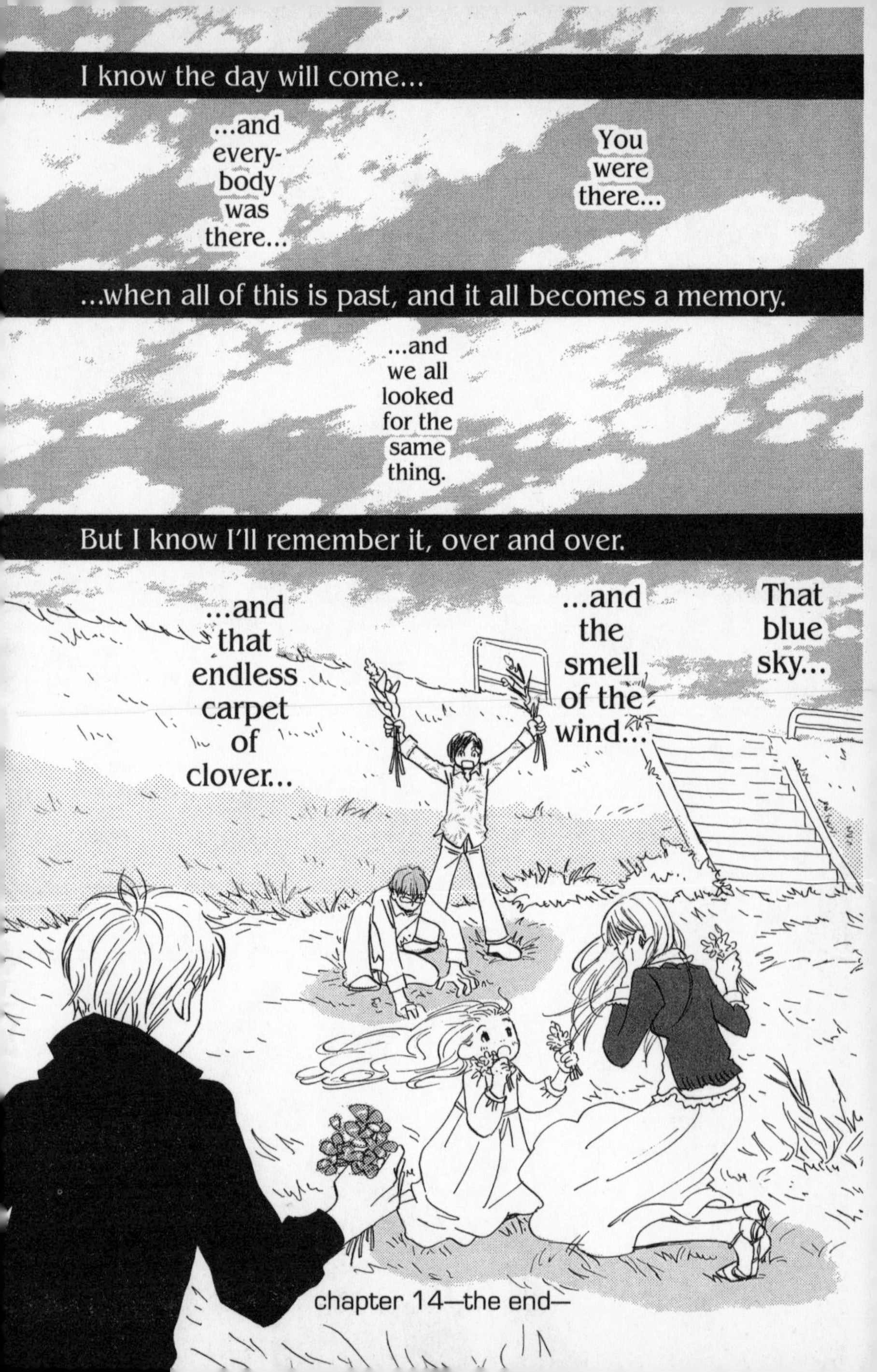
I know the day will come...
You were there...
...and everybody was there...
...when all of this is past, and it all becomes a memory.
...and we all looked for the same thing.
But I know I'll remember it, over and over.
That blue sky...
...and the smell of the wind...
...and that endless carpet of clover...
chapter 14—the end—

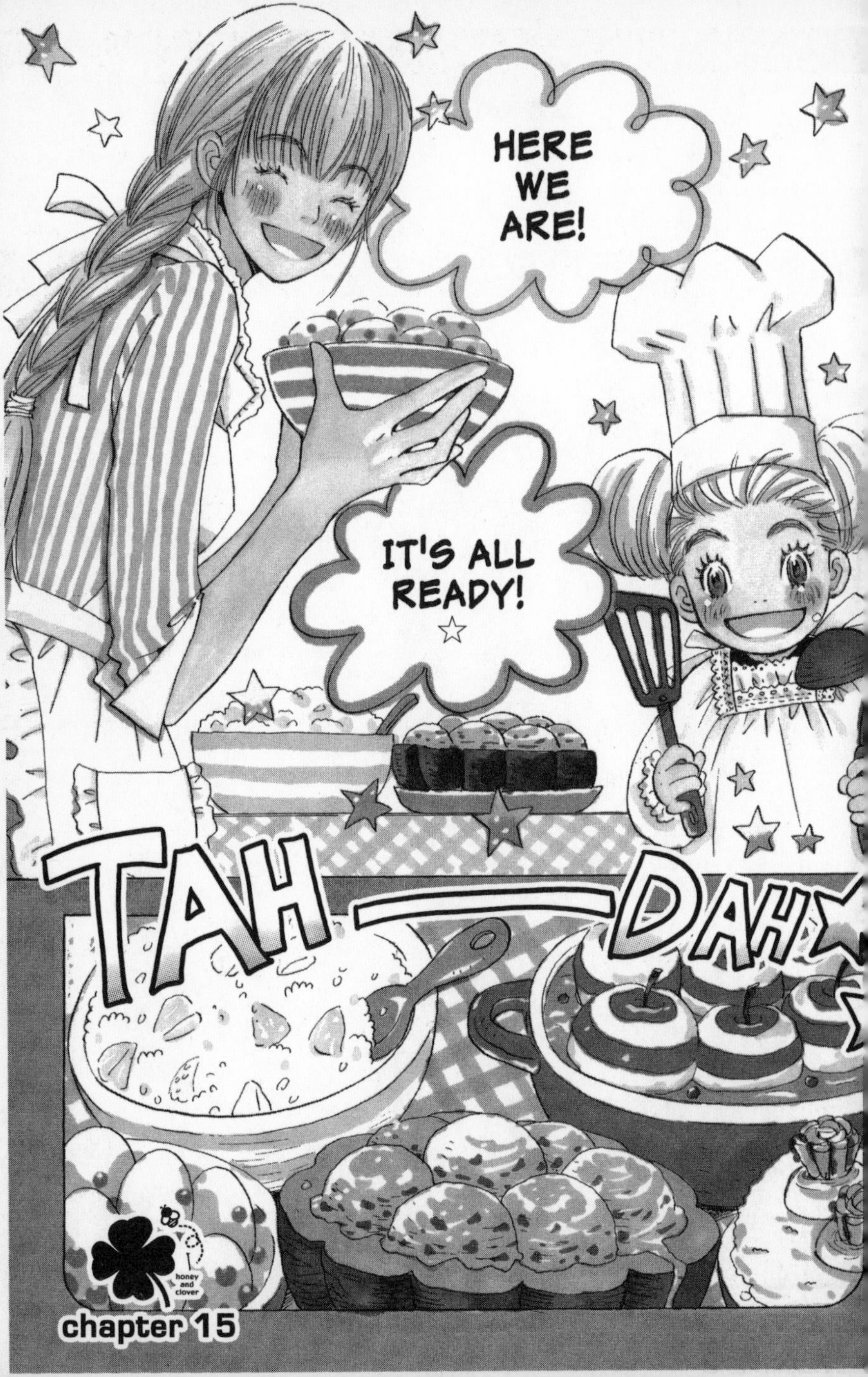
HERE WE ARE!
IT'S ALL READY!
TAH—DAH
honey and clover
chapter 15

honey and clover™

chapter 15

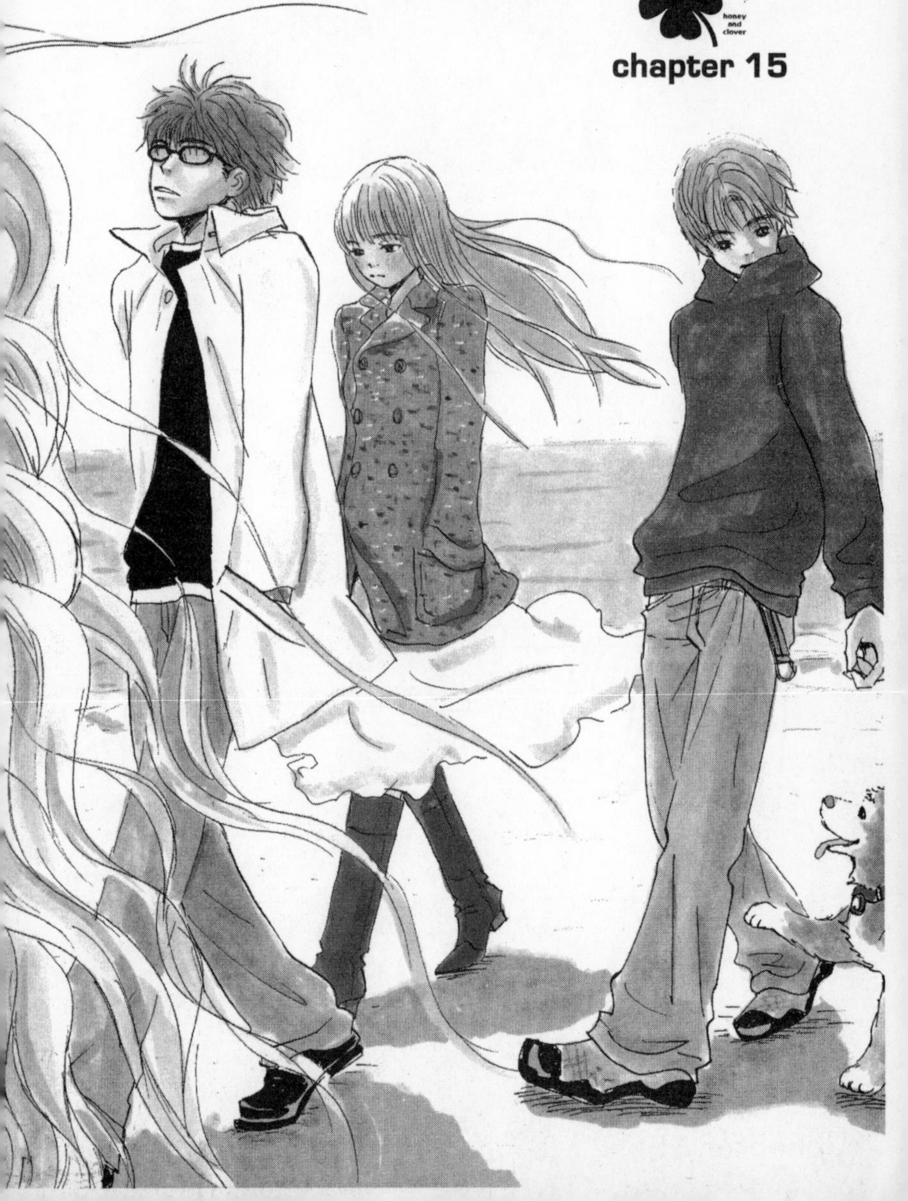

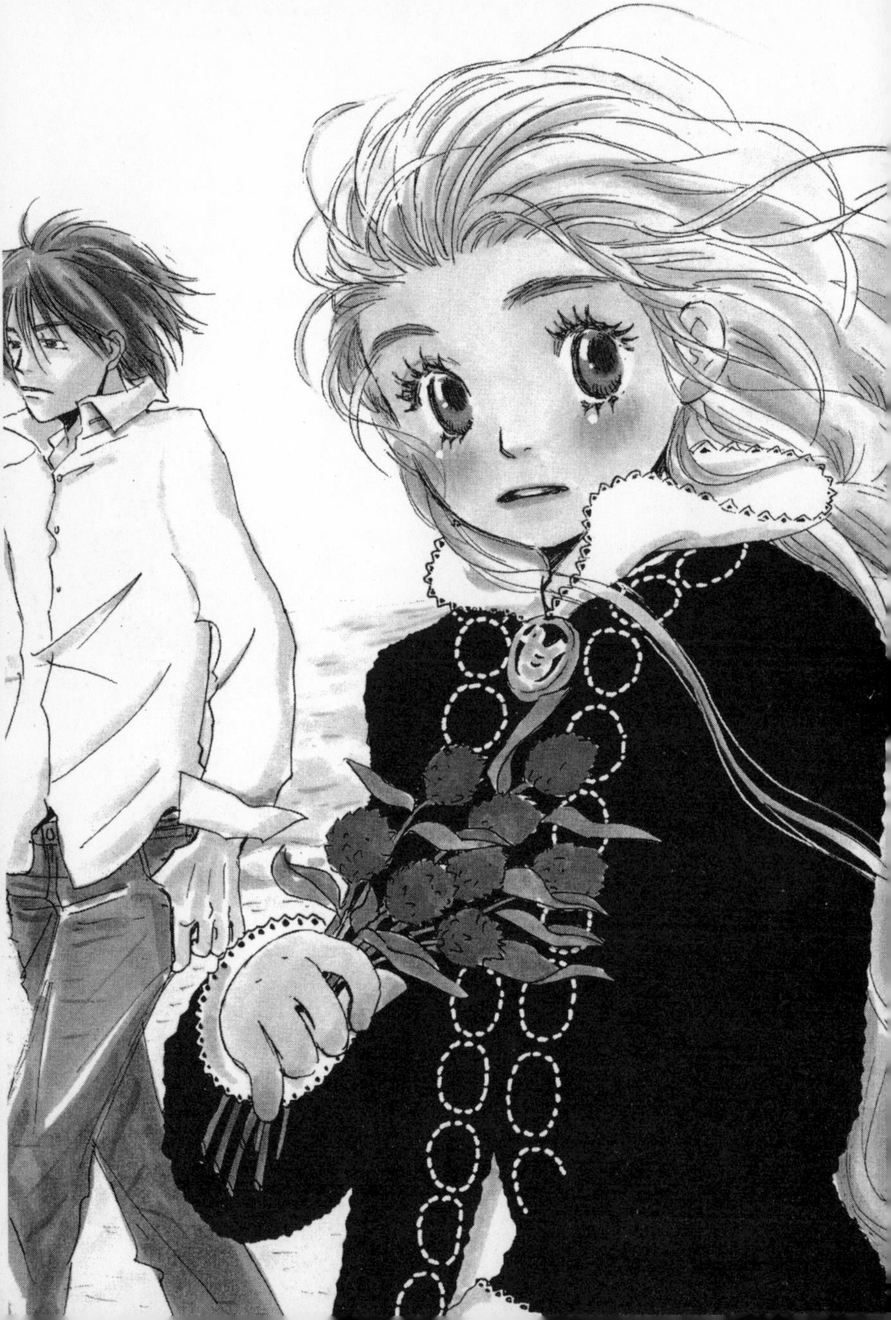

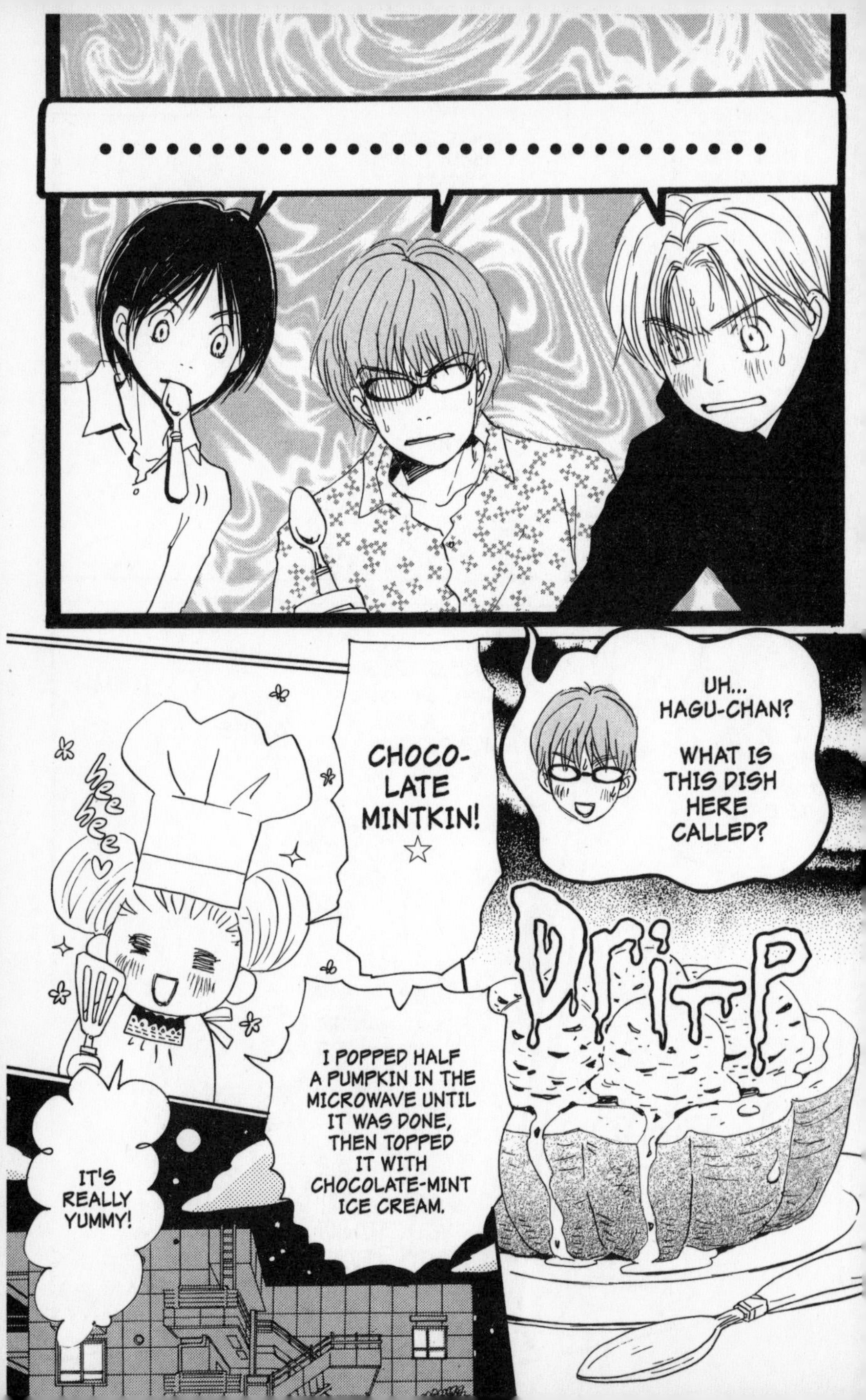

•••••••••••••••••••••••••••••
UH... HAGU-CHAN? WHAT IS THIS DISH HERE CALLED?
DRIP
CHOCO-LATE MINTKIN! ☆
hee hee ♥
I POPPED HALF A PUMPKIN IN THE MICROWAVE UNTIL IT WAS DONE, THEN TOPPED IT WITH CHOCOLATE-MINT ICE CREAM.
IT'S REALLY YUMMY!

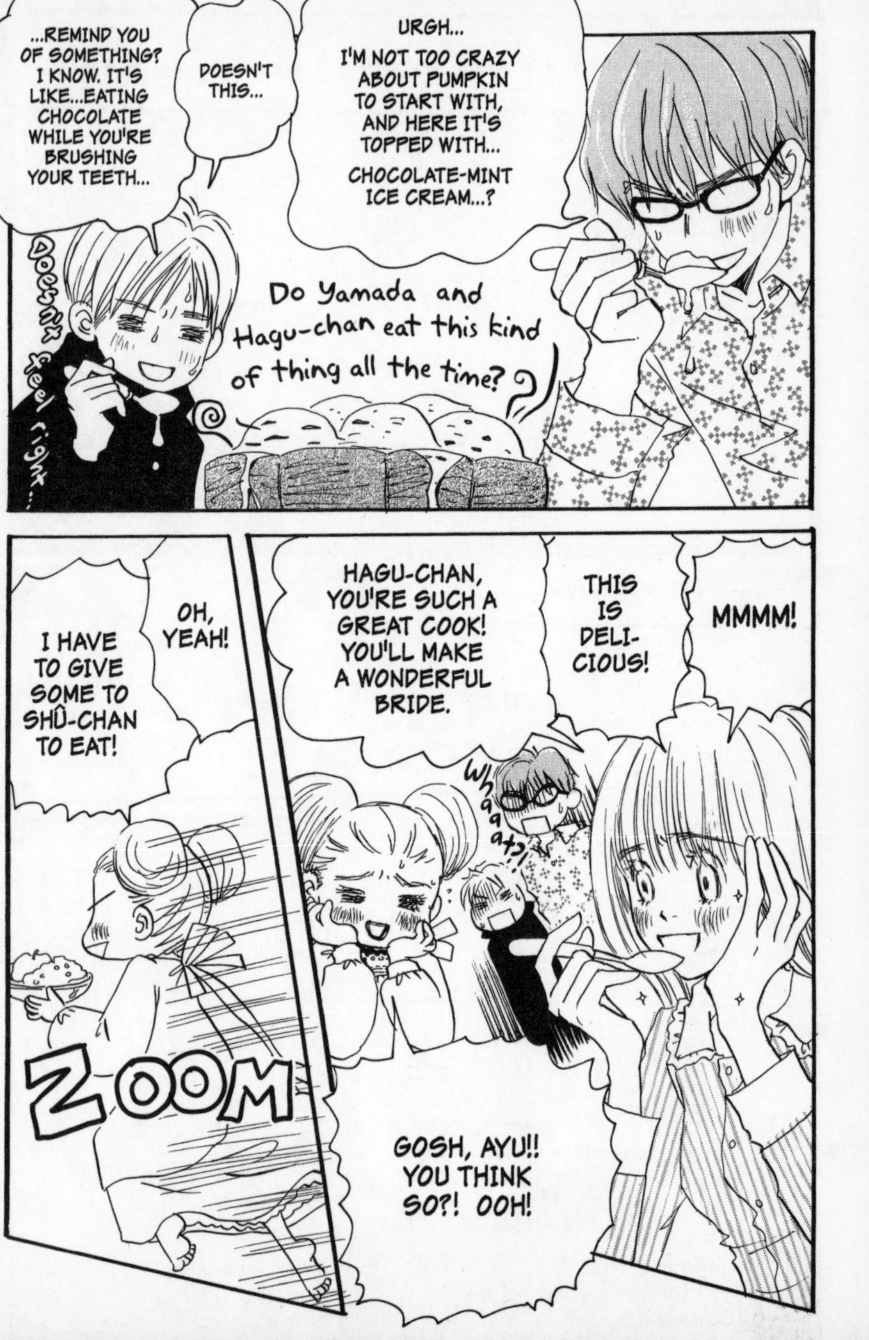
URGH... I'M NOT TOO CRAZY ABOUT PUMPKIN TO START WITH, AND HERE IT'S TOPPED WITH... CHOCOLATE-MINT ICE CREAM...?
DOESN'T THIS...
...REMIND YOU OF SOMETHING? I KNOW. IT'S LIKE...EATING CHOCOLATE WHILE YOU'RE BRUSHING YOUR TEETH...
Do Yamada and Hagu-chan eat this kind of thing all the time?
Doesn't feel right...
MMMM!
THIS IS DELICIOUS!
HAGU-CHAN, YOU'RE SUCH A GREAT COOK! YOU'LL MAKE A WONDERFUL BRIDE.
Whaaat?!
GOSH, AYU!! YOU THINK SO?! OOH!
OH, YEAH!
I HAVE TO GIVE SOME TO SHÛ-CHAN TO EAT!
ZOOM

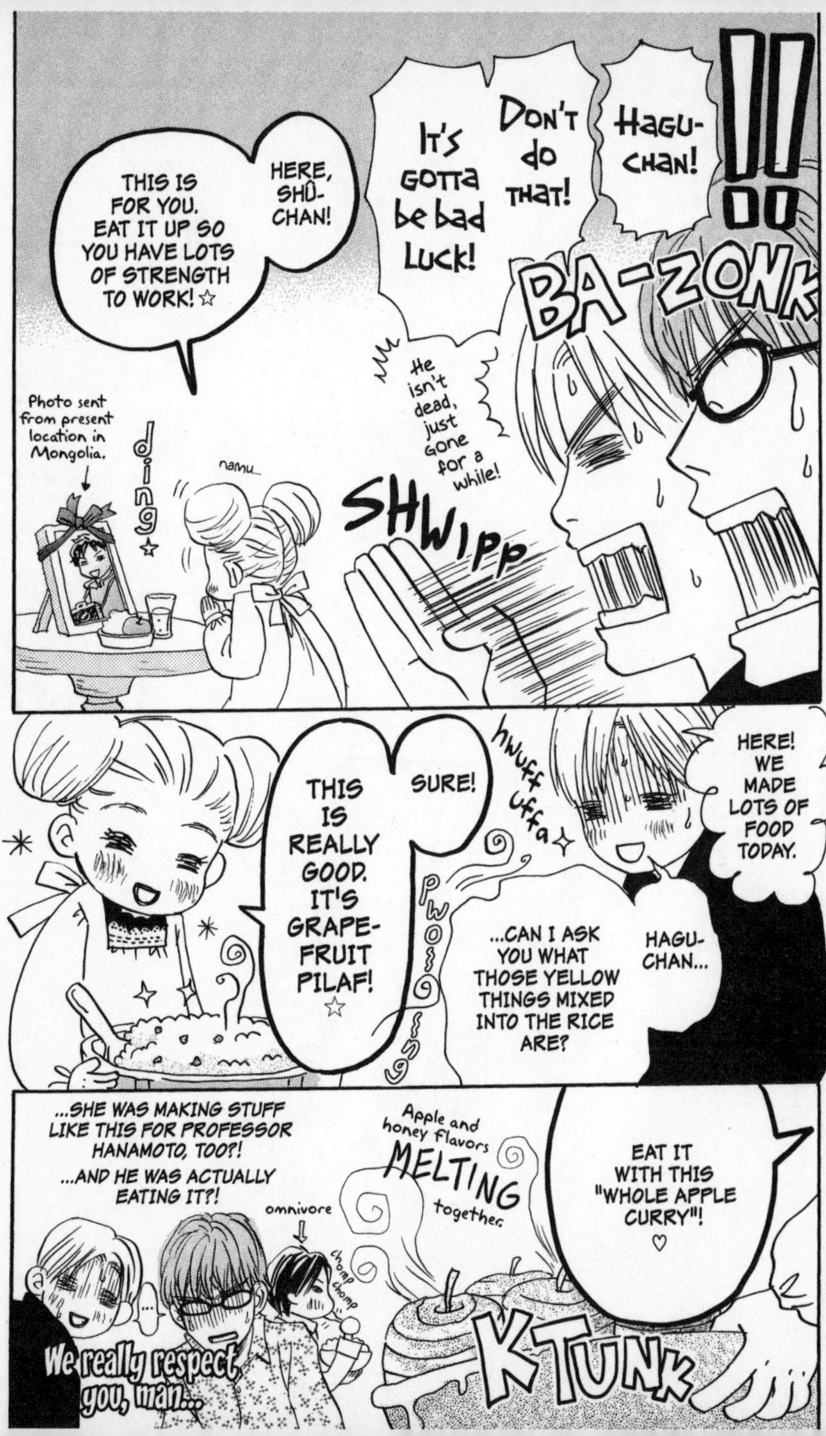

!!
Hagu-chan!
Don't do that!
It's gotta be bad luck!
BA-ZONK
Here, Shû-chan!
This is for you. Eat it up so you have lots of strength to work! ☆
He isn't dead, just gone for a while!
SHWIPP
namu...
ding☆
Photo sent from present location in Mongolia.
Here! We made lots of food today.
Hagu-chan...
...Can I ask you what those yellow things mixed into the rice are?
hwuff uffa
Sure!
This is really good. It's grapefruit pilaf! ☆
Eat it with this "whole apple curry"! ♡
KTUNK
Apple and honey flavors MELTING together.
...She was making stuff like this for Professor Hanamoto, too?!
...And he was actually eating it?!
omnivore
chomp chomp
...
We really respect you, man...

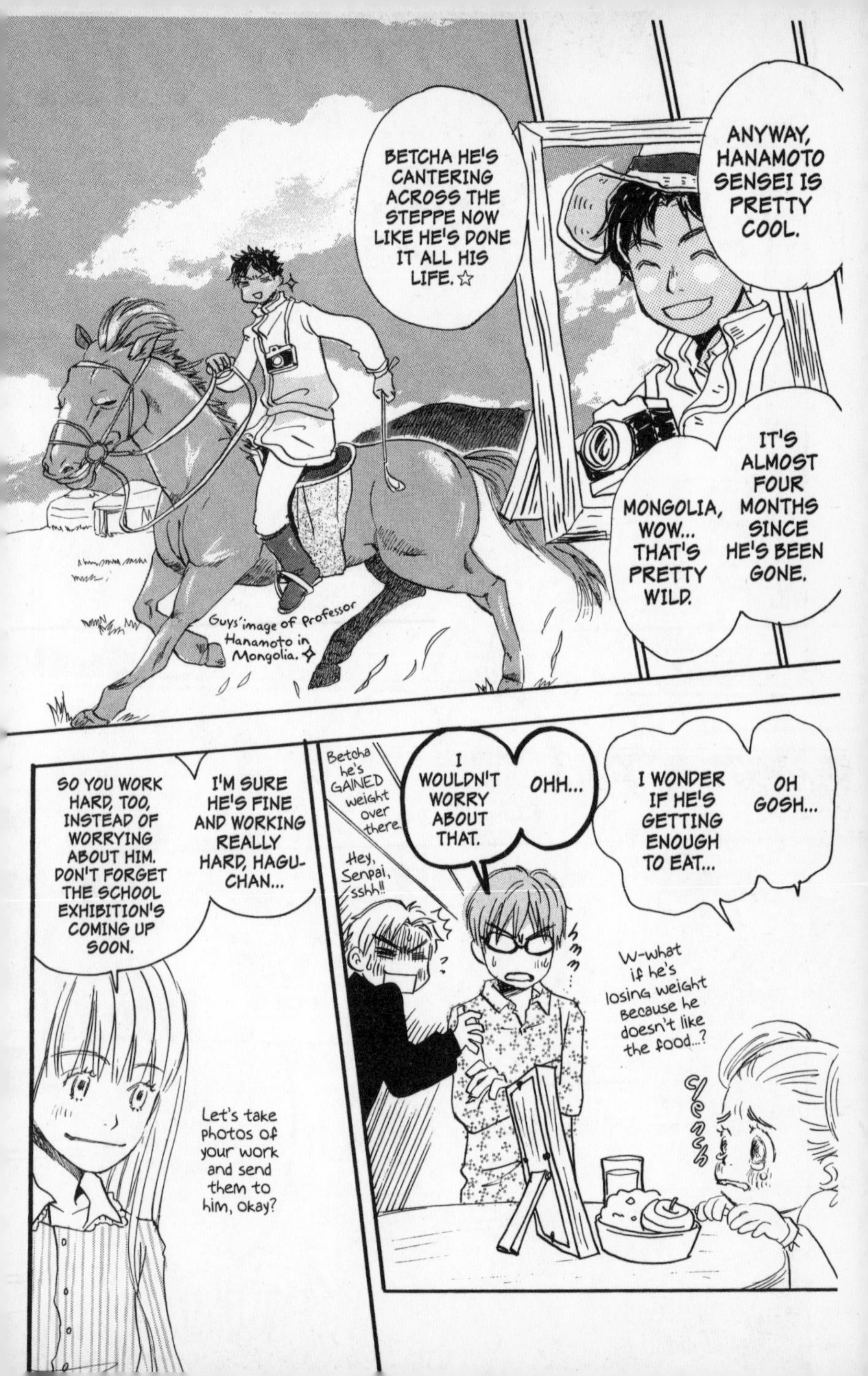
ANYWAY, HANAMOTO SENSEI IS PRETTY COOL.
IT'S ALMOST FOUR MONTHS SINCE HE'S BEEN GONE.
MONGOLIA, WOW... THAT'S PRETTY WILD.
BETCHA HE'S CANTERING ACROSS THE STEPPE NOW LIKE HE'S DONE IT ALL HIS LIFE. ☆
Guys' image of Professor Hanamoto in Mongolia.
OH GOSH...
I WONDER IF HE'S GETTING ENOUGH TO EAT...
OHH...
I WOULDN'T WORRY ABOUT THAT.
Betcha he's GAINED weight over there.
Hey, Senpai, sshh!!
hmm...
W-what if he's losing weight because he doesn't like the food...?
clench
I'M SURE HE'S FINE AND WORKING REALLY HARD, HAGU-CHAN...
SO YOU WORK HARD, TOO, INSTEAD OF WORRYING ABOUT HIM. DON'T FORGET THE SCHOOL EXHIBITION'S COMING UP SOON.
Let's take photos of your work and send them to him, okay?

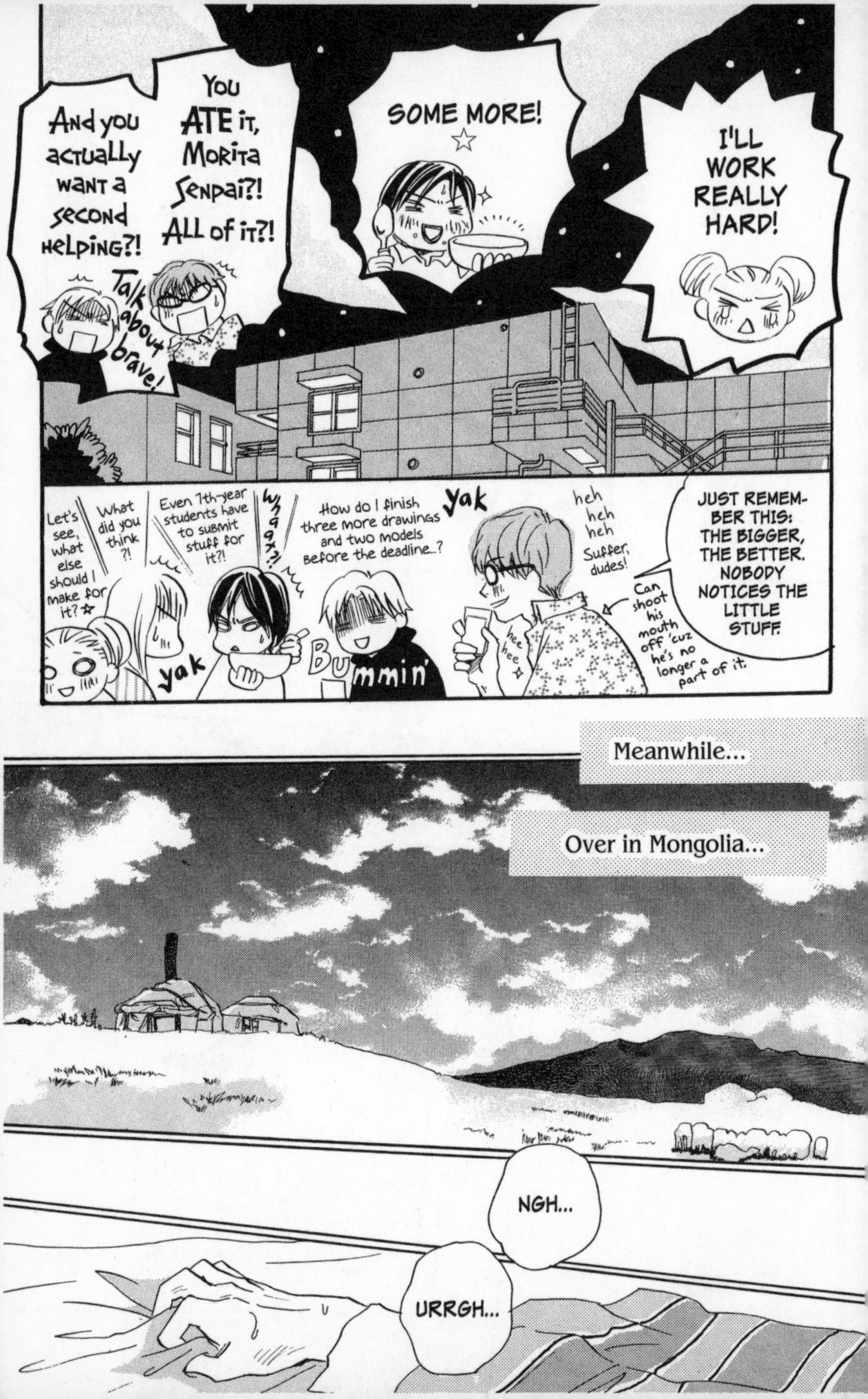
I'LL WORK REALLY HARD!
SOME MORE! ☆
You ATE it, Morita Senpai?! ALL of it?!
And you actually want a second helping?!
Talk about brave!
JUST REMEMBER THIS: THE BIGGER, THE BETTER. NOBODY NOTICES THE LITTLE STUFF.
Can shoot his mouth off 'cuz he's no longer a part of it.
heh heh heh Suffer, dudes!
hee hee
yak
How do I finish three more drawings and two models before the deadline...?
Bummin'
whaaat?!
Even 7th-year students have to submit stuff for it?!
What did you think?!
yak
Let's see, what else should I make for it? ☆
Meanwhile...
Over in Mongolia...
NGH...
URRGH...

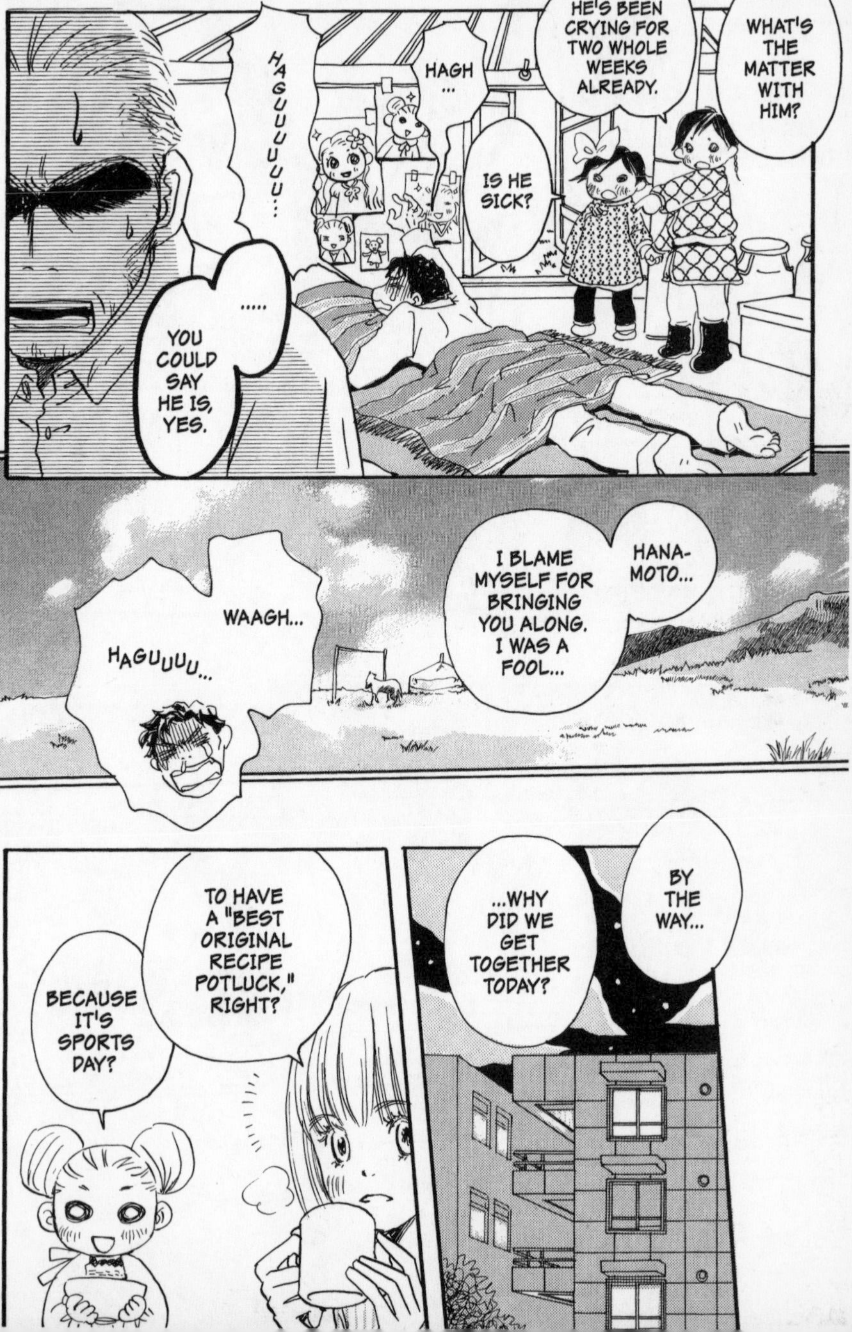
WHAT'S THE MATTER WITH HIM?
HE'S BEEN CRYING FOR TWO WHOLE WEEKS ALREADY.
HAGH...
IS HE SICK?
HAGUUUUUU...
.....
YOU COULD SAY HE IS, YES.
HANA-MOTO...
I BLAME MYSELF FOR BRINGING YOU ALONG. I WAS A FOOL...
WAAGH...
HAGUUUU...
BY THE WAY...
...WHY DID WE GET TOGETHER TODAY?
TO HAVE A "BEST ORIGINAL RECIPE POTLUCK," RIGHT?
BECAUSE IT'S SPORTS DAY?

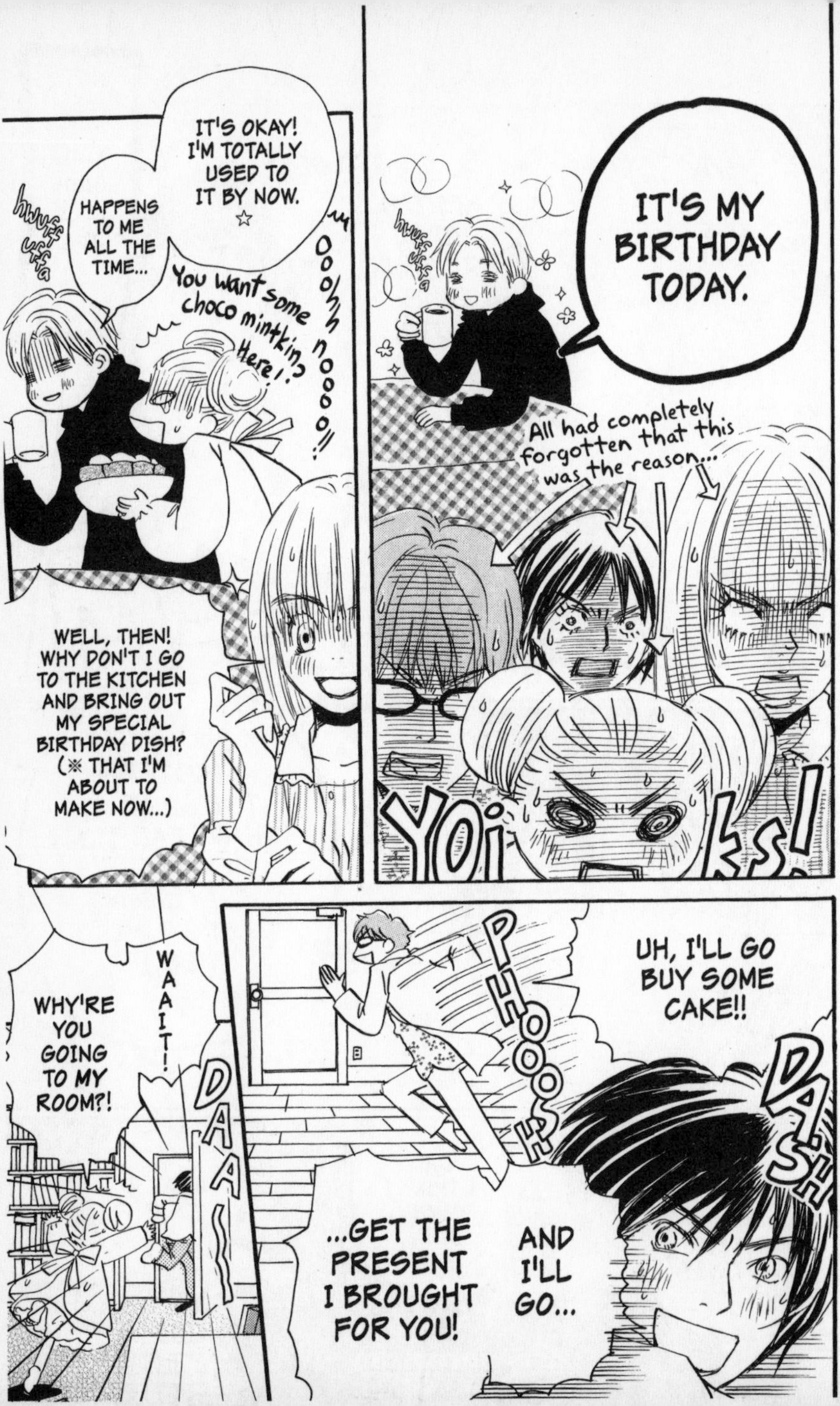
IT'S MY BIRTHDAY TODAY.
hwuff uffa
All had completely forgotten that this was the reason...
YOIKS!
OOOOHH NOOOO!!
IT'S OKAY! I'M TOTALLY USED TO IT BY NOW. ☆
HAPPENS TO ME ALL THE TIME...
hwuff uffa
You want some choco mintkin? Here!
WELL, THEN! WHY DON'T I GO TO THE KITCHEN AND BRING OUT MY SPECIAL BIRTHDAY DISH? (※ THAT I'M ABOUT TO MAKE NOW...)
UH, I'LL GO BUY SOME CAKE!!
DASH
PHOOOSH
AND I'LL GO...
...GET THE PRESENT I BROUGHT FOR YOU!
WAAAIT!
WHY'RE YOU GOING TO MY ROOM?!
DAAA!

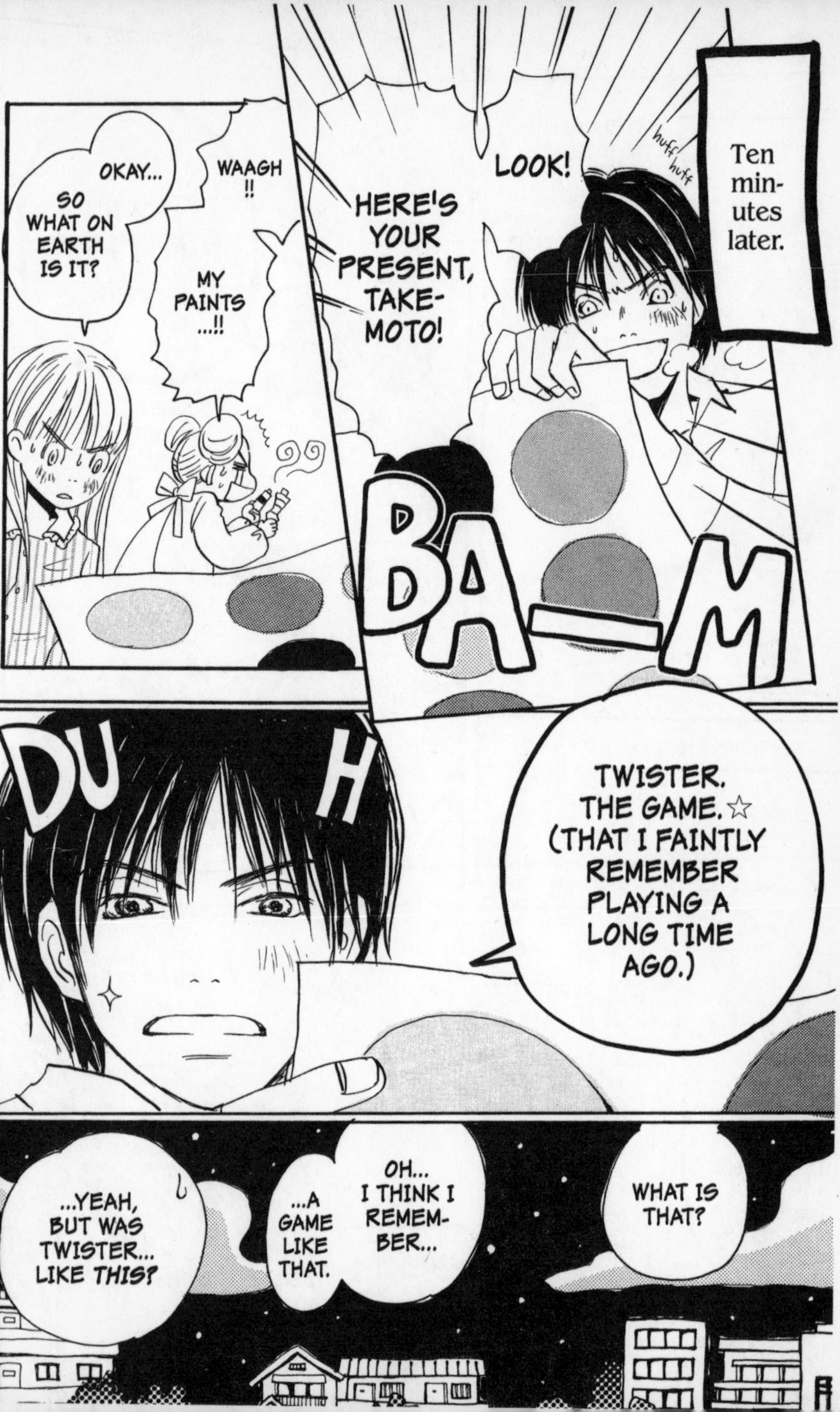
Ten minutes later.
huff huff
LOOK!
HERE'S YOUR PRESENT, TAKE-MOTO!
BA-M
WAAGH!!
MY PAINTS...!!
OKAY... SO WHAT ON EARTH IS IT?
TWISTER. THE GAME.☆ (THAT I FAINTLY REMEMBER PLAYING A LONG TIME AGO.)
DUH
WHAT IS THAT?
OH... I THINK I REMEMBER...
...A GAME LIKE THAT.
...YEAH, BUT WAS TWISTER... LIKE THIS?

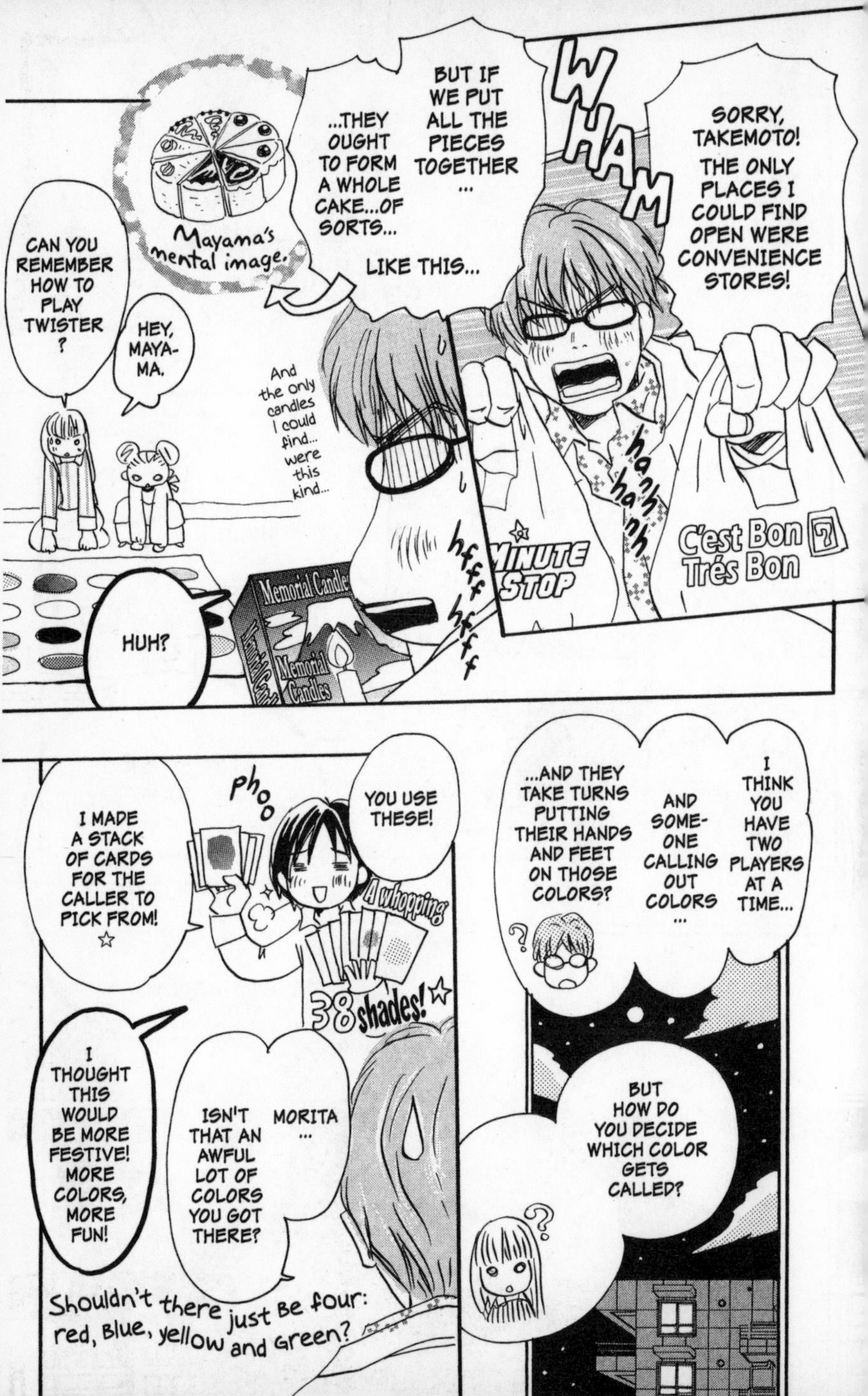
SORRY, TAKEMOTO! THE ONLY PLACES I COULD FIND OPEN WERE CONVENIENCE STORES!
WHAM
hanh hanh
C'est Bon 7 Trés Bon
MINUTE STOP
BUT IF WE PUT ALL THE PIECES TOGETHER ...
...THEY OUGHT TO FORM A WHOLE CAKE...OF SORTS...
LIKE THIS...
Mayama's mental image.
And the only candles I could find... were this kind...
hfff hfff
Memorial Candles
HEY, MAYA-MA.
CAN YOU REMEMBER HOW TO PLAY TWISTER?
HUH?
I THINK YOU HAVE TWO PLAYERS AT A TIME...
AND SOME-ONE CALLING OUT COLORS ...
...AND THEY TAKE TURNS PUTTING THEIR HANDS AND FEET ON THOSE COLORS?
BUT HOW DO YOU DECIDE WHICH COLOR GETS CALLED?
YOU USE THESE!
phoo
I MADE A STACK OF CARDS FOR THE CALLER TO PICK FROM! ☆
A whopping 38 shades! ☆
MORITA ...
ISN'T THAT AN AWFUL LOT OF COLORS YOU GOT THERE?
I THOUGHT THIS WOULD BE MORE FESTIVE! MORE COLORS, MORE FUN!
Shouldn't there just be four: red, blue, yellow and green?

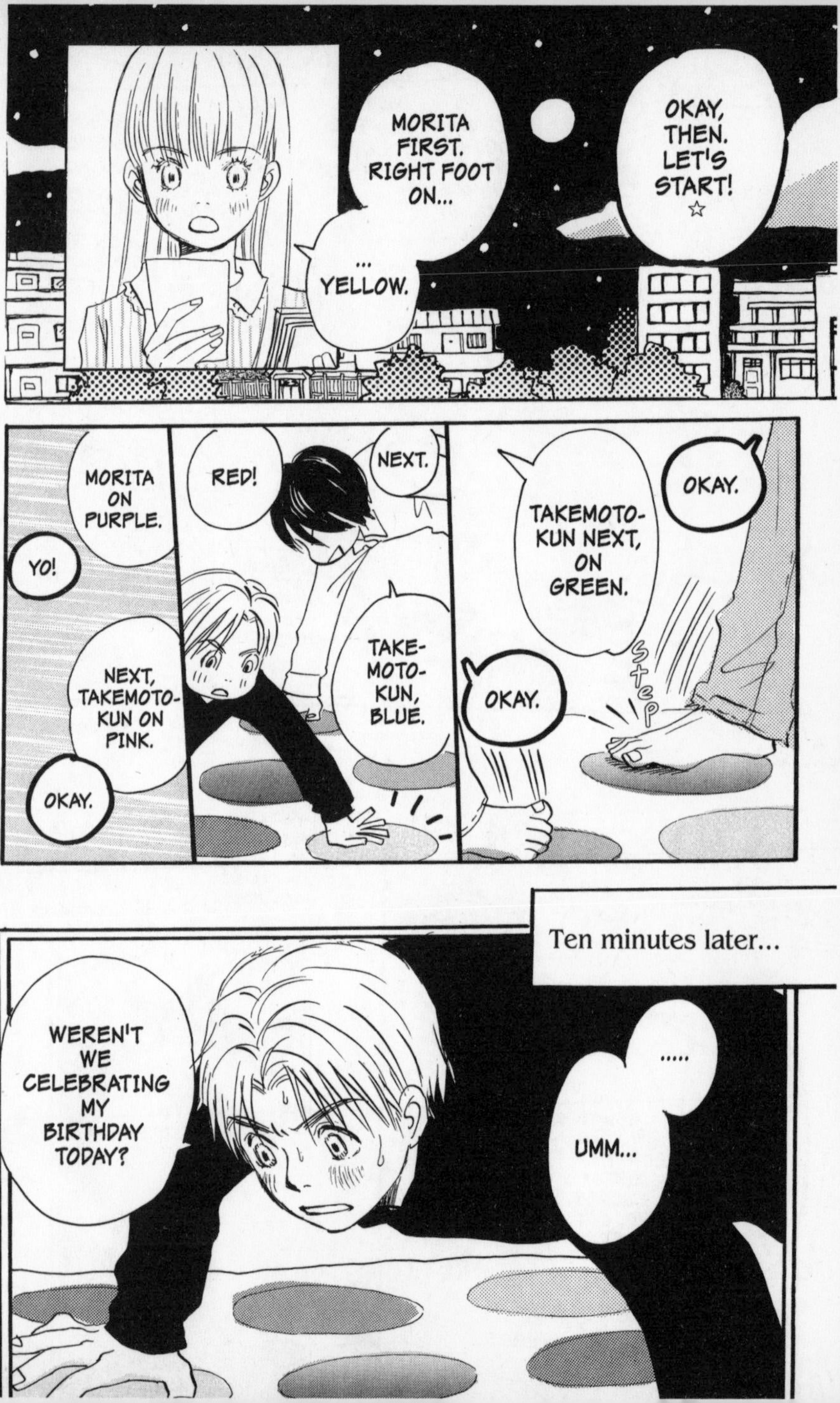
OKAY, THEN. LET'S START! ☆
MORITA FIRST. RIGHT FOOT ON...
... YELLOW.
OKAY.
TAKEMOTO-KUN NEXT, ON GREEN.
OKAY.
step
NEXT.
RED!
TAKE-MOTO-KUN, BLUE.
MORITA ON PURPLE.
YO!
NEXT, TAKEMOTO-KUN ON PINK.
OKAY.
Ten minutes later...
.....
UMM...
WEREN'T WE CELEBRATING MY BIRTHDAY TODAY?

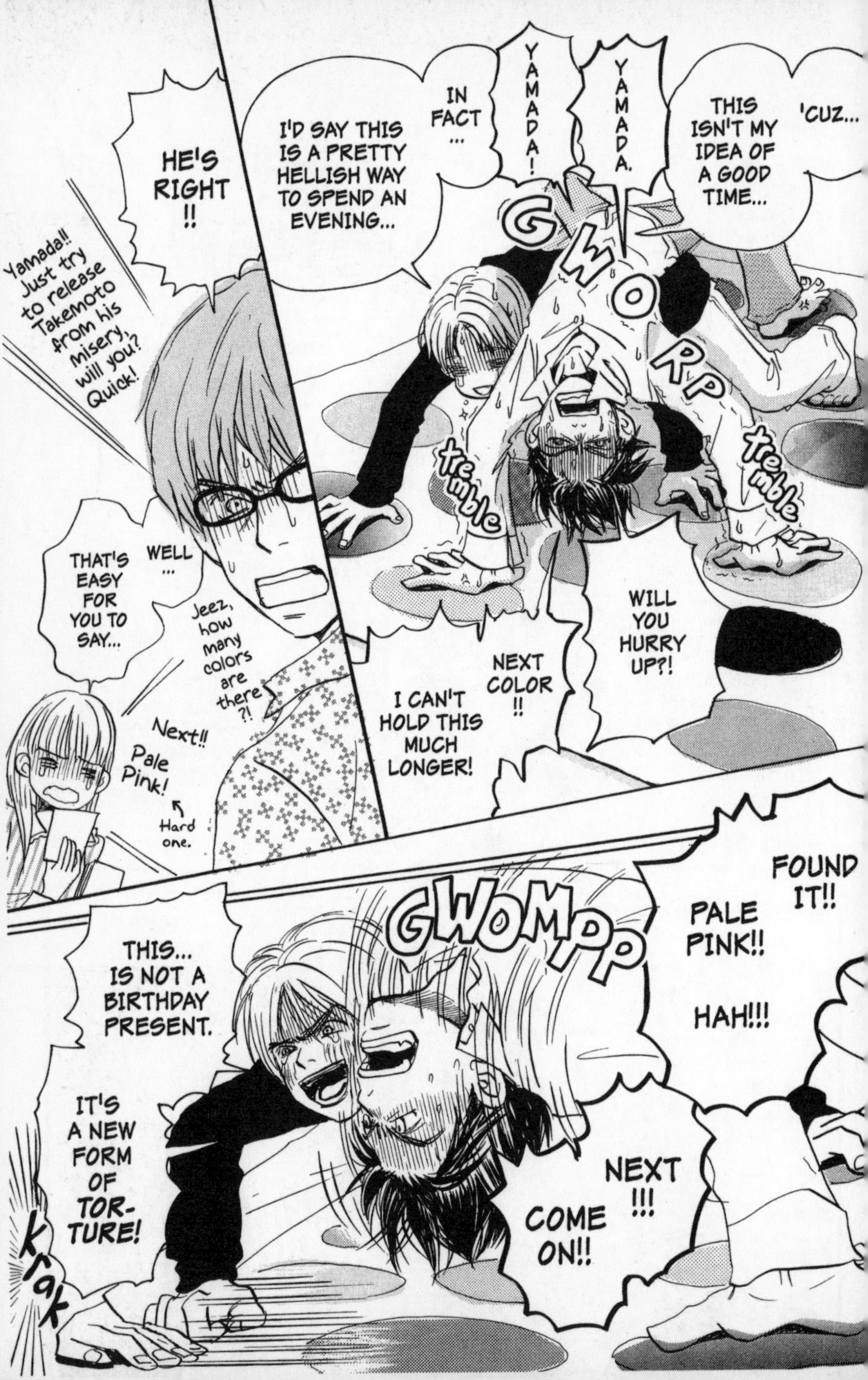
'CUZ...
THIS ISN'T MY IDEA OF A GOOD TIME...
YAMADA.
YAMADA!
IN FACT...
I'D SAY THIS IS A PRETTY HELLISH WAY TO SPEND AN EVENING...
GWORP
tremble
tremble
WILL YOU HURRY UP?!
NEXT COLOR!!
I CAN'T HOLD THIS MUCH LONGER!
HE'S RIGHT!!
Yamada!! Just try to release Takemoto from his misery, will you? Quick!
WELL...
THAT'S EASY FOR YOU TO SAY...
Jeez, how many colors are there?!
Next!!
Pale Pink!
Hard one.
FOUND IT!!
PALE PINK!!
HAH!!!
GWOMPP
THIS... IS NOT A BIRTHDAY PRESENT.
NEXT!!!
COME ON!!
IT'S A NEW FORM OF TOR-TURE!
krak

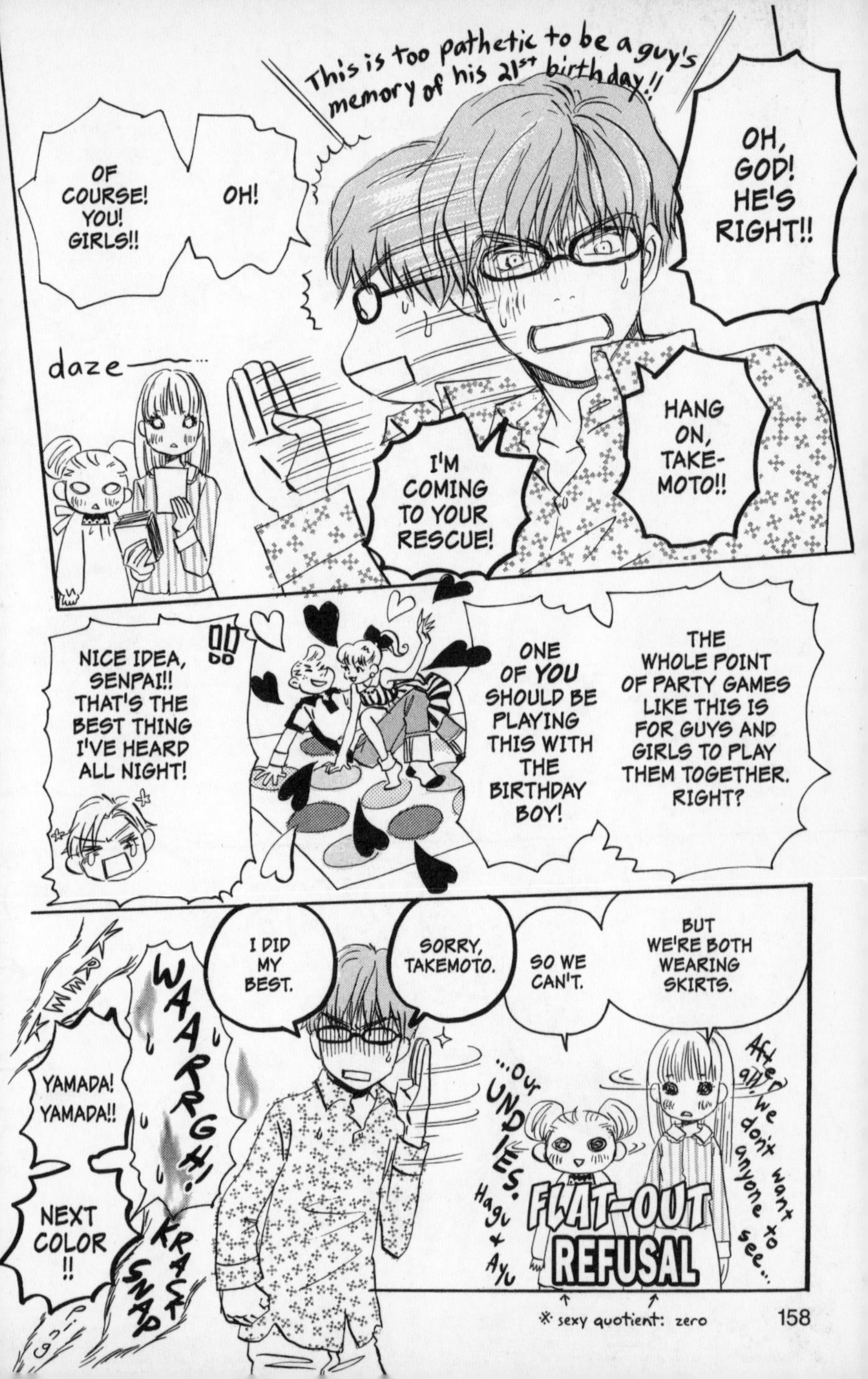

This is too pathetic to be a guy's memory of his 21st birthday!!
OH, GOD! HE'S RIGHT!!
HANG ON, TAKEMOTO!!
I'M COMING TO YOUR RESCUE!
OH!
OF COURSE! YOU! GIRLS!!
daze
THE WHOLE POINT OF PARTY GAMES LIKE THIS IS FOR GUYS AND GIRLS TO PLAY THEM TOGETHER. RIGHT?
ONE OF YOU SHOULD BE PLAYING THIS WITH THE BIRTHDAY BOY!
NICE IDEA, SENPAI!! THAT'S THE BEST THING I'VE HEARD ALL NIGHT!
!!
BUT WE'RE BOTH WEARING SKIRTS.
SO WE CAN'T.
After all, we don't want anyone to see...
...our UNDIES.
Hagu & Ayu
FLAT-OUT REFUSAL
※ sexy quotient: zero
SORRY, TAKEMOTO.
I DID MY BEST.
WAAARGH!
KRACK
SNAP
YAMADA! YAMADA!!
NEXT COLOR !!

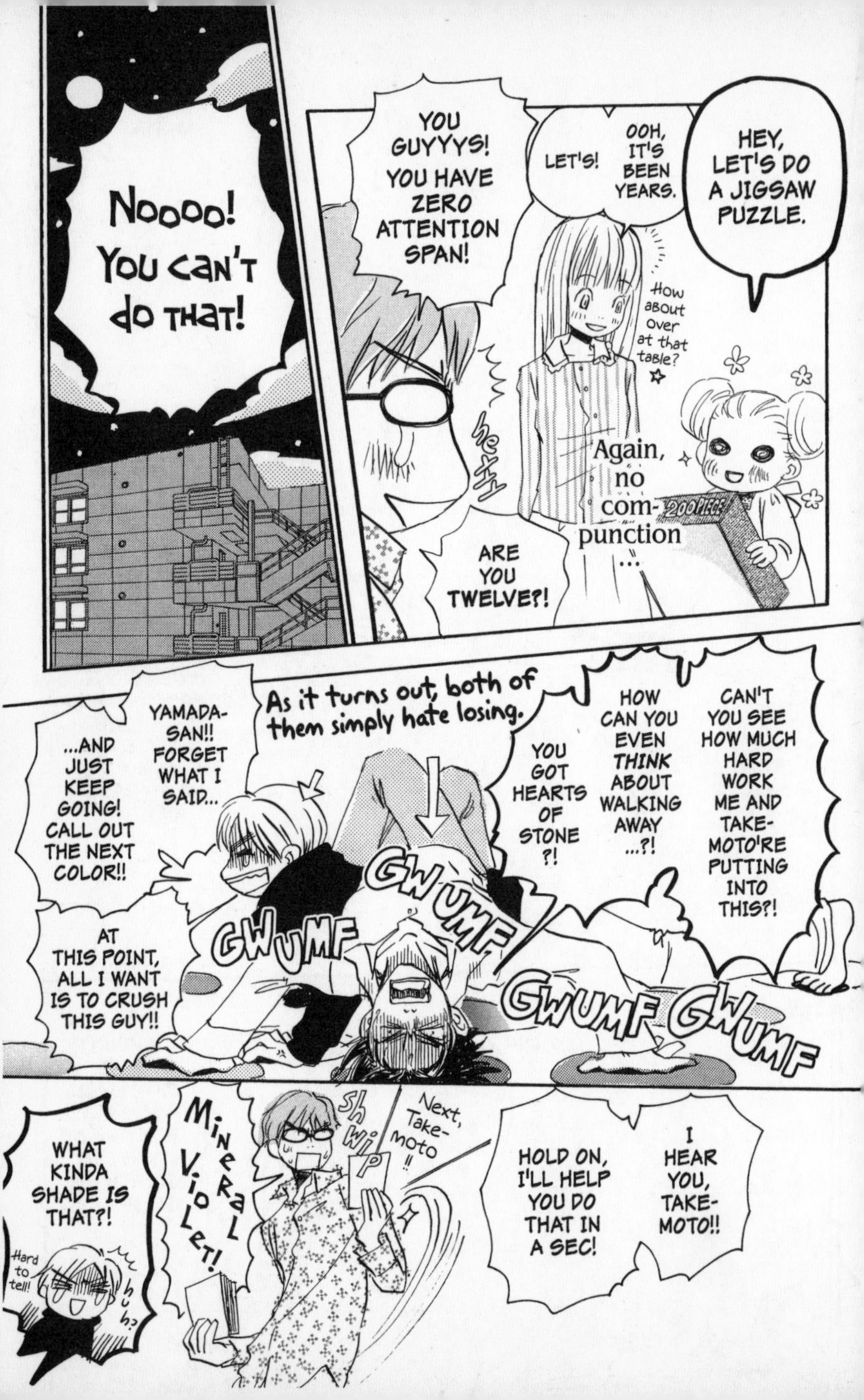
HEY, LET'S DO A JIGSAW PUZZLE.
How about over at that table?
OOH, IT'S BEEN YEARS.
LET'S!
Again, no com-punction...
YOU GUYYYS! YOU HAVE ZERO ATTENTION SPAN!
ARE YOU TWELVE?!
200 PIECE
Noooo! You can't do that!
CAN'T YOU SEE HOW MUCH HARD WORK ME AND TAKE-MOTO'RE PUTTING INTO THIS?!
HOW CAN YOU EVEN THINK ABOUT WALKING AWAY ...?!
YOU GOT HEARTS OF STONE ?!
As it turns out, both of them simply hate losing.
YAMADA-SAN!! FORGET WHAT I SAID...
...AND JUST KEEP GOING! CALL OUT THE NEXT COLOR!!
AT THIS POINT, ALL I WANT IS TO CRUSH THIS GUY!!
GWUMF
GWUMF
GWUMF GWUMF
I HEAR YOU, TAKE-MOTO!!
HOLD ON, I'LL HELP YOU DO THAT IN A SEC!
Next, Take-moto!!
SHWIP
Mineral Violet!
WHAT KINDA SHADE IS THAT?!
Hard to tell!
huh?

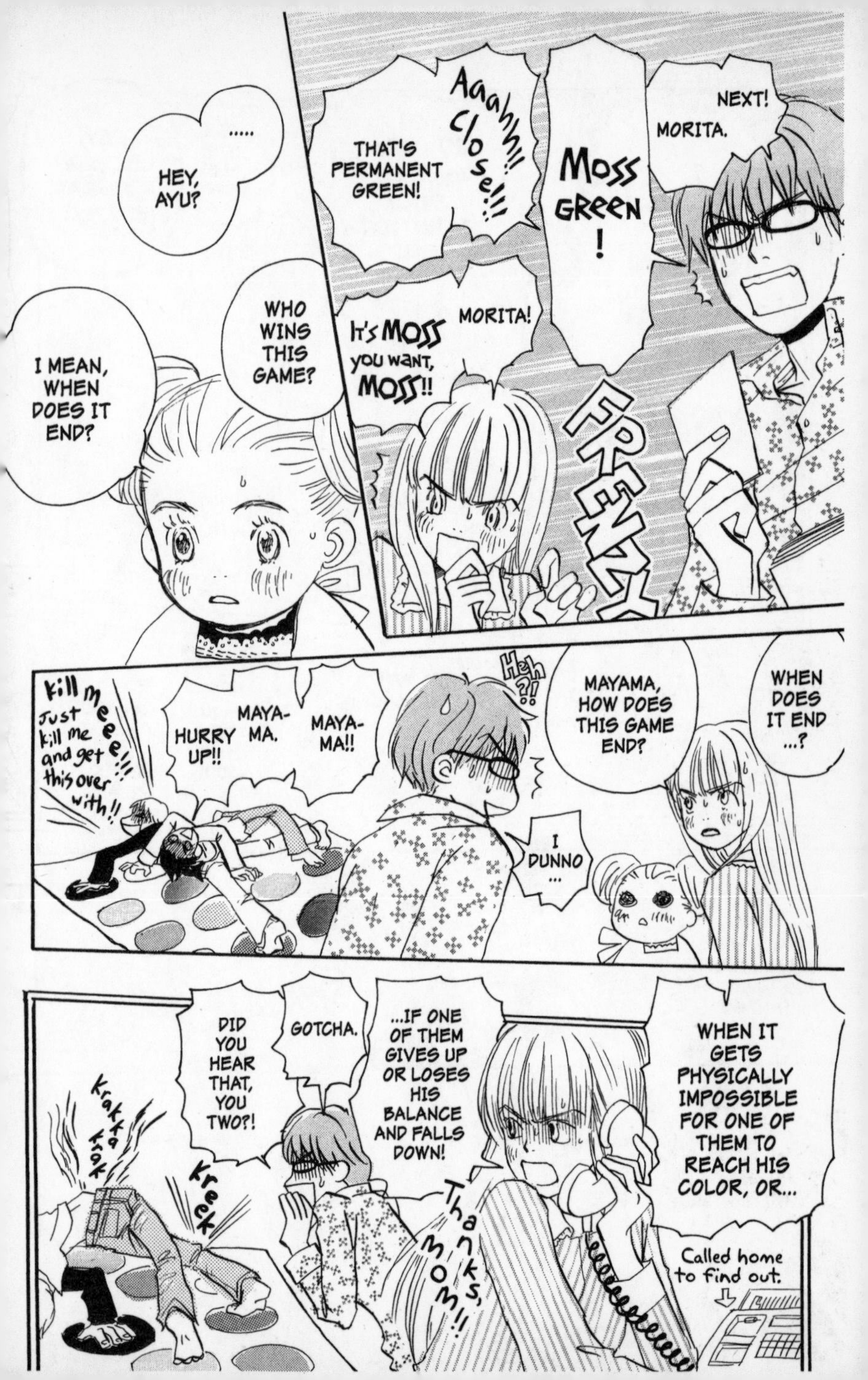

NEXT! MORITA.
MOSS GREEN!
Aaahh!! Close!!!
THAT'S PERMANENT GREEN!
MORITA!
It's MOSS you want, MOSS!!
FRENZY
.....
HEY, AYU?
WHO WINS THIS GAME?
I MEAN, WHEN DOES IT END?
WHEN DOES IT END ...?
MAYAMA, HOW DOES THIS GAME END?
Heh ?!
I DUNNO ...
MAYA-MA!!
MAYA-MA.
HURRY UP!!
kill meee!!!
Just kill me and get this over with!!
WHEN IT GETS PHYSICALLY IMPOSSIBLE FOR ONE OF THEM TO REACH HIS COLOR, OR...
Called home to find out.
...IF ONE OF THEM GIVES UP OR LOSES HIS BALANCE AND FALLS DOWN!
Thanks, MOM!!
GOTCHA.
DID YOU HEAR THAT, YOU TWO?!
Krek
Krakka krak

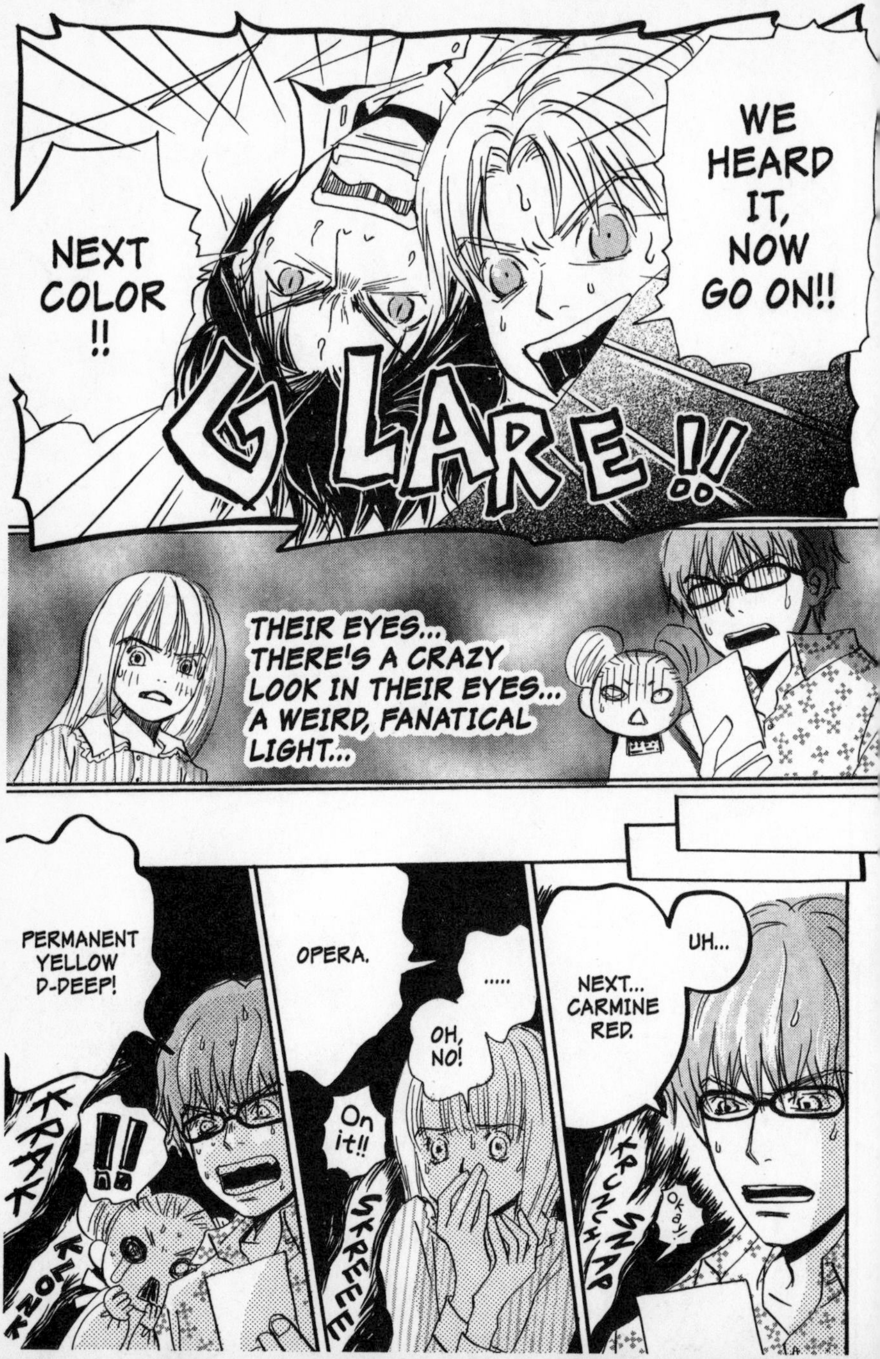
WE HEARD IT, NOW GO ON!!
NEXT COLOR !!
GLARE!!
THEIR EYES... THERE'S A CRAZY LOOK IN THEIR EYES... A WEIRD, FANATICAL LIGHT...
UH...
NEXT... CARMINE RED.
KRUNCH SNAP
Okay!
.....
OPERA.
OH, NO!
On it!!
SKREEEE
PERMANENT YELLOW D-DEEP!
!!
KRAK
KLONK

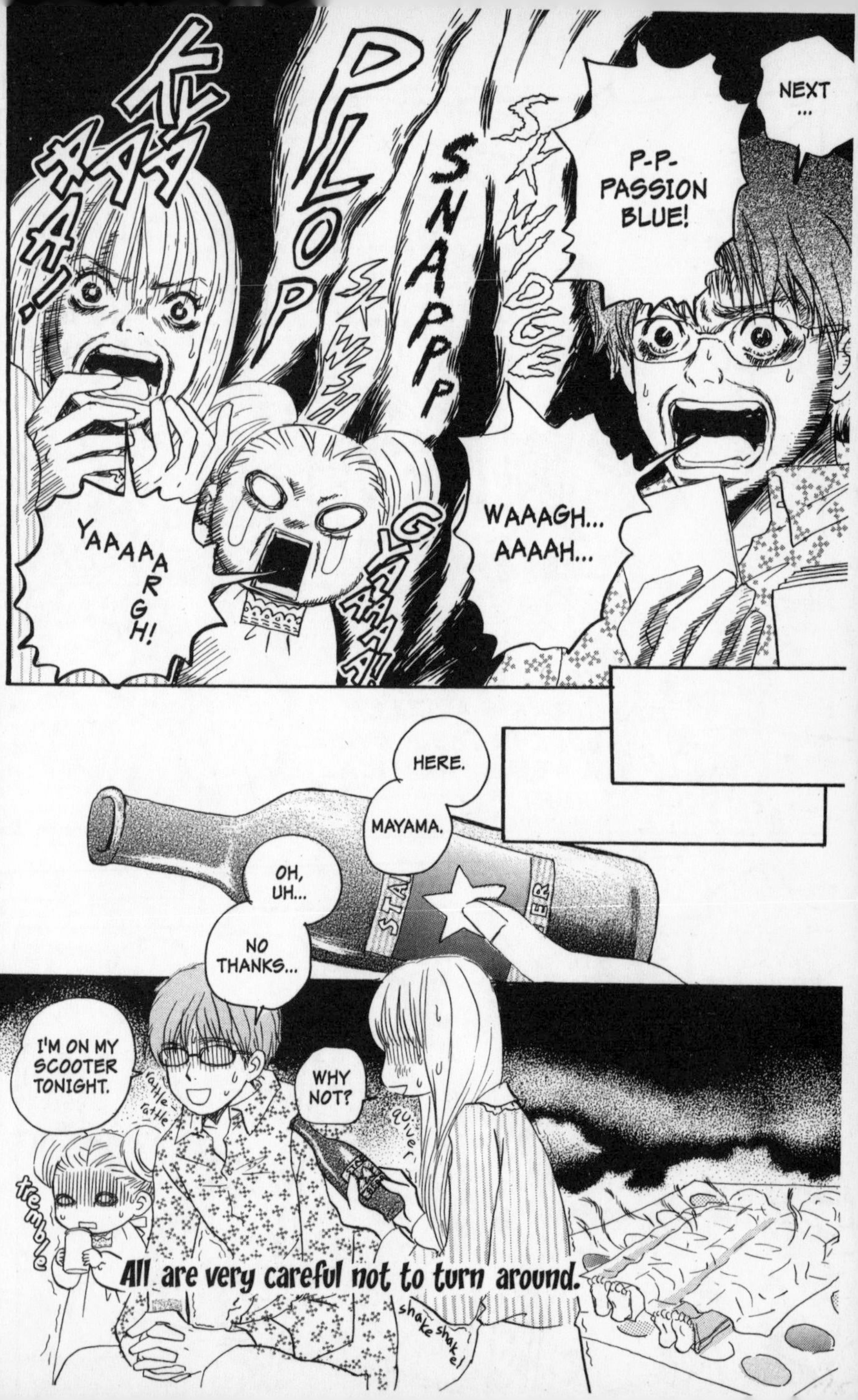
NEXT ...
P-P-PASSION BLUE!
SKWIDGE
SNAPPP
SKWISH
PLOP
KYAAAAAA!
WAAAGH... AAAAH...
GYAAAAAA!
YAAAAARGH!
HERE.
MAYAMA.
OH, UH...
NO THANKS...
WHY NOT?
I'M ON MY SCOOTER TONIGHT.
quiver
rattle rattle
tremble
shake shake
All are very careful not to turn around.

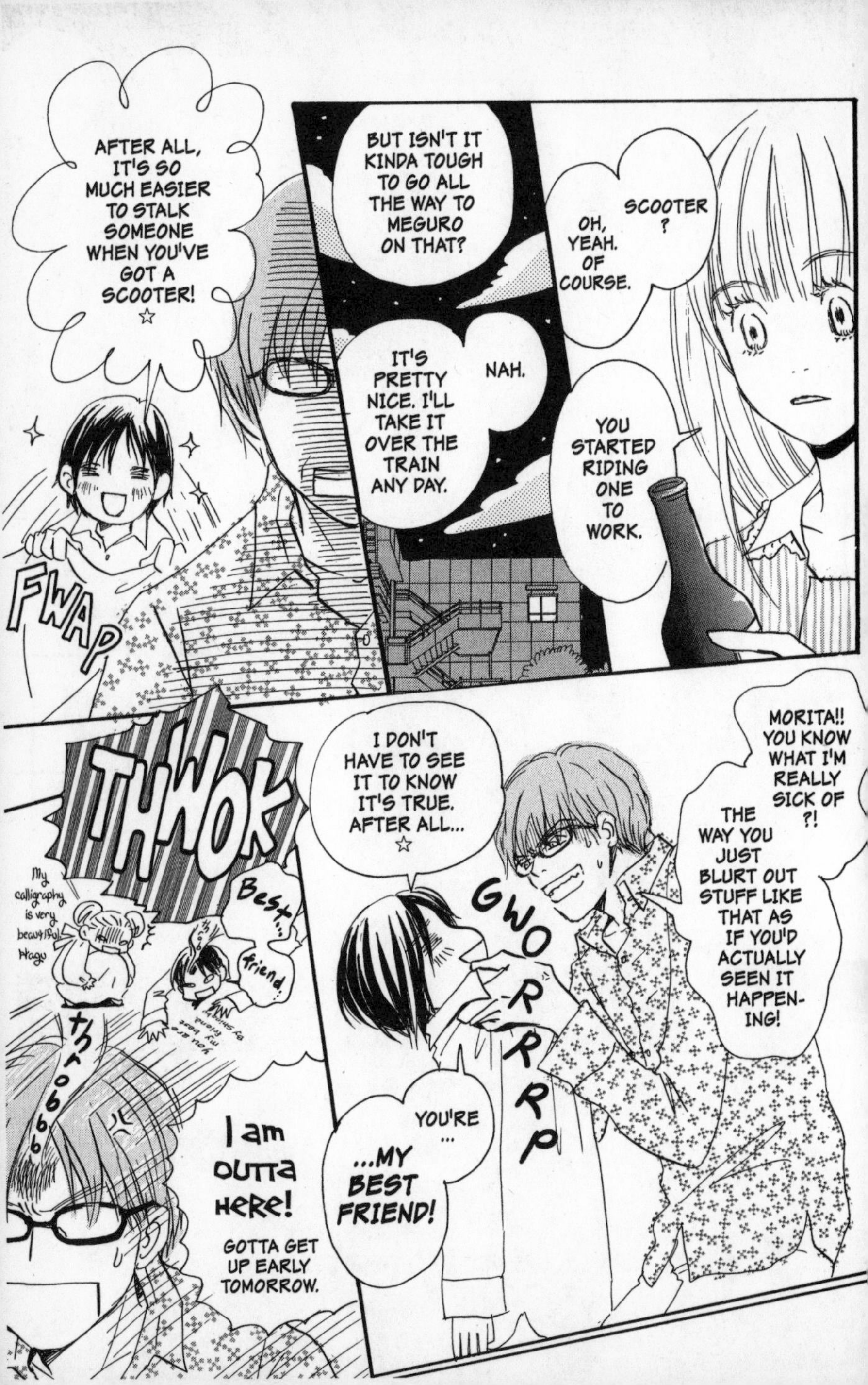
SCOOTER ?
OH, YEAH. OF COURSE.
YOU STARTED RIDING ONE TO WORK.
BUT ISN'T IT KINDA TOUGH TO GO ALL THE WAY TO MEGURO ON THAT?
NAH.
IT'S PRETTY NICE. I'LL TAKE IT OVER THE TRAIN ANY DAY.
AFTER ALL, IT'S SO MUCH EASIER TO STALK SOMEONE WHEN YOU'VE GOT A SCOOTER! ☆
FWAP
MORITA!! YOU KNOW WHAT I'M REALLY SICK OF ?!
THE WAY YOU JUST BLURT OUT STUFF LIKE THAT AS IF YOU'D ACTUALLY SEEN IT HAPPENING!
GWORRRRP
I DON'T HAVE TO SEE IT TO KNOW IT'S TRUE. AFTER ALL... ☆
YOU'RE ...
...MY BEST FRIEND!
THWOK
Best... friend.
My calligraphy is very beautiful Hagu
throbbb
I am outta here!
GOTTA GET UP EARLY TOMORROW.

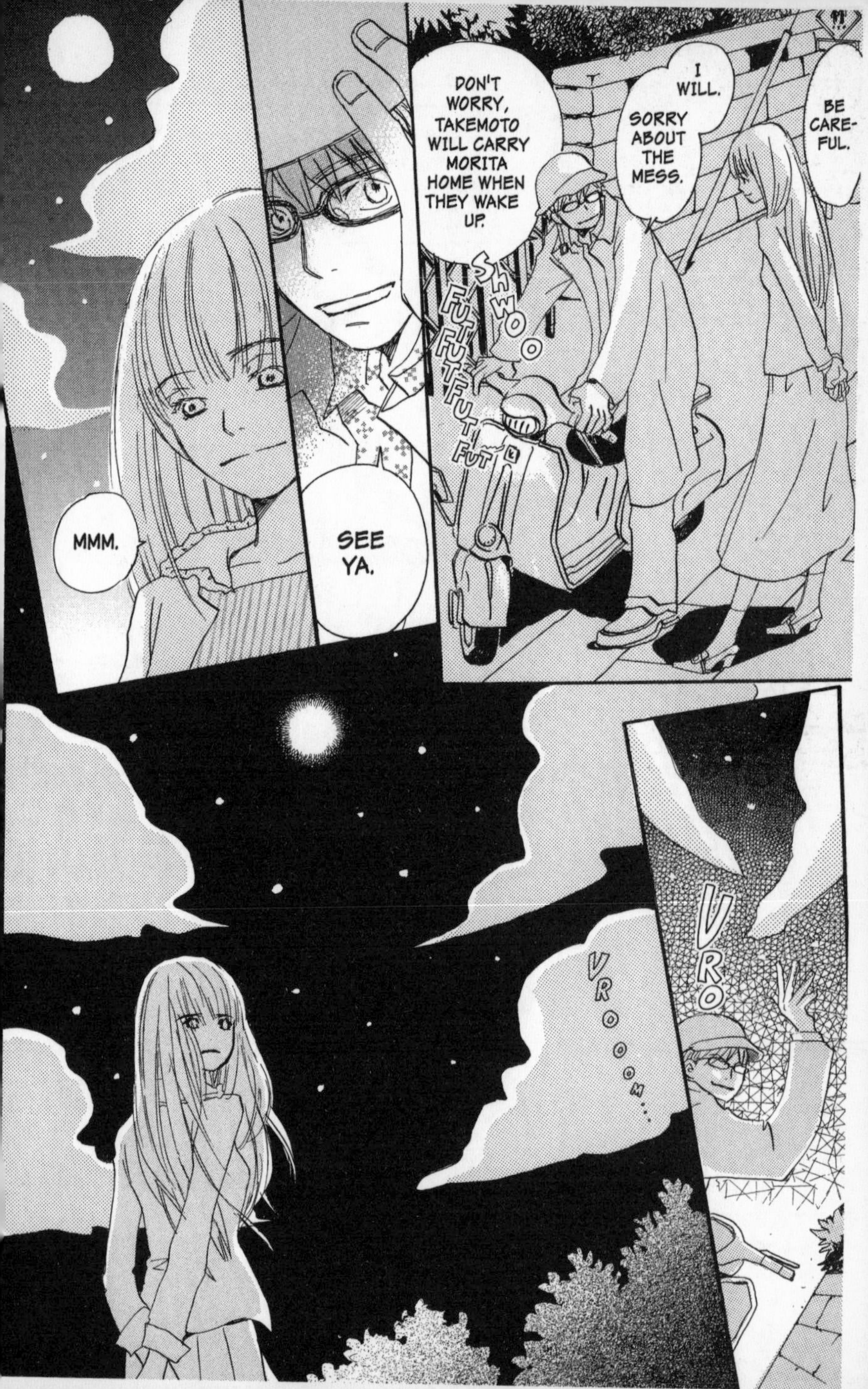
BE CAREFUL.
I WILL.
SORRY ABOUT THE MESS.
DON'T WORRY, TAKEMOTO WILL CARRY MORITA HOME WHEN THEY WAKE UP.
SHWOO
FUT FUT FUT FUT FUT
SEE YA.
MMM.
VRO
VROOOOM...

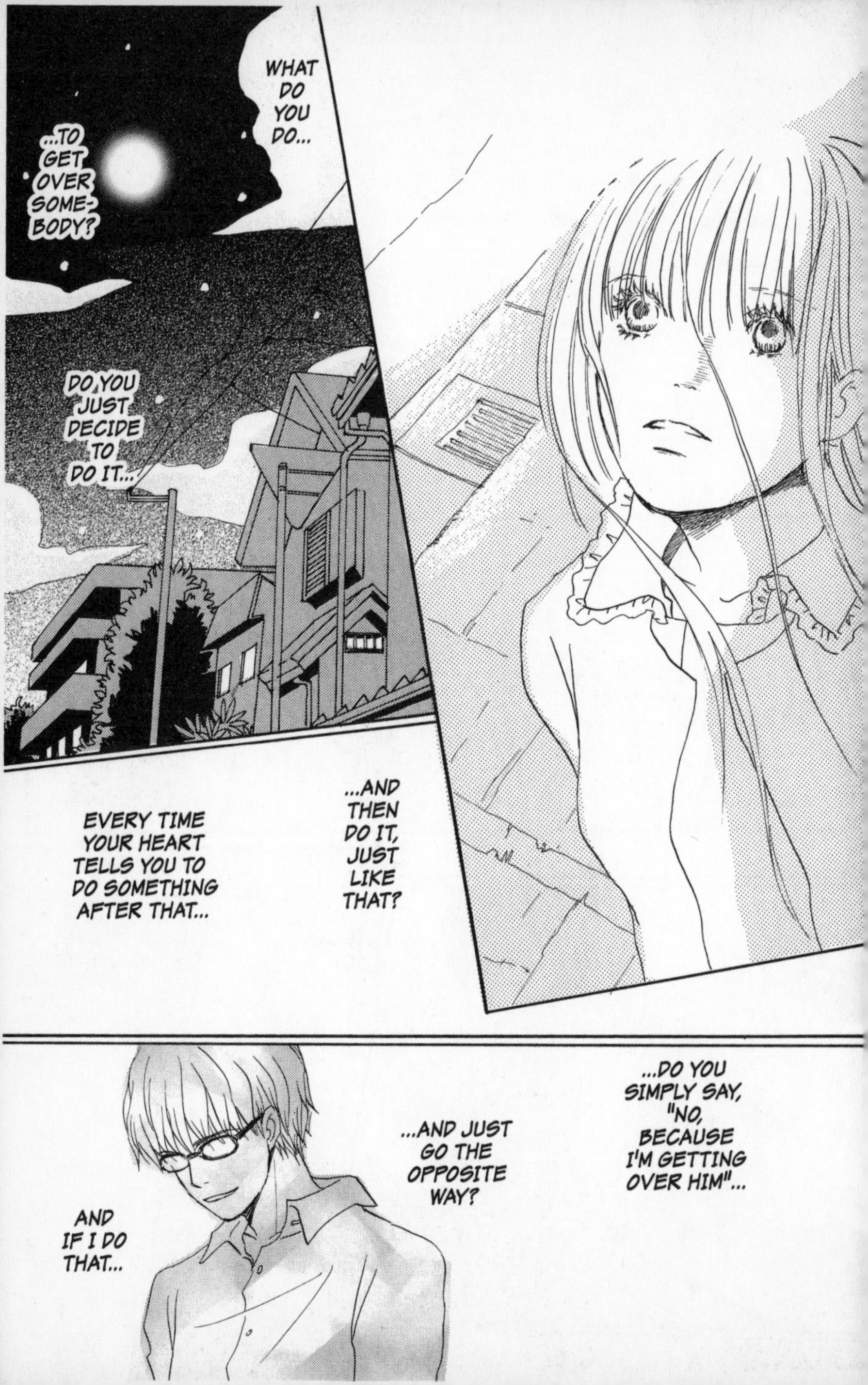
WHAT DO YOU DO...
...TO GET OVER SOME-BODY?
DO YOU JUST DECIDE TO DO IT...
...AND THEN DO IT, JUST LIKE THAT?
EVERY TIME YOUR HEART TELLS YOU TO DO SOMETHING AFTER THAT...
...DO YOU SIMPLY SAY, "NO, BECAUSE I'M GETTING OVER HIM"...
...AND JUST GO THE OPPOSITE WAY?
AND IF I DO THAT...

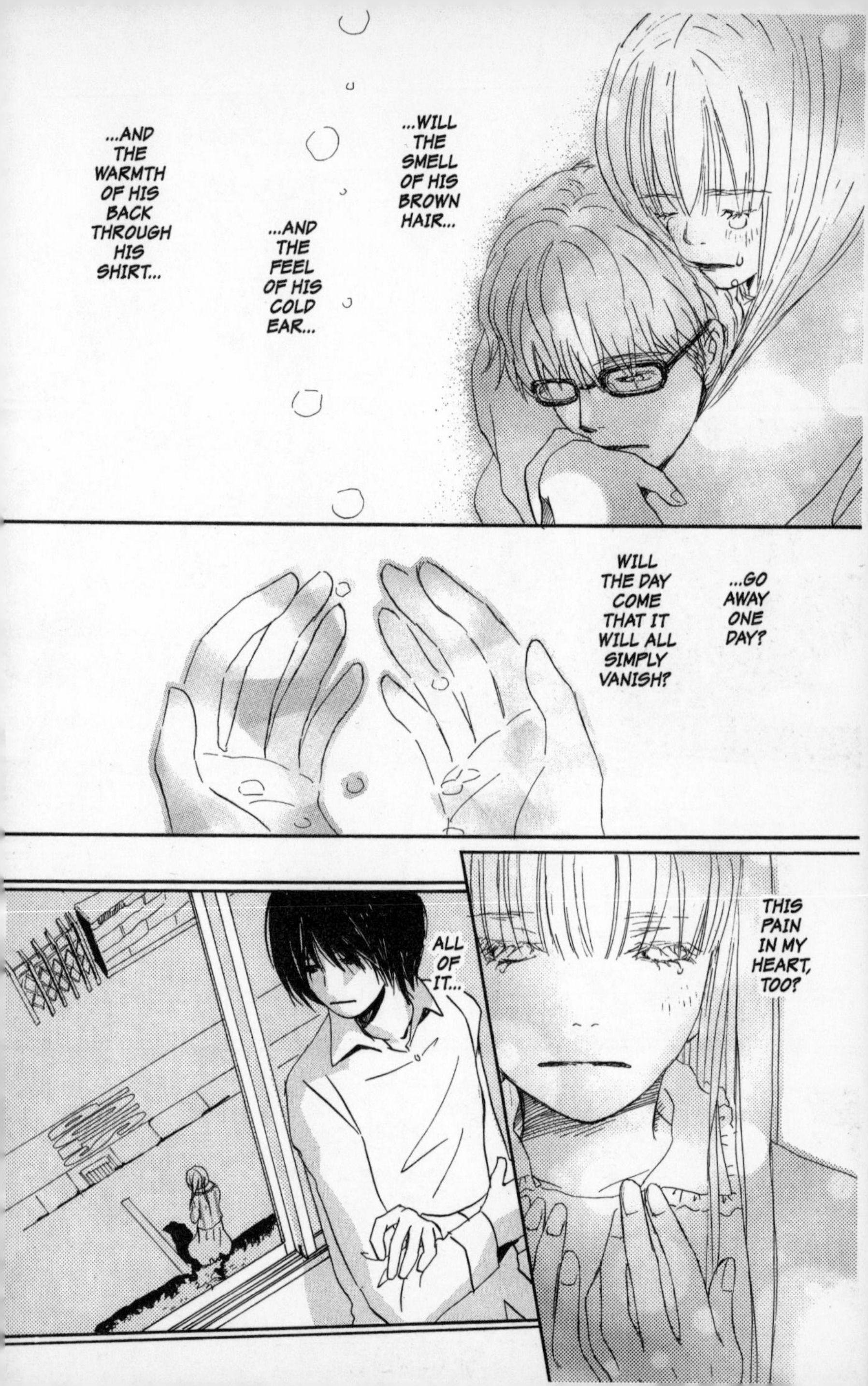
...WILL THE SMELL OF HIS BROWN HAIR...
...AND THE FEEL OF HIS COLD EAR...
...AND THE WARMTH OF HIS BACK THROUGH HIS SHIRT...
...GO AWAY ONE DAY?
WILL THE DAY COME THAT IT WILL ALL SIMPLY VANISH?
THIS PAIN IN MY HEART, TOO?
ALL OF IT...

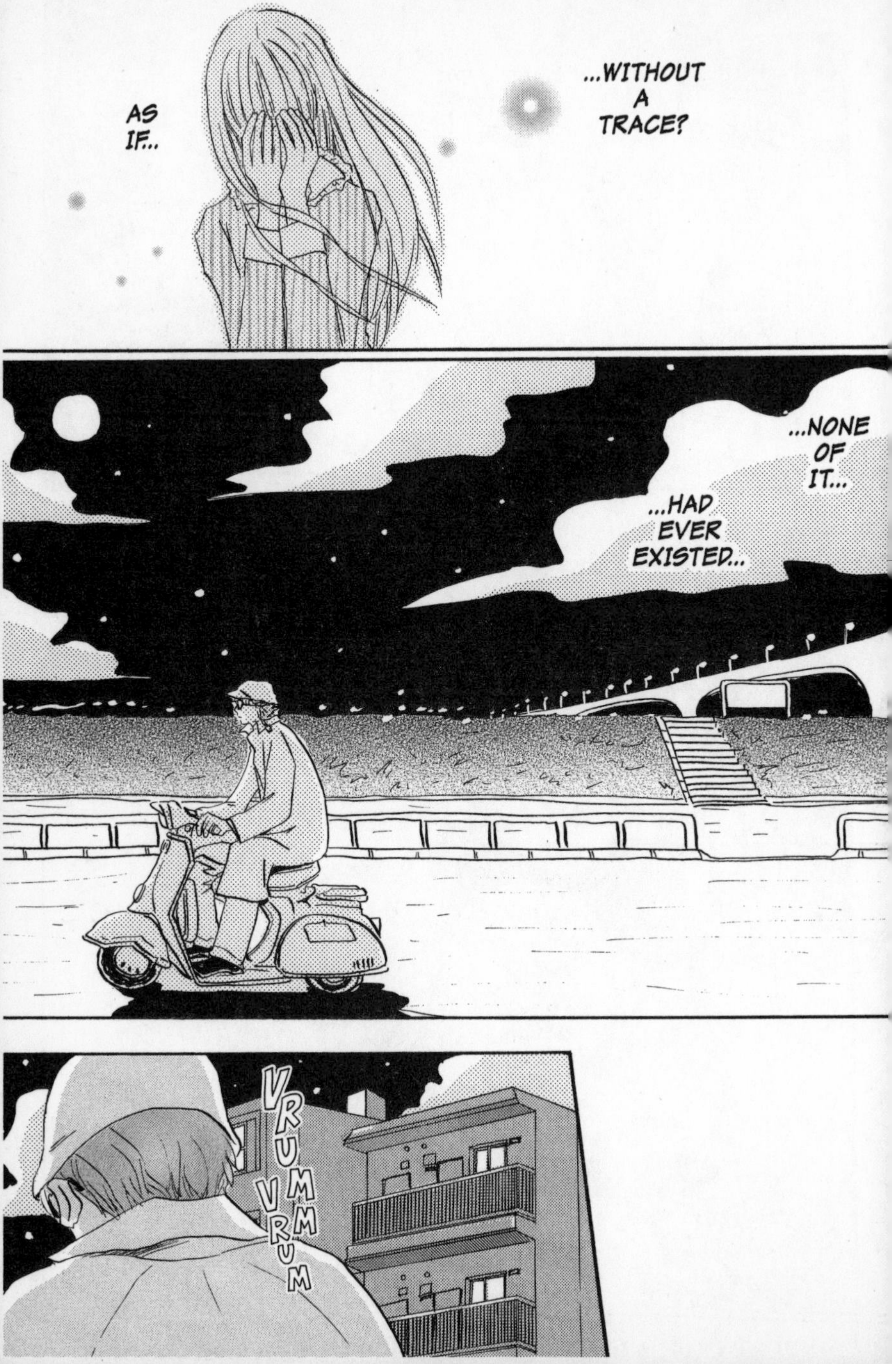
AS IF...
...WITHOUT A TRACE?
...NONE OF IT...
...HAD EVER EXISTED...
VRUMMM
VRUM

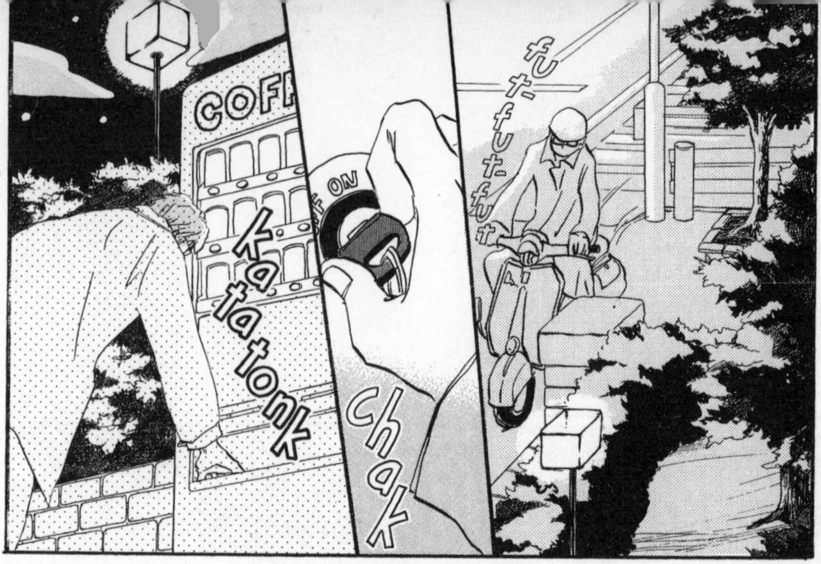
chak
katatonk
COFF

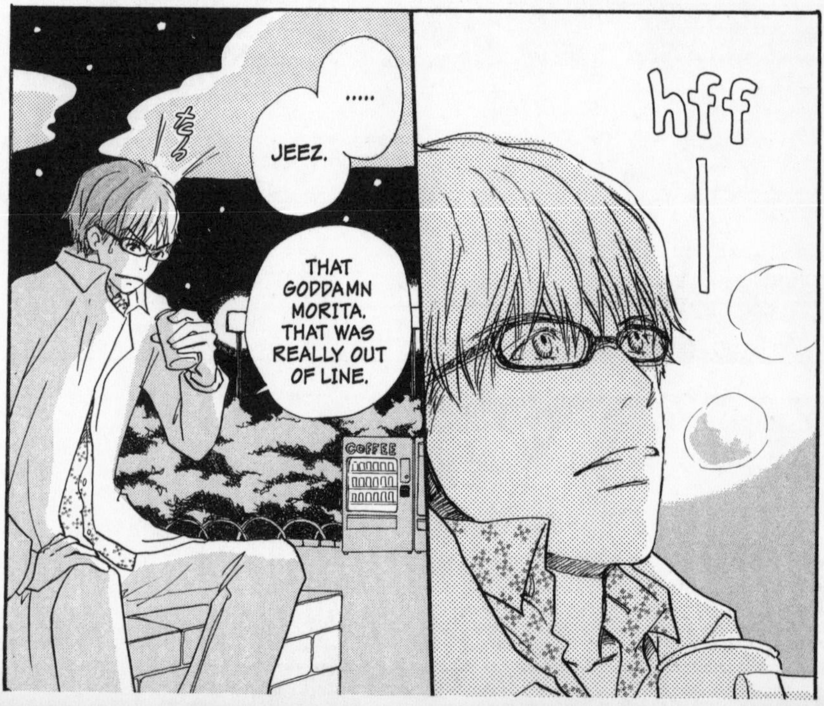
hff
.....
JEEZ.
THAT GODDAMN MORITA. THAT WAS REALLY OUT OF LINE.
COFFEE

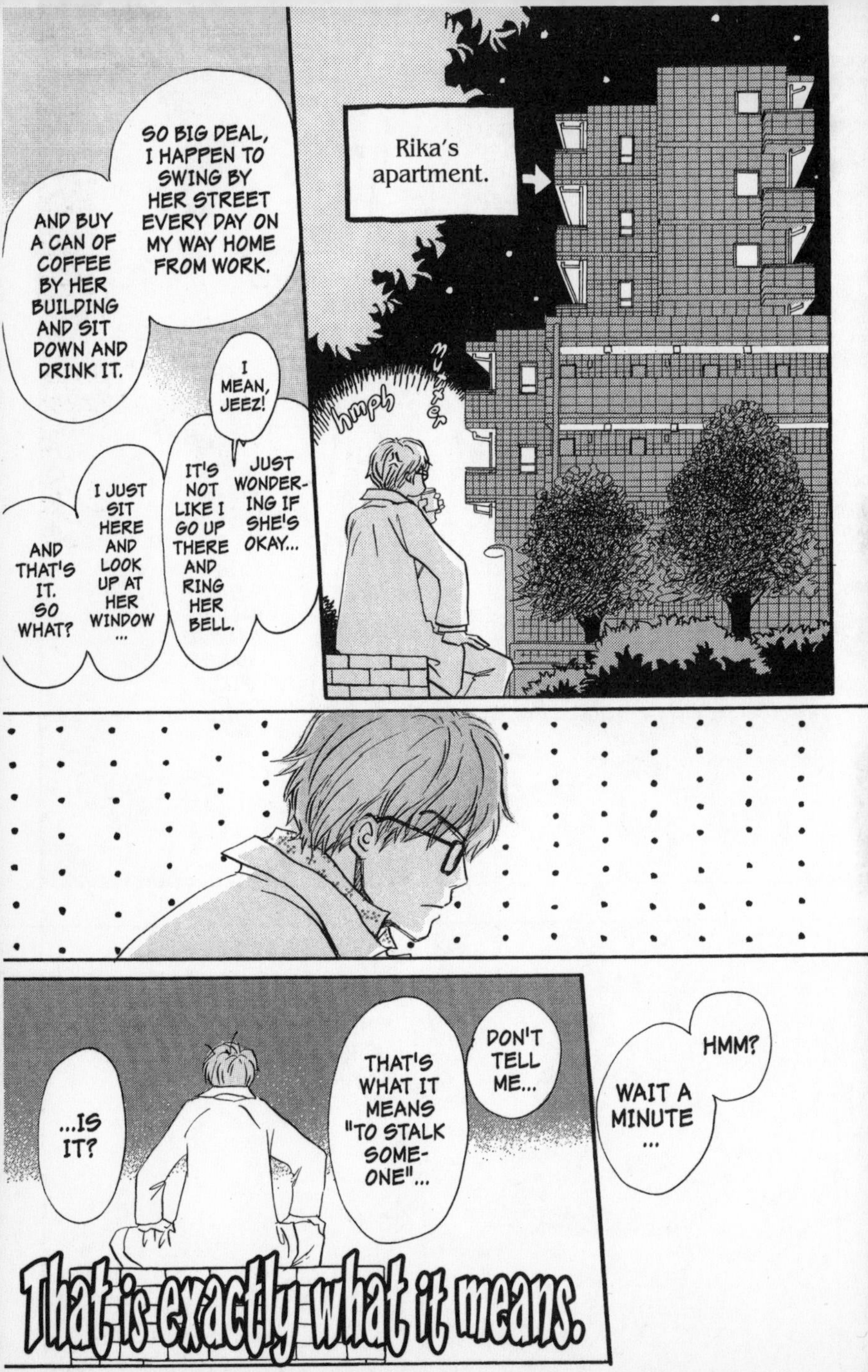
Rika's apartment.
hmph
mutter
SO BIG DEAL, I HAPPEN TO SWING BY HER STREET EVERY DAY ON MY WAY HOME FROM WORK.
AND BUY A CAN OF COFFEE BY HER BUILDING AND SIT DOWN AND DRINK IT.
I MEAN, JEEZ!
JUST WONDERING IF SHE'S OKAY...
IT'S NOT LIKE I GO UP THERE AND RING HER BELL.
I JUST SIT HERE AND LOOK UP AT HER WINDOW...
AND THAT'S IT. SO WHAT?
HMM?
WAIT A MINUTE...
DON'T TELL ME...
THAT'S WHAT IT MEANS "TO STALK SOME-ONE"...
...IS IT?
That is exactly what it means.

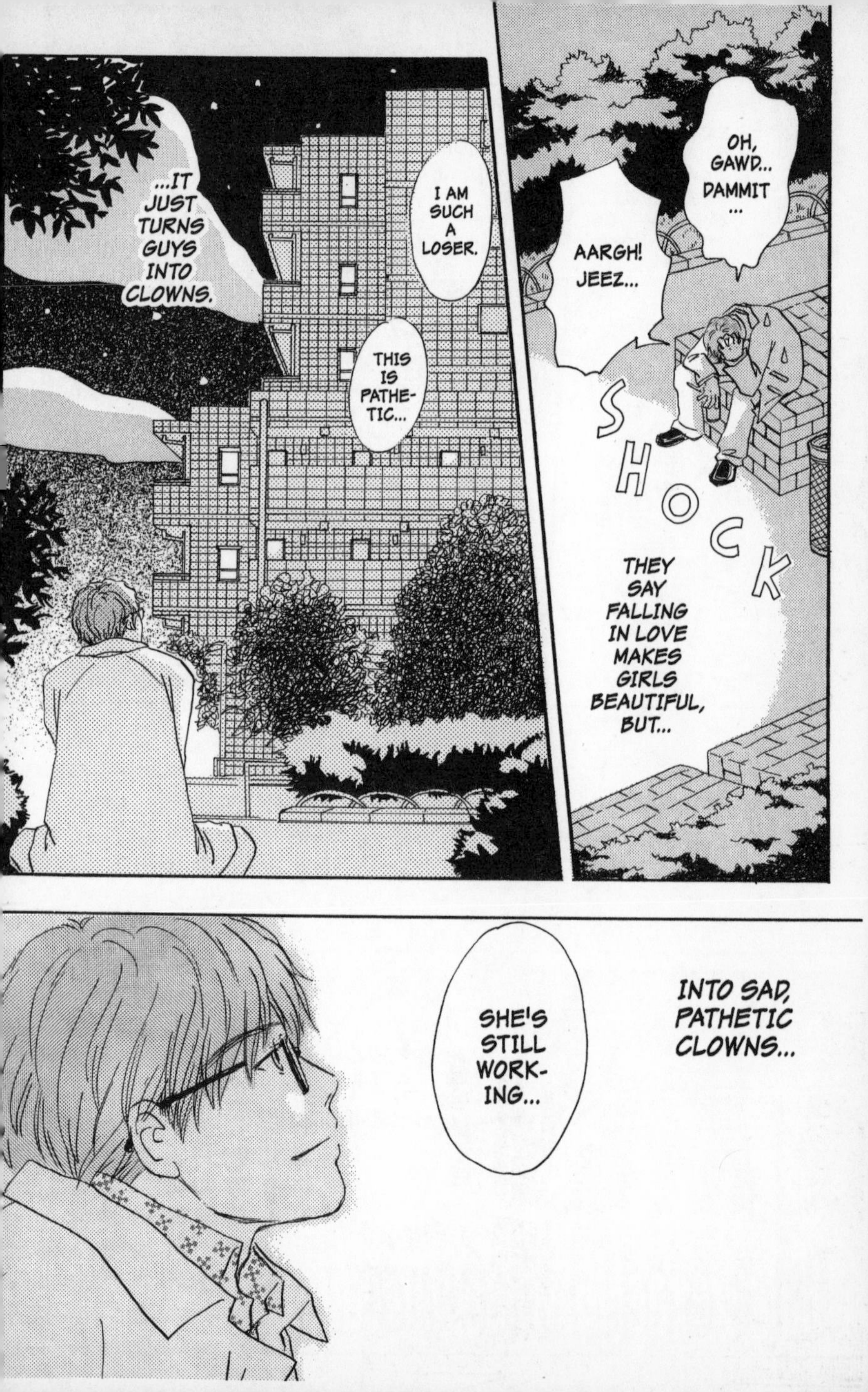

OH, GAWD... DAMMIT...
AARGH! JEEZ...
SHOCK
THEY SAY FALLING IN LOVE MAKES GIRLS BEAUTIFUL, BUT...
I AM SUCH A LOSER.
...IT JUST TURNS GUYS INTO CLOWNS.
THIS IS PATHETIC...
INTO SAD, PATHETIC CLOWNS...
SHE'S STILL WORKING...

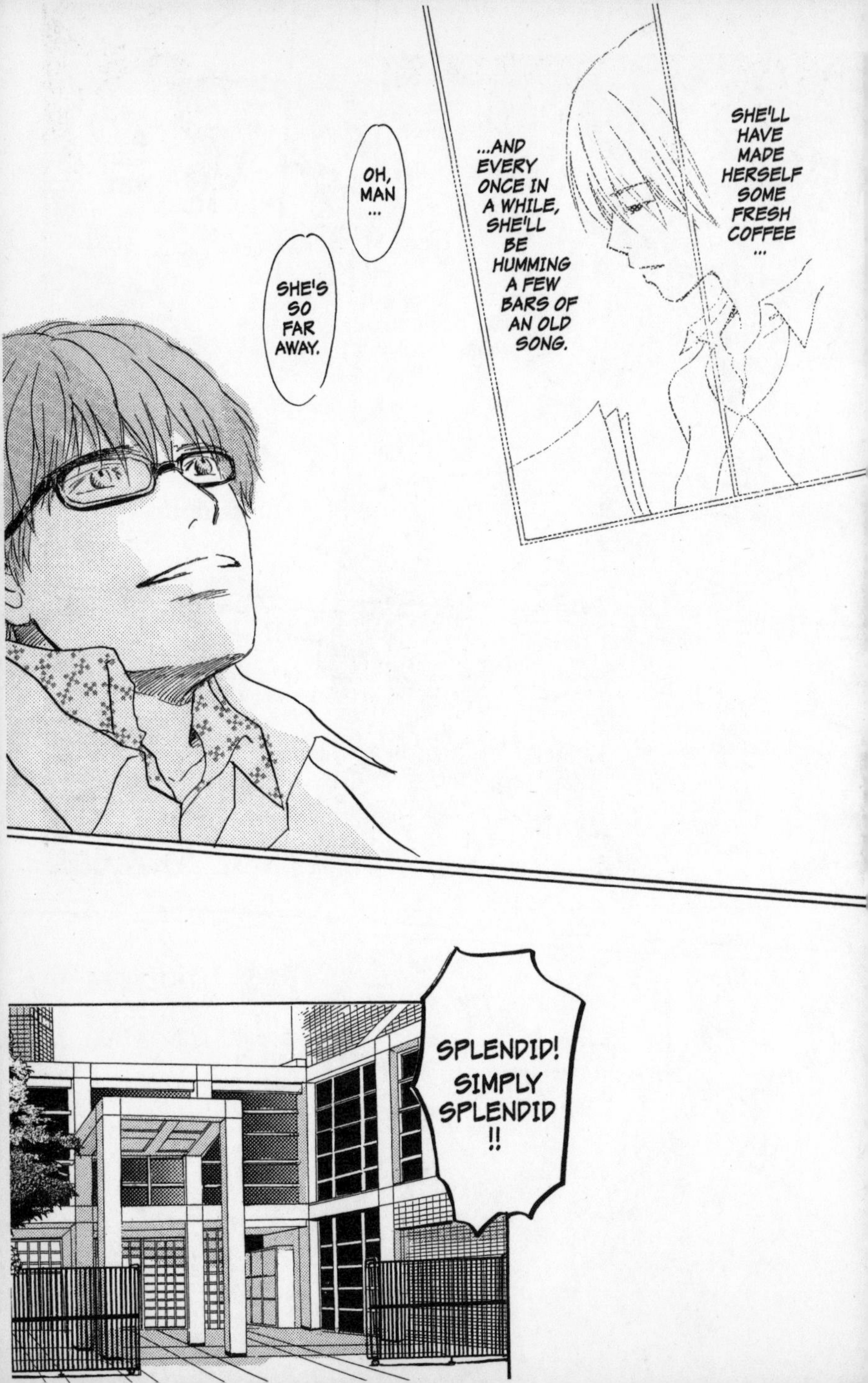
SHE'LL HAVE MADE HERSELF SOME FRESH COFFEE ...
...AND EVERY ONCE IN A WHILE, SHE'LL BE HUMMING A FEW BARS OF AN OLD SONG.
OH, MAN ...
SHE'S SO FAR AWAY.
SPLENDID! SIMPLY SPLENDID !!

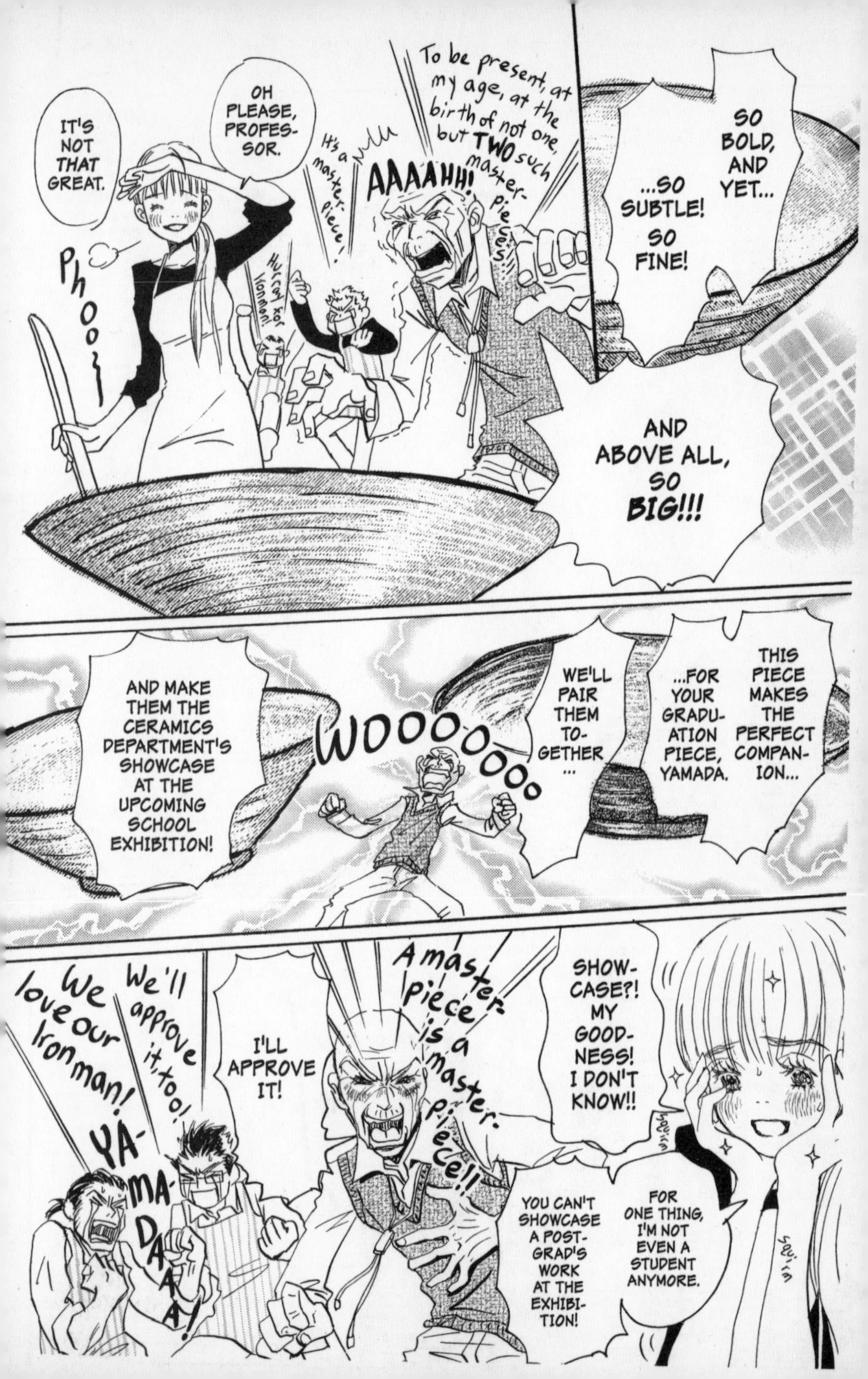
SO BOLD, AND YET...
...SO SUBTLE! SO FINE!
AND ABOVE ALL, SO BIG!!!
To be present, at my age, at the birth of not one, but TWO such master-pieces!
AAAAHH!
It's a master-piece!
Hurray for Ironman!
OH PLEASE, PROFESSOR.
IT'S NOT THAT GREAT.
Phoo~
THIS PIECE MAKES THE PERFECT COMPANION...
...FOR YOUR GRADUATION PIECE, YAMADA.
WE'LL PAIR THEM TOGETHER...
WOOOOOOOO
AND MAKE THEM THE CERAMICS DEPARTMENT'S SHOWCASE AT THE UPCOMING SCHOOL EXHIBITION!
SHOW-CASE?! MY GOODNESS! I DON'T KNOW!!
squirm
squirm
FOR ONE THING, I'M NOT EVEN A STUDENT ANYMORE.
YOU CAN'T SHOWCASE A POST-GRAD'S WORK AT THE EXHIBITION!
A master-piece is a master-piece!!
I'LL APPROVE IT!
We'll approve it, too!
We love our Ironman!
YA-MA-DAAAA!

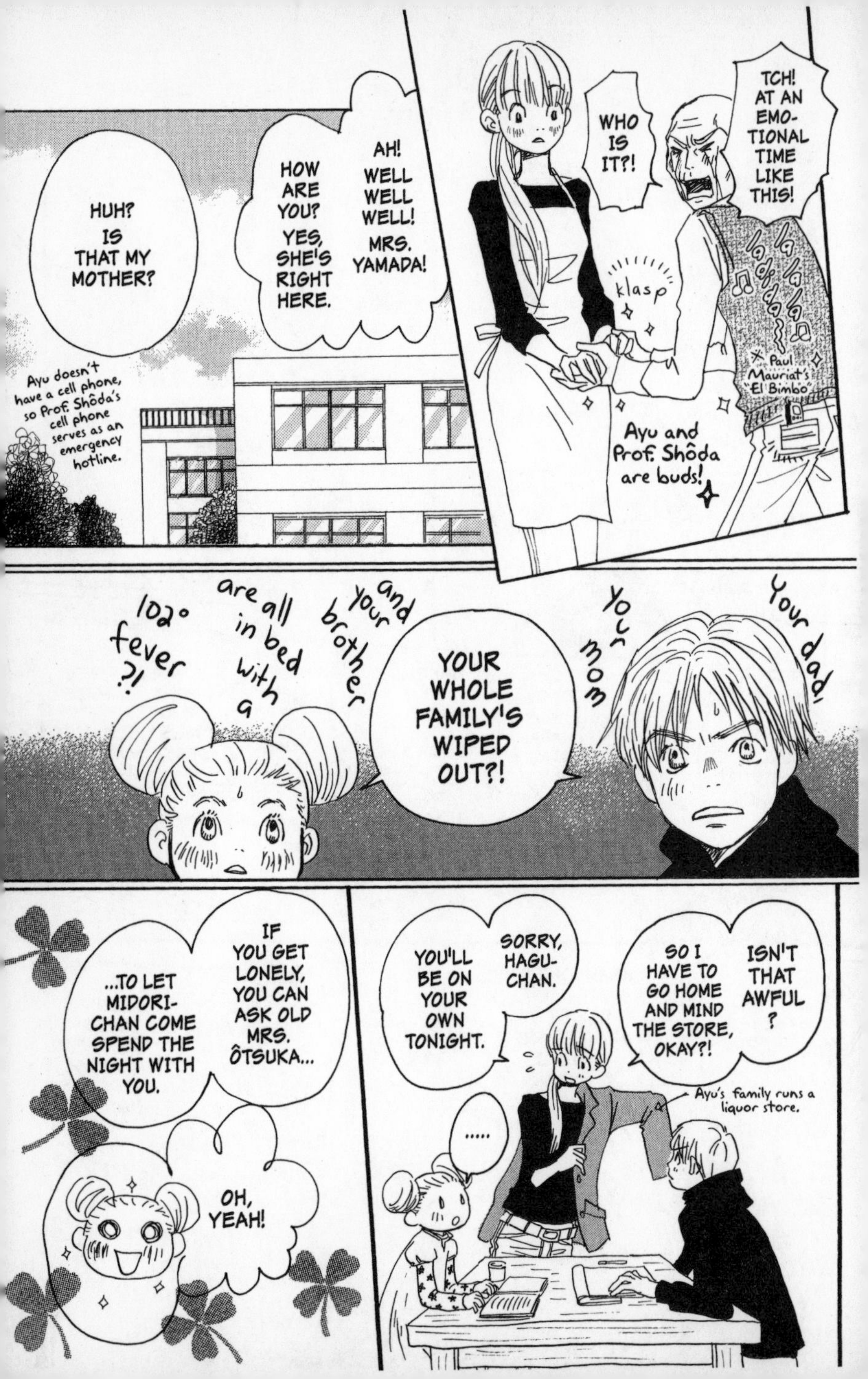
TCH! AT AN EMO-TIONAL TIME LIKE THIS!
WHO IS IT?!
lalala ladadala~
※ Paul Mauriat's "El Bimbo"
klasp
Ayu and Prof. Shôda are buds!
AH! WELL WELL WELL! MRS. YAMADA!
HOW ARE YOU? YES, SHE'S RIGHT HERE.
HUH? IS THAT MY MOTHER?
Ayu doesn't have a cell phone, so Prof. Shôda's cell phone serves as an emergency hotline.
Your dad, your mom and your brother are all in bed with a 102° fever?!
YOUR WHOLE FAMILY'S WIPED OUT?!
ISN'T THAT AWFUL?
SO I HAVE TO GO HOME AND MIND THE STORE, OKAY?!
SORRY, HAGU-CHAN.
YOU'LL BE ON YOUR OWN TONIGHT.
Ayu's family runs a liquor store.
.....
IF YOU GET LONELY, YOU CAN ASK OLD MRS. ÔTSUKA...
...TO LET MIDORI-CHAN COME SPEND THE NIGHT WITH YOU.
OH, YEAH!

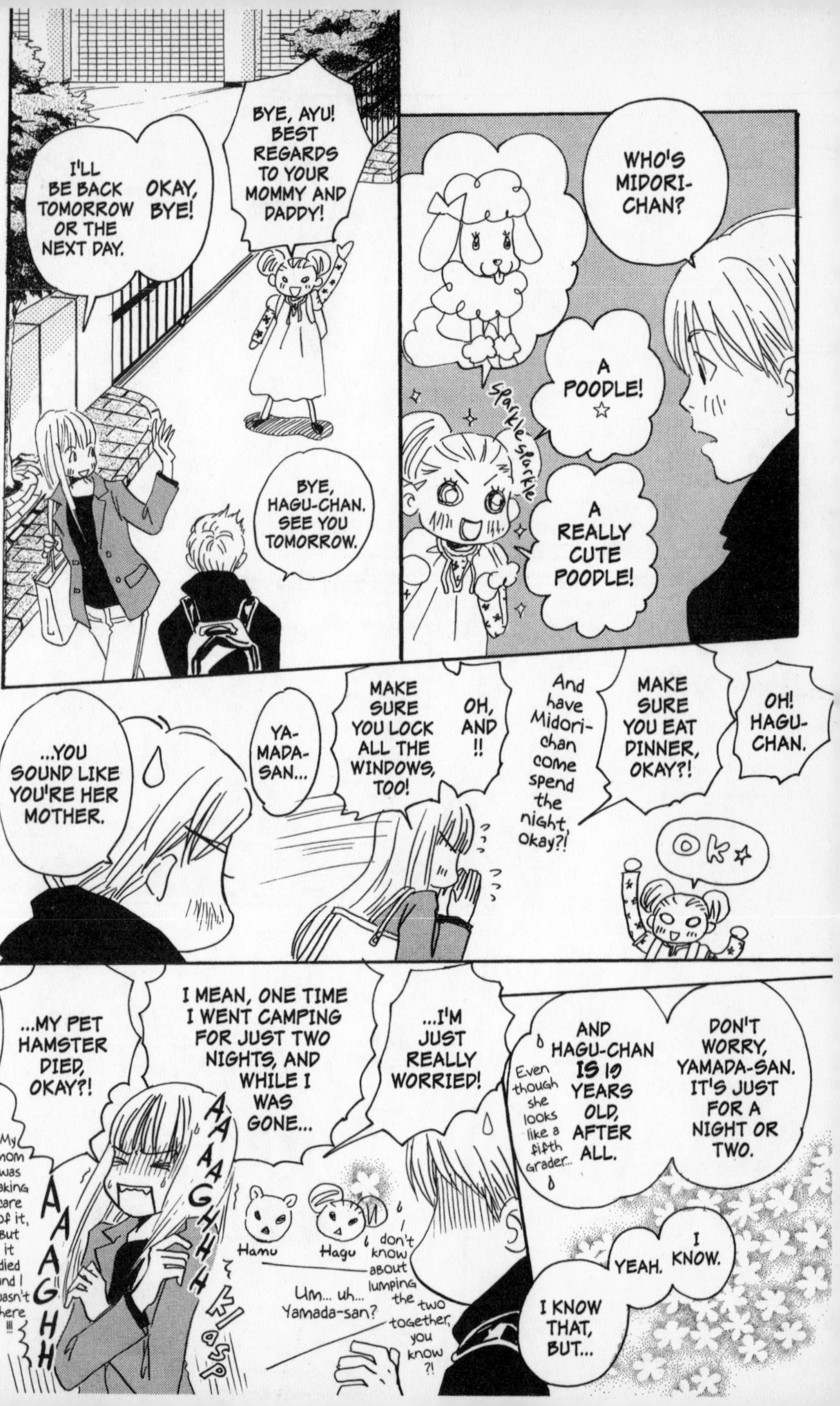
WHO'S MIDORI-CHAN?
A POODLE! ☆
sparkle sparkle
A REALLY CUTE POODLE!
BYE, AYU! BEST REGARDS TO YOUR MOMMY AND DADDY!
OKAY, BYE!
I'LL BE BACK TOMORROW OR THE NEXT DAY.
BYE, HAGU-CHAN. SEE YOU TOMORROW.
OH! HAGU-CHAN.
MAKE SURE YOU EAT DINNER, OKAY?!
And have Midori-chan come spend the night, okay?!
OH, AND!!
MAKE SURE YOU LOCK ALL THE WINDOWS, TOO!
OK☆
YA-MADA-SAN...
...YOU SOUND LIKE YOU'RE HER MOTHER.
DON'T WORRY, YAMADA-SAN. IT'S JUST FOR A NIGHT OR TWO.
AND HAGU-CHAN IS 19 YEARS OLD, AFTER ALL.
Even though she looks like a fifth grader...
I KNOW.
YEAH.
I KNOW THAT, BUT...
...I'M JUST REALLY WORRIED!
I MEAN, ONE TIME I WENT CAMPING FOR JUST TWO NIGHTS, AND WHILE I WAS GONE...
...MY PET HAMSTER DIED, OKAY?!
My mom was taking care of it, but it died and I wasn't there!!!
AAAGHH
AAAAGHHHH
Hamu
Hagu
I don't know about lumping the two together, you know?!
Um... uh... Yamada-san?
KI
ASP

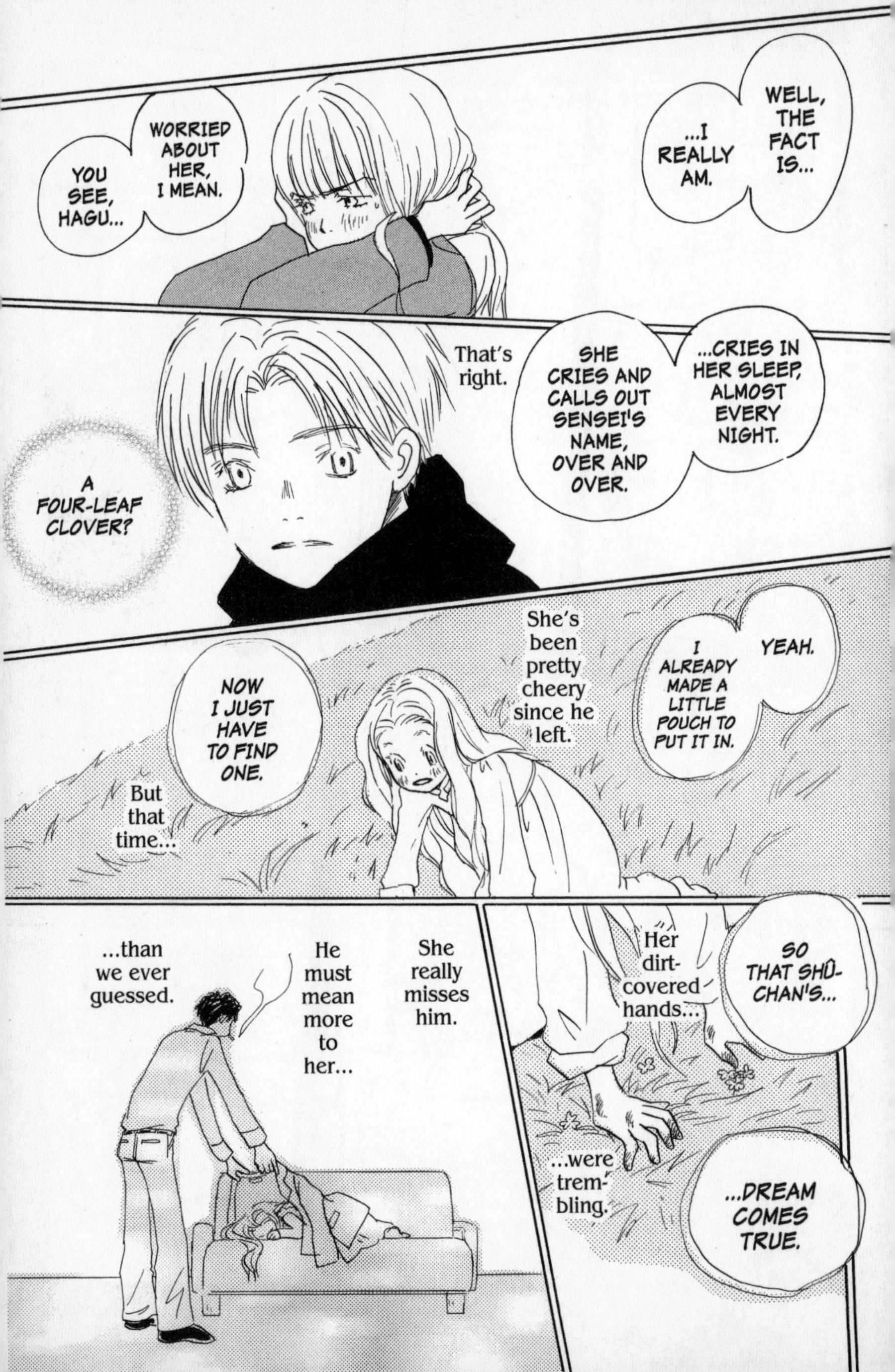
WELL, THE FACT IS...
...I REALLY AM.
WORRIED ABOUT HER, I MEAN.
YOU SEE, HAGU...
...CRIES IN HER SLEEP, ALMOST EVERY NIGHT.
SHE CRIES AND CALLS OUT SENSEI'S NAME, OVER AND OVER.
That's right.
A FOUR-LEAF CLOVER?
YEAH.
I ALREADY MADE A LITTLE POUCH TO PUT IT IN.
She's been pretty cheery since he left.
NOW I JUST HAVE TO FIND ONE.
But that time...
SO THAT SHŌ-CHAN'S...
Her dirt-covered hands...
...DREAM COMES TRUE.
...were trembling.
She really misses him.
He must mean more to her...
...than we ever guessed.

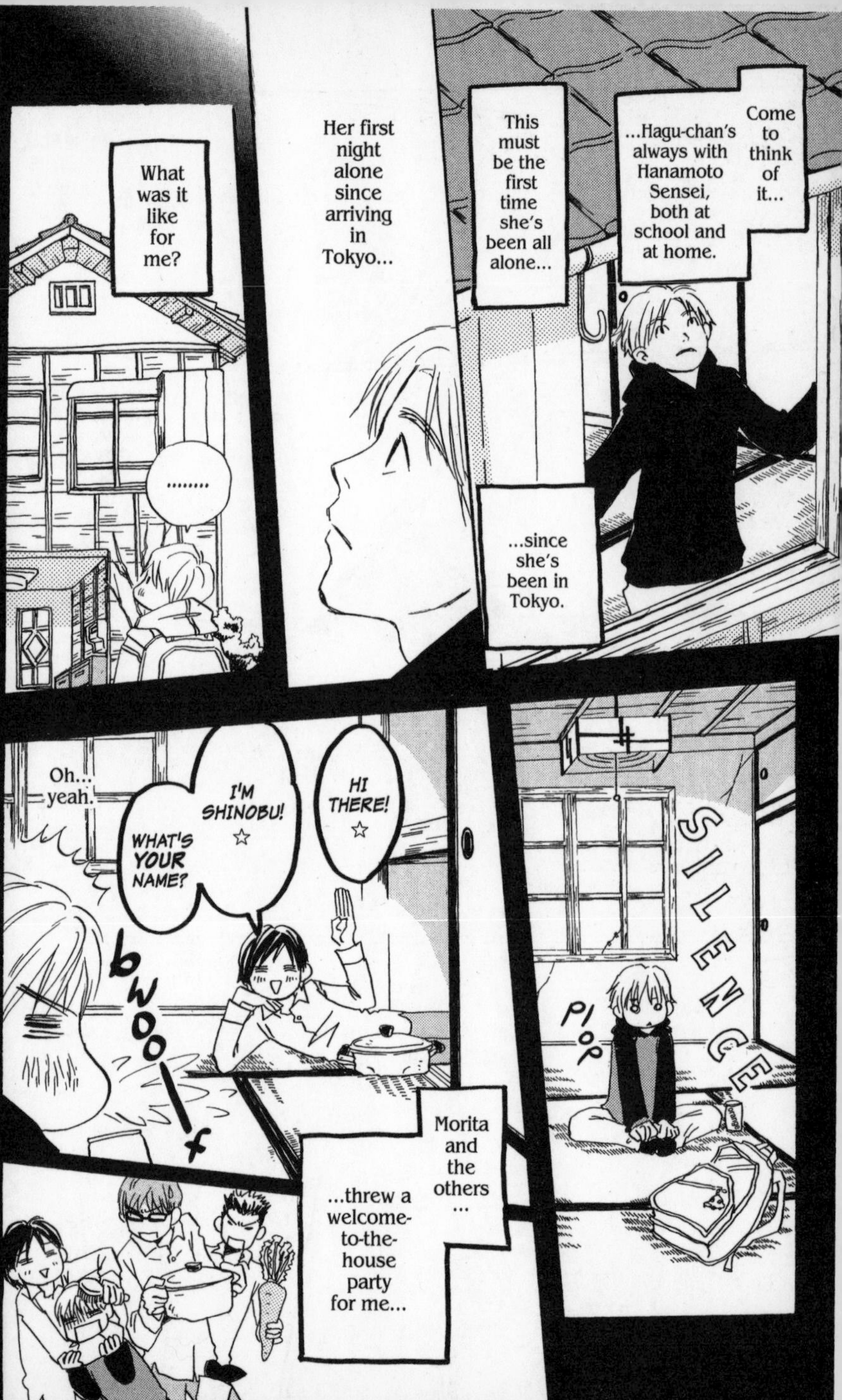
Come to think of it...
...Hagu-chan's always with Hanamoto Sensei, both at school and at home.
This must be the first time she's been all alone...
...since she's been in Tokyo.
Her first night alone since arriving in Tokyo...
What was it like for me?
....
SILENCE
PLOP
HI THERE! ☆
I'M SHINOBU! ☆
WHAT'S YOUR NAME?
Oh... yeah.
bwoof
Morita and the others...
...threw a welcome-to-the-house party for me...

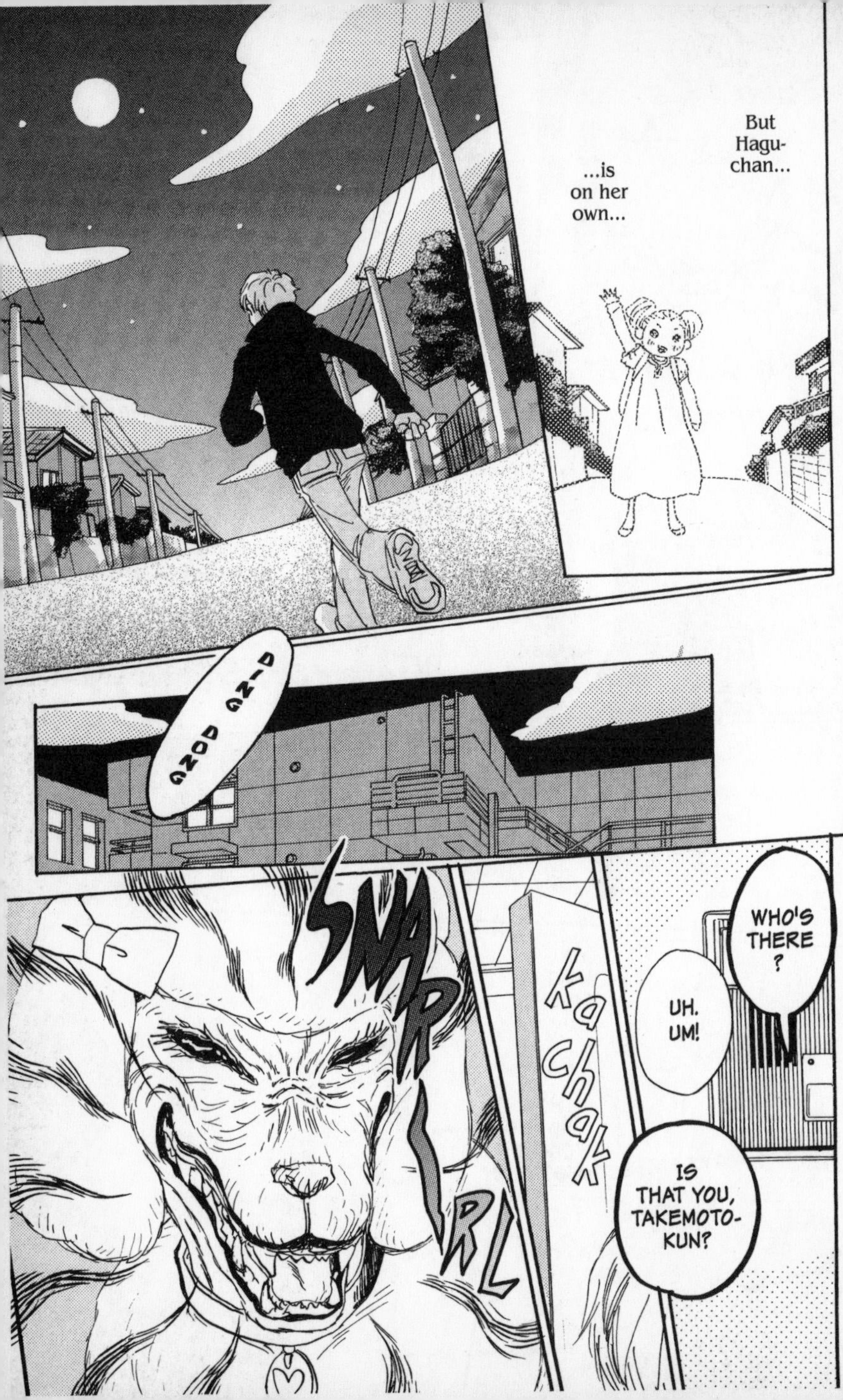
But Hagu-chan...
...is on her own...
DING DONG
WHO'S THERE?
UH. UM!
IS THAT YOU, TAKEMOTO-KUN?
kachak
SNARL

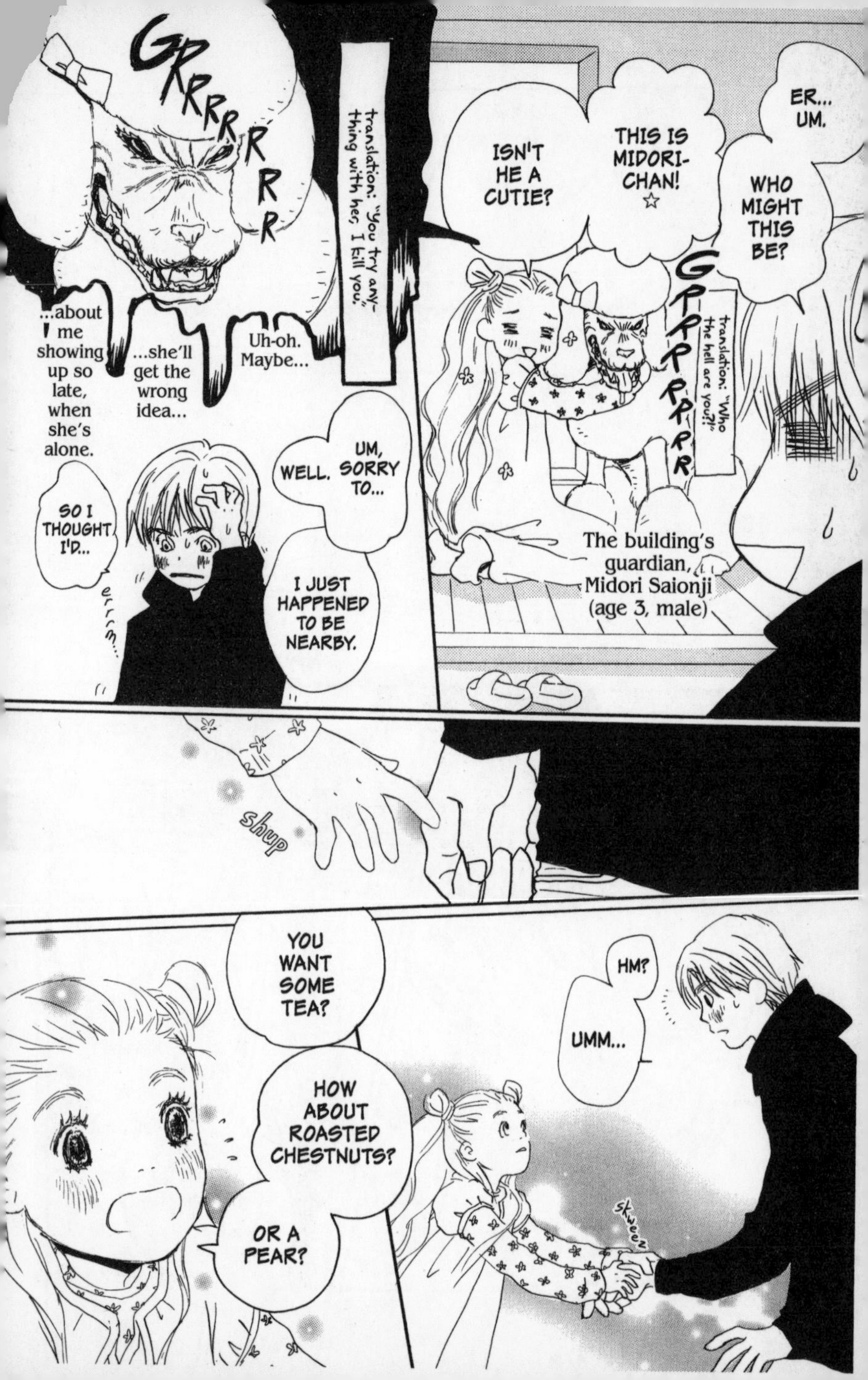
ER... UM.
WHO MIGHT THIS BE?
THIS IS MIDORI-CHAN! ☆
ISN'T HE A CUTIE?
GRRRRRRR
translation: "Who the hell are you?!"
The building's guardian, Midori Saionji (age 3, male)
GRRRRRRR
translation: "You try anything with her, I kill you."
Uh-oh. Maybe...
...she'll get the wrong idea...
...about me showing up so late, when she's alone.
WELL. UM, SORRY TO...
I JUST HAPPENED TO BE NEARBY.
SO I THOUGHT I'D...
errrm...
shup
HM?
UMM...
skweez
YOU WANT SOME TEA?
HOW ABOUT ROASTED CHESTNUTS?
OR A PEAR?

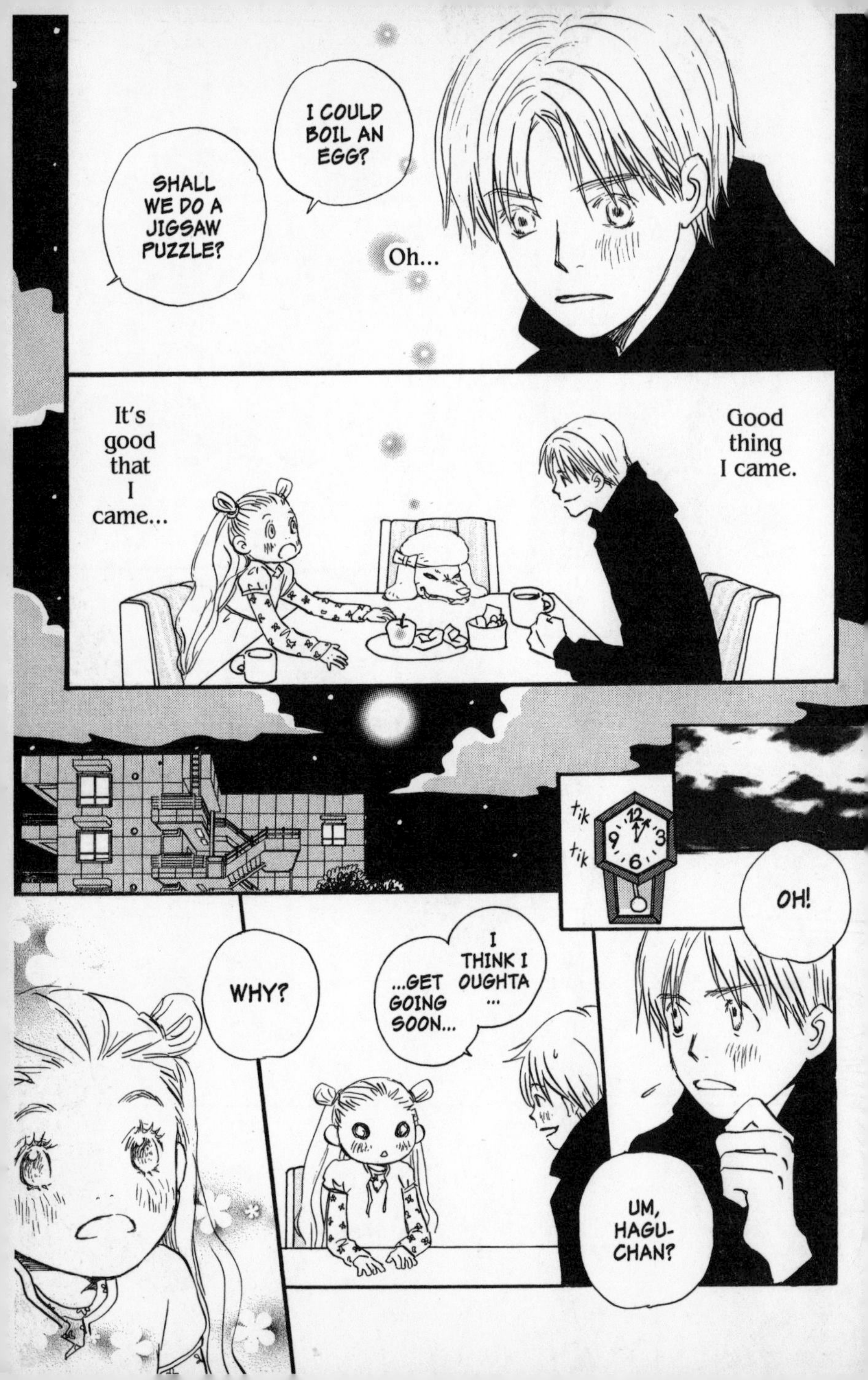

I COULD BOIL AN EGG?
SHALL WE DO A JIGSAW PUZZLE?
Oh...
Good thing I came.
It's good that I came...
tik tik
OH!
UM, HAGU-CHAN?
I THINK I OUGHTA ...
...GET GOING SOON...
WHY?

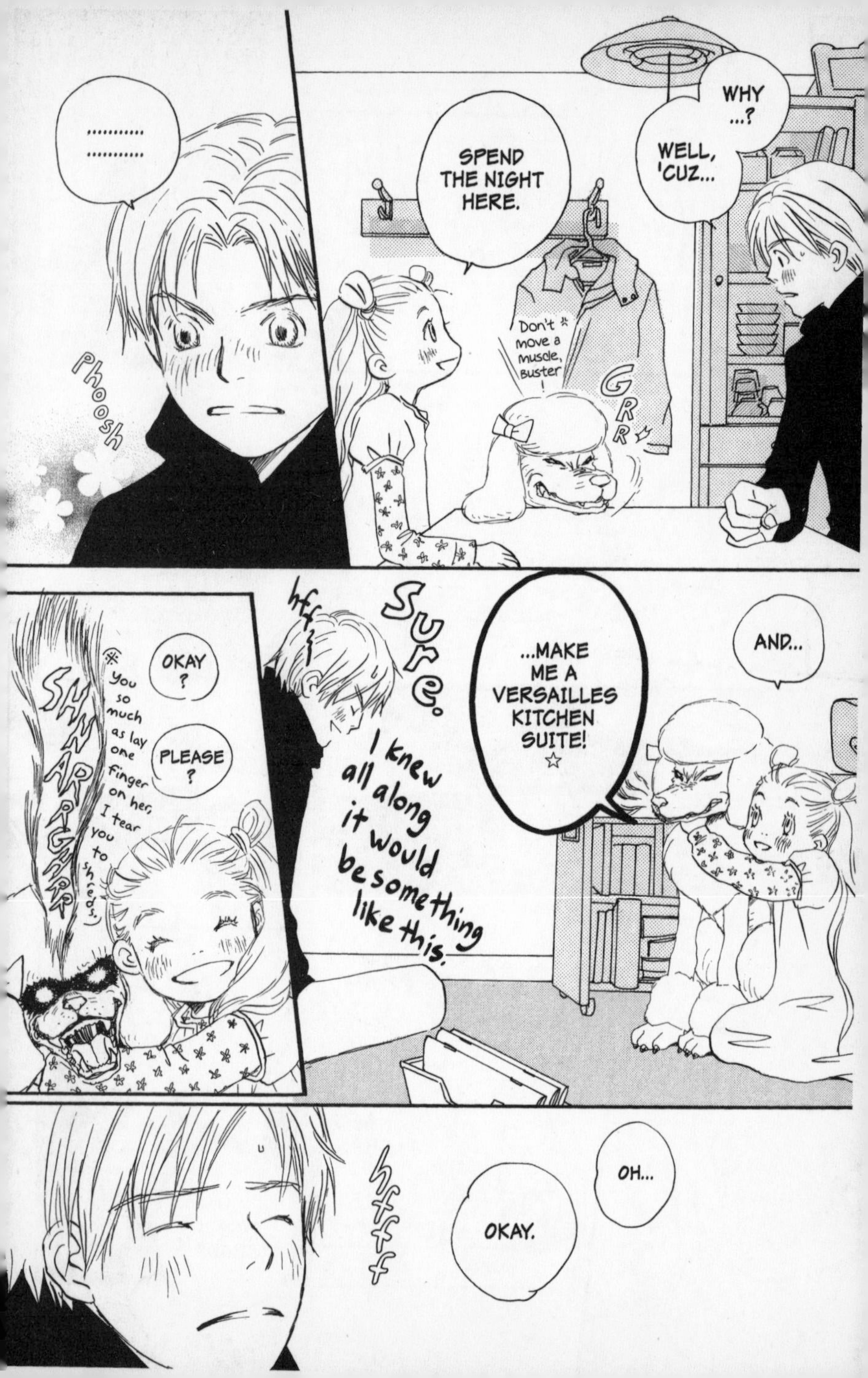
WHY ...?
WELL, 'CUZ...
SPEND THE NIGHT HERE.
Don't ※ move a muscle, Buster!
GRR
....
....
Phoosh
AND...
...MAKE ME A VERSAILLES KITCHEN SUITE! ☆
Sure.
hff
I knew all along it would be something like this.
OKAY?
PLEASE?
SHNARRGHRR
※ You so much as lay one finger on her, I tear you to shreds.
OH...
OKAY.
hfff

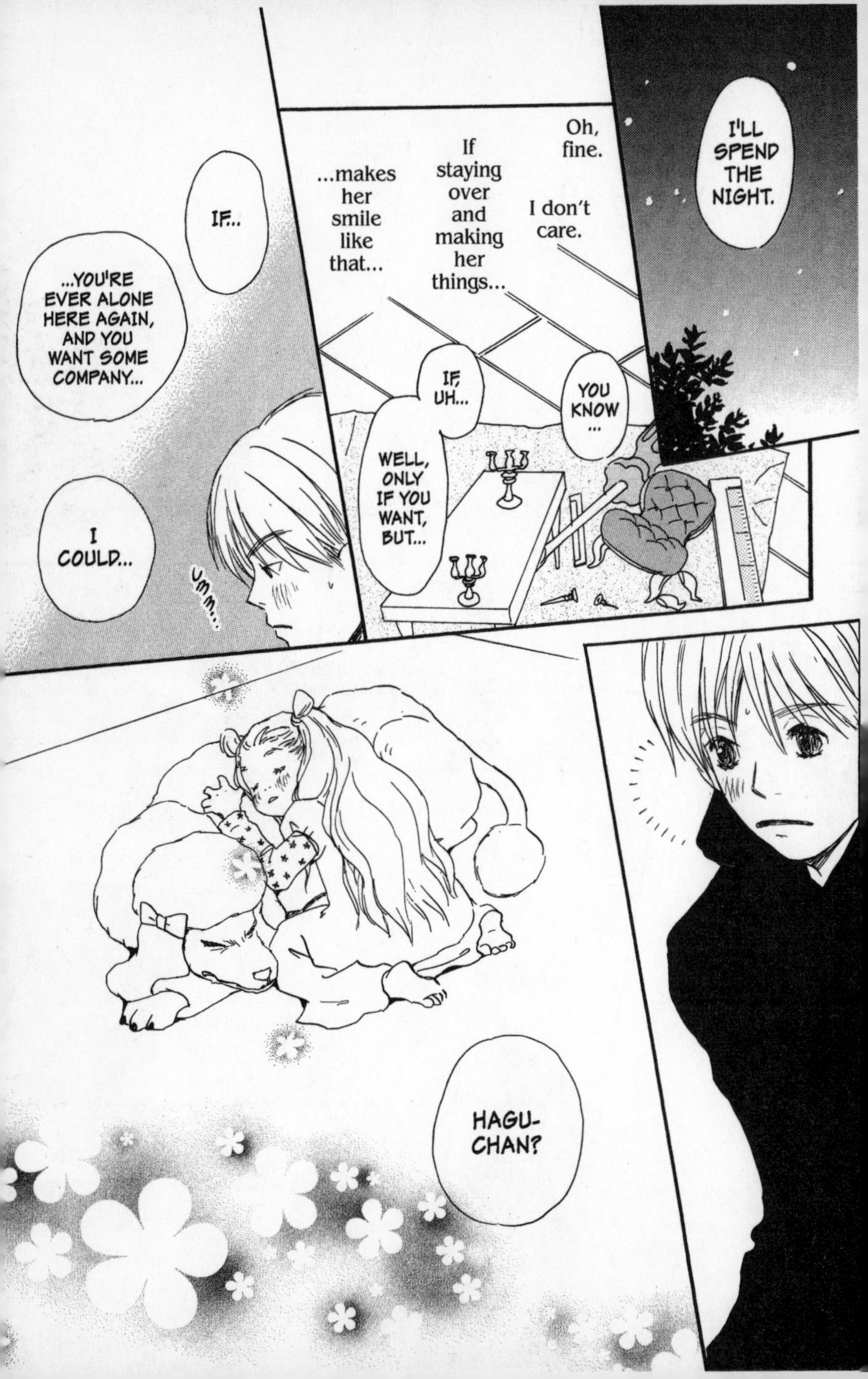
I'LL SPEND THE NIGHT.
Oh, fine.
I don't care.
If staying over and making her things...
...makes her smile like that...
YOU KNOW...
IF, UH...
WELL, ONLY IF YOU WANT, BUT...
IF...
...YOU'RE EVER ALONE HERE AGAIN, AND YOU WANT SOME COMPANY...
I COULD...
UMM...
HAGU-CHAN?

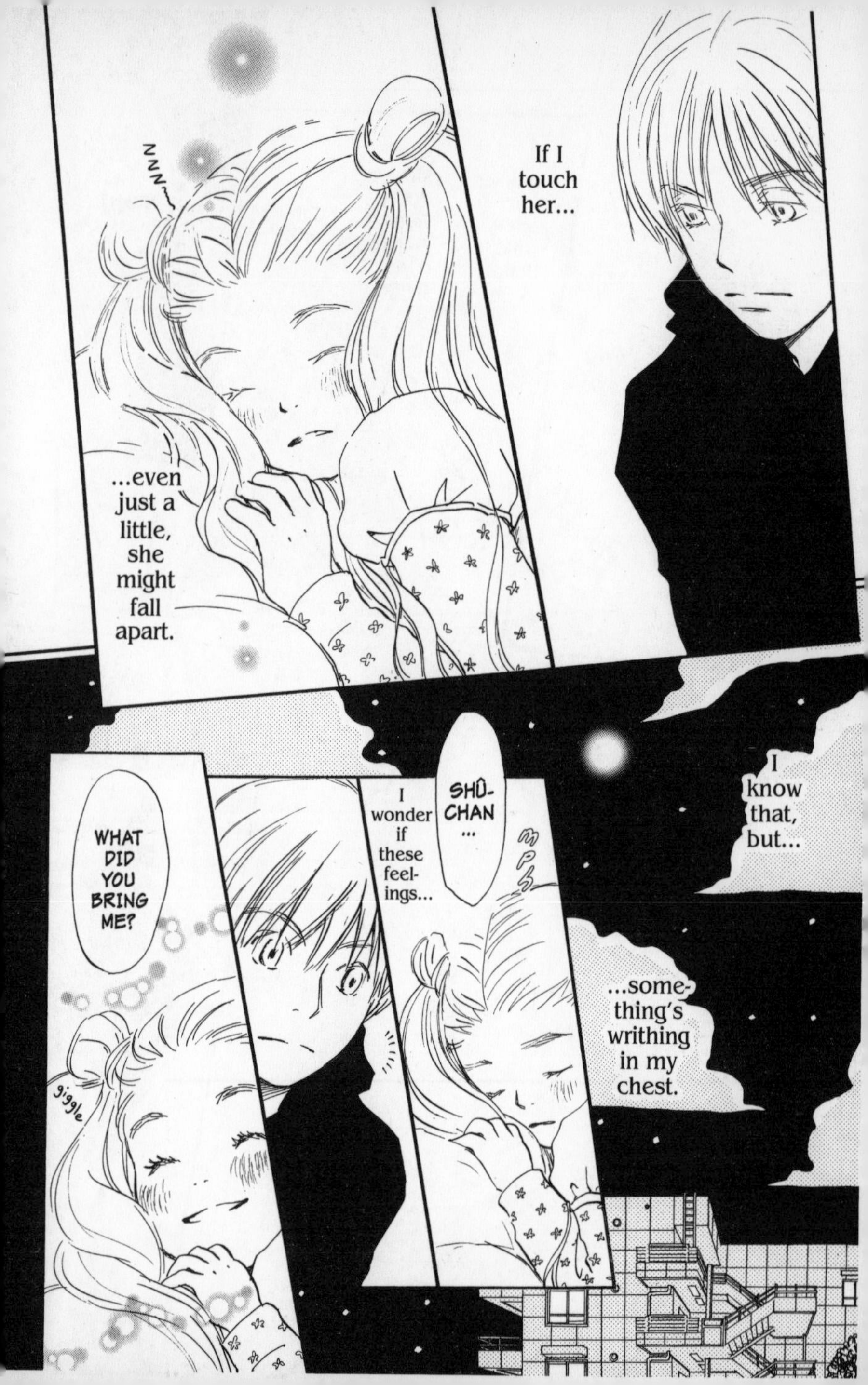
If I touch her...
...even just a little, she might fall apart.
I know that, but...
...something's writhing in my chest.
SHŪ-CHAN...
mph
I wonder if these feelings...
WHAT DID YOU BRING ME?
giggle

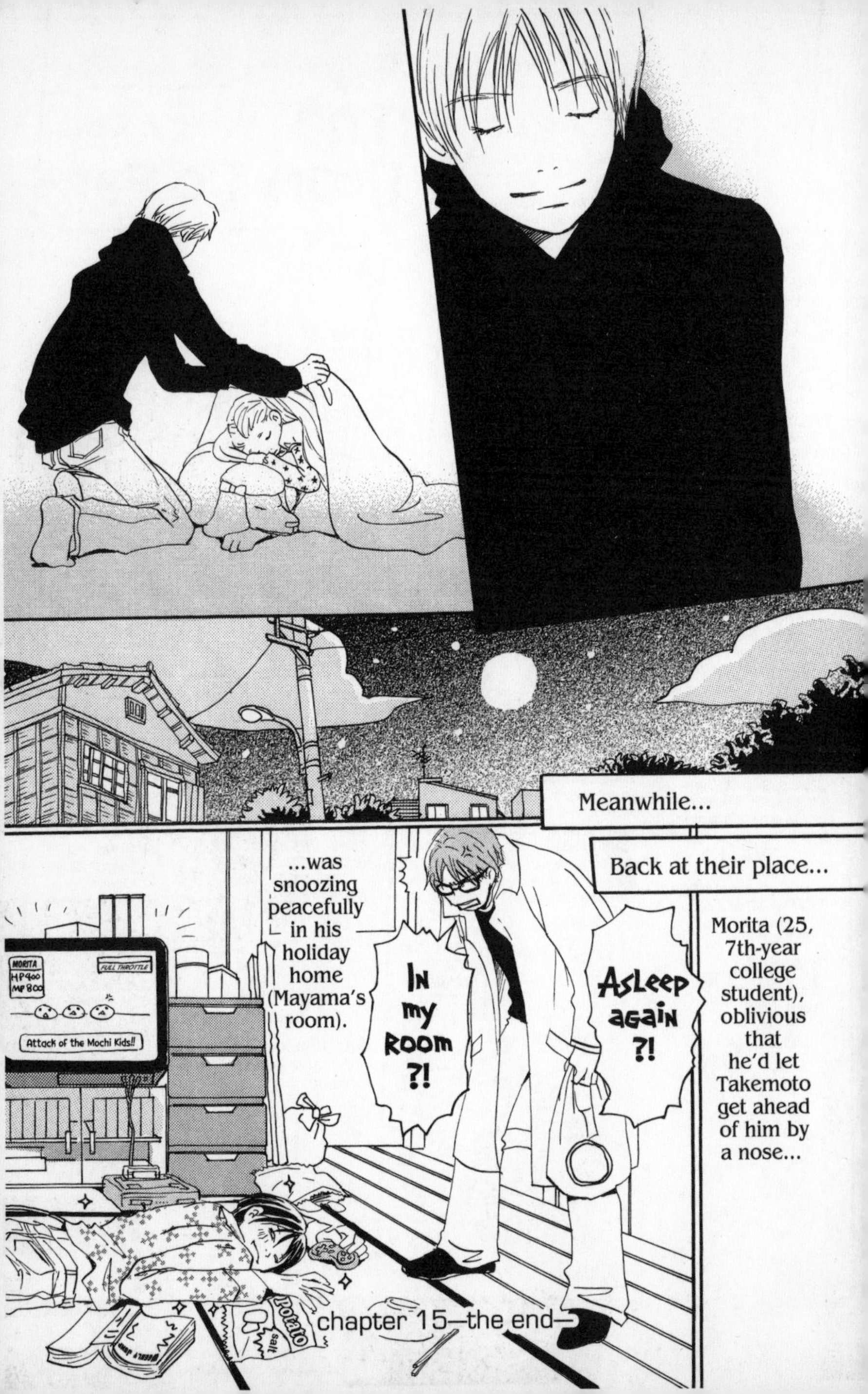
Meanwhile...
Back at their place...
Morita (25, 7th-year college student), oblivious that he'd let Takemoto get ahead of him by a nose...
Asleep again?!
In my ROOM?!
...was snoozing peacefully in his holiday home (Mayama's room).
MORITA
HP400
MP800
FULL THROTTLE
Attack of the Mochi Kids!!
Potato
salt
chapter 15—the end—

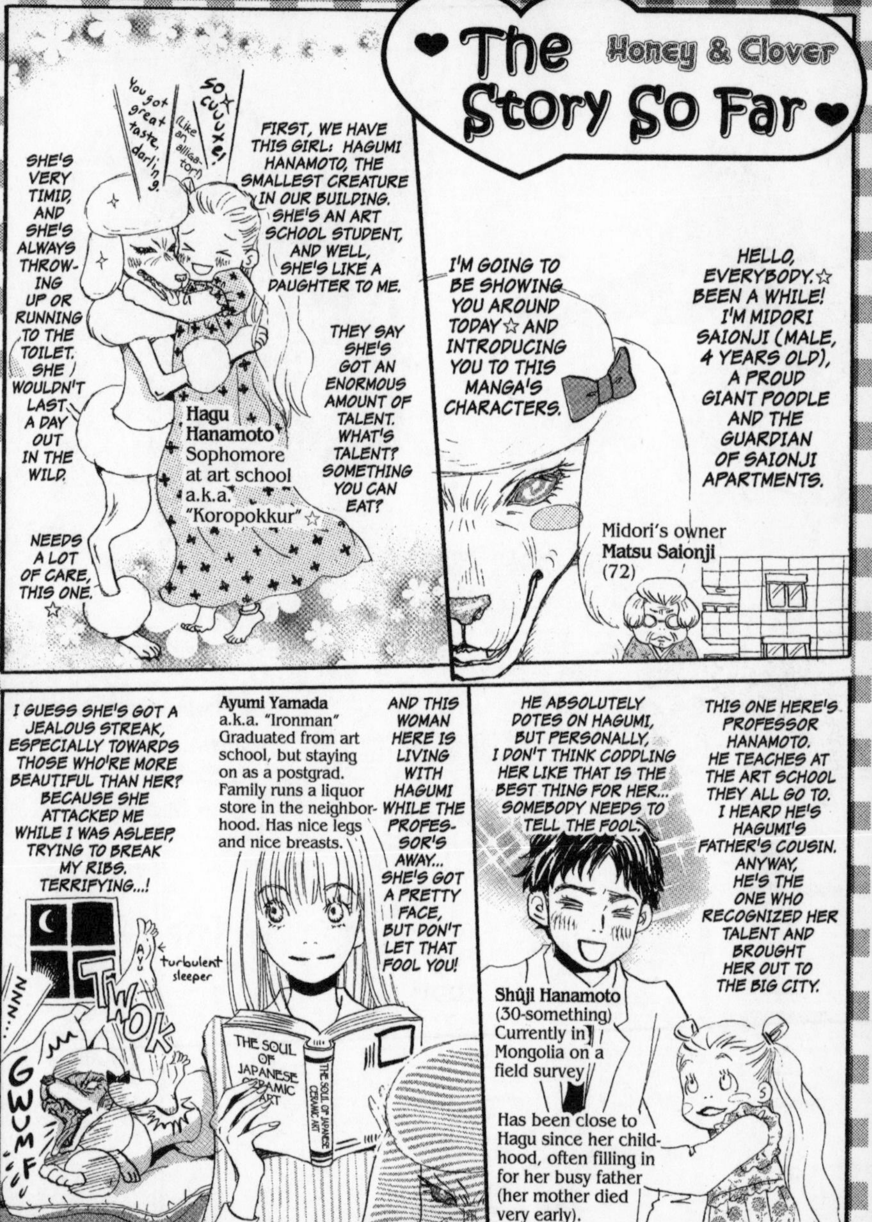
The Story So Far
Honey & Clover
HELLO, EVERYBODY.☆ BEEN A WHILE! I'M MIDORI SAIONJI (MALE, 4 YEARS OLD), A PROUD GIANT POODLE AND THE GUARDIAN OF SAIONJI APARTMENTS.
I'M GOING TO BE SHOWING YOU AROUND TODAY☆ AND INTRODUCING YOU TO THIS MANGA'S CHARACTERS.
Midori's owner **Matsu Saionji** (72)
FIRST, WE HAVE THIS GIRL: HAGUMI HANAMOTO, THE SMALLEST CREATURE IN OUR BUILDING. SHE'S AN ART SCHOOL STUDENT, AND WELL, SHE'S LIKE A DAUGHTER TO ME.
THEY SAY SHE'S GOT AN ENORMOUS AMOUNT OF TALENT. WHAT'S TALENT? SOMETHING YOU CAN EAT?
So cuuute!
(Like an alligator!)
You got great taste, darling.
SHE'S VERY TIMID, AND SHE'S ALWAYS THROWING UP OR RUNNING TO THE TOILET. SHE WOULDN'T LAST A DAY OUT IN THE WILD.
Hagu Hanamoto Sophomore at art school a.k.a. "Koropokkur"☆
NEEDS A LOT OF CARE, THIS ONE.☆
THIS ONE HERE'S PROFESSOR HANAMOTO. HE TEACHES AT THE ART SCHOOL THEY ALL GO TO. I HEARD HE'S HAGUMI'S FATHER'S COUSIN. ANYWAY, HE'S THE ONE WHO RECOGNIZED HER TALENT AND BROUGHT HER OUT TO THE BIG CITY.
HE ABSOLUTELY DOTES ON HAGUMI, BUT PERSONALLY, I DON'T THINK CODDLING HER LIKE THAT IS THE BEST THING FOR HER... SOMEBODY NEEDS TO TELL THE FOOL.
Shûji Hanamoto (30-something) Currently in Mongolia on a field survey
Has been close to Hagu since her childhood, often filling in for her busy father (her mother died very early).
AND THIS WOMAN HERE IS LIVING WITH HAGUMI WHILE THE PROFESSOR'S AWAY... SHE'S GOT A PRETTY FACE, BUT DON'T LET THAT FOOL YOU!
Ayumi Yamada a.k.a. "Ironman" Graduated from art school, but staying on as a postgrad. Family runs a liquor store in the neighborhood. Has nice legs and nice breasts.
I GUESS SHE'S GOT A JEALOUS STREAK, ESPECIALLY TOWARDS THOSE WHO'RE MORE BEAUTIFUL THAN HER? BECAUSE SHE ATTACKED ME WHILE I WAS ASLEEP, TRYING TO BREAK MY RIBS. TERRIFYING...!
AY
turbulent sleeper
TWOK
NNN...
GWUMF
THE SOUL OF JAPANESE CERAMIC ART

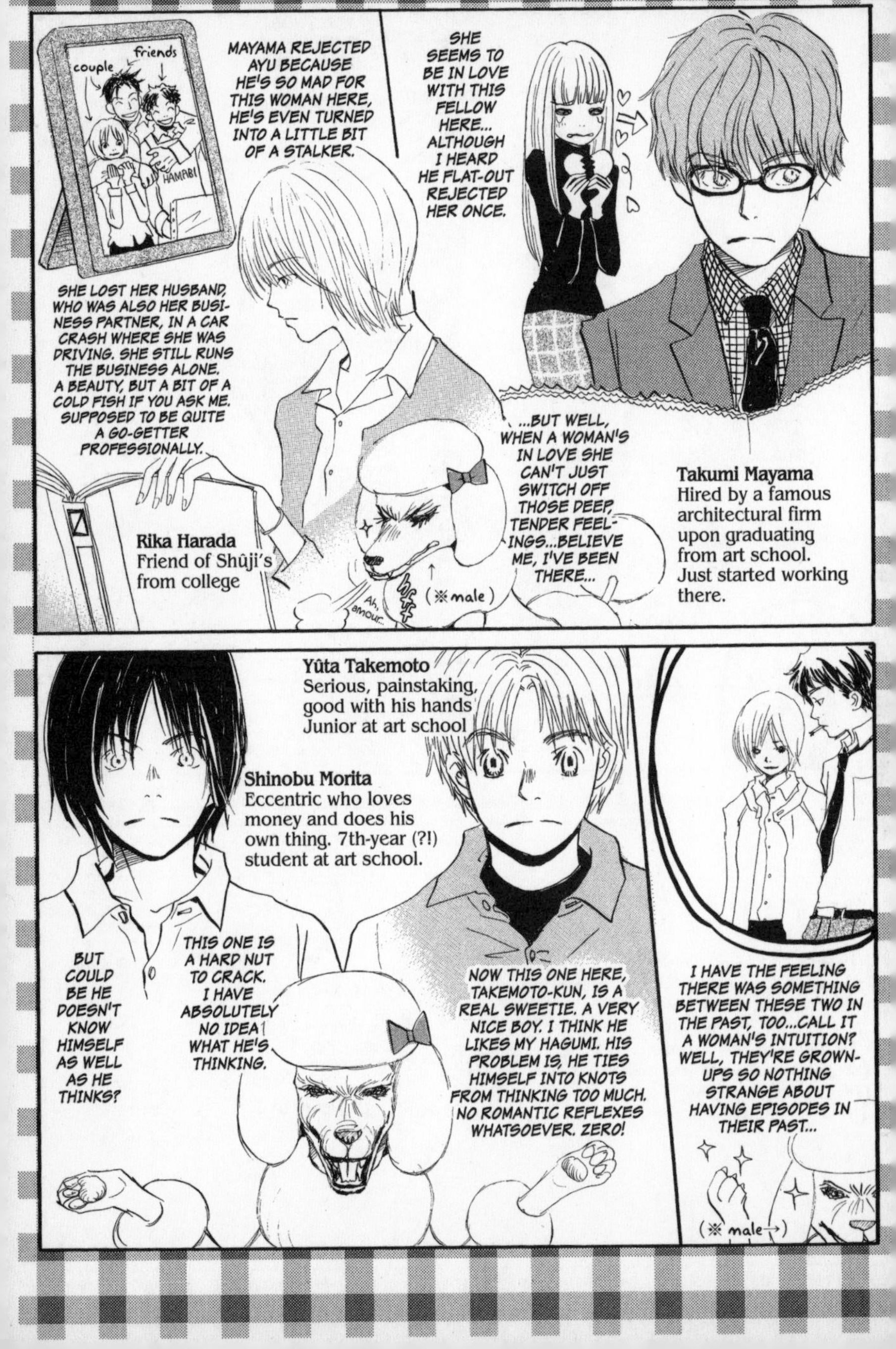
SHE SEEMS TO BE IN LOVE WITH THIS FELLOW HERE... ALTHOUGH I HEARD HE FLAT-OUT REJECTED HER ONCE.
Takumi Mayama
Hired by a famous architectural firm upon graduating from art school. Just started working there.
...BUT WELL, WHEN A WOMAN'S IN LOVE SHE CAN'T JUST SWITCH OFF THOSE DEEP, TENDER FEELINGS...BELIEVE ME, I'VE BEEN THERE...
(※male)
Ah, amour...
MAYAMA REJECTED AYU BECAUSE HE'S SO MAD FOR THIS WOMAN HERE, HE'S EVEN TURNED INTO A LITTLE BIT OF A STALKER.
friends
couple
HAMABI
SHE LOST HER HUSBAND, WHO WAS ALSO HER BUSINESS PARTNER, IN A CAR CRASH WHERE SHE WAS DRIVING. SHE STILL RUNS THE BUSINESS ALONE. A BEAUTY, BUT A BIT OF A COLD FISH IF YOU ASK ME. SUPPOSED TO BE QUITE A GO-GETTER PROFESSIONALLY.
Rika Harada
Friend of Shûji's from college
I HAVE THE FEELING THERE WAS SOMETHING BETWEEN THESE TWO IN THE PAST, TOO...CALL IT A WOMAN'S INTUITION? WELL, THEY'RE GROWN-UPS SO NOTHING STRANGE ABOUT HAVING EPISODES IN THEIR PAST...
(※male→)
Yûta Takemoto
Serious, painstaking, good with his hands
Junior at art school
NOW THIS ONE HERE, TAKEMOTO-KUN, IS A REAL SWEETIE. A VERY NICE BOY. I THINK HE LIKES MY HAGUMI. HIS PROBLEM IS, HE TIES HIMSELF INTO KNOTS FROM THINKING TOO MUCH. NO ROMANTIC REFLEXES WHATSOEVER. ZERO!
Shinobu Morita
Eccentric who loves money and does his own thing. 7th-year (?!) student at art school.
THIS ONE IS A HARD NUT TO CRACK. I HAVE ABSOLUTELY NO IDEA WHAT HE'S THINKING.
BUT COULD BE HE DOESN'T KNOW HIMSELF AS WELL AS HE THINKS?

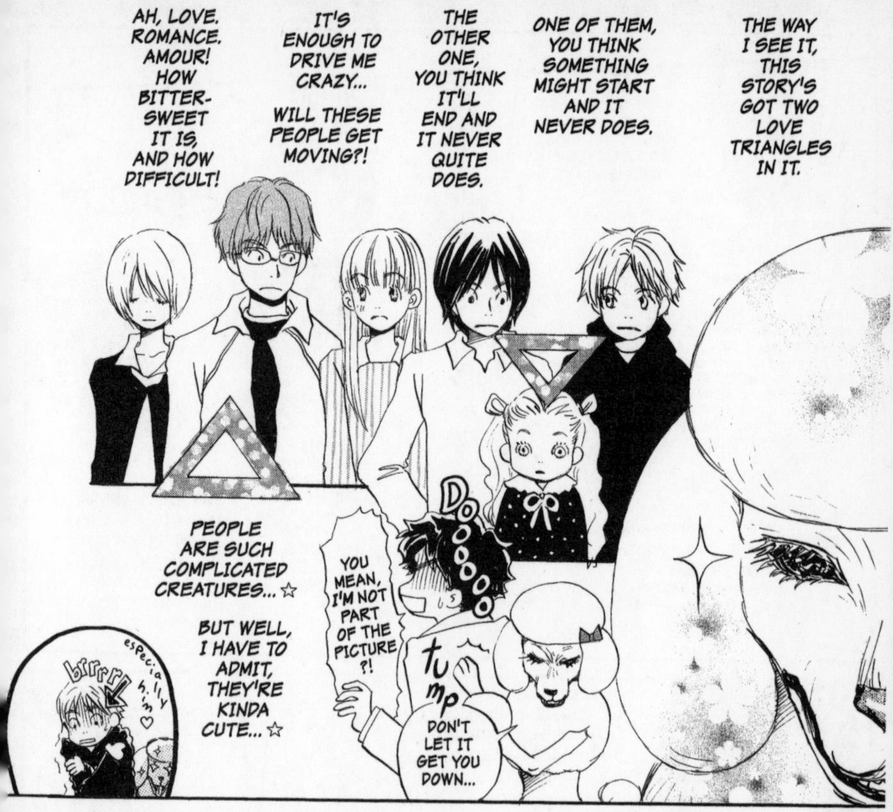
THE WAY I SEE IT, THIS STORY'S GOT TWO LOVE TRIANGLES IN IT.
ONE OF THEM, YOU THINK SOMETHING MIGHT START AND IT NEVER DOES.
THE OTHER ONE, YOU THINK IT'LL END AND IT NEVER QUITE DOES.
IT'S ENOUGH TO DRIVE ME CRAZY...
WILL THESE PEOPLE GET MOVING?!
AH, LOVE. ROMANCE. AMOUR! HOW BITTER-SWEET IT IS, AND HOW DIFFICULT!
PEOPLE ARE SUCH COMPLICATED CREATURES... ☆
BUT WELL, I HAVE TO ADMIT, THEY'RE KINDA CUTE... ☆
DOOOOOOO
YOU MEAN, I'M NOT PART OF THE PICTURE?!
tump
DON'T LET IT GET YOU DOWN...
brrrr
especially him ♡

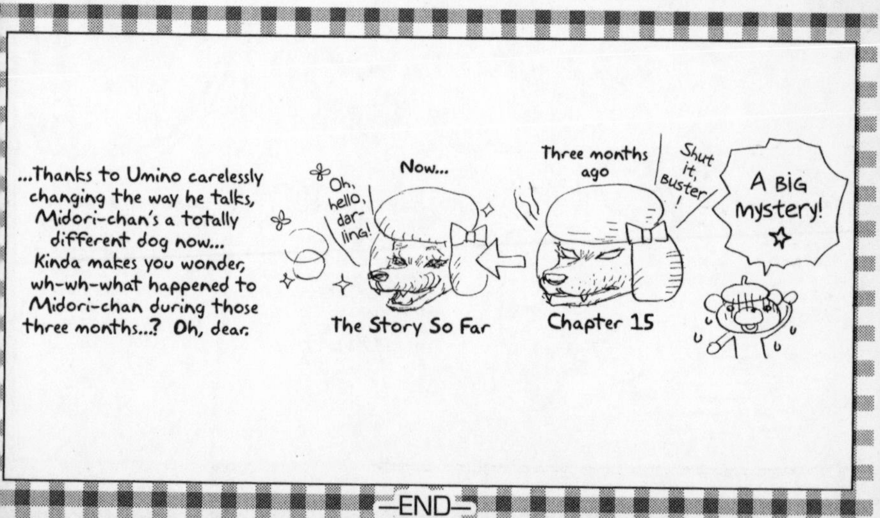
A BIG Mystery! ☆
Shut it, Buster!
Three months ago
Chapter 15
Now...
Oh, hello, darling!
The Story So Far
...Thanks to Umino carelessly changing the way he talks, Midori-chan's a totally different dog now... Kinda makes you wonder, wh-wh-what happened to Midori-chan during those three months...? Oh, dear.

—END—

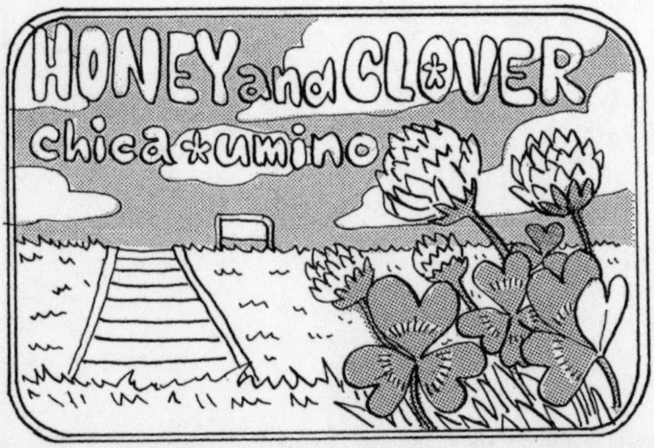
HONEY and CLOVER
chica*umino

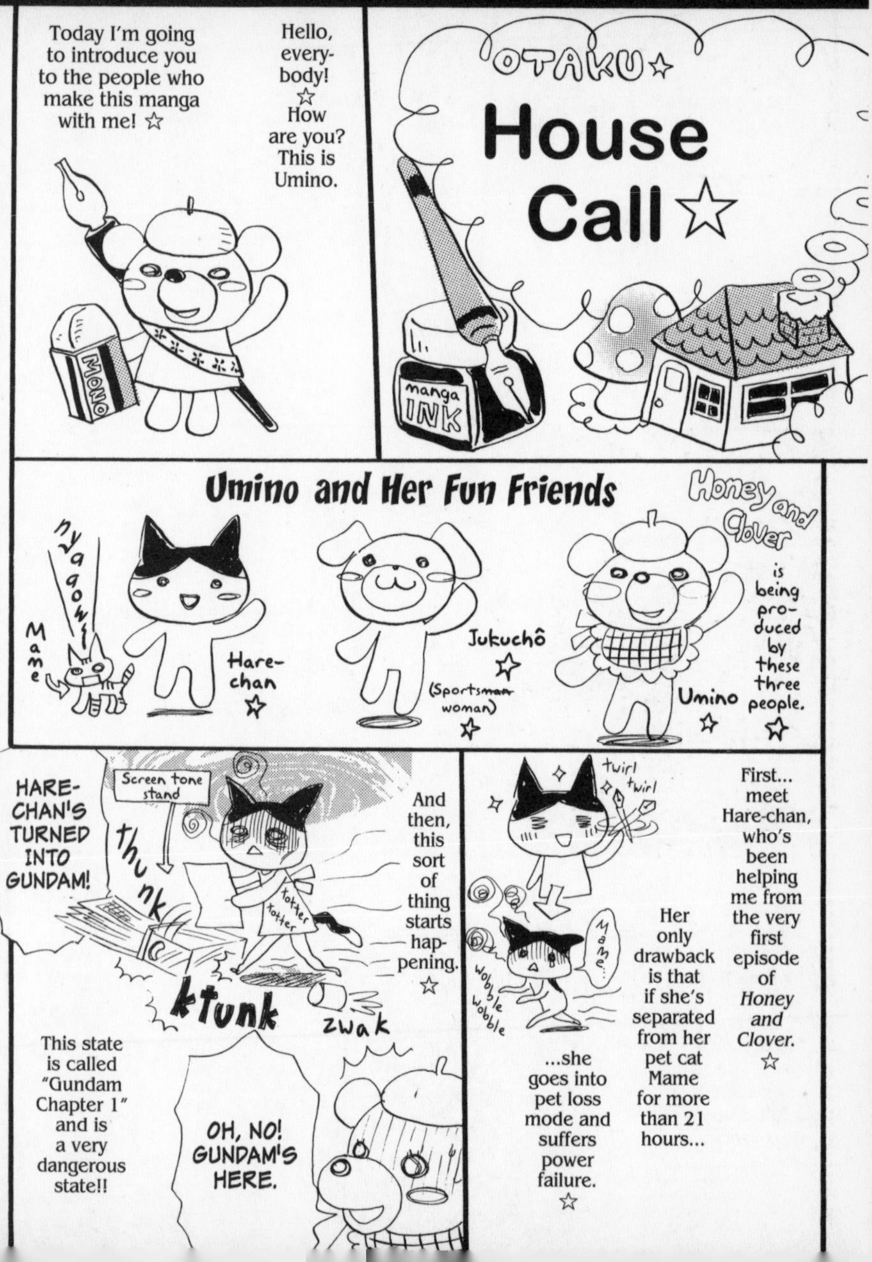
OTAKU☆
House Call☆
manga INK
Hello, everybody! ☆ How are you? This is Umino.
Today I'm going to introduce you to the people who make this manga with me! ☆
MONO
Umino and Her Fun Friends
Honey and Clover is being produced by these three people. ☆
Umino ☆
Jukuchô ☆ (Sportsman woman) ☆
Hare-chan ☆
nyaaoow!
Mame
First... meet Hare-chan, who's been helping me from the very first episode of Honey and Clover. ☆
twirl twirl
Her only drawback is that if she's separated from her pet cat Mame for more than 21 hours...
Mame...
wobble wobble
...she goes into pet loss mode and suffers power failure. ☆
And then, this sort of thing starts happening. ☆
Screen tone stand
HARE-CHAN'S TURNED INTO GUNDAM!
thunk
xotter xotter
ktunk
zwak
OH, NO! GUNDAM'S HERE.
This state is called "Gundam Chapter 1" and is a very dangerous state!!

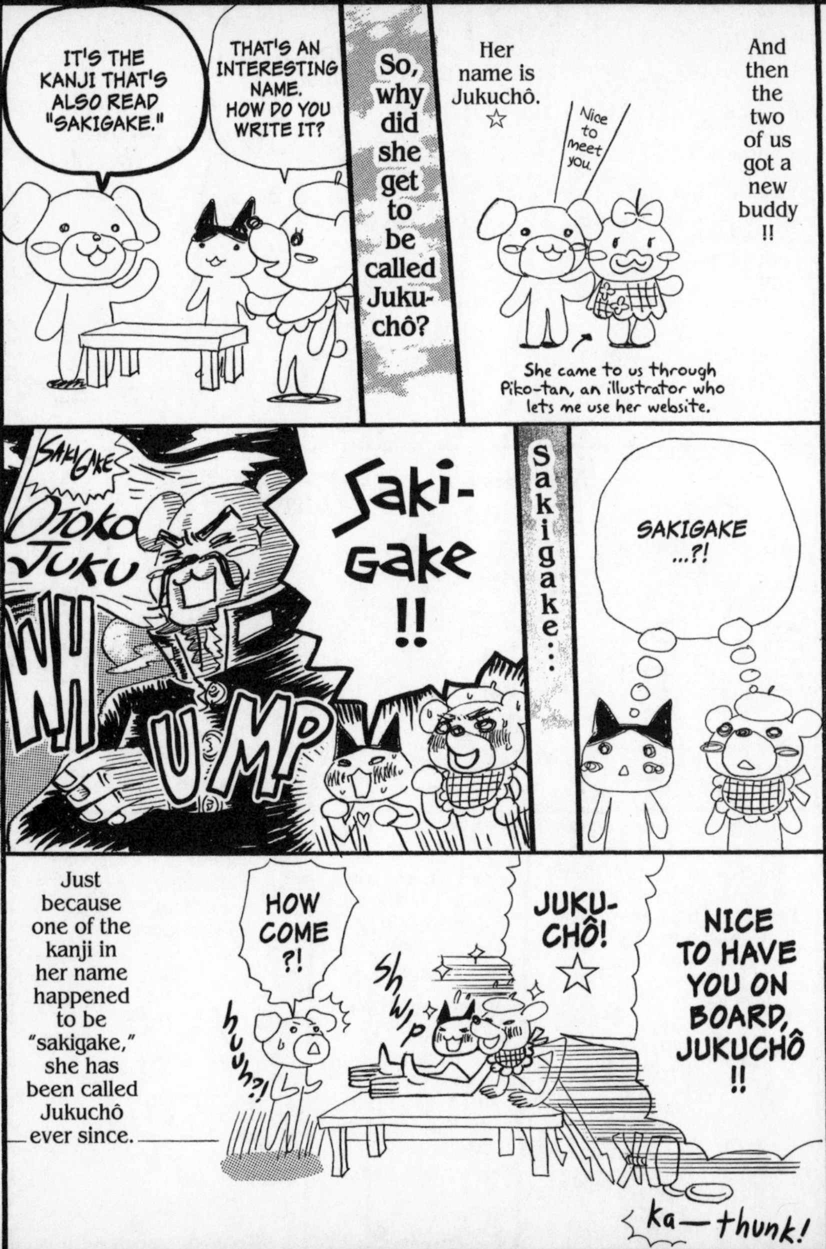
And then the two of us got a new buddy !!
Her name is Jukuchô. ☆
Nice to meet you.
She came to us through Piko-tan, an illustrator who lets me use her website.
So, why did she get to be called Juku-chô?
THAT'S AN INTERESTING NAME. HOW DO YOU WRITE IT?
IT'S THE KANJI THAT'S ALSO READ "SAKIGAKE."
SAKIGAKE ...?!
Sakigake...
Saki-gake !!
SAKIGAKE
OTOKO JUKU
WHUMP
NICE TO HAVE YOU ON BOARD, JUKUCHÔ !!
JUKU-CHÔ! ☆
SHWIP
HOW COME ?!
huuh?!
Just because one of the kanji in her name happened to be "sakigake," she has been called Jukuchô ever since.
ka—thunk!

a Shonen Jump manga

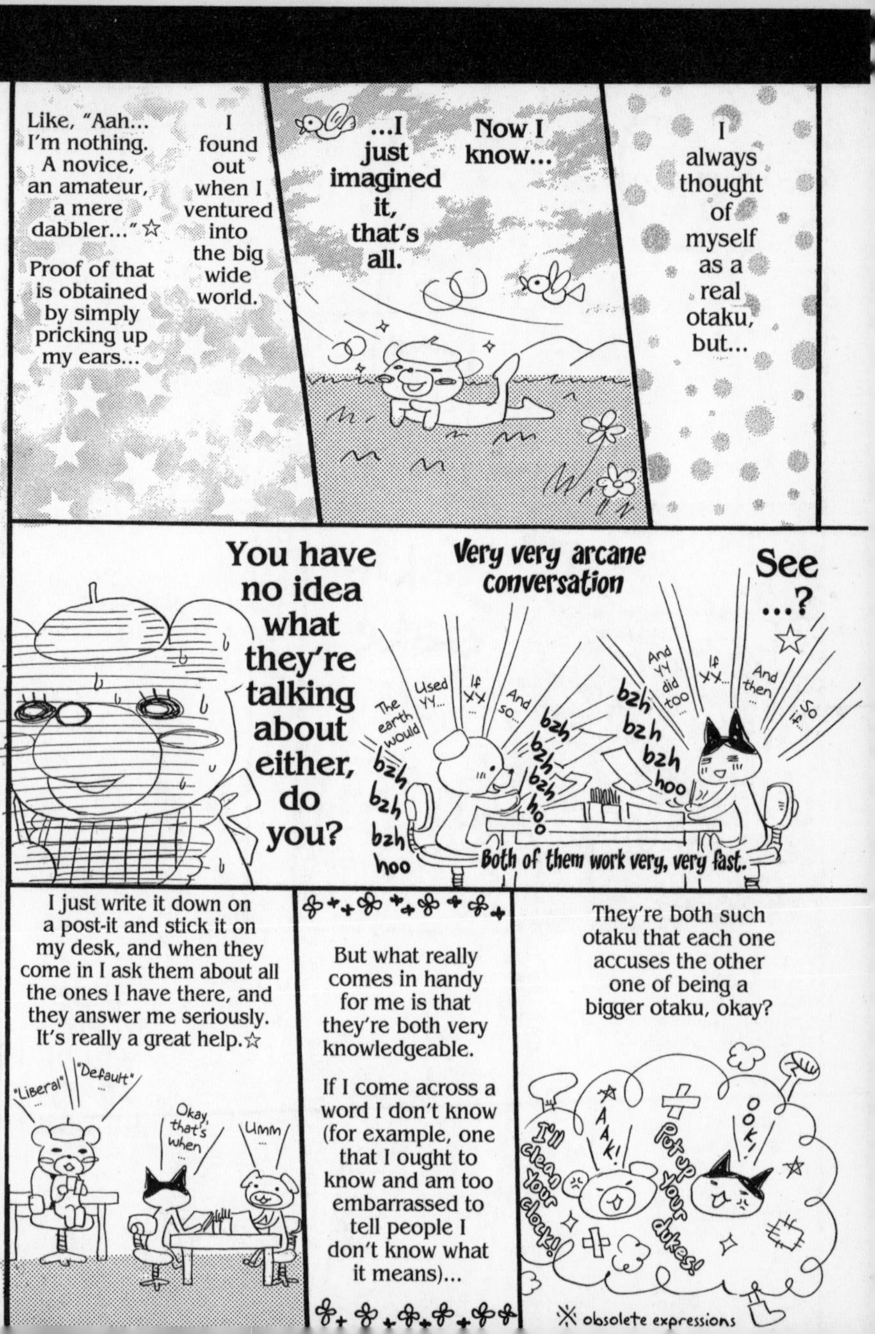
I always thought of myself as a real otaku, but...
Now I know...
...I just imagined it, that's all.
I found out when I ventured into the big wide world.
Like, "Aah... I'm nothing. A novice, an amateur, a mere dabbler..."☆
Proof of that is obtained by simply pricking up my ears...
See ...? ☆
Very very arcane conversation
So if...
And then...
If XX...
And YY did too
And so...
If XX...
Used YY...
The earth would...
bzh bzh bzh hoo
bzh bzh bzh hoo
bzh bzh bzh bzh hoo
Both of them work very, very fast.
You have no idea what they're talking about either, do you?
They're both such otaku that each one accuses the other one of being a bigger otaku, okay?
OOK!
Put up your dukes!
AAK!
I'll clean your clock!
※obsolete expressions
But what really comes in handy for me is that they're both very knowledgeable.
If I come across a word I don't know (for example, one that I ought to know and am too embarrassed to tell people I don't know what it means)...
I just write it down on a post-it and stick it on my desk, and when they come in I ask them about all the ones I have there, and they answer me seriously. It's really a great help.☆
"Default"...
"Liberal"...
Umm...
Okay, that's when...

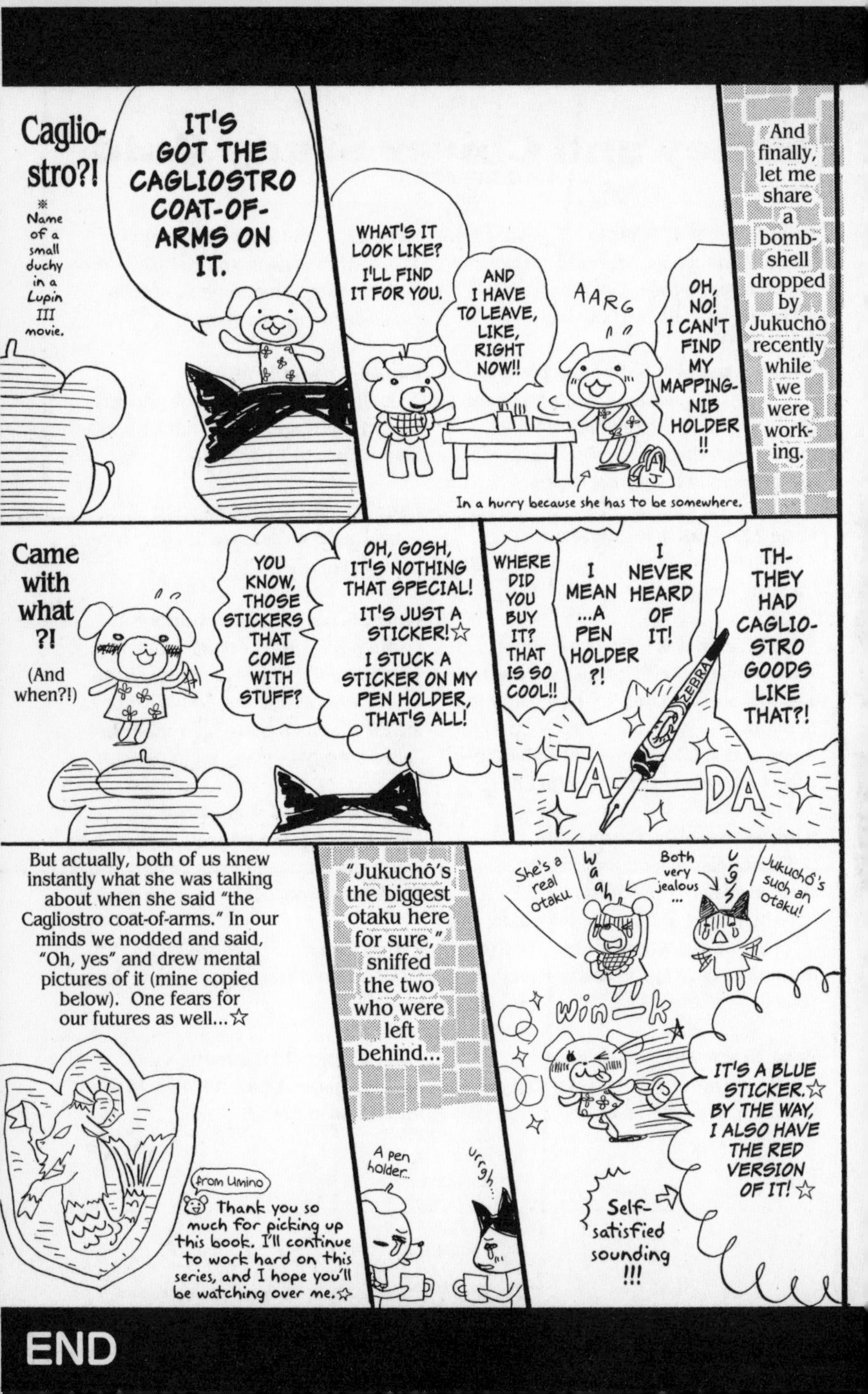

And finally, let me share a bombshell dropped by Jukuchô recently while we were working.
OH, NO! I CAN'T FIND MY MAPPING-NIB HOLDER!!
AARG
WHAT'S IT LOOK LIKE? I'LL FIND IT FOR YOU.
AND I HAVE TO LEAVE, LIKE, RIGHT NOW!!
In a hurry because she has to be somewhere.
IT'S GOT THE CAGLIOSTRO COAT-OF-ARMS ON IT.
Caglio-stro?!
※ Name of a small duchy in a Lupin III movie.
TH-THEY HAD CAGLIOSTRO GOODS LIKE THAT?!
I NEVER HEARD OF IT!
I MEAN ...A PEN HOLDER?!
WHERE DID YOU BUY IT? THAT IS SO COOL!!
ZEBRA
TA—DA
OH, GOSH, IT'S NOTHING THAT SPECIAL! IT'S JUST A STICKER!☆ I STUCK A STICKER ON MY PEN HOLDER, THAT'S ALL!
YOU KNOW, THOSE STICKERS THAT COME WITH STUFF?
Came with what?!
(And when?!)
Jukuchô's such an otaku!
ugh
Both very jealous ...
Waah
She's a real otaku.
IT'S A BLUE STICKER.☆ BY THE WAY, I ALSO HAVE THE RED VERSION OF IT!☆
win—k
Self-satisfied sounding!!!
"Jukuchô's the biggest otaku here for sure," sniffed the two who were left behind...
A pen holder...
urrgh...
But actually, both of us knew instantly what she was talking about when she said "the Cagliostro coat-of-arms." In our minds we nodded and said, "Oh, yes" and drew mental pictures of it (mine copied below). One fears for our futures as well...☆
from Umino
Thank you so much for picking up this book. I'll continue to work hard on this series, and I hope you'll be watching over me.☆
END

Honey and Clover Study Guide

Page 4, panel 4: Takasaki
Located about 65 miles north of Tokyo, or one hour on the bullet train. Takasaki is home to about 340,000 people.

Page 22, panel 1: Shimonita leeks
A type of Japanese leek or spring onion grown in the Kanto region. They are thicker than the *shironegi* and *naganegi* leeks grown in the Kansai region.

Page 22, panel 4: Konnyaku
A firm jelly with little natural flavor, made from the konjac plant.

Page 22, panel 6: Mizusawa
A city in Iwate prefecture, on the northeast of Honshu Island. It is home to one of the six International Latitude Observatories, and in 2006 it merged with other cities in the area to create Oshu City.

Page 23, panel 2: Daruma doll
Dolls modeled after Bohdidharma, the founder of Zen. The egg-shaped dolls have no pupils, and it is traditional to color in one eye while making a wish or resolution. When your goal is achieved, you fill in the other eye.

Page 25, panel 1: Nozawa-na
A leafy Japanese vegetable related to the turnip. It is often pickled.

Page 25, panel 2: Otoshidama
The custom of giving money to children on New Year's. The money comes in small, decorated envelopes.

Page 26, panel 1: Yaizu
A city in Shizuoka prefecture and an important fishing port. It has a population of about 120,000.

Page 26, panel 1: Kamaboko
A steamed fishcake, like the kind served in ramen.

Page 26, panel 1: Kuro-hanpen
Hanpen is a square of *surimi*, or fish puree, usually served in oden or soup. In Shizuoka prefecture, whole sardines are used, resulting in a blue-gray puree called kuro-hanpen, or black hanpen.

Page 26, panel 1: Kanazawa
Capital of Ishikawa prefecture; it is surrounded by the Japanese Alps and two national parks.

Page 26, panel 1: Kabura-zushi
Pickled turnip and yellowtail fish, served in layers.

Page 26, panel 1: Namafu
A wheat gluten product similar to the seitan sold in the U.S.

Page 26, panel 4: Azumino
A city in Nagano prefecture. It was founded October 1, 2005, when Akashina, Horigane, Hotaka, Misato, and Toyoshina merged. It has a population of about 100,000.

Page 40, panel 2: Dokudami
A strong-smelling plant renowned for its medicinal properties. It is often served as a medicinal tea. It is know as heartleaf and lizardtail in English.

Page 89, panel 5: Postgrad
In Japanese the term is *kenkyusei*, which means "research student." They are students who have graduated but remain on at the university to continue work in their field or for special studies. Kenkyusei work does not count towards another degree.

Page 92, panel 3: Angkor Wat
Temple complex in Cambodia built in the 12th century by King Suryavarman II and dedicated to the Hindu god Vishnu. Around the 14th or 15th century it was converted to a Buddhist site. The name comes from the Sanskrit *nokor* (capital) and the Khmer *wat* (temple).

Page 93, panel 2: Cappadocia
An area of modern Turkey known for its "fairy chimney" rock formations. It was the home of the Hittite empire in the Bronze Age. The name comes from the Persian *katpataka* and means "land of beautiful horses."

Page 93, panel 4: Abu Simbel
A temple complex carved out of the mountainside near Lake Nasser during the reign of Ramses II in the 13th century BC.

Page 117, panel 5: Beef bowl
Called *gyûdon* in Japanese (which literally means beef bowl), this dish is a bowl of rice topped with beef and onion that has been cooked in a mild soy sauce broth. It is often served with pickled ginger, shichimi, and a side of miso soup.

Page 155, panel : C'est Bon Très Bon
A spoof of the Japanese pronunciation of 7-11.

Page 158, panel 3: After all
This poem and the one on page 163 are spoofs of the calligraphy homilies by 20th century artist Mitsuo Aida, whose most famous piece reads "*Ningen damono*," or "*I am human, after all.*" Hagu, Ayumi, and Morita's efforts all end in "damono" in Japanese, and are signed the way Aida's are.

I have 20 pencils at home, as well as eight rulers, five utility blades, five or six erasers, and five staplers. And yet, whenever I need any of these items, they all vanish without a trace. Once I've given up looking for them, I go out to buy replacements; when I return, they suddenly reappear. What kind of magic is at work here?
-Chica Umino

Chica Umino was born in Tokyo and started out as a product designer and illustrator. Her beloved *Honey and Clover* debuted in 2000 and received the Kodansha Manga Award in 2003. *Honey and Clover* was also nominated for the Tezuka Culture Prize and an award from the Japan Media Arts Festival.

HONEY AND CLOVER
VOL. 2
The Shojo Beat Manga Edition

This manga volume contains material that was originally published in English in *Shojo Beat* magazine, January-April 2008. Artwork in the magazine may have been slightly altered from that presented here.

STORY AND ART BY CHICA UMINO

English Translation & Adaptation/Akemi Wegmuller
Touch-up Art & Lettering/Sabrina Heep
Design/Yukiko Whitley
Editor/Pancha Diaz

Editor in Chief, Books/Alvin Lu
Editor in Chief, Magazines/Marc Weidenbaum
VP of Publishing Licensing/Rika Inouye
VP of Sales/Gonzalo Ferreyra
Sr. VP of Marketing/Liza Coppola
Publisher/Hyoe Narita

Printed in Canada

Published by VIZ Media, LLC
P.O. Box 77010
San Francisco, CA 94107

Shojo Beat Manga Edition
10 9 8 7 6 5 4 3 2 1
First printing, June 2008

store.viz.com

PARENTAL ADVISORY
HONEY AND CLOVER is rated T+ for Older Teen and is recommended for ages 16 and up. This volume contains strong language, alcohol use and adult situations.

ratings.viz.com

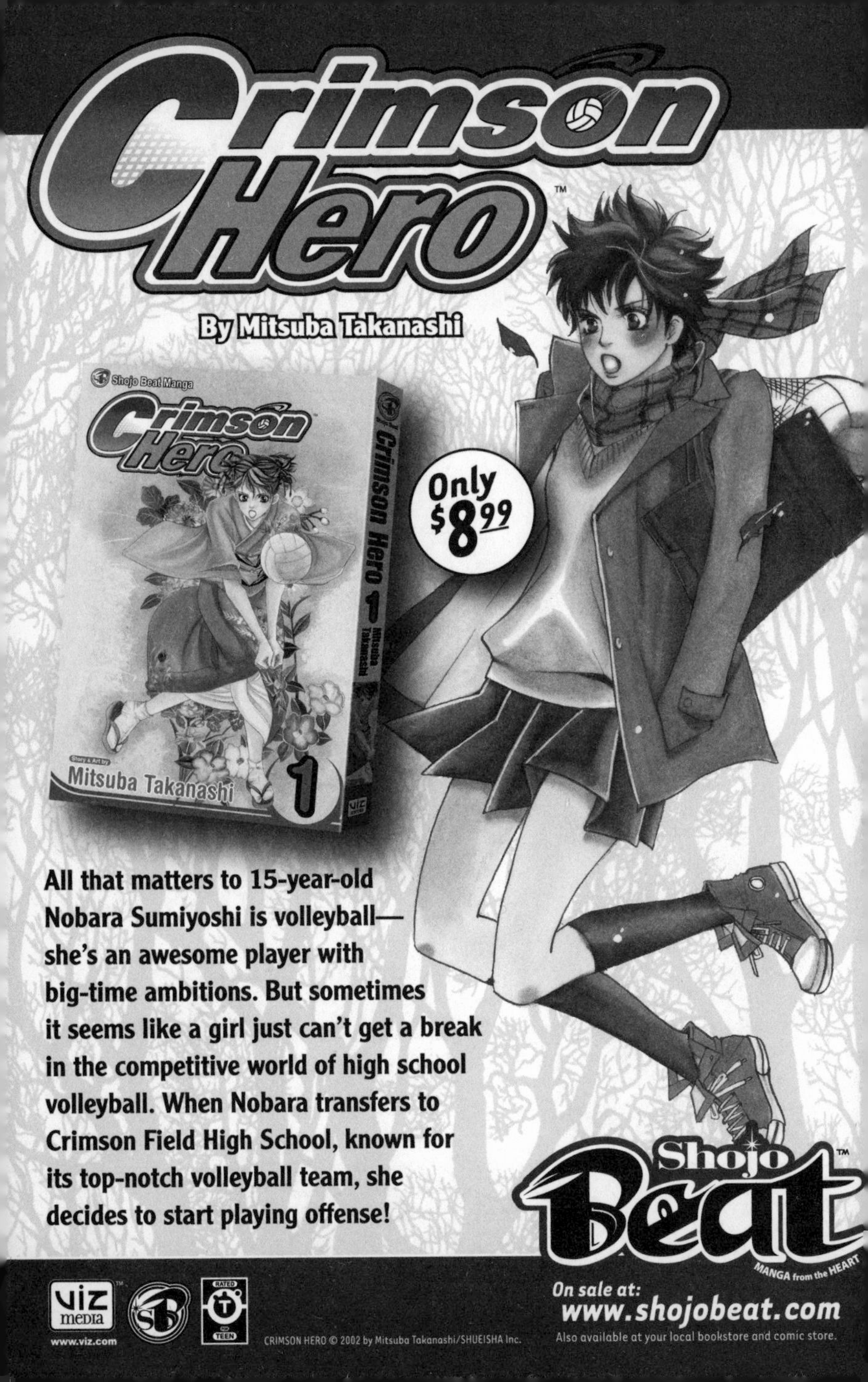

Crimson Hero™
By Mitsuba Takanashi
Shojo Beat Manga
Crimson Hero
Story & Art by
Mitsuba Takanashi
1
Crimson Hero 1
Mitsuba Takanashi
Only $8.99
All that matters to 15-year-old Nobara Sumiyoshi is volleyball—she's an awesome player with big-time ambitions. But sometimes it seems like a girl just can't get a break in the competitive world of high school volleyball. When Nobara transfers to Crimson Field High School, known for its top-notch volleyball team, she decides to start playing offense!
Shojo Beat™
MANGA from the HEART
On sale at:
www.shojobeat.com
Also available at your local bookstore and comic store.
VIZ media
www.viz.com
RATED T TEEN
CRIMSON HERO © 2002 by Mitsuba Takanashi/SHUEISHA Inc.

you think
Beat Manga!

Our survey is now
available online. Go to:

shojobeat.com/mangasurvey

Help us make our
product offerings
better!

Shojo Beat™
MANGA from the HEART

The Shojo Manga Authority

12 GIANT issues for ONLY $34.99*

That's 51% OFF the cover price!

The most **ADDICTIVE** shojo manga stories from Japan **PLUS** unique editorial coverage on the arts, music, culture, fashion, and much more!